Get the eBook FREE!

(PDF, ePub, Kindle, and liveBook all included)

We believe that once you buy a book from us, you should be able to read it in any format we have available. To get electronic versions of this book at no additional cost to you, purchase and then register this book at the Manning website.

Go to https://www.manning.com/freebook and follow the instructions to complete your pBook registration.

That's it!
Thanks from Manning!

Learn Quantum Computing with Python and Q#

Learn Quantum Computing with Python and Q#

A HANDS-ON APPROACH

SARAH KAISER
AND CHRIS GRANADE

MANNING

SHELTER ISLAND

Manning Publications Co.
20 Baldwin Road
PO Box 761
Shelter Island, NY 11964

Development editor:	Dustin Archibald
Technical development editors:	Alain Couniot and Joel Kotarski
Review editor:	Ivan Martinović
Production editor:	Deirdre S. Hiam
Copy editor:	Tiffany Taylor
Proofreader:	Katie Tennant
Technical proofreader:	Krzysztof Kamyczek
Typesetter:	Dennis Dalinnik
Cover designer:	Marija Tudor

ISBN: 9781617296130
Printed in the United States of America

We dedicate this book to the next generation of quantum developers who are working to make this field a safer and more inclusive space.

brief contents

PART 1 GETTING STARTED WITH QUANTUM 1

    1 ▪ Introducing quantum computing 3

    2 ▪ Qubits: The building blocks 17

    3 ▪ Sharing secrets with quantum key distribution 54

    4 ▪ Nonlocal games: Working with multiple qubits 75

    5 ▪ Nonlocal games: Implementing a multi-qubit simulator 90

    6 ▪ Teleportation and entanglement: Moving
        quantum data around 108

PART 2 PROGRAMMING QUANTUM ALGORITHMS IN Q# 131

    7 ▪ Changing the odds: An introduction to Q# 133

    8 ▪ What is a quantum algorithm? 152

    9 ▪ Quantum sensing: It's not just a phase 185

PART 3 APPLIED QUANTUM COMPUTING 217

    10 ▪ Solving chemistry problems with quantum computers 219

    11 ▪ Searching with quantum computers 249

    12 ▪ Arithmetic with quantum computers 278

contents

foreword xv
preface xvii
acknowledgments xix
about this book xxi
about the authors xxv
about the cover illustration xxvi

PART 1 GETTING STARTED WITH QUANTUM 1

1 Introducing quantum computing 3

1.1 Why does quantum computing matter? 4

1.2 What is a quantum computer? 5

1.3 How will we use quantum computers? 8

What can quantum computers do? 10 ▪ *What can't quantum computers do?* 11

1.4 What is a program? 13

What is a quantum program? 14

2   *Qubits: The building blocks*   17

   2.1   Why do we need random numbers?   19
   2.2   What are classical bits?   22

         *What can we do with classical bits?   23 ▪ Abstractions are
         our friend   26*

   2.3   Qubits: States and operations   27

         *State of the qubit   28 ▪ The game of operations   30
         Measuring qubits   34 ▪ Generalizing measurement: Basis
         independence   38 ▪ Simulating qubits in code   41*

   2.4   Programming a working QRNG   46

3   *Sharing secrets with quantum key distribution   54*

   3.1   All's fair in love and encryption   54

         *Quantum NOT operations   58 ▪ Sharing classical bits
         with qubits   62*

   3.2   A tale of two bases   63
   3.3   Quantum key distribution: BB84   66
   3.4   Using a secret key to send secret messages   71

4   *Nonlocal games: Working with multiple qubits   75*

   4.1   Nonlocal games   76

         *What are nonlocal games?   76 ▪ Testing quantum physics:
         The CHSH game   76 ▪ Classical strategy   80*

   4.2   Working with multiple qubit states   81

         *Registers   81 ▪ Why is it hard to simulate quantum
         computers?   83 ▪ Tensor products for state preparation   85
         Tensor products for qubit operations on registers   86*

5   *Nonlocal games: Implementing a multi-qubit simulator   90*

   5.1   Quantum objects in QuTiP   91

         *Upgrading the simulator   96 ▪ Measuring up: How can
         we measure multiple qubits?   99*

   5.2   CHSH: Quantum strategy   103

6 *Teleportation and entanglement: Moving quantum data around 108*

    6.1   Moving quantum data   109

        Swapping out the simulator   112 ▪ *What other two-qubit gates are there?   115*

    6.2   All the single (qubit) rotations   117

        Relating rotations to coordinates: The Pauli operations   119

    6.3   Teleportation   126

PART 2   PROGRAMMING QUANTUM ALGORITHMS IN Q# ...131

7 *Changing the odds: An introduction to Q#   133*

    7.1   Introducing the Quantum Development Kit   134

    7.2   Functions and operations in Q#   137

        Playing games with quantum random number generators in Q#   138

    7.3   Passing operations as arguments   143

    7.4   Playing Morgana's game in Q#   149

8 *What is a quantum algorithm?   152*

    8.1   Classical and quantum algorithms   153

    8.2   Deutsch–Jozsa algorithm: Moderate improvements for searching   156

        Lady of the (quantum) Lake   156

    8.3   Oracles: Representing classical functions in quantum algorithms   161

        Merlin's transformations   162 ▪ *Generalizing our results   165*

    8.4   Simulating the Deutsch–Jozsa algorithm in Q#   170

    8.5   Reflecting on quantum algorithm techniques   174

        Shoes and socks: Applying and undoing quantum operations   175 Using Hadamard instructions to flip control and target   178

    8.6   Phase kickback: The key to our success   180

9 **Quantum sensing: It's not just a phase 185**

9.1 Phase estimation: Using useful properties of qubits for measurement 186

Part and partial application 186

9.2 User-defined types 191

9.3 Run, snake, run: Running Q# from Python 197

9.4 Eigenstates and local phases 202

9.5 Controlled application: Turning global phases into local phases 206

Controlling any operation 210

9.6 Implementing Lancelot's best strategy for the phase-estimation game 212

9.7 Summary 215

9.8 Part 2: Conclusion 215

PART 3 APPLIED QUANTUM COMPUTING 217

10 **Solving chemistry problems with quantum computers 219**

10.1 Real chemistry applications for quantum computing 220

10.2 Many paths lead to quantum mechanics 222

10.3 Using Hamiltonians to describe how quantum systems evolve in time 225

10.4 Rotating around arbitrary axes with Pauli operations 229

10.5 Making the change we want to see in the system 237

10.6 Going through (very small) changes 239

10.7 Putting it all together 242

11 **Searching with quantum computers 249**

11.1 Searching unstructured data 250

11.2 Reflecting about states 256

Reflection about the all-ones state 257 ▪ Reflection about an arbitrary state 258

11.3 Implementing Grover's search algorithm 264

11.4 Resource estimation 271

12 *Arithmetic with quantum computers* 278

12.1 Factoring quantum computing into security 279

12.2 Connecting modular math to factoring 283

Example of factoring with Shor's algorithm 287

12.3 Classical algebra and factoring 288

12.4 Quantum arithmetic 291

Adding with qubits 292 ▪ Multiplying with qubits in superposition 293 ▪ Modular multiplication in Shor's algorithm 296

12.5 Putting it all together 299

appendix A Installing required software 307
appendix B Glossary and quick reference 314
appendix C Linear algebra refresher 327
appendix D Exploring the Deutsch–Jozsa algorithm by example 341

index 351

foreword

For most of its history, quantum computing was a field for physicists—perhaps a few having a proclivity for computer science, but not necessarily so. The popular textbook, *Quantum Computation and Quantum Information*, by Michael A. Nielsen and Isaac L. Chuang, is still considered the go-to textbook, and was written by two quantum physicists. To be sure, computer scientists have always been around, but some theoreticians wear how few lines of code they have written as a badge of honor. This is the quantum world myself, Kaiser, and Granade came of age in. I could easily shake my fist at the new cohort of students and yell, "When I was your age, we didn't write code—we choked on chalk dust!"

I met Chris Granade while we were both graduate students. Back then we wrote academic journal articles for physics journals that contained lines of code which were rejected for being "not physics." But we were not deterred. And now, many years later, this book represents for me the ultimate vindication! This is a book that teaches you everything you'll ever want and need to know about quantum computing, without the need for physics—though, if you really want to know the connection back to physics, Kaiser and Granade offer that as well 😆? There are also emojis 😊!

I've come a long way since then, and I owe much to Granade, as does the field of quantum computing, for showing many of us that between the "quantum" and the "computing," there is more than just theorems and proofs. Kaiser has also taught me more than I thought existed about the need for the software engineer's touch in developing quantum technology. Kaiser and Granade have turned their expertise into words and lines of code so all can benefit from it, as I have.

Though the goal was to create "not a textbook," this book could certainly be used as such in a university lecture as introductions to quantum computing shift from physics departments to schools of computer science. There is immense growing interest in quantum computing, and the majority of it is not coming from physics—software developers, operations managers, and financial executives all want to know what quantum computing is about and how to get their hands on it. Gone are the days of quantum computing as a purely academic pursuit. This book serves the needs of the growing quantum community.

Though I've alluded to the decreasing proportion of physicists in the field of quantum computing, I don't want to discount them. Just as I was once a software development Luddite, this book is really for anyone—especially those already in the field who want to learn about the software side of quantum computing in a familiar setting.

Fire up your favorite code editor and get ready to print ("Hello quantum world!").

CHRIS FERRIE, PhD
Associate Professor, Centre for Quantum Software and Information
Sydney, NSW, Australia

preface

Quantum computing has been our jam for more than 20 years combined, and we are passionate about taking that experience and using it to help more folks get involved in quantum technologies. We completed our doctoral degrees together, and while doing so, we struggled through research questions, pun competitions, and board games, helping to push the boundaries of what was possible with qubits. For the most part, this meant developing new software and tools to help us and our teams do better research, which was a great bridge between the "quantum" and "computing" parts of the subject. However, while developing various software projects, we needed to teach our developer colleagues what we were working on. We kept wondering, "Why isn't there a good book for quantum computing that's technical but not a textbook?" What you are currently looking at is the result. 😺

We've written the book to be accessible to developers, rather than writing it in the textbook style that is so typical in other quantum computing books. When we were learning quantum computing ourselves, it was very exciting but also a bit scary and intimidating. It doesn't have to be that way, as a lot of what makes quantum computing topics confusing is the *way* they are presented, not the content.

 Unfortunately, quantum computing is often described as "weird," "spooky," or beyond our understanding, when the truth is that quantum computing has become quite well understood during its 35-year history. Using a combination of software development and math, *you* can build up the basic concepts you need to make sense of quantum computing and explore this amazing new field.

Our goal with this book is to help *you* learn the basics about the technology and equip you with tools you can use to build the quantum solutions of tomorrow. We focus on hands-on experience with developing code for quantum computing. In part 1, you'll build your own quantum device simulator in Python; in part 2, you'll learn how to apply your new skills to writing quantum applications with Q# and the Quantum Development Kit; and in part 3, you'll learn to implement an algorithm that factors integers exponentially faster than the best-known conventional algorithm—and throughout, *you* are the one doing it, and this is *your* quantum journey.

We have included as many practical applications as we can, but the truth is, that's where you come in! Quantum computing is at a cusp where to go forward, we need a bridge between the immense amount that's known about what quantum computers can and can't do and the problems that people need to solve. Building that bridge takes us from quantum algorithms that make for great research to quantum algorithms that can impact all of society. You can help build that bridge. Welcome to your quantum journey; we're here to help make it fun!

acknowledgments

We didn't know what we were getting into with this book at the start; all we knew was that a resource like this needed to exist. Writing the book gave us a huge opportunity to refine and develop our skills in explaining and teaching the content we were familiar with. All the folks we worked with at Manning were wonderful—Deirdre Hiam, our production editor; Tiffany Taylor, our copyeditor; Katie Tennant, our proofreader; and Ivan Martinović, our reviewing editor—and they helped us make sure this was the best book it could be for our readers.

We thank Olivia Di Matteo and Chris Ferrie for all of their valuable feedback and notes, which helped keep our explanations both accurate and clear.

We also thank all the reviewers of the manuscript who looked at it in various stages of development and whose thoughtful feedback made this a much better book: Alain Couniot, Clive Harber, David Raymond, Debmalya Jash, Dimitri Denisjonok, Domingo Salazar, Emmanuel Medina Lopez, Geoff Clark, Javier, Karthikeyarajan Rajendran, Krzysztof Kamyczek, Kumar Unnikrishnan, Pasquale Zirpoli, Patrick Regan, Paul Otto, Raffaella Ventaglio, Ronald Tischliar, Sander Zegveld, Steve Sussman, Tom Heiman, Tuan A. Tran, Walter Alexander Mata López, and William E. Wheeler.

Our thanks go to all of the Manning Early Access Program (MEAP) subscribers who helped find bugs, typos, and places to improve the explanations. Many folks also provided feedback by filing issues on our sample code repo: our thanks go to them!

We would like to acknowledge the many great establishments around the Seattle area (notably Caffe Ladro, Miir, Milstead & Co., and Downpour Coffee Bar) that tolerated us drinking coffee after coffee and talking animatedly about qubits, as well as the wonderful folks at Fremont Brewing, who were always there when we needed a pint. It was always a welcome interruption when a random passerby would ask us questions about what we were working on!

We'd also like to thank the talented members of the Quantum Systems team at Microsoft for working to provide developers with the best tools possible for onboarding to quantum computing. In particular, our thanks go to Bettina Heim for working to make Q# an amazing language, as well as for being a good friend.

Finally, we thank our German Shepherd, Chewie, who provided much-needed distractions and excuses to take breaks from the computer.

SARAH KAISER

My family has always been there for me, and I thank them for all their patience and encouragement as I worked my way through this project. I would like to thank my therapist, without whom this book would never have come to be. Most of all, I want to thank my coauthor and partner, Chris. They have been there with me through thick and thin and always encouraged and inspired me to do what they knew I could. ♡

CHRIS GRANADE

This book would not have been possible without the amazing love and support of my partner and coauthor, Dr. Sarah Kaiser. Together, we've been through more and have accomplished more than I'd have ever dreamed. Our story together has always been about making a better, safer, and more inclusive quantum community, and this book is a wondrous opportunity to take another step on that journey. Thank you for making this happen, Sarah.

Nor would this have been possible without the support of my family and friends. Thank you for being there, whether by sharing cute puppy photos, commiserating over the latest headlines, or joining late-night meteor watching in Animal Crossing. Finally, I also thank the fantastic online community that I've relied on over the years to help me understand the world from many new perspectives.

about this book

Welcome to *Learn Quantum Computing with Python and Q#*! This book will introduce you to the world of quantum computing by using Python as a comfortable starting point, building to solutions written in Q#, a domain-specific programming language developed by Microsoft. We take an example- and game-driven approach to teaching quantum computing and development concepts that get you hands-on with writing code right away.

> ### Deep dive: It's OK to snorkel!
>
> Quantum computing is a richly interdisciplinary area of study, bringing together ideas from programming, physics, mathematics, engineering, and computer science. From time to time throughout the book, we'll take a moment to point to how quantum computing draws on ideas from these other fields to put the concepts we're learning about into that richer context.
>
> While these asides are meant to spark curiosity and further exploration, they are by nature tangential. You'll get everything you need to enjoy quantum programming in Python and Q# from this book regardless of whether you plunge into these deep dives. Taking a deep dive can be fun and enlightening, but if deep dives aren't your thing, that's OK; it's perfectly fine to snorkel.

Who should read this book

This book is intended for people who are interested in quantum computing and have little to no experience with quantum mechanics but do have some programming background. As you learn to write quantum simulators in Python and quantum programs in Q#, Microsoft's specialized language for quantum computing, we use traditional programming ideas and techniques to help you out. A general understanding of programming concepts like loops, functions, and variable assignments will be helpful.

Similarly, we use some mathematical concepts from linear algebra, such as vectors and matrices, to help us describe quantum concepts; if you're familiar with computer graphics or machine learning, many of the concepts are similar. We use Python to review the most important mathematical concepts along the way, but familiarity with linear algebra will be helpful.

How this book is organized: A roadmap

This text aims to enable you to start exploring and using practical tools for quantum computing. The book is broken into three parts that build on each other:

- Part 1 gently introduces the concepts needed to describe *qubits*, the fundamental unit of a quantum computer. This part describes how to simulate qubits in Python, making it easy to write simple quantum programs.
- Part 2 describes how to use the Quantum Development Kit and the Q# programming language to compose qubits and run quantum algorithms that perform differently from any known classical algorithms.
- In part 3, we apply the tools and methods from the previous two parts to learn how quantum computers can be applied to real-world problems such as simulating chemical properties.

There are also four appendixes. Appendix A has all the installation instructions for setting up the tools we use in the book. Appendix B is a quick reference section with a quantum glossary, notation reminders, and code snippets that may be helpful as you progress through the book. Appendix C is a linear algebra refresher, and appendix D is a deep dive into one of the algorithms you will be implementing.

About the code

All the code used in this book can be found at https://github.com/crazy4pi314/learn-qc-with-python-and-qsharp. Full installation instructions are available at the repository for this book and in appendix A.

The book's samples can also be run online without installing anything, using the mybinder.org service. To get started, go to https://bit.ly/qsharp-book-binder.

liveBook discussion forum

Purchase of *Learn Quantum Computing with Python and Q#* includes free access to a private web forum run by Manning Publications where you can make comments about the book, ask technical questions, and receive help from the authors and from other users. To access the forum, go to https://livebook.manning.com/#!/book/learn-quantum-computing-with-python-and-q-sharp/discussion. You can also learn more about Manning's forums and the rules of conduct at https://livebook.manning.com/#!/discussion.

Manning's commitment to our readers is to provide a venue where a meaningful dialogue between individual readers and between readers and authors can take place. It is not a commitment to any specific amount of participation on the part of the authors, whose contribution to the forum remains voluntary (and unpaid).We suggest you try asking them some challenging questions lest their interest stray! The forum and the archives of previous discussions will be accessible from the publisher's website as long as the book is in print.

Other online resources

As you start your quantum computing journey by reading this book and working through the provided sample code, you may find the following online resources helpful:

- *Quantum Development Kit documentation* (https://docs.microsoft.com/azure/quantum/)—Conceptual documentation and a full reference to everything about Q#, including changes and additions since this book was printed
- *Quantum Development Kit samples* (https://github.com/microsoft/quantum)—Complete samples for using Q#, both on its own and with host programs in Python and .NET, covering a wide range of different applications
- *QuTiP.org* (http://qutip.org)—Full user's guide for the QuTiP package we used to help with the math in this book

There are also some great communities for quantum computing experts and novices alike. Joining a quantum development community like the following can help resolve questions you have along the way and will also let you assist others with their journeys:

- *qsharp.community* (https://qsharp.community)—A community of Q# users and developers, complete with chat room, blog, and project repositories
- *Quantum Computing Stack Exchange* (https://quantumcomputing.stackexchange.com/)—A great place to ask for answers to quantum computing questions, including any Q# questions you may have
- *Women in Quantum Computing and Applications* (https://wiqca.dev)—An inclusive community for people of all genders to celebrate quantum computing and the people who make it possible
- *Quantum Open Source Foundation* (https://qosf.org/)—A community supporting the development and standardization of open tools for quantum computing

- *Unitary Fund* (https://unitary.fund/)—A nonprofit working to create a quantum technology ecosystem that benefits the most people

Going further

Quantum computing is a fascinating new field that offers new ways of thinking about computation and new tools for solving difficult problems. This book can help you get a start in quantum computing so that you can continue to explore and learn. That said, this book isn't a textbook and isn't intended to prepare you for quantum computing research all on its own. As with classical algorithms, developing new quantum algorithms is a mathematical art as much as anything else; while we touch on math in this book and use it to explain algorithms, a variety of textbooks are available that can help you build on the ideas we cover.

Once you've read this book and gotten started with quantum computing, if you want to continue your journey into physics or mathematics, we suggest one of the following resources:

- The Complexity Zoo (https://complexityzoo.net/Complexity_Zoo)
- The Quantum Algorithm Zoo (http://quantumalgorithmzoo.org)
- *Complexity Theory: A Modern Approach* by Sanjeev Arora and Boaz Barak (Cambridge University Press, 2009)
- *Quantum Computing: A Gentle Introduction* by Eleanor G. Rieffel and Wolfgang H. Polak (MIT Press, 2011)
- *Quantum Computing since Democritus* by Scott Aaronson (Cambridge University Press, 2013)
- *Quantum Computation and Quantum Information* by Michael A. Nielsen and Isaac L. Chuang (Cambridge University Press, 2000)
- *Quantum Processes Systems, and Information* by Benjamin Schumacher and Michael Westmoreland (Cambridge University Press, 2010)

about the authors

SARAH KAISER completed her PhD in physics (quantum information) at the University of Waterloo's Institute for Quantum Computing. She has spent much of her career developing new quantum hardware in the lab, from building satellites to hacking quantum cryptography hardware. Communicating what is so exciting about quantum is her passion, and she loves building new demos and tools to help enable the quantum community to grow. When not at her mechanical keyboard, she loves kayaking and writing books about science for all ages.

CHRIS GRANADE completed their PhD in physics (quantum information) at the University of Waterloo's Institute for Quantum Computing and now works in the Quantum Systems group at Microsoft. They work in developing the standard libraries for Q# and are an expert in the statistical characterization of quantum devices from classical data. Chris also helped Scott Aaronson prepare his lectures as a book, *Quantum Computing Since Democritus* (Cambridge University Press, 2013).

about the cover illustration

The figure on the cover of *Learn Quantum Computing with Python and Q#* is captioned "Hongroise," or Hungarian woman. The illustration is taken from a collection of dress costumes from various countries by Jacques Grasset de Saint-Sauveur (1757–1810), titled Costumes de Différents Pays, published in France in 1797. Each illustration is finely drawn and colored by hand. The rich variety of Grasset de Saint-Sauveur's collection reminds us vividly of how culturally apart the world's towns and regions were just 200 years ago.

Isolated from each other, people spoke different dialects and languages. In the streets or in the countryside, it was easy to identify where they lived and what their trade or station in life was just by their dress. The way we dress has changed since then and the diversity by region, so rich at the time, has faded away. Itis now hard to tell apart the inhabitants of different continents, let alone different towns, regions, or countries. Perhaps we have traded cultural diversity for a more varied personal life—certainly for a more varied and fast-paced technological life.

At a time when it is hard to tell one computer book from another, Manning celebrates the inventiveness and initiative of the computer business with book covers based on the rich diversity of regional life of two centuries ago, brought back to life by Grasset de Saint-Sauveur's pictures.

Part 1

Getting started with quantum

This part of the book helps set the stage for the rest of our quantum journey. In chapter 1, we gain more context about quantum computing, the approach to learning quantum computing in this book, and where we can expect to use this to apply the skills we learn. In chapter 2, we start getting into writing code by developing a quantum simulator in Python. We then use the simulator to program a quantum random number generator. Next, in chapter 3, we extend the simulator to program cryptographic applications of quantum technology, such as the BB84 quantum key exchange protocol. In chapter 4, we use nonlocal games to learn about entanglement and extend the simulator once again to support multiple qubits. In chapter 5, we learn how to use a new Python package to help implement quantum strategies for playing the nonlocal games from chapter 4. Finally, in chapter 6, we extend the simulator one last time, adding new quantum operations so that we can simulate techniques like *quantum teleportation* and practice moving data in our quantum devices.

Introducing
quantum computing

This chapter covers

- Why people are excited about quantum computing
- What a quantum computer is
- What a quantum computer can and cannot do
- How quantum computers relate to classical programming

Quantum computing has been an increasingly popular research field and source of hype over the last few years. By using quantum physics to perform computation in new and wonderful ways, *quantum computers* can impact society, making it an exciting time to get involved and learn how to program quantum computers and apply quantum resources to solve problems that matter.

In all the buzz about the advantages quantum computing offers, however, it is easy to lose sight of the *real* scope of those benefits. We have some interesting historical precedent for what can happen when promises about a technology outpace reality. In the 1970s, machine learning and artificial intelligence suffered from dramatically reduced funding, as the hype and excitement around AI outstripped its results; this would later be called the "AI winter." Similarly, internet companies faced the same danger when trying to overcome the dot-com bust.

One way forward is to critically understand the promise offered by quantum computing, how quantum computers work, and what is and is not in scope for quantum computing. In this chapter, we help you develop that understanding so that you can get hands-on and write your own quantum programs in the rest of the book.

All that aside, though, it's just really cool to learn about an entirely new computing model! As you read this book, you'll learn how quantum computers work by programming simulations that you can run on your laptop today. These simulations will show many essential elements of what we expect real commercial quantum programming to be like while useful commercial hardware is coming online. This book is intended for folks who have some basic programming and linear algebra experience but no prior knowledge about quantum physics or computing. If you have some quantum familiarity, you can jump into parts 2 and 3, where we get into quantum programming and algorithms.

1.1 Why does quantum computing matter?

Computing technology is advancing at a truly stunning pace. Three decades ago, the 80486 processor allowed users to execute 50 MIPS (million instructions per second). Today, small computers like the Raspberry Pi can reach 5,000 MIPS, while desktop processors can easily reach 50,000 to 300,000 MIPS. If we have an exceptionally difficult computational problem we'd like to solve, a very reasonable strategy is to simply wait for the next generation of processors to make our lives easier, our videos stream faster, and our games more colorful.

For many problems that we care about, however, we're not so lucky. We might hope that getting a CPU that's twice as fast will let us solve problems that are twice as big, but as with so much in life, "more is different." Suppose we sort a list of 10 million numbers and find that it takes about 1 second. Later, if we want to sort a list of 1 billion numbers in 1 second, we'll need a CPU that's 130 times faster, not just 100 times. When solving some kinds of problems, this gets even worse: for some graphics problems, going from 10 million to 1 billion points would take 13,000 times longer.

Problems as widely varied as routing traffic in a city and predicting chemical reactions become more difficult *much* more quickly. If quantum computing was about making a computer that runs 1,000 times as fast, we would barely make a dent in the daunting challenges that we want to solve. Fortunately, quantum computers are *much* more interesting. We expect that quantum computers will be much *slower* than classical computers but that the resources required to solve many problems will *scale* differently, such that if we look at the right kinds of problems, we can break through "more is different." At the same time, quantum computers aren't a magic bullet—some problems will remain hard. For example, while it is likely that quantum computers can help us immensely with predicting chemical reactions, they may not be much help with other difficult problems.

Investigating exactly which problems we can obtain such an advantage in and developing quantum algorithms to do so has been a large focus of quantum computing research. Up until this point, it has been very difficult to assess quantum approaches this way, as doing so required extensive mathematical skill to write out quantum algorithms and understand all the subtleties of quantum mechanics.

As industry has started developing platforms to help connect developers to quantum computing, however, this situation has begun to change. By using Microsoft's entire Quantum Development Kit, we can abstract away most of the mathematical complexities of quantum computing and begin actually *understanding* and *using* quantum computers. The tools and techniques taught in this book allow developers to explore and understand what writing programs for this new hardware platform will be like.

Put differently, quantum computing is not going away, so understanding what problems we can solve with it matters quite a lot indeed! Independent of whether a quantum "revolution" happens, quantum computing has factored—and will continue to factor—heavily into decisions about how to develop computing resources over the next several decades. Decisions like these are strongly impacted by quantum computing:

- What assumptions are reasonable in information security?
- What skills are useful in degree programs?
- How can we evaluate the market for computing solutions?

For those of us working in tech or related fields, we increasingly must make such decisions or provide input for them. We have a responsibility to understand what quantum computing is and, perhaps more important, what it is not. That way, we will be best prepared to step up and contribute to these new efforts and decisions.

All that aside, another reason quantum computing is such a fascinating topic is that it is both similar to and very different from classical computing. Understanding both the similarities and differences between classical and quantum computing helps us understand what is fundamental about computing in general. Both classical and quantum computation arise from different descriptions of physical laws such that understanding computation can help us understand the universe in a new way.

What's absolutely critical, though, is that there is no one right or even best reason to be interested in quantum computing. Whatever brings you to quantum computing research or applications, you'll learn something interesting along the way.

1.2 What is a quantum computer?

Let's talk a bit about what actually makes up a quantum computer. To facilitate this discussion, let's briefly talk about what the term *computer* means.

> **DEFINITION** A *computer* is a device that takes data as input and does some sort of operations on that data.

There are many examples of what we have called a *computer*; see figure 1.1 for some examples.

All of these have in common that we can model them with classical physics—that is, in terms of Newton's laws of motion, Newtonian gravity, and electromagnetism.

Figure 1.1   **Several examples of different kinds of computers, including the UNIVAC mainframe operated by Rear Admiral Hopper, a room of "human computers" working to solve flight calculations, a mechanical calculator, and a LEGO-based Turing machine. Each computer can be described by the same mathematical model as computers like cell phones, laptops, and servers. Sources: Photo of "human computers" by NASA. Photo of LEGO Turning machine by Projet Rubens, used under CC BY 3.0 (https://creativecommons.org/licenses/by/3.0/).**

This will help us tell apart the kinds of computers we're used to (e.g., laptops, phones, bread machines, houses, cars, and pacemakers) and the computers we're learning about in this book. To tell the two apart, we'll call computers that can be described using classical physics *classical computers*. What's nice about this is that if we replace the term *classical physics* with *quantum physics*, we have a great definition for what a quantum computer is!

> **DEFINITION**   A *quantum computer* is a device that takes data as input and does some sort of operations on that data with a process that can only be described using quantum physics.

Put differently, the distinction between classical and quantum computers is precisely that between classical and quantum physics. We will get into this more later in the book. But the primary difference is one of scale: our everyday experience is largely with objects that are large enough and hot enough that even though quantum effects still exist, they don't do much on average. While quantum mechanics works even at the scale of everyday objects like coffee mugs, bags of flour, and baseball bats, it turns out that we can do a very good job of describing how these objects interact using classical physics alone.

Deep dive: What happened to relativity?

Quantum physics applies to objects that are very small and very cold or well isolated. Similarly, another branch of physics called *relativity* describes objects that are large enough for gravity to play an important role or that are moving very fast—near the speed of light. Many computers rely on relativistic effects; indeed, global positioning satellites depend critically on relativity. So far, we have primarily been comparing classical and quantum physics, so what about relativity?

As it turns out, all computation that is implemented using relativistic effects can also be described using purely classical models of computing such as Turing machines. By contrast, quantum computation cannot be described as faster classical computation but requires a different mathematical model. There has not yet been a proposal for a "gravitic computer" that uses relativity in the same way, so we're safe to set relativity aside in this book.

If we focus on a much smaller scale where quantum mechanics *is* needed to describe our systems, then quantum computing is the art of using small, well-isolated devices to usefully transform data in ways that cannot be described in terms of classical physics alone. One way to build quantum devices is to use small classical computers such as digital signal processors (DSPs) to control the properties of exotic materials.

Physics and quantum computing

The exotic materials used to build quantum computers have names that can sound intimidating, like *superconductors* and *topological insulators*. We can take solace, though, from how we learn to understand and use classical computers.

We can program classical computers without knowing what a semiconductor is. Similarly, the physics behind how we build quantum computers is a fascinating subject, but it's not required for us to learn how to program and use quantum devices.

Quantum devices may differ in the details of how they are controlled, but ultimately all quantum devices are controlled from and read out by classical computers and control electronics of some kind. After all, we are interested in classical data, so there must eventually be an interface with the classical world.

NOTE Most quantum devices must be kept very cold and well isolated, since they can be extremely susceptible to noise.

By applying quantum operations using embedded classical hardware, we can manipulate and transform quantum data. The power of quantum computing then comes from carefully choosing which operations to apply in order to implement a useful transformation that solves a problem of interest.

1.3   How will we use quantum computers?

Figure 1.2   Ways we wish we could use quantum computers. Comic used with permission from xkcd.com.

It is important to understand both the potential and the limitations of quantum computers, especially given the hype surrounding quantum computation. Many of the misunderstandings underlying this hype stem from extrapolating analogies beyond where they make any sense—all analogies have their limits, and quantum computing is no different. Simulating how a quantum program acts in practice can be a great way to help test and refine the understanding provided by analogies. Nonetheless, we will still use analogies in this book, as they can help provide intuition for how quantum computation works.

> **TIP**   If you've ever seen descriptions of new results in quantum computing that read like "We can teleport cats that are in two places at once using the power of infinitely many parallel universes all working together to cure cancer," then you've seen the danger of extrapolating too far from where analogies are useful.

One especially common point of confusion regarding quantum computing is how users will use quantum computers. As a society, we've come to understand what a *computer* is: something you can use to run web applications, write documents, and run simulations. In fact, classical computers do so many different things in our life that we don't always even notice what is and isn't a computer. Cory Doctorow made this observation by noting that "Your car is a computer you sit inside of" (DrupalCon Amsterdam 2014 keynote, www.youtube.com/watch?v=iaf3Sl2r3jE).

Quantum computers, however, are likely to be much more special-purpose—we expect quantum computers to be pointless for some tasks. A great model for how quantum computing will fit into our existing classical computing stack is GPUs. GPUs are specialized hardware devices designed to speed up particular types of calculations like graphics drawing, machine learning tasks, and anything easily parallelizable. You want a GPU for those specific tasks but likely do not want to use it for everything, as we have much more flexible CPUs for general tasks like checking email. Quantum computers will be exactly the same: they will be good at accelerating specific types of tasks but will not be appropriate for broad use.

> **NOTE** Programming a quantum computer comes with some restrictions, so classical computers will be preferable when there's no particular quantum advantage to be found.

Classical computing will still be around and will be the primary way we communicate and interact with each other, as well as our quantum hardware. Even to get the classical computing resource to interface with the quantum devices, in most cases, we will also need a digital-to-analog signal processor, as shown in figure 1.3.

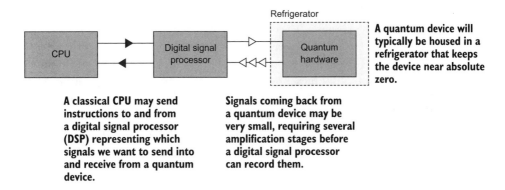

Figure 1.3 An example of how a quantum device might interact with a classical computer through the use of a digital signal processor (DSP). The DSP sends low-power signals into the quantum device and amplifies very low-power signals coming back to the device.

Moreover, quantum physics describes things at very small scales (both size and energy) that are well isolated from their surroundings. This puts some hard limitations on the environments in which we can run a quantum computer. One possible solution is to keep quantum devices in cryogenic fridges, often near absolute 0 K (–459.67°F, or –273.15°C). While this is not a problem in a data center, maintaining a dilution refrigerator isn't really something that makes sense on a desktop, much less on a laptop or a cell phone. For this reason, quantum computers will likely be used through the cloud, at least for quite a while after they first become commercially available.

Using quantum computers as a cloud service resembles other advances in specialized computing hardware. By centralizing exotic computing resources like the following in data centers, it's possible to explore computing models that are difficult for all but the largest users to deploy on-premises:

- Specialized gaming hardware (PlayStation Now, Xbox One)
- Extremely low-latency, high-performance computing (e.g., Infiniband) clusters for scientific problems

- Massive GPU clusters
- Reprogrammable hardware (e.g., Catapult/Brainwave)
- Tensor processing unit (TPU) clusters
- High-permanence, high-latency archival storage (e.g., Amazon Glacier)

Going forward, cloud services like Azure Quantum (https://azure.com/quantum) will make the power of quantum computing available in much the same way.

Just as high-speed, high-availability internet connections have made cloud computing accessible for large numbers of users, we will be able to use quantum computers from the comfort of our favorite WiFi-blanketed beach or coffee shop or even from a train as we view majestic mountain ranges in the distance.

1.3.1   *What can quantum computers do?*

As quantum programmers, if we have a particular problem, *how do we know it makes sense to solve it with a quantum computer?*

We are still learning about the exact extent of what quantum computers are capable of, and thus we don't have any concrete rules to answer this question yet. So far, we have found some examples of problems where quantum computers offer significant advantages over the best-known classical approaches. In each case, the quantum algorithms that have been found to solve these problems exploit quantum effects to achieve the advantages, sometimes referred to as a *quantum advantage*. The following are two useful quantum algorithms:

- Grover's algorithm (discussed in chapter 11) searches a list of N items in $\sqrt{N}$ steps.
- Shor's algorithm (chapter 12) quickly factors large integers, such as those used by cryptography to protect private data.

We'll see several more in this book, but Grover's and Shor's are good examples of how quantum algorithms work: each uses quantum effects to separate correct answers to computational problems from invalid solutions. One way to realize a quantum advantage is to find ways of using quantum effects to separate correct and incorrect solutions to classical problems.

> **What are quantum advantages?**
> Grover's and Shor's algorithms illustrate two distinct kinds of quantum advantages. Factoring integers might be easier classically than we suspect. Many people have tried very hard to factor integers quickly and haven't succeeded, but that doesn't mean we can *prove* that factoring is difficult. On the other hand, we can prove that Grover's algorithm is faster than *any* classical algorithm; the catch is that it uses a different kind of input.
>
> Finding a *provable* advantage for a practical problem is an active area of research in quantum computing. That said, quantum computers can be powerful tools for solving

problems, even if we can't prove that there will never be a better classical algorithm. After all, Shor's algorithm challenges the assumptions underlying large swaths of information security—a mathematical proof is necessary only because we haven't yet built a quantum computer large enough to run Shor's algorithm.

Quantum computers also offer significant benefits for simulating properties of quantum systems, opening up applications to quantum chemistry and materials science. For instance, quantum computers could make it much easier to learn about the ground-state energies of chemical systems. These ground-state energies then provide insight into reaction rates, electronic configurations, thermodynamic properties, and other properties of immense interest in chemistry.

Along the way to developing these applications, we have also seen significant advantages in spin-off technologies such as quantum key distribution and quantum metrology, some of which we will see in the next few chapters. In learning to control and understand quantum devices for the purpose of computing, we have also learned valuable techniques for imaging, parameter estimation, security, and more. While these are not applications for quantum computing in a strict sense, they go a long way toward showing the values of *thinking* in terms of quantum computation.

Of course, new applications of quantum computers are much easier to discover when we have a concrete understanding of how quantum algorithms work and how to build new algorithms from basic principles. From that perspective, quantum programming is a great resource to learn how to discover entirely new applications.

1.3.2   *What can't quantum computers do?*

Like other forms of specialized computing hardware, quantum computers won't be good at everything. For some problems, classical computers will simply be better suited to the task. In developing applications for quantum devices, it's helpful to note what tasks or problems are out of scope for quantum computing.

The short version is that we don't have any hard-and-fast rules to quickly decide which tasks are best run on classical computers and which tasks can take advantage of quantum computers. For example, the storage and bandwidth requirements for Big Data–style applications are very difficult to map onto quantum devices, where we may only have a relatively small quantum system. Current quantum computers can only record inputs of no more than a few dozen bits, and this limitation will become more relevant as quantum devices are used for more demanding tasks. Although we expect to eventually build much larger quantum systems than we can now, classical computers will likely always be preferable for problems that require large amounts of input/output to solve.

Similarly, machine learning applications that depend heavily on random access to large sets of classical inputs are conceptually difficult to solve with quantum computing. That said, there *may* be other machine learning applications that map much more naturally onto quantum computation. Research efforts to find the best ways to apply quantum resources to solve machine learning tasks are still ongoing. In general, problems that have small input and output data sizes but require large amounts of computation to get from input to output are good candidates for quantum computers.

In light of these challenges, it might be tempting to conclude that quantum computers *always* excel at tasks that have small inputs and outputs but very intense computation between the two. Notions like *quantum parallelism* are popular in media, and quantum computers are sometimes even described as using parallel universes to compute.

> **NOTE** The concept of "parallel universes" is a great example of an analogy that can help make quantum concepts understandable but can lead to nonsense when taken to its extreme. It can sometimes be helpful to think of the different parts of a quantum computation as being in different universes that can't affect each other, but this description makes it harder to think about some of the effects we will learn in this book, such as interference. When taken too far, the parallel-universes analogy also lends itself to thinking of quantum computing in ways that are closer to a particularly pulpy and fun episode of a sci-fi show like *Star Trek* than to reality.

What this fails to communicate, however, is that it isn't always obvious how to use quantum effects to extract useful answers from a quantum device, even if the state of the quantum device appears to contain the desired output. For instance, one way to factor an integer N using a classical computer is to list each *potential* factor and check whether it's actually a factor or not:

1 Let $i = 2$.
2 Check if the remainder of N / i is zero.
   - If so, return that i factors N.
   - If not, increment i and loop.

We can speed up this classical algorithm by using a large number of different classical computers, one for each potential factor that we want to try. That is, this problem can be easily parallelized. A quantum computer can try each potential factor within the same device, but as it turns out, this isn't *yet* enough to factor integers faster than the classical approach. If we use this approach on a quantum computer, the output will be one of the potential factors chosen at random. The actual correct factors will occur with probability about $1 / \sqrt{N}$, which is no better than the classical algorithm.

As we'll see in chapter 12, though, we can use other quantum effects to factor integers with a quantum computer faster than the best-known classical factoring algorithms. Much of the heavy lifting done by Shor's algorithm is to make sure that the probability of measuring a correct factor at the end is much larger than the probability of measuring an incorrect factor. Canceling out incorrect answers this way is where much of the art of quantum programming comes in; it's not easy or even possible to do for all problems we might want to solve.

To understand more concretely what quantum computers can and can't do and how to do cool things with quantum computers despite these challenges, it's helpful to take a more concrete approach. Thus, let's consider what a quantum program even **is**, so that we can start writing our own.

1.4 What is a program?

Throughout this book, we will often find it useful to explain a quantum concept by first reexamining the analogous classical concept. In particular, let's take a step back and examine what a classical program is.

> **DEFINITION** A *program* is a sequence of instructions that can be interpreted by a classical computer to perform a desired task. Tax forms, driving directions, recipes, and Python scripts are all examples of programs.

We can write classical programs to break down a wide variety of different tasks for interpretation by all sorts of different computers. See figure 1.4 for some example programs.

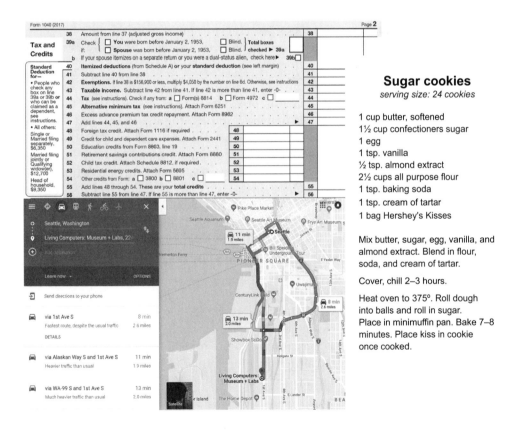

Figure 1.4 Examples of classical programs. Tax forms, map directions, and recipes are all examples in which a sequence of instructions is interpreted by a classical computer such as a person. These may look very different, but each uses a list of steps to communicate a procedure.

Let's take a look at what a simple "hello, world" program might look like in Python:

```
>>> def hello():
...     print("Hello, world!")
...
>>> hello()
Hello, world!
```

At its most basic, this program can be thought of as a sequence of instructions given to the Python *interpreter*, which then executes each instruction in turn to accomplish some effect—in this case, printing a message to the screen. That is, the program is a *description* of a task that is then *interpreted* by Python and, in turn, by our CPU to accomplish our goal. This interplay between description and interpretation motivates calling Python, C, and other such programming tools *languages*, emphasizing that programming is how we communicate with our computers.

In the example of using Python to print "Hello, world!" we are effectively communicating with Guido van Rossum, the founding designer of the Python language. Guido then effectively communicates on our behalf with the designers of the operating system we are using. These designers in turn communicate on our behalf with Intel, AMD, ARM, or whatever company designed the CPU we are using, and so forth.

1.4.1   *What is a quantum program?*

Like classical programs, quantum programs consist of sequences of instructions that are interpreted by classical computers to perform a particular task. The difference, however, is that in a quantum program, the task we wish to accomplish involves controlling a quantum system to perform a computation.

As a result, the instructions used in classical and quantum programs differ as well. A classical program may describe a task such as loading some cat pictures from the internet in terms of instructions to a networking stack and eventually in terms of assembly instructions such as mov (move). By contrast, quantum languages like Q# allow programmers to express quantum tasks in terms of instructions like M (measure). When run using quantum hardware, these programs may instruct a digital signal processor to send microwaves, radio waves, or lasers into a quantum device and amplify signals coming out of the device.

Throughout the rest of this book, we will see many examples of the kinds of tasks a quantum program is faced with solving, or at least addressing, and what kinds of classical tools we can use to make quantum programming easier. For example, figure 1.5 shows an example of writing a quantum program in Visual Studio Code, a classical integrated development environment (IDE).

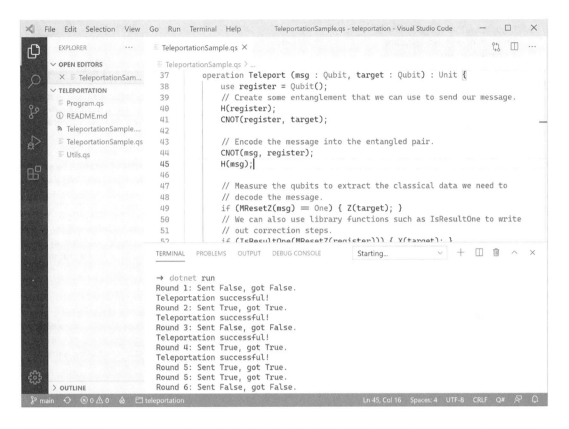

Figure 1.5 Writing a quantum program with the Quantum Development Kit and Visual Studio Code. We will get to the content of this program in chapter 7, but you can see at a high level that it looks similar to other software projects you may have worked on.

We will build up the concepts we need to write quantum programs chapter by chapter; figure 1.6 shows a roadmap. In the next chapter, we kick things off by learning about the basic building blocks that make up a quantum computer and using them to write our first quantum program.

Domain areas like chemistry simulation, cryptography, and machine learning are potential applications for quantum computers.

Just like learning any other programming language, when learning Q# it is important to learn things like syntax, patterns, and types for Q#.

To help build understanding as well as test programs, simulators for quantum hardware are a core piece of the quantum development stack.

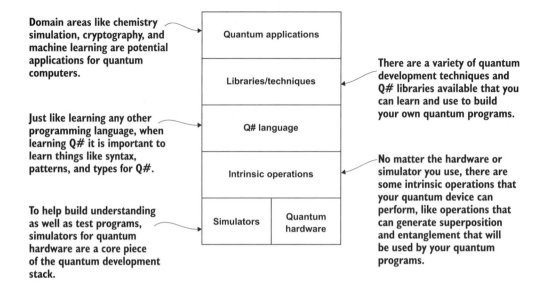

There are a variety of quantum development techniques and Q# libraries available that you can learn and use to build your own quantum programs.

No matter the hardware or simulator you use, there are some intrinsic operations that your quantum device can perform, like operations that can generate superposition and entanglement that will be used by your quantum programs.

Figure 1.6   This book builds up the concepts we need to write quantum programs. We start in part 1 with lower-level descriptions of simulators and intrinsic operations (think hardware API) by building our own simulator in Python. Part 2 examines the Q# language and quantum development techniques that will help us develop our own applications. Part 3 shows some known applications for quantum computing and the challenges and opportunities we have with this technology moving forward.

Summary

- Quantum computing is important because quantum computers potentially will allow us to solve problems that are too difficult to solve with conventional computers.
- Quantum computers can provide advantages over classical computers for some kinds of problems, such as factoring large numbers.
- Quantum computers are devices that use quantum physics to process data.
- Programs are sequences of instructions that can be interpreted by a classical computer to perform tasks.
- Quantum programs are programs that perform computation by sending instructions to quantum devices.

Qubits:
The building blocks

2

This chapter covers

- Why random numbers are an important resource
- What is a qubit?
- What basic operations can we perform on a qubit?
- Programming a quantum random number generator in Python

In this chapter, we'll start to get our feet wet with some quantum programming concepts. The main concept we will explore is the *qubit*, the quantum analogue of a classical bit. We'll use qubits as an abstraction or model to describe the new kinds of computing that are possible with quantum physics. Figure 2.1 shows a model of using a quantum computer as well as the simulator setup that we use in this book. Real or simulated qubits will live on the target machine and interact with the quantum programs that we will be writing! Those quantum programs can be sent by various host programs that then wait to receive the results from the quantum program.

17

**Quantum computer
mental model**

A host program such as Jupyter Notebook
or a custom program in Python can send a
quantum program to a target machine, such
as a device offered through cloud services like
Azure Quantum.

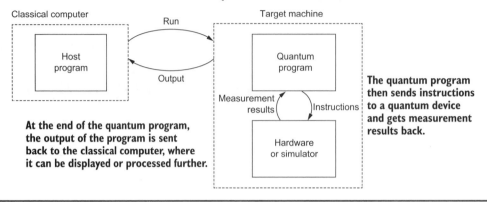

At the end of the quantum program,
the output of the program is sent
back to the classical computer, where
it can be displayed or processed further.

The quantum program
then sends instructions
to a quantum device
and gets measurement
results back.

**Implementation
on a simulator**

When working on a simulator, as we'll
be doing in this book, the simulator can
run on the same computer as our host
program, but our quantum program still
sends instructions to the simulator and
gets results back.

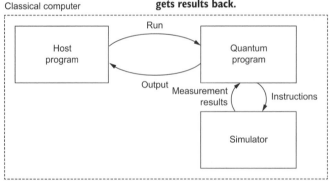

Figure 2.1   A mental model for how we can use a quantum computer. The top half of the figure is the general model for a quantum computer. We will be using local simulators for this book, and the bottom half represents what we will be building and using.

To help learn about what qubits are and how we interact with them, we will use an example of how they are used today: random number generation. While we can build up much more interesting devices from qubits, the simple example of a *quantum random number generator* (QRNG) is a good way to get familiar with the qubit.

2.1 Why do we need random numbers?

Humans like certainty. We like it when pressing a key on our keyboard does the same thing every time. However, there are some contexts in which we want randomness:

- Playing games
- Simulating complex systems (such as the stock market)
- Picking secure secrets (for example, passwords and cryptographic keys)

In all of these situations where we want randomness, we can describe the chances of each outcome. For random events, describing the chances is all we can say about the situation until the die is cast (or the coin is flipped or the password is reused). When we describe the chances of each example, we say things like this:

- *If* I roll this die, *then* I will get a six *with probability* 1 out of 6.
- *If* I flip this coin, *then* I will get heads *with probability* 1 out of 2.

We can also describe cases where the probabilities aren't the same for every outcome. On *Wheel of Fortune*, (figure 2.2), the probability that *if* we spin the wheel, *then* we will get a $1,000,000 prize is much smaller than the probability that *if* we spin the wheel, *then* we will go bankrupt.

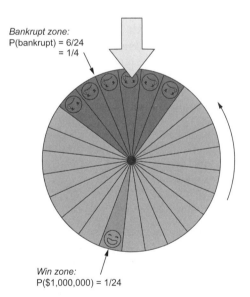

Bankrupt zone:
P(bankrupt) = 6/24
= 1/4

Win zone:
P($1,000,000) = 1/24

Figure 2.2 **Probabilities of $1,000,000 and Bankrupt on *Wheel of Fortune*. Before spinning the wheel, we don't know exactly where it will land, but we do know by looking at the wheel that the probability of getting Bankrupt is much larger than the probability of winning big.**

As on game shows, there are many contexts in computer science where randomness is critical, especially when security is required. If we want to keep some information private, cryptography lets us do so by combining our data with random numbers in different ways. If our random number generator isn't very good—that is to say, if an attacker can predict what numbers we use to protect our private data—then cryptography doesn't help us much. We can also imagine using a poor random number generator to run a raffle or a lottery; an attacker who figures out how our random numbers are generated can take us straight to the bank.

What are the odds?

We can lose a lot of money by using random numbers that our adversaries can predict. Just ask the producers of *Press Your Luck!*, a popular 1980s game show.

A contestant found that he could predict where the game's new electronic "wheel" would land, which allowed him to win more than $250,000 in today's money. To learn more, read "The Man Who Got No Whammies" by Zachary Crockett at https://priceonomics.com/the-man-who-got-no-whammies.

As it turns out, quantum mechanics lets us build some really unique sources of randomness. If we build them right, the randomness of our results is guaranteed by *physics*, not an assumption about how long it would take for a computer to solve a difficult problem. This means a hacker or adversary would have to break the laws of physics to break the security! This does not mean we should use quantum random numbers for everything; humans are still the weakest link in security infrastructure 😺.

Deep dive: Computational security and information theoretic security

Some ways of protecting private information rely on assumptions about what problems are easy or hard for an attacker to solve. For instance, the RSA algorithm is a commonly used encryption algorithm and is based on the difficulty of finding prime factors for large numbers. RSA is used on the web and in other contexts to protect user data, under the assumption that adversaries can't easily factor very large numbers. So far, this has proven to be a good assumption, but it is entirely possible that a new factoring algorithm may be discovered, undermining the security of RSA. New models of computation like quantum computing also change how reasonable or unreasonable it is to make computational assumptions like "factoring is hard." As we'll see in chapter 11, a quantum algorithm known as *Shor's algorithm* allows for solving some kinds of cryptographic problems much faster than classical computers can, challenging the assumptions that are commonly used to promise computational security.

By contrast, if an adversary can only ever randomly guess at secrets, even with very large amounts of computing power, then a security system provides much better guarantees about its ability to protect private information. Such systems are said to be *informationally secure*. Later in this chapter, we'll see that generating random numbers in a hard-to-predict fashion allows us to implement an informationally secure procedure called a *one-time pad*.

This gives us some confidence that we can use quantum random numbers for vital tasks, such as to protect private data, run lotteries, and play *Dungeons and Dragons*. Simulating how quantum random number generators work lets us learn many of the basic concepts underlying quantum mechanics, so let's jump right in and get started!

As mentioned earlier, one great way to get started is to look at an example of a quantum program that generates random numbers: a quantum random number generator (QRNG). Don't worry if the following algorithm (also shown in figure 2.3) doesn't make a lot of sense right now—we'll explain the different pieces as we go through the rest of the chapter:

1 Ask the quantum device to allocate a qubit.
2 Apply an instruction called the *Hadamard instruction* to the qubit; we learn about this later in the chapter.
3 Measure the qubit, and return the result.

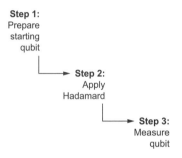

Figure 2.3   Quantum random number generator algorithm. To sample random numbers with a quantum computer, our program will prepare a fresh qubit and then use a Hadamard instruction to prepare the superposition we need. Finally, we can measure and return the random result that we get at the end.

In the rest of the chapter, we'll develop a Python class called `QuantumDevice` to let us write programs that implement algorithms like this one. Once we have a `Quantum-Device` class, we'll be able to write QRNG as a Python program similar to classical programs that we're used to.

NOTE Please see appendix A for instructions on how to set up Python on your device to run quantum programs.

Note that the following sample will not run until you have written the simulator in this chapter 😊.

Listing 2.1   qrng.py: a quantum program that generates random numbers

Quantum programs are written just like classical programs. In this case, we're using Python, so our quantum program is a Python function qrng that implements a QRNG.

```
def qrng(device : QuantumDevice) -> bool:

    with device.using_qubit() as q:

        q.h()

        return q.measure()
```

Quantum programs work by asking quantum computing hardware for qubits: quantum analogues of bits that we can use to perform computations.

Once we have a qubit, we can issue instructions to that qubit. Similar to assembly languages, these instructions are often denoted by short abbreviations; we'll see what h() stands for later in this chapter.

To get data back from our qubits, we can measure them. In this case, half of the time, our measurement will return True, and the other half of the time, we'll get back False.

That's it! Four steps, and we've just created our first quantum program. This QRNG returns true or false. In Python terms, this means we get a 1 or a 0 each time we run qrng. It's not a very sophisticated random number generator, but the number it returns is truly random.

To run the qrng program, we need to give the function a `QuantumDevice` that provides access to qubits and implements the different instructions we can send to qubits. Although we need only one qubit, to start, we're going to build our own quantum computer simulator. Existing hardware could be used for this modest task, but what we will look at later will be beyond the scope of available hardware. It will run locally on a laptop or desktop and behave like actual quantum hardware. Throughout the rest of the chapter, we'll build the different pieces we need to write our own simulator and run qrng.

2.2   *What are classical bits?*

When learning about the concepts of quantum mechanics, it often helps to step back and reexamine *classical* concepts to make the connection to how they are expressed in quantum computing. With that in mind, let's take another look at what *bits* are.

Suppose we'd like to send our dear friend Eve an important message, such as "♡". How can we represent our message in a way that it can be easily sent?

We might start by making a list of every letter and symbol that we could use to write messages. Fortunately, the Unicode Consortium (https://unicode.org) has already done this for us and assigned *codes* to an extensive variety of characters used for communication around the world. For instance, *I* is assigned the code 0049, while ✾ is denoted by A66E, ⚖ by 2E0E, and ♡ by 1F496. These codes may not seem helpful at first glance, but they're useful recipes for how to send each symbol as a message. If we know how to send two messages (let's call them "0" and "1"), these recipes let us build more complicated messages like "✾", "⚖", and "♡" as sequences of "0" and "1" messages:

0	0000	8	1000
1	0001	9	1001
2	0010	A	1010
3	0011	B	1011
4	0100	C	1100
5	0101	D	1101
6	0110	E	1110
7	0111	F	1111

Now we can send whatever we want if we know how to send just two messages to Eve: a "0" message and a "1" message. Using these recipes, our message "♡" becomes "0001 1111 0100 1001 0110" or Unicode 1F496.

TIP Don't send "0001 1111 0100 1001 0100" by mistake, or Eve will get a 💔 from you!

We call each of the two messages "0" and "1" a *bit*.

NOTE To distinguish bits from the quantum bits we'll see throughout the rest of the book, we'll often emphasize that we're talking about *classical* bits.

When we use the word *bit*, we generally mean one of two things:

- Any physical system that can be completely described by answering one true/false question
- The information stored in such a physical system

For example, padlocks, light switches, transistors, the left or right spin on a curveball, and wine in wine glasses can all be thought of as bits, as we can use all of them to send or record messages (see table 2.1).

Table 2.1 Examples of bits

Label	Padlock	Light switch	Transistor	Wine glass	Baseball
0	Unlocked	Off	Low voltage	Contains white wine	Rotating to the left
1	Locked	On	High voltage	Contains red wine	Rotating to the right

These examples are all bits because we can fully describe them to someone else by answering a single true/false question. Put differently, each example lets us send either a 0 or a 1 message. Like all conceptual models, a bit has limitations—how would we describe a rosé wine, for instance?

That said, a bit is a useful tool because we can describe ways of interacting with a bit that are independent of how we actually build the bit.

2.2.1 *What can we do with classical bits?*

Now that we have a way of describing and sending classical information, what can we do to process and modify it? We describe the ways that we can process information in terms of *operations*, which we define as the ways of describing how a model can be changed or acted upon.

To visualize the NOT operation, let's imagine labeling two points as 0 and 1, as shown in figure 2.4. The NOT operation is then any transformation that turns 0 bits

This bit is in the 0 setting.

Figure 2.4 A classical bit can be in one of two different states, typically called 0 and 1. We can depict a classical bit as a black dot in either the 0 or 1 position.

into 1 bits and vice versa. In classical storage devices like hard drives, a NOT gate flips the magnetic field that stores our bit value. As shown in figure 2.5, we can think of NOT as implementing a 180° rotation between the 0 and 1 points we drew in figure 2.4.

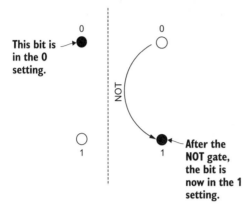

This bit is in the 0 setting.

NOT

After the NOT gate, the bit is now in the 1 setting.

Figure 2.5   The classical NOT operation flips a classical bit between 0 and 1. For instance, if a bit starts in the 0 state, NOT flips it to the 1 state.

Visualizing classical bits this way also lets us extend the notion of bits slightly to include a way to describe *random* bits (which will be helpful later). If we have a *fair coin* (that is, a coin that lands heads half the time and tails the other half), then it wouldn't be correct to call that coin a 0 or a 1. We only know what bit value our coin bit has if we set it with a particular side face up on a surface; we can also flip it to get a random bit value. Every time we flip a coin, we know that eventually, it will land, and we will get heads or tails. Whether it lands heads or tails is governed by a probability called the *bias* of the coin. We have to pick a side of the coin to describe the bias, which is easy to phrase as a question like "What is the probability that the coin will land heads?" Thus a fair coin has a bias of 50% because it lands with the value heads half of the time, which is mapped to the bit value 0 in figure 2.6.

Using this visualization, we can take our previous two dots indicating the bit values 0 and 1 and connect them with a line on which we can plot our coin's bias. It becomes

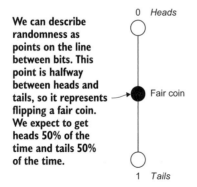

We can describe randomness as points on the line between bits. This point is halfway between heads and tails, so it represents flipping a fair coin. We expect to get heads 50% of the time and tails 50% of the time.

0 *Heads*

Fair coin

1 *Tails*

Figure 2.6   We can use the same picture as before to extend our concept of a bit to describe a coin. Unlike a bit, a coin has a probability of being either 0 or 1 each time it is tossed. We graphically represent that probability as a point between 0 and 1.

easier to see that a NOT operation (which still works on our new probabilistic bit) doesn't do anything to a fair coin. If 0 and 1 occur with the same probability, then it doesn't matter if we rotate a 0 to a 1 or a 1 to a 0: we'll still wind up with 0 and 1 having the same probability.

What if our bias is not in the middle? If we know that someone is trying to cheat by using a weighted or modified coin that almost always lands on heads, we can say the bias of the coin is 90% and plot it on our line by drawing a point much closer to 0 than to 1.

> **DEFINITION** The point on a line where we would draw each classical bit is the *state* of that bit.

Let's consider a scenario. Say I want to send you a bunch of bits stored using padlocks. What is the cheapest way I can do so?

One approach is to mail a box containing many padlocks that are either open or closed and hope that they arrive in the same state in which I sent them. On the other hand, we can agree that all padlocks start in the 0 (unlocked) state, and I can send you instructions on which padlocks to close. This way, you can buy your own padlocks, and I only need to send a *description* of how to prepare those padlocks using classical NOT gates. Sending a piece of paper or an email is much cheaper than mailing a box of padlocks!

This illustrates a principle we will rely on throughout the book: *the state of a physical system can also be described in terms of instructions for how to prepare that state.* Thus, the operations allowed on a physical system also define what states are possible.

Although it may sound completely trivial, there is one more thing we can do with classical bits that will turn out to be critical for how we understand quantum computing: we can look at them. If I look at a padlock and conclude, "Aha! That padlock is unlocked," then I can now think of my brain as a particularly squishy kind of bit. The 0 message is stored in my brain by my thinking, "Aha! That padlock is unlocked," while a 1 message would be stored by my thinking, "Ah, well, that padlock is locked ☹." In effect, by looking at a classical bit, I have *copied* it into my brain. We say that the act of *measuring* the classical bit copies that bit.

More generally, modern life is built around the ease with which we copy classical bits by looking at them. We copy classical bits with truly reckless abandon, measuring many billions of classical bits every second that we copy data from our video game consoles to our TVs.

On the other hand, if a bit is stored as a coin, then the process of measuring involves flipping it. Measuring doesn't quite copy the coin, as I might get a different measurement result the next time I flip. If I only have one measurement of a coin, I can't conclude the probability of getting heads or tails. We didn't have this ambiguity with padlock bits because we knew the state of the padlocks was either 0 or 1. If I measured a padlock and found it to be in the 0 state, I would know that it would always be in the 0 state unless I did something to the padlock.

The situation isn't precisely the same in quantum computing, as we'll see later in the chapter. While measuring classical information is cheap enough that we complain about precisely how many billions of bits a $5 cable lets us measure, we have to be much more careful with how we approach quantum measurements.

2.2.2 *Abstractions are our friend*

Regardless of how we physically build a bit, we can (fortunately) represent them the same way in both math and code. For instance, Python provides the `bool` type (short for Boolean, in honor of the logician George Boole), which has two valid values: `True` and `False`. We can represent transformations on bits such as NOT and OR as operations acting on `bool` variables. Importantly, we can specify a classical operation by describing how that operation transforms each possible input, often called a *truth table*.

> **DEFINITION**   A *truth table* is a table describing the output of a classical operation for every possible combination of inputs. For example, figure 2.7 shows the truth table for the AND operation.

Truth tables are one way to show what happens to classical bits in functions or logical circuits.

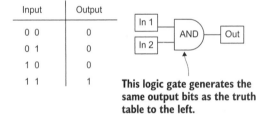

Input	Output
0 0	0
0 1	0
1 0	0
1 1	1

This logic gate generates the same output bits as the truth table to the left.

Figure 2.7   Truth table for the logical operation AND. If we know the entire truth table for a logical operation, then we know what that operation does for any possible input.

We can find the truth table for the NAND (short for NOT-AND) operation in Python by iterating over combinations of `True` and `False`.

Listing 2.2   Using Python to print out a truth table for NAND

```
>>> from itertools import product
>>> for inputs in product([False, True], repeat=2):
...     output = not (inputs[0] and inputs[1])
...     print(f"{inputs[0]}\t{inputs[1]}\t->\t{output}")
False   False   ->      True
False   True    ->      True
True    False   ->      True
True    True    ->      False
```

> **NOTE**   Describing an operation as a truth table holds for more complicated operations. In principle, even an operation like addition between two 64-bit

integers can be written as a truth table. This isn't very practical, though, as a truth table for two 64-bit inputs would have $2^{128} \approx \times 10^{38}$ entries and would take 10^{40} bits to write. By comparison, recent estimates put the size of the entire internet at closer to 10^{27} bits.

Much of the art of classical logic and hardware design is making *circuits* that can provide very compact representations of classical operations rather than relying on potentially massive truth tables. In quantum computing, we use the name *unitary operators* for similar truth tables for quantum bits, which we will expand on as we go along.

In summary:

- Classical bits are physical systems that can be in one of two different *states*.
- Classical bits can be manipulated through *operations* to process information.
- The act of *measuring* a classical bit makes a copy of the information contained in the state.

NOTE In the next section, we'll use linear algebra to learn about *qubits*, the basic unit of information in a quantum computer. If you need a refresher on linear algebra, this would be a great time to take a detour to appendix C. We'll refer to an analogy from this appendix throughout the book, where we'll think of vectors as directions on a map. We'll be right here when you get back!

2.3   *Qubits: States and operations*

Just as classical bits are the most basic unit of information in a classical computer, *qubits* are the basic unit of information in a quantum computer. They can be physically implemented by systems that have two states, just like classical bits, but they behave according to the laws of quantum mechanics, which allows for some behaviors that classical bits are not capable of. Let's treat qubits like we would any other fun new computer part: plug it in and see what happens!

Simulated qubits

For all of this book, we won't be using actual qubits. Instead, we will use *classical simulations* of qubits. This lets us learn how quantum computers work and get started programming small instances of the kinds of problems that quantum computers can solve, even if we don't yet have access to the quantum hardware we'd need to solve practical problems.

The trouble with this approach is that simulating qubits on classical computers takes an exponential amount of classical resources in the number of qubits. The most powerful classical computing services can simulate up to about 40 qubits before having to simplify or reduce the types of quantum programs being run. For comparison, current commercial hardware maxes out at about 70 qubits at the time of this writing. Devices with that many qubits are extremely difficult to simulate with classical computers, but currently available devices are still too noisy to complete most useful computational tasks.

(continued)
Imagine having to write a classical program with only 40 classical bits to work with! While 40 bits is quite small compared to the gigabytes we are used to working with in classical programming, we can still do some really interesting things with only 40 qubits that will help us prototype what an actual quantum advantage might look like.

2.3.1   State of the qubit

To implement our QRNG, we need to work out how to describe our qubit. We have used locks, baseballs, and other classical systems to represent *classical* bit values of 0 or 1. We can use many physical systems to act as our qubit, and *states* are the "values" our qubit can have.

Similar to the 0 and 1 states of classical bits, we can write labels for quantum states. The qubit states that are most similar to the classical 0 and 1 are $|0\rangle$ and $|1\rangle$, as shown in figure 2.8. These are referred to as *ket 0* and *ket 1*, respectively.

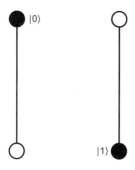

Figure 2.8   Using Dirac (bra-ket) notation for qubits, we can graphically represent the $|0\rangle$ and $|1\rangle$ states for qubits the same way as we represented the 0 and 1 states of classical bits. In particular, we'll draw the $|0\rangle$ and $|1\rangle$ states as opposite points along an axis, as shown here.

Ket?

The term *ket* comes from a kind of whimsical naming in quantum computing that owes its history to a particularly silly pun. As we'll see when we look at measurements, there's another kind of object called a *bra* that is written $\langle 0|$. When we put a bra and a ket together, we get a pair of brackets: $\langle\rangle$.

The use of bras and kets to write out math for quantum mechanics is often called *Dirac notation* after Paul Dirac, who invented both the notation and the truly groanworthy pun that we're now stuck with. We will see more of this style of whimsy throughout the book.

One thing to be mindful of, though, is that a state is a convenient model used to predict how a qubit behaves, not an inherent property of the qubit. This distinction becomes especially important when we consider measurement later in the chapter—as we will see, we cannot directly measure the state of a qubit.

WARNING   In real systems, we can never extract or perfectly learn the state of a qubit given a finite number of copies.

Don't worry if this doesn't all make sense yet; we'll see plenty of examples as we go through the book. What's important to keep in mind for now is that qubits aren't states.

If we want to simulate how a baseball moves once it's thrown, we might start by writing down its current location, how fast it's going and in what direction, which way it's spinning, and so forth. That list of numbers helps us represent a baseball on a piece of paper or in a computer to predict what that baseball will do, but we wouldn't say that the baseball *is* that list of numbers. To get our simulation started, we'd have to take a baseball we're interested in and *measure* where it is, how fast it's going, and so forth.

We say that the full set of data we need to simulate the behavior of a baseball accurately is the *state* of that baseball. Similarly, the state of a qubit is the full set of data we need to simulate it and to predict what results we'll get when we measure it. Just as we need to update the state of a baseball in our simulator as it goes along, we'll update the state of a qubit when we apply operations to it.

TIP   One way to remember this subtle distinction is that a qubit *is described by a* state, but it is not true that a qubit *is a* state.

Where things get a little more subtle is that while we can measure a baseball without doing anything to it other than copying some classical information, as we'll see throughout the rest of the book, we can't perfectly copy the quantum information stored in a qubit—when we measure a qubit, we have an effect on its state. This can be confusing, as we record the full state of a qubit when we simulate it, such that we can look at the memory in our simulator whenever we want. Nothing we can do with actual qubits lets us look at their state, so if we "cheat" by looking at the memory of a simulator, we won't be able to run our program on real hardware.

Put differently, while looking at states directly can be useful for debugging classical simulators as we build them, we have to make sure we are only writing algorithms based on information we could plausibly learn from real hardware.

Cheating with our eyes shut

When we are using a quantum simulator, the simulator must store the state of our qubits internally—this is why simulating quantum systems can be so difficult. Every qubit could, in principle, be correlated with every other qubit, so we need exponential resources in general to write down the state in our simulator (we'll see more about this in chapter 4).

If we "cheat" by looking directly at the state stored by a simulator, then we can only ever run our program on a simulator, not on actual hardware. We'll see in later chapters how to cheat more safely by using assertions and making cheating unobservable 😺.

2.3.2   *The game of operations*

Now that we have names for these states, let's show how to represent the information they contain. With classical bits, we can record the information contained in the bit at any time as simply a value on a line: 0 or 1. This works because the only operations we can do consist of flips (or 180° rotations) on this line. Quantum mechanics allows us to apply more kinds of operations to qubits, including rotations by less than 180°. That is, qubits differ from classical bits in what operations we can do with them.

> **NOTE**   While operations on classical bits are logical operations that can be made by combining NOT, AND, and OR in different ways, quantum operations consist of *rotations*.

For instance, if we want to turn the state of a qubit from $|0\rangle$ to $|1\rangle$ and vice versa, the quantum analogue of a NOT operation, we rotate the qubit clockwise by 180°, as shown in figure 2.9.

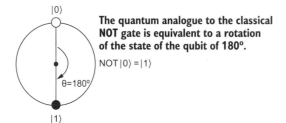

The quantum analogue to the classical **NOT** gate is equivalent to a rotation of the state of the qubit of 180°.

NOT $|0\rangle = |1\rangle$

$\theta = 180°$

Figure 2.9   A visualization of the quantum equivalent of a NOT operation operating on a qubit in the $|0\rangle$ state, leaving the qubit in the $|1\rangle$ state. We can think of this operation as a rotation of 180° about the center of the line connecting the $|0\rangle$ and $|1\rangle$ states.

We have seen how rotation by 180° is the analogue to a NOT gate, but what other rotations can we do?

Reversibility

When we rotate a quantum state, we can always get back to the same state we started in by rotating backward. This property, known as *reversibility*, turns out to be fundamental to quantum computing. With the exception of measurement, which we'll learn more about later in this chapter, all quantum operations must be reversible.

Not all of the classical operations we're used to are reversible, though. Operations like AND and OR aren't reversible as they are typically written, so they cannot be implemented as quantum operations without a little more work. We'll see how to do this in chapter 8 when we introduce the "uncompute" trick for expressing other classical operations as rotations.

On the other hand, classical operations like XOR can easily be made reversible, so we can write them out as rotations using a quantum operation called *controlled NOT*, as we will see in chapter 8.

If we rotate a qubit in the $|0\rangle$ state clockwise by 90° instead of 180°, we get a quantum operation that we can think of as the square root of a NOT operation, as shown in figure 2.10.

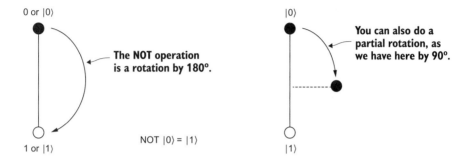

Figure 2.10 We can also rotate a state by less than 180 degrees. Doing so, we get a state that is neither $|0\rangle$ nor $|1\rangle$ but that lies halfway around the circle between them.

Just as we earlier defined the square root $\sqrt{x}$ of a number x as being a number y such that $y^2 = x$, we can define the square root of a quantum operation. If we apply a 90° rotation twice, we get back the NOT operation, so we can think of the 90° rotation as the square root of NOT.

Halves and halve-nots

Every field has its stumbling blocks. Ask a graphics programmer whether positive y means "up" or "down," for instance. In quantum computing, the rich history and interdisciplinary nature of the field sometimes come across as a double-edged sword in that each different way of thinking about quantum computing comes with conventions and notations.

One way this manifests is that it's really easy to make mistakes about where to put factors of two. In this book, we've chosen to follow the convention used by Microsoft's Q# language.

We now have a new state that is neither $|0\rangle$ nor $|1\rangle$, but an equal combination of them both. In precisely the same sense that we can describe "northeast" by adding together the directions "north" and "east," we can write this new state as shown in figure 2.11.

The state of a qubit can be represented as a point on a circle that has two labeled states on the poles: $|0\rangle$ and $|1\rangle$. More generally, we will picture rotations using arbitrary angles θ between qubit states, as shown in figure 2.12.

Just as we can point ourselves northeast by looking north and then rotating toward the east, we get a new state that points between $|0\rangle$ and $|1\rangle$ by starting in $|0\rangle$ and rotating toward $|1\rangle$.

In the same way we might think of directions like north and east, quantum states like $|0\rangle$ and $|1\rangle$ are directions.

$$\cos(90°/2)\ |0\rangle + \sin(90°/2)\ |1\rangle = (|0\rangle + |1\rangle)/\sqrt{2}$$

We can rotate between states using the same math we use to describe rotations of map directions; we just have to watch out for factors of 2.

For example, if we want to rotate the $|0\rangle$ state by 90°, we use the cosine and sine functions to find the new state.

Figure 2.11   We can write the state we get when we rotate by 90° by thinking of the $|0\rangle$ and $|1\rangle$ states as *directions*. Doing so, and using some trigonometry, we get that rotating the $|0\rangle$ state by 90° gives us a new state, $(|0\rangle + |1\rangle)/\sqrt{2}$. For more details on how to write out the math for this kind of rotation, check out appendix B for a refresher on linear algebra.

$|+\rangle$, $|-\rangle$, and superposition

We call the state that is an equal combination of $|0\rangle$ and $|1\rangle$ the $|+\rangle = (|0\rangle + |1\rangle)/\sqrt{2}$ state (due to the sign between the terms). We say that the $|+\rangle$ state is a *superposition* of $|0\rangle$ and $|1\rangle$.

If the rotation is by −90° (counterclockwise), then we call the resulting state $|-\rangle = (|0\rangle - |1\rangle)/\sqrt{2}$. Try writing out these rotations using −90° to see that we get $|-\rangle$!

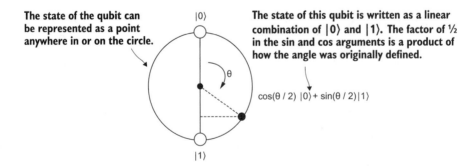

The state of the qubit can be represented as a point anywhere in or on the circle.

The state of this qubit is written as a linear combination of $|0\rangle$ and $|1\rangle$. The factor of ½ in the sin and cos arguments is a product of how the angle was originally defined.

$\cos(\theta/2)\ |0\rangle + \sin(\theta/2)|1\rangle$

Figure 2.12   If we rotate the $|0\rangle$ state by an angle other than 90° or 180°, the resulting state can be represented as a point on a circle that has $|0\rangle$ and $|1\rangle$ as its top and bottom poles. This gives us a way to visualize the possible states that a single qubit can be in.

Mathematically, we can write the state of any point on the circle that represents our qubit as $\cos(\theta\,/\,2)\,|0\rangle + \sin(\theta\,/\,2)\,|1\rangle$, where $|0\rangle$ and $|1\rangle$ are different ways of writing the vectors $[[1], [0]]$ and $[[0], [1]]$, respectively.

> **TIP** One way to think of ket notation is that it gives *names* to vectors that we commonly use. When we write $|0\rangle = [[1], [0]]$, we're saying that $[[1], [0]]$ is important enough that we name it after 0. Similarly, when we write $|+\rangle = [[1], [1]] \,/\, \sqrt{2}$, we give a name to the vector representation of a state that we will use throughout the book.

Another way to say this is that a qubit is generally the *linear combination* of the vectors of $|0\rangle$ and $|1\rangle$ with coefficients that describe the angle that $|0\rangle$ would have to be rotated to get to the state. To be useful for programming, we can write how rotating a state affects each of the $|0\rangle$ and $|1\rangle$ states, as shown in figure 2.13.

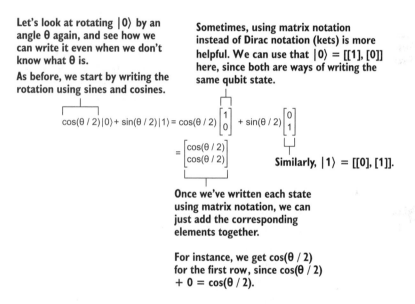

Let's look at rotating $|0\rangle$ by an angle θ again, and see how we can write it even when we don't know what θ is.

As before, we start by writing the rotation using sines and cosines.

Sometimes, using matrix notation instead of Dirac notation (kets) is more helpful. We can use that $|0\rangle = [[1], [0]]$ here, since both are ways of writing the same qubit state.

$$\cos(\theta\,/\,2)|0\rangle + \sin(\theta\,/\,2)|1\rangle = \cos(\theta\,/\,2)\begin{bmatrix}1\\0\end{bmatrix} + \sin(\theta\,/\,2)\begin{bmatrix}0\\1\end{bmatrix}$$

$$= \begin{bmatrix}\cos(\theta\,/\,2)\\\cos(\theta\,/\,2)\end{bmatrix}$$

Similarly, $|1\rangle = [[0], [1]]$.

Once we've written each state using matrix notation, we can just add the corresponding elements together.

For instance, we get $\cos(\theta\,/\,2)$ for the first row, since $\cos(\theta\,/\,2) + 0 = \cos(\theta\,/\,2)$.

Figure 2.13 Using linear algebra, we can describe the state of a single qubit as a two-element vector. In this equation, we show how that way of thinking about qubit states relates to our earlier use of Dirac (bra-ket) notation. In particular, we show the final state after rotating the $|0\rangle$ state by an arbitrary angle θ using both vector and Dirac notations; both will be helpful at different points in our quantum journey.

> **TIP** This is precisely the same as when we used a basis of vectors earlier to represent a linear function as a matrix.

We'll learn about other quantum operations in this book, but these are the easiest to visualize as rotations. Table 2.2 summarizes the states we have learned to create from these rotations.

Table 2.2   State labels, expansions in Dirac notation, and representations as vectors

State label	Dirac notation	Vector representation
$\lvert 0 \rangle$	$\lvert 0 \rangle$	[[1], [0]]
$\lvert 1 \rangle$	$\lvert 1 \rangle$	[[0], [1]]
$\lvert + \rangle$	$(\lvert 0 \rangle + \lvert 1 \rangle) / \sqrt{2}$	[[1 / $\sqrt{2}$], [1 / $\sqrt{2}$]]
$\lvert - \rangle$	$(\lvert 0 \rangle - \lvert 1 \rangle) / \sqrt{2}$	[[1 / $\sqrt{2}$], [–1 / $\sqrt{2}$]]

A mouthful of math

At first glance, something like $\lvert + \rangle = (\lvert 0 \rangle + \lvert 1 \rangle) / \sqrt{2}$ would be terrible to have to say out loud, making it useless in conversation. In practice, however, quantum programmers often take some shortcuts when speaking out loud or sketching things on a whiteboard.

For instance, the "$\sqrt{2}$" part always has to be there, since vectors representing quantum states must always be length one; that means we can sometimes be a little casual and write "$\lvert + \rangle = \lvert 0 \rangle + \lvert 1 \rangle$," relying on our audience to remember to divide by $\sqrt{2}$. If we're giving a talk or discussing quantum computing over some tea, we may say, "Ket plus is ket 0 plus ket 1," but the reuse of the word *plus* gets a little confusing without bras and kets to help. To emphasize verbally that addition allows us to represent superposition, we might say, "The plus state is an equal superposition of zero and one," instead.

2.3.3   *Measuring qubits*

When we want to retrieve the information stored in a qubit, we need to measure the qubit. Ideally, we would like a measurement device that lets us directly read out all the information about the state at once. As it turns out, this is not possible by the laws of quantum mechanics, as we'll see in chapters 3 and 4. That said, measurement *can* allow us to learn information about the state relative to particular directions in the system. For instance, if we have a qubit in the $\lvert 0 \rangle$ state, and we look to see if it is in the $\lvert 0 \rangle$ state, we'll always get that it is. On the other hand, if we have a qubit in the $\lvert + \rangle$ state, and we look to see if it is in the $\lvert 0 \rangle$ state, we'll get a 0 outcome with 50% probability. As shown in figure 2.14, this is because the $\lvert + \rangle$ state overlaps equally with the $\lvert 0 \rangle$ and $\lvert 1 \rangle$ states, such that we'll get both outcomes with the same probability.

> **TIP**   Measurement outcomes of qubits are *always* classical bit values! Put differently, whether we measure a classical bit or a qubit, our result is always a classical bit.

Most of the time, we will choose to measure whether we have a $\lvert 0 \rangle$ or a $\lvert 1 \rangle$; that is, we'll want to measure along the line between the $\lvert 0 \rangle$ and $\lvert 1 \rangle$. For convenience, we give this

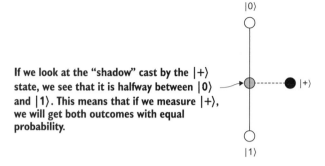

If we look at the "shadow" cast by the $|+\rangle$ state, we see that it is halfway between $|0\rangle$ and $|1\rangle$. This means that if we measure $|+\rangle$, we will get both outcomes with equal probability.

Figure 2.14 The $|+\rangle$ state overlaps equally with both $|0\rangle$ and $|1\rangle$ because the "shadow" it casts is exactly in the middle. Thus, when we look at our qubit to see if it's in the $|0\rangle$ or $|1\rangle$ state, we'll get both results with equal probability if our qubit started in the $|+\rangle$ state. We can think of the shadow the $|+\rangle$ state casts on the line between the $|0\rangle$ and $|1\rangle$ states as a kind of coin.

axis a name: the Z-axis. We can visually represent this by *projecting* our state vector onto the Z-axis (see figure 2.15) using the inner product.

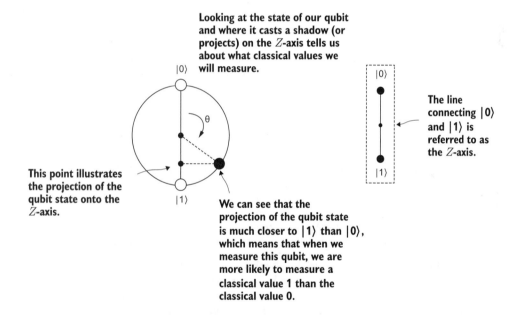

Looking at the state of our qubit and where it casts a shadow (or projects) on the Z-axis tells us about what classical values we will measure.

The line connecting $|0\rangle$ and $|1\rangle$ is referred to as the Z-axis.

This point illustrates the projection of the qubit state onto the Z-axis.

We can see that the projection of the qubit state is much closer to $|1\rangle$ than $|0\rangle$, which means that when we measure this qubit, we are more likely to measure a classical value 1 than the classical value 0.

Figure 2.15 A visualization of a quantum measurement, which can be thought of as projecting the state in a particular direction. For example, if a qubit is rotated such that its state is close to the $|1\rangle$ state, then measuring it is more likely to return 1 than 0.

TIP If you need a refresher on inner products, please check out appendix B.

Think of shining a flashlight from where we draw the state of a qubit back onto the Z-axis; the probability of getting a 0 or 1 result is determined by the shadow the state leaves on the Z-axis.

Deep dive: Why isn't measurement linear?

After having made such a big deal of the linearity of quantum mechanics, it may seem odd that we immediately introduce measurement as being nonlinear. If we're allowed nonlinear operations like measurement, can we also implement other nonlinear operations like cloning qubits?

The short version is that while everyone agrees on the math behind measurement, there's still a lot of philosophical discussion about the best way to understand why quantum measurement acts the way it does. These discussions fall under the name of *quantum foundations* and attempt to do more than simply understand what quantum mechanics is and what it predicts by also understanding *why*. For the most part, foundations explore different ways to *interpret* quantum mechanics. In the same way that we can understand classical probability by considering counterintuitive thought experiments such as game show strategies or how casinos can win even from games that seem to lose money, quantum foundations develops new interpretations through small thought experiments that probe different aspects of quantum mechanics. Fortunately, some of the results from quantum foundations can help us make sense of measurement.

In particular, one critical observation is that we can always make quantum measurements linear again by including the state of the measurement apparatus in our description; we'll see some of the mathematical tools needed to do so in chapters 4 and 6. When taken to its extreme, this observation leads to interpretations such as the *many-worlds interpretation*. The many-worlds interpretation solves the interpretation of measurement by insisting that we only consider states that include measurement devices, such that the apparent nonlinearity of measurement doesn't really exist.

At the other extreme, we can interpret measurement by noting that the nonlinearity in quantum measurement is precisely the same as in a branch of statistics known as Bayesian inference. Thus, quantum mechanics only appears nonlinear when we forget to include that an agent is performing the measurement and learns from each result. This observation leads to thinking of quantum mechanics not as a description of the world but as a description of what we know about the world.

Although these two kinds of interpretations disagree at a philosophical level, both offer different ways of resolving how a linear theory such as quantum mechanics can sometimes appear to be nonlinear. Regardless of which interpretation helps you understand the interaction between measurement and the rest of quantum mechanics, you can take solace that the measurement results are always described by the same math and simulations. Indeed, relying on simulations (sometimes sarcastically called the "shut up and calculate" interpretation) is the oldest and most celebrated of all interpretations.

The squared length of each projection *represents* the probability that the state we are measuring will be found along that direction. If we have a qubit in the $|0\rangle$ state and try to measure it along the direction of the $|1\rangle$ state, we will get a probability of zero because the states are opposite each other when we draw them on a circle. Thinking in terms of pictures, the $|0\rangle$ state has no projection onto the $|1\rangle$ state—in the sense of figure 2.15, $|0\rangle$ doesn't leave a shadow on $|1\rangle$.

TIP If something happens with probability 1, then that event *always* occurs. If something happens with probability 0, then that event is *impossible*. For example, the probability that a typical six-sided die rolls a 7 is zero since that roll is impossible. Similarly, if a qubit is in the $|0\rangle$ state, getting a 1 result from a *Z*-axis measurement is impossible since $|0\rangle$ has no projection onto $|1\rangle$.

If we have a $|0\rangle$ and try to measure it along the $|0\rangle$ direction, however, we will get a probability of 1 because the states are parallel (and of length 1 by definition). Let's walk through measuring a state that is neither parallel nor perpendicular.

Example
Say we have a qubit in state $(|0\rangle + |1\rangle) / \sqrt{2}$ (the same as $|+\rangle$ from table 2.1), and we want to measure it or project it along the *Z*-axis. We can then find the probability that the classical result will be a 1 by projecting $|+\rangle$ onto $|1\rangle$.

We can find the projection of one state onto another by using the *inner product* between their vector representations. In this case, we write the inner product of $|+\rangle$ and $|1\rangle$ as $\langle 1 | + \rangle$, where $\langle 1|$ is the transpose of $|1\rangle$ and where butting the two bars against each other indicates taking the inner product. Later, we'll see that $\langle 1|$ is the conjugate transpose of $|1\rangle$ and is referred to as a "bra."

We can write this out as follows:

To compute the projection, we start by writing down the "bra" that we want to project onto.

$\langle 1 | (|0\rangle + |1\rangle))/\sqrt{2}$

Next, we distribute the bra.

$= (1/\sqrt{2})(\langle 1|0\rangle + \langle 1|1\rangle)$

We can write each bra-ket pair as an inner product between two vectors.

$= (1/\sqrt{2}) ([[0], [1]] \cdot [[1], [0]] + [[0], [1]] \cdot [[0], [1]])$

Calculating each inner product makes things a lot simpler!

$= (1/\sqrt{2}))(0 + 1)$

We now have the overlap between $|0\rangle$ and $|1\rangle$.

$= 1/\sqrt{2}.$

To turn this projection into a probability, we square it, getting that the probability of observing a 1 outcome when we prepare a $|+\rangle$ state is 1 / 2.

We often project onto the *Z*-axis because it is convenient in many real experiments, but we can also measure along the *X*-axis to see if we have a $|+\rangle$ or a $|-\rangle$ state. Measuring along the *X*-axis, we get $|+\rangle$ with certainty and never get $|-\rangle$, as shown in figure 2.16.

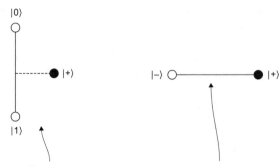

The shadow that the |+⟩ leaves on the Z-axis is halfway between |0⟩ and |1⟩, so we see both outcomes with equal probability.

On the other hand, the shadow left by |+⟩ on the X-axis is entirely on |+⟩, so we never see the outcome for |−⟩.

Figure 2.16   Measuring |+⟩ along the X-axis always results in |+⟩. To see this, note that the "shadow" left by the |+⟩ state on the X-axis (that is, the line between the |−⟩ and |+⟩ states) is precisely the |+⟩ state itself.

NOTE   We can get a fully certain measurement outcome *only* because we know the "right" direction to measure ahead of time in this case—if we are simply handed a state with no information about what the "right" measurement direction is, we cannot predict any measurement outcome perfectly.

2.3.4   *Generalizing measurement: Basis independence*

Sometimes we may not know how our qubit was prepared, so we do not know how to measure the bits properly. More generally, any pair of states that don't overlap (are opposite poles) defines a measurement the same way. The actual outcome of a measurement is a classical bit value that indicates which pole the state is aligned with when we perform the measurement.

> **Even more general measurements**
> Quantum mechanics allows for much more general kinds of measurements—we'll see a few of these as we go along, but mostly we focus in this book on the case of checking between two opposite poles. This choice is a pretty convenient way of controlling most quantum devices and can be used in almost any of the commercial platforms for quantum computing that are currently available.

Mathematically, we use notation like ⟨measurement | state⟩ to represent measuring a qubit. The left component, ⟨measurement|, is called a *bra*, and we have already seen the *ket* part on the right. Together, they are called a *braket*!

Bras are very similar to kets, except that to switch from one to the other, we have to take the transpose (turn rows to columns and vice versa) of the bra or ket we have:

$$|0\rangle^T = [[1], [0]]^T = [[1, 0]].$$

Another way to think of this is that taking the transpose turns column vectors (kets) into row vectors (bras).

> **NOTE** Since we're only working with real numbers for now, we won't need to do anything else to go between kets and bras. But when we work with complex numbers in the next chapter, we'll need the complex conjugate as well.

Bras let us write down measurements. But to see what measurements actually *do*, we need one more thing at our disposal: a rule for how to use a bra and a ket together to get the *probability* of seeing that measurement result. In quantum mechanics, measurement probabilities are found by looking at the length of the projection or shadow that the ket for a state leaves on a bra for a measurement. We know from experience that we can find projections and lengths using inner products. In Dirac notation, the inner product of a bra and a ket is written as $\langle \text{measurement} \mid \text{state} \rangle$, giving us just the rule we need.

For example, if we have prepared a state $|+\rangle$ and we want to know the probability that we observe a 1 when we measure in the Z-basis, then projecting as shown in figure 2.15, we can find the length we need. The projection of $|+\rangle$ onto $\langle 1|$ tells us that we see a 1 outcome with probability $\Pr(1|+) = |\langle 1|+\rangle|^2 = |\langle 1|0\rangle + \langle 1|1\rangle|^2 / 2 = |0 + 1|^2 / 2 = 1 / 2$. Thus, 50% of the time, we'll get a 1 outcome. The other 50% of the time, we'll get a 0 outcome.

Born's rule

If we have a quantum state $|\text{state}\rangle$ and we perform a measurement along the $\langle\text{measurement}|$ direction, we can write the probability that we will observe *measurement* as our result as

$$\Pr(\text{measurement}|\text{state}) = |\langle\text{measurement}|\text{state}\rangle|^2$$

In other words, the probability is the square of the magnitude of the inner product of the measurement bra and the state ket.

This expression is called *Born's rule*.

In table 2.3, we've listed several other examples of using Born's rule to predict what classical bits we will get when we measure qubits.

Table 2.3 Examples of using Born's rule to find measurement probabilities

If we prepare...	...and we measure...	...then we see that outcome with this probability.
$|0\rangle$	$\langle 0|$	$|\langle 0 \mid 0 \rangle|^2 = 1$
$|0\rangle$	$\langle 1|$	$|\langle 1 \mid 0 \rangle|^2 = 0$
$|0\rangle$	$\langle +|$	$|\langle + \mid 0 \rangle|^2 = |(\langle 0| + \langle 1|) \, |0\rangle / \sqrt{2}|^2 = (1 / \sqrt{2} + 0)^2 = 1 / 2$

Table 2.3   Examples of using Born's rule to find measurement probabilities *(continued)*

If we prepare...	...and we measure...	...then we see that outcome with this probability.
$|+\rangle$	$\langle+|$	$|\langle+\,|\,+\rangle|^2 = |(\langle 0| + \langle 1|)\,(|0\rangle + |1\rangle) / 2|^2 = |\langle 0\,|\,0\rangle + \langle 1\,|\,0\rangle + \langle 0\,|\,1\rangle + \langle 1\,|\,1\rangle|^2 / 4 = |1 + 0 + 0 + 1|^2 / 4 = 2^2 / 4 = 1$
$|+\rangle$	$\langle-|$	$|\langle-\,|\,+\rangle|^2 = 0$
$-|0\rangle$	$\langle 0|$	$|-\langle 0\,|\,0\rangle|^2 = |-1|^2 = 1^2$
$-|+\rangle$	$\langle-|$	$|-\langle+\,|\,-\rangle|^2 = |(-\langle 0| - \langle 1|)\,(|0\rangle - |1\rangle) / 2|^2 = |-\langle 0\,|\,0\rangle - \langle 1\,|\,0\rangle + \langle 0\,|\,1\rangle + \langle 1\,|\,1\rangle|^2 / 4 = |-1 - 0 + 0 + 1|^2 / 4 = 0^2 / 4 = 0$

TIP   In table 2.3, we use the fact that $\langle 0\,|\,0\rangle = \langle 1\,|\,1\rangle = 1$ and $\langle 0\,|\,1\rangle = \langle 1\,|\,0\rangle = 0$. (Try checking this for yourself!) When two states have an inner product of zero, we say that they are *orthogonal* (or *perpendicular*). The fact that $|0\rangle$ and $|1\rangle$ are orthogonal makes a lot of calculations easier to do quickly.

We have now covered everything we need to know about qubits to be able to simulate them! Let's review the requirements we needed to satisfy to make sure we have working qubits.

> **Qubit**
>
> A qubit is any physical system satisfying three properties:
>
> - The system can be perfectly simulated given knowledge of the vector of numbers (the state).
> - The system can be transformed using quantum operations (for example, rotations).
> - Any measurement of the system produces a single classical bit of information, following Born's rule.

Anytime we have a qubit (a system with the previous three properties), we can describe it using the same math or simulation code without further reference to what kind of system we are working with. This is similar to how we do not need to know whether a bit is defined by the direction of a pinball's motion or the voltage in a transistor to write NOT and AND gates or to write software that uses those gates to do interesting computations.

NOTE   Similar to how we use the word *bit* to mean both a physical system that stores information and the information stored in a bit, we also use the word *qubit* to mean both a quantum device and the quantum information stored in that device.

Phase

In the last two rows of table 2.3, we saw that multiplying a state by a phase of –1 doesn't affect measurement probabilities. This isn't a coincidence but rather points to one of the more interesting things about qubits. Because Born's rule only cares about the squared absolute value of the inner product of a state and a measurement, multiplying a number by (–1) doesn't affect its absolute value. We call numbers such as +1 or –1, whose absolute value is equal to 1, *phases*. In the next chapter, we'll see a lot more about phases when we work more with complex numbers.

For now, we say that multiplying an entire vector by –1 is an example of applying a *global phase*, while changing from $|+\rangle$ to $|-\rangle$ is an example of applying a *relative phase* between $|0\rangle$ and $|1\rangle$. While global phases don't ever affect measurement results, there's a big difference between the states $|+\rangle = (|0\rangle + |1\rangle) / \sqrt{2}$ and $|-\rangle = (|0\rangle - |1\rangle) / \sqrt{2}$: the coefficients in front of $|0\rangle$ and $|1\rangle$ are the same in $|+\rangle$ and are different by a phase of (–1) in $|-\rangle$. We will see much more of the difference between these two concepts in chapters 3, 4, 6, and 7.

2.3.5 *Simulating qubits in code*

Now that we have looked at how we can describe qubit states, operations, and measurements, it's time to see how to represent all of these concepts in code. We will use a scenario with our friend Eve to motivate the code we write.

Suppose we would like to keep our 💟 for Eve a secret, lest anyone else find out. How can we scramble our message to Eve so that only she can read it?

We'll explore this application more in the next chapter, but the most basic step we need for any good *encryption* algorithm is a source of random numbers that's difficult to predict. Let's write down exactly how we would combine our secret and random bits to make a secure message to send to Eve. Figure 2.17 shows that if both you and Eve know the same secret sequence of random classical bits, we can use that sequence to communicate securely. At the start of the chapter, we saw how to write the message, or *plaintext*, that we want to send to Eve (in this case, "💟") as a string of classical bits. The one-time pad is a sequence of random classical bits that acts as a way to scramble or encrypt our message. This scrambling is done by taking the bitwise XOR of the message and one-time pad bits for each position in the sequence. This then produces a sequence of classical bits called the *ciphertext*. To anyone else trying to read our message, the ciphertext will look like random bits. For example, it's impossible to tell if a bit in the ciphertext is 1 because of the plaintext or the one-time pad.

You may ask how we get the random bit strings for our one-time pad. We can make our own QRNG with qubits! It may seem odd, but we will simulate qubits with classical bits to make our QRNG. The random numbers it generates won't be any more secure than the computer we use to do our simulation, but this approach gives us a good start in understanding how qubits work.

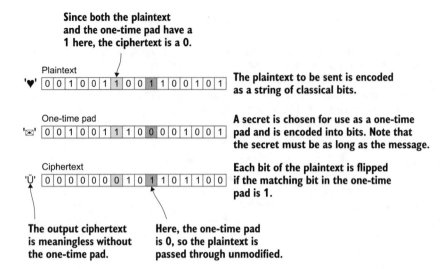

Figure 2.17 **An example of how to use random bits to encrypt secrets, even over the internet or another untrusted network. Here, we're trying to securely send the message "♥". If we and Eve start with the shared secret "✉", then we can use that as a *one-time pad* to protect our message.**

Let's send Eve our message! Just as a classical bit can be represented in code by the values `True` and `False`, we've seen that we can represent the two qubit states $|0\rangle$ and $|1\rangle$ as *vectors*. That is, qubit states are represented in code as lists of lists of numbers.

Listing 2.3   Representing qubits in code with NumPy

```
>>> import numpy as np
>>> ket0 = np.array(
...        [[1], [0]]
... )
>>> ket0
array([[1],
       [0]])
>>> ket1 = np.array(
...        [[0], [1]]
... )
>>> ket1
array([[0],
       [1]])
```

We use the NumPy library for Python to represent vectors, as NumPy is highly optimized and will make our lives much easier.

We name our variable ket0 after the notation $|0\rangle$, in which we label qubit states by the ket half of $\langle\rangle$ brakets.

NumPy will print 2 × 1 vectors as columns.

As we saw earlier, we can construct other states such as $|+\rangle$ by using linear combinations of $|0\rangle$ and $|1\rangle$. In exactly the same sense, we can use NumPy to add the vector representations of $|0\rangle$ and $|1\rangle$ to construct the vector representation of $|+\rangle$.

Listing 2.4 The vector representation of |+⟩

```
>>> ket_plus = (ket0 + ket1) / np.sqrt(2)
>>> ket_plus
array([[0.70710678+0.j],
       [0.70710678+0.j]])
```

NumPy uses vectors to store the |+⟩ state, which is a linear combination of |0⟩ and |1⟩.

We will see the number 0.70710678 a lot in this book, as it is a good approximation of $\sqrt{2}$, the length of the vector [[1], [1]].

In classical logic, if we wanted to simulate how an operation would transform a list of bits, we could use a truth table. Similarly, since quantum operations other than measurement are always linear, to simulate how an operation transforms the state of a qubit, we can use a matrix that tells us how each state is transformed.

Linear operators and quantum operations

Describing quantum operations as linear operators is a good start, but not all linear operators are valid quantum operations! If we could implement an operation described by a linear operator such as $2 \times \mathbb{1}$ (that is, twice the identity operator), then we would be able to violate that probabilities are always numbers between zero and one. We also require that all quantum operations other than measurement are *reversible*, as this is a fundamental property of quantum mechanics.

It turns out that the operations realizable in quantum mechanics are described by matrices U whose inverses U^{-1} can be computed by taking the conjugate transpose, $U^{-1} = U^{\dagger}$. Such matrices are called *unitary matrices*.

Not all linear operators describe valid operations in quantum mechanics.

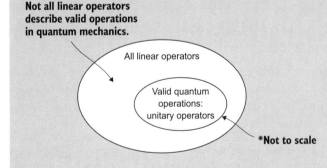

Visualizing types of valid quantum operations. All unitary operators are linear, but not all linear operators are unitary. Reversible quantum operations (that is, other than measurement) are represented by operators that are not just linear but unitary.

One particularly important quantum operation is the *Hadamard operation*, which transforms |0⟩ to |+⟩ and |1⟩ to |−⟩. As we saw earlier, measuring |+⟩ along the Z-axis gives either a 0 or a 1 result with equal probability. Since we want random bits in order to send secret messages, the Hadamard operation is really useful for making our QRNG.

Using vectors and matrices, we can define the Hadamard operation by making a table of how it acts on the |0⟩ and |1⟩ states, as shown in table 2.4.

Because quantum mechanics is linear, this is a fully complete description of the Hadamard operation!

Table 2.4 Representing the Hadamard operation as a table

Input state	Output state
$\lvert 0 \rangle$	$\lvert + \rangle = (\lvert 0 \rangle + \lvert 1 \rangle) / \sqrt{2}$
$\lvert 1 \rangle$	$\lvert - \rangle = (\lvert 0 \rangle - \lvert 1 \rangle) / \sqrt{2}$

In matrix form, we write table 2.4 as `H = np.array([[1, 1], [1, -1]]) / np.sqrt(2)`.

Listing 2.5 Defining the Hadamard operation

```
>>> H = np.array([[1, 1], [1, -1]]) / np.sqrt(2)
>>> H @ ket0
array([[0.70710678],
       [0.70710678]])
>>> H @ ket1
array([[ 0.70710678],
       [-0.70710678]])
```

We define a variable **H** to hold the matrix representation **H** of the Hadamard operation that we saw in table 2.4. We'll need **H** throughout the rest of this chapter, so it's helpful to define it here.

Hadamard operation

The Hadamard operation is a quantum operation that can be simulated by this linear transformation:

$$H = \frac{1}{\sqrt{2}} \begin{pmatrix} 1 & 1 \\ 1 & -1 \end{pmatrix}.$$

Any operation on quantum data can be written as a matrix in this way. If we wish to transform $\lvert 0 \rangle$ to $\lvert 1 \rangle$ and vice versa (the quantum generalization of the classical NOT operation that we saw earlier, corresponding to a 180° rotation), we do the same thing we did to define the Hadamard operation.

Listing 2.6 Representing the quantum NOT gate

```
>>> X = np.array([[0, 1], [1, 0]])
>>> X @ ket0
array([[0],
       [1]])
>>> (X @ ket0 == ket1).all()
True
```

The quantum operation corresponding to the classical **NOT** operation is typically called the **x** operation; we represent the matrix for **x** with a Python variable **X**.

We can confirm that **X** transforms $\lvert 0 \rangle$ to $\lvert 1 \rangle$. The NumPy method all() returns **True** if every element of **X** @ ket0 == ket1 is True: that is, if every element of the array **X** @ ket0 is equal to the corresponding element of ket1.

```
>>> X @ H @ ket0
array([[0.70710678],
       [0.70710678]])
```

The x operator doesn't do anything to $H|0\rangle$. We can confirm this by using the @ operator again to multiply X by a Python value representing the state $|+\rangle = H|0\rangle$. We can express that value as **H @ ket0**.

The x operation doesn't do anything on the last input because the x operation swaps $|0\rangle$ and $|1\rangle$. The $H|0\rangle$ state, also called $|+\rangle$, is already a sum of the two kets: $(|0\rangle + |1\rangle)$ / $\sqrt{2} = (|1\rangle + |0\rangle)$ / $\sqrt{2}$, so a swap action of the x operation doesn't do anything.

Recalling the map analogy from appendix C, we can think of the matrix H as a *reflection* about the ↗ direction, as illustrated in figure 2.18.

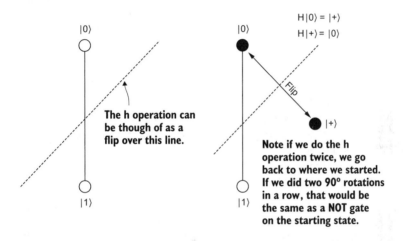

Figure 2.18 The h operation as a reflection or flip about ↗. Unlike a rotation of 90°, applying h twice returns a qubit to the state it started in. Another way to think of h is that the reflection about ↗ swaps the role of the *X*- and *Z*-axes.

The third dimension awaits!

For qubits, the map analogy from appendix C helps us understand how to write and manipulate the states of single qubits. So far, however, we've only looked at states that can be written using real numbers. In general, quantum states can use complex numbers. If we rearrange our map and make it three-dimensional, we can include complex numbers without any problem. This way of thinking about qubits is called the *Bloch sphere* and can be very useful for considering quantum operations such as rotations and reflections, as we'll see in chapter 6.

(continued)

The state of the qubit now is represented as a point anywhere on the Bloch sphere.

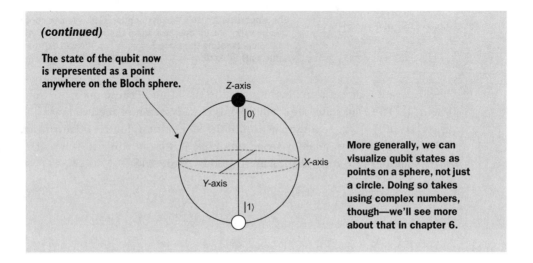

More generally, we can visualize qubit states as points on a sphere, not just a circle. Doing so takes using complex numbers, though—we'll see more about that in chapter 6.

Deep dive: Infinitely many states?

It may seem from the figure in the previous sidebar that there are infinitely many different states of a qubit. For any two different points on a sphere, we can always find a point that's "between" them. While this is true, it can also be a little misleading. Thinking of the classical situation for a moment, a coin that lands heads 90% of the time is distinct from a coin that lands heads 90.0000000001% of the time. In fact, we can always make a coin whose bias is "between" the bias of two other coins. Flipping a coin can only ever give us one classical bit of information, though. On average, it would take about 10^{23} flips to tell a coin that lands heads 90% of the time apart from one that lands heads 90.0000000001% of the time. We can treat these two coins as identical because we cannot do an experiment that reliably tells them apart. Similarly, for quantum computing, there are limits to our ability to tell apart the infinitely many different quantum states that we recognize from the Bloch sphere picture.

The fact that a qubit has infinitely many states is not what makes it unique. Sometimes people say that a quantum system can be "in infinitely many states at once," which is why they say quantum computers can offer speedups. *This is false!* As pointed out previously, we can't distinguish states that are very close together, so the "infinitely many" part of the statement can't be what gives quantum computing an advantage. We will talk more about the "at once" part in upcoming chapters, but suffice to say it is not the number of states that our qubit can be in that makes quantum computers cool!

2.4   Programming a working QRNG

Now that we have a few quantum concepts to play with, let's apply what we've learned to program a QRNG so that we can send ♡s with no worries. We are going to build a QRNG that returns either a 0 or a 1.

Random bits or random numbers?

It may seem limiting that our QRNG can only output one of two numbers, 0 or 1. On the contrary: this is enough to generate random numbers in the range 0 to N for any positive integer N. It's easiest to see this starting with the special case that N is $2^n - 1$ for some positive integer n, in which case we simply write down our random numbers as n-bit strings. For example, we can make random numbers between 0 and 7 by generating three random bits r_0, r_1, and r_2 and then returning $4r_2 + 2r_1 + r_0$.

The case is slightly more tricky if N isn't given by a power of two, in that we have "left-over" possibilities that we need to deal with. For instance, if we need to roll a six-sided die but only have an eight-sided die (maybe we played a druid at the latest RPG night), then we need to decide what to do when that die rolls a 7 or an 8. The best thing we can do if we want a fair six-sided die is to simply reroll when that happens. Using this approach, we can build arbitrary fair dice from coin flips—handy for what-ever game we want to play. Long story short, we aren't limited by having just two out-comes from our QRNG!

As with any quantum program, our QRNG program will be a sequence of instructions to a device that performs operations on a qubit (see figure 2.19). In pseudocode, a quantum program for implementing a QRNG consists of three instructions:

1. Prepare a qubit in the state $|0\rangle$.
2. Apply the Hadamard operation to our qubit so it is in the state $|+\rangle = H|0\rangle$.
3. Measure the qubit to get either a 0 or a 1 result with 50/50 probability.

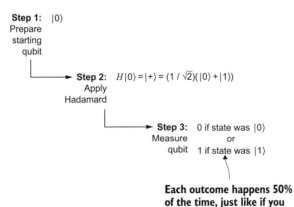

Step 1: $|0\rangle$
Prepare starting qubit

Step 2: $H|0\rangle = |+\rangle = (1 / \sqrt{2})(|0\rangle + |1\rangle)$
Apply Hadamard

Step 3: 0 if state was $|0\rangle$
Measure or
qubit 1 if state was $|1\rangle$

Each outcome happens 50% of the time, just like if you flipped a coin!

Figure 2.19 Steps for writing the QRNG program that we want to test. Revisiting figure 2.3, we can use what we've learned so far to write the state of our qubit after each step in the QRNG algorithm.

That is, we want a program that looks something like the following.

Listing 2.7   Example pseudocode for a QRNG program

```
def qrng():
    q = Qubit()
    H(q)
    return measure(q)
```

Using matrix multiplication, we can use a classical computer like a laptop to simulate how qrng() would act on an ideal quantum device. Our qrng program calls into a software stack (see figure 2.20) that abstracts away whether we're using a classical simulator or an actual quantum device.

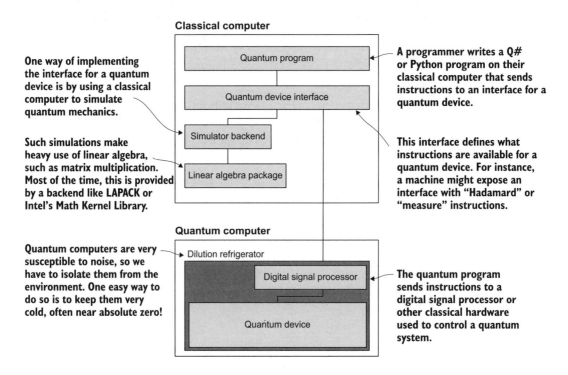

One way of implementing the interface for a quantum device is by using a classical computer to simulate quantum mechanics.

Such simulations make heavy use of linear algebra, such as matrix multiplication. Most of the time, this is provided by a backend like **LAPACK** or Intel's Math Kernel Library.

Classical computer

Quantum program

Quantum device interface

Simulator backend

Linear algebra package

A programmer writes a **Q#** or **Python** program on their classical computer that sends instructions to an interface for a quantum device.

This interface defines what instructions are available for a quantum device. For instance, a machine might expose an interface with "Hadamard" or "measure" instructions.

Quantum computer

Quantum computers are very susceptible to noise, so we have to isolate them from the environment. One easy way to do so is to keep them very cold, often near absolute zero!

Dilution refrigerator

Digital signal processor

Quantum device

The quantum program sends instructions to a digital signal processor or other classical hardware used to control a quantum system.

Figure 2.20   An example of what a software stack for a quantum program might look like

There are many parts to the stack, but don't worry—we will talk about them as we go. For now, we are focusing on the top section (labeled "Classical computer" in the figure) and will start by writing code for a quantum program as well as a simulator backend in Python.

> **NOTE**   In chapter 7, we'll pivot to using the simulator backend provided with Microsoft's Quantum Development Kit, instead.

With this view of a software stack in mind, then, we can write our simulation of a QRNG by first writing a `QuantumDevice` class with abstract methods for allocating qubits, performing operations, and measuring qubits. We can then implement this class with a simulator and call into that simulator from `qrng()`.

To design the interface for our simulator in a way that looks like figure 2.20, let's list what we need our quantum device to do. First, users must be able to allocate and return qubits.

Listing 2.8 interface.py: interface into a quantum device as abstract methods

```
class QuantumDevice(metaclass=ABCMeta):
    @abstractmethod
    def allocate_qubit(self) -> Qubit:     ◁
        pass

    @abstractmethod
    def deallocate_qubit(self, qubit: Qubit):   ◁
        pass

    @contextmanager
    def using_qubit(self):      ◁
        qubit = self.allocate_qubit()
        try:
            yield qubit
        finally:
            qubit.reset()      ◁
            self.deallocate_qubit(qubit)
```

> Any implementation of a quantum device must implement this method, allowing users to obtain qubits.

> When users are done with a qubit, implementations of deallocate_qubit will allow users to return the qubit to the device.

> We can provide a Python context manager to make it easy to allocate and deallocate qubits safely.

> The context manager makes sure that no matter what exceptions are raised, each qubit is reset and deallocated before being returned to the classical computer.

The qubits themselves can then expose the actual transformations that we need:

- Users must be able to perform Hadamard operations on qubits.
- Users must be able to measure qubits to get classical data.

Listing 2.9 interface.py: interface into the qubits on a quantum device

```
from abc import ABCMeta, abstractmethod
from contextlib import contextmanager
class Qubit(metaclass=ABCMeta):
    @abstractmethod
    def h(self): pass      ◁

    @abstractmethod
    def measure(self) -> bool: pass     ◁

    @abstractmethod
    def reset(self): pass      ◁
```

> The h method transforms a qubit in place (not making a copy) using the Hadamard operation np.array([[1, 1], [1, −1]]) / np.sqrt(2).

> The measure method allows users to measure qubits and extract classical data.

> The reset method makes it easy for users to prepare the qubit from scratch again.

With this in place, we can return to our definition of `qrng` using these new classes.

Listing 2.10   qrng.py: definition of the `qrng` device

```
def qrng(device: QuantumDevice) -> bool:
    with device.using_qubit() as q:
        q.h()
        return q.measure()
```

If we implement the `QuantumDevice` interface with a class called `SingleQubitSimulator`, then we can pass this to qrng to run our QRNG implementation on a simulator.

Listing 2.11   qrng.py: definition of `main` for qrng.py

```
if __name__ == "__main__":
    qsim = SingleQubitSimulator()
    for idx_sample in range(10):
        random_sample = qrng(qsim)
        print(f"Our QRNG returned {random_sample}.")
```

We now have everything to write `SingleQubitSimulator`. We start by defining a couple of constants for the vector $|0\rangle$ and the matrix representation of the Hadamard operation.

Listing 2.12   simulator.py: defining useful constants

```
KET_0 = np.array([
    [1],
    [0]
], dtype=complex)
H = np.array([
    [1, 1],
    [1, -1]
], dtype=complex) / np.sqrt(2)
```

Since we'll be using $|0\rangle$ a lot in our simulator, we define a constant for it.

Similarly, we'll use the Hadamard matrix H to define how the Hadamard operation transforms states, so we define a constant for that as well.

Next, we define what a simulated qubit looks like. From the perspective of a simulator, a qubit wraps a vector that stores the qubit's current state. We use a NumPy array to represent our qubit's state.

Listing 2.13   simulator.py: defining a class to represent qubits in our device

```
class SimulatedQubit(Qubit):
    def __init__(self):
        self.reset()

    def h(self):
        self.state = H @ self.state
```

As a part of the Qubit interface, we ensure that the reset method prepares our qubit in the $|0\rangle$ state. We can use that when we create the qubit to ensure that qubits always start in the correct state.

The Hadamard operation can be simulated by applying the matrix representation H to the state that we're storing at the moment and then updating to our new state.

```
def measure(self) -> bool:
    pr0 = np.abs(self.state[0, 0]) ** 2
    sample = np.random.random() <= pr0
    return bool(0 if sample else 1)

def reset(self):
    self.state = KET_0.copy()
```

We stored our qubit's state as a vector, so we know the inner product with |0⟩ is simply the first element of that vector. For instance, if the state is np.array([[a], [b]]) for some numbers a and b, then the probability of observing a 0 outcome is $|a|^2$. We can find this using np.abs(a) ** 2. This gives us the probability that a measurement of our qubit returns 0.

To turn the probability of getting a 0 into a measurement result, we generate a random number between 0 and 1 using np.random.random and check whether it's less than pr0.

Finally, we return 0 to the caller if we got a 0 and 1 if we got a 1.

What random number came first: 0 or 1?

In making this QRNG, we have to call a *classical* random number generator. This may feel a bit circular, but it comes about because our classical simulation is just that: a simulation. A simulation of a QRNG is no more random than the hardware and software we use to implement that simulator.

That said, the quantum program qrng.py itself does not need to call a classical RNG but calls into the simulator. If we were to run qrng.py on an actual quantum device, the simulator and the classical RNG would be substituted for operations on the actual qubit. At that point, we would have a stream of random numbers that would be impossible to predict, thanks to the laws of quantum mechanics.

Running our program, we now get the random numbers we expected!

```
$ python qrng.py
Our QRNG returned False.
Our QRNG returned True.
Our QRNG returned True.
Our QRNG returned False.
Our QRNG returned False.
Our QRNG returned True.
Our QRNG returned False.
Our QRNG returned False.
Our QRNG returned False.
Our QRNG returned True.
```

Congratulations! We've not only written our first quantum program but also written a simulation backend and used it to run our quantum program the same way we'd run it on an actual quantum computer.

Deep dive: Schrödinger's cat

You may have already seen or heard of this quantum program under a very different name. The QRNG program is often described in terms of the *Schrödinger's cat* thought experiment. Suppose a cat is in a closed box with a vial of poison that will be released if a particular random particle decays. Before we open the box to check, how do we know if it is alive or dead?

> The [state] of the entire system would express this by having in it the living and dead cat (pardon the expression) mixed or smeared out in equal parts.
>
> —*Erwin Schrödinger*

Historically, Schrödinger proposed this description in 1935 to express his view that some implications of quantum mechanics are "ridiculous" by means of a thought experiment that highlights how counterintuitive these implications are. Such thought experiments, known as *gedankenexperiment*, are a celebrated tradition in physics and can help us understand or critique different theories by pushing them to extreme or absurd limits.

Reading about Schrödinger's cat nearly a century later, however, it's helpful to remember everything that's happened in the intervening years. Since his original letter, the world has seen

- War on a scale never before imagined
- The first steps that humanity has taken to explore beyond our planet
- The rise of commercial jet travel
- The understanding and first effects of anthropogenic climate change
- A fundamental shift in how we communicate (from television all the way to the internet)
- A wide availability of affordable computing devices
- The discovery of a wondrous variety of subatomic particles

The world we live in isn't the same world in which Schrödinger tried to make sense of quantum mechanics! We have many advantages in trying to understand, not the least of which is that we can quickly get our hands on quantum mechanics by programming simulations using classical computers. For example, the h instruction we saw earlier puts our qubit in a situation similar to the cat in the gedankenexperiment, but with the advantage that it's much easier to experiment with our program than with a thought experiment. Throughout the rest of the book, we'll use quantum programs to learn the parts of quantum mechanics we need to write quantum algorithms.

Summary

- Random numbers help in a wide range of applications, such as playing games, simulating complex systems, and securing data.
- Classical bits can be in one of two states, which we traditionally call 0 and 1.
- Quantum analogues to classical bits, called *qubits*, can be in either the $|0\rangle$ or $|1\rangle$ state, or in superpositions of $|0\rangle$ and $|1\rangle$; for example, $|+\rangle = 1 / \sqrt{2} \; (|0\rangle + |1\rangle)$.
- By using the Hadamard operation, we can prepare qubits in the $|+\rangle$ state; we can then measure the qubits to generate numbers that are guaranteed to be random by the laws of quantum mechanics.

Sharing secrets with quantum key distribution

This chapter covers

- Recognizing the implications of quantum resources for security
- Programming a Python simulator for a quantum key distribution protocol
- Implementing the quantum NOT operation

In the previous chapter, we started playing around with qubits and used them to build a quantum random number generator with a simulator that we built in Python. In this chapter, we see that qubits can help us with encryption (or other cryptographic tasks) by letting us securely *distribute* secret keys. There are classical methods for sharing random keys (e.g., RSA), but they have different guarantees about the security of the sharing.

3.1 All's fair in love and encryption

We have a quantum random number generator from chapter 2, but that's only half of what we need to share secrets with our friends. We need to share those random numbers with our friends if we want to use the quantum random numbers to communicate securely with them. Those random numbers (often called a *key*) can be used with *encryption* algorithms that combine the randomness of the key with information people want to keep secret in such a way that only someone else with the key can see the information. We can see in figure 3.1 how two people could use a key (here, a random binary string) to encrypt and decrypt messages between themselves.

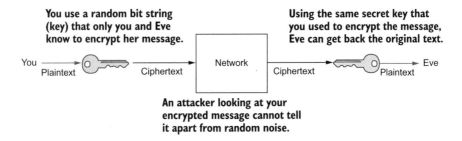

Figure 3.1 Mental model for how we and Eve might use encryption to communicate secretly, even over the internet or another untrusted network

If we want to get qubits involved, we can show that using quantum key distribution (QKD) is *provably* secure, whereas classical key distribution methods are often *computationally* secure.

> **DEFINITION** *Quantum key distribution* (QKD) is a communication protocol that allows users to share quantum random numbers by exchanging qubits and authenticated classical information.

This difference doesn't matter for most use cases. But if we are a government, activist group, bank, journalist, spy, or any other entity where information security is a life-and-death matter, this is a huge deal.

Computational vs. provable security

Provable security for cryptographic protocols is the dream. A method or protocol for a cryptographic task is *provably secure* if we can write a proof showing it is secure using no assumptions about an adversary: i.e., that they can have all the time and computing power in the universe and our protocol is still secure! Most of our current cryptographic infrastructure is *computationally secure*, which guarantees the security of a method or protocol with reasonable assumptions about an adversary's capabilities. The designer or user of the protocol can choose thresholds for what finite computer resources look like (e.g., the largest current supercomputer or all the computers on the planet) and what a reasonable time is (100 years, 10,000 years, the age of the universe).

When we share a key using QKD, it does not guarantee that the key will get to the other person. This is because someone can always do a denial of service attack (such as cutting the optical fiber between sender and receiver), which is the same for any other classical protocol. A good analogy for what QKD can promise is similar to the tamper-proof seal on food products. When a peanut butter manufacturer wants to ensure that when we open the jar, it is exactly as it was when it left the factory floor, the company puts a tamper-proof seal on the container. The company makes a promise that if the seal makes it to us (the consumer) intact, the peanut butter is good and no third party has done anything to it. Transmitting a cryptographic key with a QKD protocol is like putting a tamper-proof seal on the bits in transit. If someone tries to compromise the key in transit, the receiver will know and won't use that key. However, sealing the bits in transit does *not* guarantee that the bits make it to the receiver.

We can use many protocols to implement the general QKD scheme. In this chapter, we will be working with one of the most common QKD protocols—BB84—but there are many others that we won't have time to get into. Throughout this chapter, we build up to this, but figure 3.2 shows the steps to the BB84 protocol.

QKD is an example of a quantum program that uses a single qubit and a spin-off technology from quantum computing. What makes it attractive to develop is that we

BB84 protocol

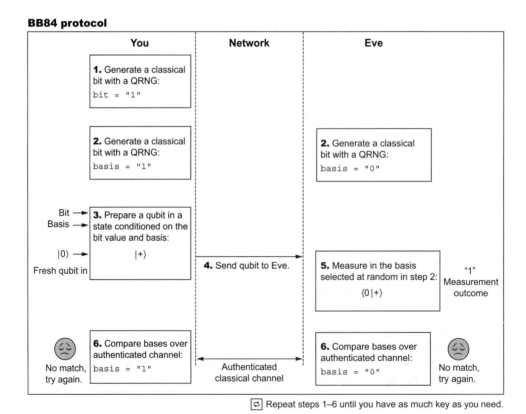

Figure 3.2   Timing diagram for the BB84 protocol, a variant of a QKD protocol

already have the hardware to implement it today! A number of companies have been commercially selling QKD hardware for about 15 years, but the important next steps for the technology involve hardware and software security vetting of these systems.

> **WARNING**   The examples we are implementing and using in this book *simulate* provably secure protocols. Given that we are not running the examples on quantum devices, they are *not* provably secure. Even when implementing these protocols with real quantum hardware, these security proofs do nothing to stop side-channel attacks or social engineering from separating us from our key 😈. We talk more about these proofs later in this chapter when we discuss the no-cloning theorem.

Let's dive into how QKD works! For our purposes, let's say we and Eve are the two people from the previous chapter who want to exchange a key so we can send secret messages 😊. The scenario is as follows:

> *We wish to send a secret message to our friend. Using our quantum random number generator from chapter 2, the QKD protocol BB84, and one-time pad encryption, design a program to send messages that can be provably secure.*

We can visualize the scenario as a kind of timing diagram, like figure 3.3.

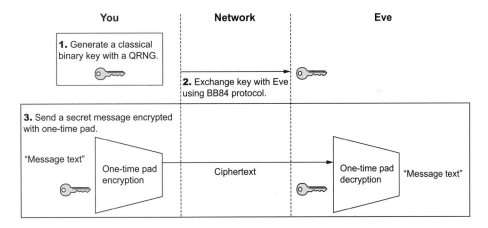

Figure 3.3   The scenario for this chapter: sending a secret message to Eve with BB84 and one-time pad encryption. We first have to exchange a secret key with Eve so we can use it to encrypt the message we want to send. We can use qubits and superposition states to help with the key-exchange step!

Note that the key we need to send is a string of classical bits. How can we use qubits to send those classical bits? We start by seeing how to encode classical information in qubits and then learn the specific steps of the BB84 protocol. In the next section, we'll look at a new quantum operation that will help us encode classical bits with qubits.

3.1.1 *Quantum NOT operations*

If we have some classical information, say a single binary bit, how can we encode it with a quantum resource like a qubit? Take a look at the following algorithm for sending a random classical bit string encoded in qubits:

1 Use a quantum random number generator to generate a random key bit to send.
2 Start with a qubit in the $|0\rangle$ state and then prepare it in a state that represents that bit value from step 1. Here, use $|0\rangle$ if the classical bit was a 0 and $|1\rangle$ if the classical bit was a 1.
3 That prepared qubit is sent to Eve, who then measures it and records the classical bit value.
4 Repeat steps 1–3 until we and Eve have as much key as we want (usually dictated by the cryptographic protocol we want to use after).

Figure 3.4 shows a timing diagram for this algorithm.

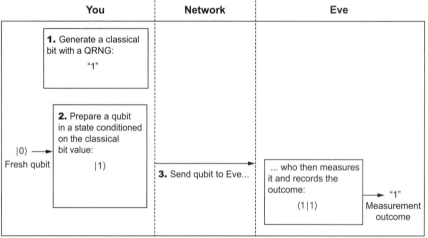

Figure 3.4 **A visualization of the algorithm for sending a classical bit string with qubits. We start by using our QRNG to generate a classical bit value, encode that on a fresh qubit, and then send it to Eve. She can then measure it and record the classical measurement result.**

Now, to switch the qubit from $|0\rangle$ to $|1\rangle$, we need another quantum operation in our toolbox. In step 2, we can use a *quantum* NOT operation—which is similar to a classical NOT operation—that rotates the qubit from $|0\rangle$ to $|1\rangle$ (see figure 2.9).

We refer to this quantum NOT operation as the x operation.

DEFINITION The x operation or *quantum NOT* takes a qubit in the $|0\rangle$ state to the $|1\rangle$ state and vice versa.

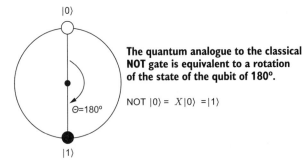

The quantum analogue to the classical **NOT** gate is equivalent to a rotation of the state of the qubit of 180°.

NOT $|0\rangle = X|0\rangle = |1\rangle$

Figure 3.5   A visualization of the quantum equivalent of a NOT operation operating on a qubit in the |0⟩ state, leaving the qubit in the |1⟩ state

Step 2 can be rewritten as follows:

1 If our classical bit from step 1 was a 0, do nothing. If it was a 1, apply a quantum NOT operation (aka x operation) to our qubit.

This algorithm works 100% of the time because when Eve measures the qubit she receives, the $|0\rangle$ and $|1\rangle$ states can be perfectly distinguished with a measurement in the Z-axis. It may seem like we and Eve have done a lot of work just to share some random classical bits, but we will see how adding some quantum behaviors to this basic protocol will make it more useful! Let's look at how we could implement this in code.

Listing 3.1   qkd.py: exchanging classical bits via qubits

To prepare our qubit with the classical bit we want to send, we need as input the bit value and a qubit to use. This function does not return anything because the consequences of the operations we apply to our qubit are tracked in the single-qubit simulator.

```
def prepare_classical_message(bit: bool, q: Qubit) -> None:
    if bit:
        q.x()

def eve_measure(q: Qubit) -> bool:
    return q.measure()

def send_classical_bit(device: QuantumDevice, bit: bool) -> None:
    with device.using_qubit() as q:
        prepare_classical_message(bit, q)
        result = eve_measure(q)
        q.reset()
    assert result == bit
```

If we're sending a 1, we can use the NOT operation x to prepare q in the |1⟩ state because the x operation will rotate |0⟩ to |1⟩ and vice versa.

We can check that measuring q gives the same classical bit we sent.

It seems silly to separate measuring as another function, given its one line. But we will change how Eve measures the qubit in the future, so this is a helpful setup.

The simulator we wrote in the previous chapter *almost* has what we need to implement this. We just need to add an instruction corresponding to the x operation. The x instruction can be represented with a matrix X, just as we represented the h instruction using the matrix H. In the same way we wrote H in chapter 2, we can write the matrix X as follows:

$$X = \begin{pmatrix} 0 & 1 \\ 1 & 0 \end{pmatrix}.$$

Exercise 3.1: Truth tables and matrices

In chapter 2, we saw that unitary matrices play the same role in quantum computing that *truth tables* play in classical computing. We can use that to figure out what the matrix X has to look like to represent the quantum NOT operation, x. Let's start by making a table of what the matrix X has to do to each input state to represent what the x instruction does.

Input	Output
$|0\rangle$	$|1\rangle$
$|1\rangle$	$|0\rangle$

This table tells us that if we multiply the matrix X by the vector $|0\rangle$, we need to get $|1\rangle$, and similarly that $X|1\rangle = |0\rangle$.

Either by using NumPy or by hand, check that the matrix

$$X = \begin{pmatrix} 0 & 1 \\ 1 & 0 \end{pmatrix}$$

matches what we have in the previous truth table.

Exercise solutions

All solutions for exercises in this book can be found in the companion code repo: https://github.com/crazy4pi314/learn-qc-with-python-and-qsharp. Just go to the folder for the chapter you are in and open the Jupyter notebook with the name that mentions exercise solutions.

Let's go on and add the functionality we need to our simulator to run listing 3.1. We will be working with the simulator we wrote in the previous chapter, but if you need a refresher, you can find the code in the GitHub repo for this book: https://github.com/crazy4pi314/learn-qc-with-python-and-qsharp. First, we need to update our quantum device's interface by adding a new method our qubit must have.

Listing 3.2   interface.py: adding x to the qubit interface

```python
class Qubit(metaclass=ABCMeta):
    @abstractmethod
    def h(self): pass

    @abstractmethod
    def x(self): pass              ◁─────

    @abstractmethod
    def measure(self) -> bool: pass

    @abstractmethod
    def reset(self): pass
```

We can model implementing the
quantum **NOT** operation after the h
operation from chapter 1.

Now that our interface for a qubit knows that we want an implementation of the x operation, let's add that implementation!

Listing 3.3   simulator.py: adding x to the qubit simulator

```python
KET_0 = np.array([
    [1],
    [0]
], dtype=complex)
H = np.array([
    [1, 1],
    [1, -1]
], dtype=complex) / np.sqrt(2)
X = np.array([              ◁─────
    [0, 1],
    [1, 0]
], dtype=complex) / np.sqrt(2)

class SimulatedQubit(Qubit):
    def __init__(self):
        self.reset()

    def h(self):
        self.state = H @ self.state

    def x(self):               ◁─────
        self.state = X @ self.state

    def measure(self) -> bool:
        pr0 = np.abs(self.state[0, 0]) ** 2
        sample = np.random.random() <= pr0
        return bool(0 if sample else 1)

    def reset(self):
        self.state = KET_0.copy()
```

Adds a variable **X** to store
the matrix X that we need
to represent the x operation

Just like the h function, we want to
implement the quantum operation x
by applying the matrix stored in **X** to
the state vector.

3.1.2   *Sharing classical bits with qubits*

Awesome! Let's try out using our upgraded Python qubit simulator to share a secret classical bit with a qubit.

> **NOTE**   In the code we will be writing for this chapter, the qubits we and Eve share live in the same simulated device. This might make it awkward to think about *sending* qubits to each other if we both are using the same device! In reality, our devices would be using *photons* (single particles of light) as qubits, and those are really easy to send in optical fibers or through the air with telescopes.

This is not yet quite the same as a quantum key distribution protocol, but it serves as a good foundation for the types of functions and steps that our end goal QKD protocol has.

Open an IPython session where we keep the code for our simulator by running `ipython` in our terminal. After importing the Python files, create an instance of the single-qubit simulator and generate a random bit to use as the classical bit to send. (Good thing we have a quantum random number generator!) Using a fresh qubit, prepare it based on the classical bit value we want to send Eve. Eve then measures the qubit, and we can see if we both have the same classical bit value.

Listing 3.4   Sending classical bits with a single-qubit simulator

We'll are using a new qubit simulator instance here for the key exchange, but strictly speaking, we don't need to. We'll see in chapter 4 how to expand the simulator to work with multiple qubits.

```
>>> qrng_simulator = SingleQubitSimulator()          ◁——  We need a simulated qubit
                                                            to use for our QRNG.
>>> key_bit = int(qrng(qrng_simulator))              ◁——
                                                          Reusing the qrng function that
>>> qkd_simulator = SingleQubitSimulator()                we wrote in chapter 2, we can
                                                          generate a random classical bit
>>> with qkd_simulator.using_qubit() as q:                to use for our key.
...     prepare_classical_message(key_bit, q)
...     print(f"You prepared the classical key bit: {key_bit}")
...     eve_measurement = int(eve_measure(q))        ◁——
...     print(f"Eve measured the classical key bit: {eve_measurement}")
...

You prepared the classical key bit: 1                      Eve measures the qubit
Eve measured the classical key bit: 1                      from qkd_simulator and
                                                          then stores the bit value
                                                          as eve_measurement.
```

We encode our classical bit in the qubit provided by qkd_simulator. If the classical bit was a 0, we do nothing to qkd_simulator; and if the classical bit was a 1, we use the x method to change the qubit to the |1⟩ state.

Our example of secret sharing with qubits should be deterministic, which is to say that every time we'll prepare and send a bit, Eve will correctly measure the same value. Is this secure? If you suspect it is not secure, you are definitely onto something. In the next section, we'll discuss the security of our prototype secret-sharing scheme and look at ways to improve it.

3.2 A tale of two bases

We and Eve now have a way to send classical bits using qubits, but what happens if an adversary gets hold of that qubit? They could use the `measure` instruction to get the same classical data that Eve does. That's a huge problem and would reasonably make us wonder why anyone would use qubits to share keys in the first place.

Fortunately, quantum mechanics offers a way to make this exchange more secure! What are some modifications we could make to our protocol? For instance, we could represent a classical "0" message with a qubit in the $|+\rangle$ state and a "1" message with a qubit in the $|-\rangle$ state.

> **Listing 3.5 qkd.py: encoding the message with $|+\rangle$ / $|-\rangle$ states**

```
def prepare_classical_message_plusminus(bit: bool, q: Qubit) -> None:
    if bit:
        q.x()
    q.h()          ◁──┐  Everything before this line of prepare_classical_message_plusminus is the
                      │  same as before with prepare_classical_message. Applying the Hadamard
                      │  gate at this point rotates the |0⟩ / |1⟩ states to |+⟩ / |−⟩ states.

def eve_measure_plusminus(q: Qubit) -> bool:
    q.h()
    return q.measure()

def send_classical_bit_plusminus(device: QuantumDevice, bit: bool) -> None:
    with device.using_qubit() as q:
        prepare_classical_message_plusminus(bit, q)
        result = eve_measure_plusminus(q)
        assert result == bit
```

Uses the h operation to rotate our $|+\rangle$ / $|-\rangle$ states back to the $|0\rangle$ / $|1\rangle$ states because our measure operation is defined to only measure the $|0\rangle$ / $|1\rangle$ states correctly

> **TIP** Another way of thinking about the measurement in listing 3.5 is that we are rotating the measurement to match the basis we are currently working in ($|+\rangle$ / $|-\rangle$). It's all a matter of perspective!

Now we have two different ways of sending qubits that we and Eve could use when sending qubits (see table 3.1 for a summary). We call these two different ways of sending messages *bases*, and each contains two completely distinguishable (orthogonal) states. This is similar to appendix C, where we look at map directions (such as North and West) that define a convenient *basis* for describing directions.

Table 3.1 Different classical messages we want to send, and how to encode them in the Z- and X-bases

	"0" message	"1" message
"0" (or Z) basis	$|0\rangle$	$|1\rangle = X|0\rangle$
"1" (or X) basis	$|+\rangle = H|0\rangle$	$|-\rangle = H|1\rangle = HX|0\rangle$

> **TIP** For a refresher on bases, see appendix C.

We have used the $|0\rangle$ and $|1\rangle$ states as one basis (called the Z-basis) and $|+\rangle$ and $|-\rangle$ as another (called the X-basis). The names for these bases refer to the axis along which we can perfectly distinguish the states (see figure 3.6).

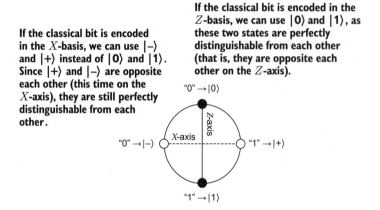

If the classical bit is encoded in the X-basis, we can use $|-\rangle$ and $|+\rangle$ instead of $|0\rangle$ and $|1\rangle$. Since $|+\rangle$ and $|-\rangle$ are opposite each other (this time on the X-axis), they are still perfectly distinguishable from each other.

If the classical bit is encoded in the Z-basis, we can use $|0\rangle$ and $|1\rangle$, as these two states are perfectly distinguishable from each other (that is, they are opposite each other on the Z-axis).

"0" → $|0\rangle$

"0" → $|-\rangle$ X-axis Z-axis   "1" → $|+\rangle$

"1" → $|1\rangle$

Figure 3.6   Now, in addition to using the Z-basis to encode a classical bit on a qubit, we can use the X-basis.

NOTE In quantum computing, there is never really a *correct* basis as much as there are convenient bases that we choose to use by convention.

If neither we nor Eve knows which way of sending we are using for a particular bit, we both have a problem. What happens if we mix sending our messages in the Z-basis and X-basis? Good news: we can use our simulator to try it and see what happens.

Listing 3.6   Exchanging bits but not using the same basis

```
def prepare_classical_message(bit: bool, q: Qubit) -> None:
    if bit:
        q.x()

def eve_measure_plusminus(q: Qubit) -> bool:
    q.h()
    return q.measure()

def prepare_classical_message(bit: bool, q: Qubit) -> None:
    if bit:
        q.x()

def eve_measure_plusminus(q: Qubit) -> bool:
    q.h()
    return q.measure()

def send_classical_bit_wrong_basis(device: QuantumDevice, bit: bool) -> None:
    with device.using_qubit() as q:
        prepare_classical_message(bit, q)
```

Uses the method we saw before to prepare our qubit in the Z-basis by using the h method

Eve measures in the X-basis because she does a Hadamard gate on her qubit before measuring.

```
result = eve_measure_plusminus(q)
assert result == bit, "Two parties do not have the same bit value"
```

The function does not return anything, so if we and Eve end up with key bits that don't match, it will raise an error.

Running the previous code, we can see that if we send in the Z-basis and Eve measures in the X-basis, we may not wind up with matching classical bits at the end.

Listing 3.7   Sending in the Z-basis; measuring in the X-basis

We picked our bit value as 0. You may have to run this line a few times before you get the error.

```
>>> qsim = SingleQubitSimulator()
>>> send_classical_bit_wrong_basis(qsim, 0)
AssertionError: Two parties do not have the same bit value
```

You can try this out experimentally. You will find that you get the `AssertionError` (the key exchange failed) about half of the time. Why is that? To start with, Eve is measuring in the X-basis, so she can only tell $|+\rangle$ and $|-\rangle$ apart perfectly. What will she measure if she is not given a perfectly distinguishable state for her basis (as in this case, where she is given a $|0\rangle$)? We can write the $|0\rangle$ state in the X-basis as

$$|0\rangle = (|+\rangle + |-\rangle) / \sqrt{2}.$$

Recall that in chapter 2, we defined $|+\rangle$ in a similar way by adding together $|0\rangle$ and $|1\rangle$. The $|+\rangle$ state is also called a *superposition* of the $|0\rangle$ and $|1\rangle$ states.

NOTE   Any time a state can be written as a linear combination of states like this, it is considered a superposition of the states that are added together.

Exercise 3.2: Verifying that $|0\rangle$ is a superposition of $|+\rangle$ and $|-\rangle$
Try using what you learned about vectors in the previous chapter to verify that $|0\rangle = (|+\rangle + |-\rangle) / \sqrt{2}$, either by hand or by using Python. Hint: recall that $|+\rangle = (|0\rangle + |1\rangle) / \sqrt{2}$ and that $|-\rangle = (|0\rangle - |1\rangle) / \sqrt{2}$.

Now to calculate the actual measurement with Born's rule from chapter 2. Recall that we can calculate the probability of a measurement outcome by measuring a particular state with the following expression:

$$\text{Pr}(\text{measurement}|\text{state}) = |\langle\text{measurement} \mid \text{state}\rangle|^2.$$

Writing out the measurement of the $|0\rangle$ state in the X-basis, we can see that we will get 0 (or $|+\rangle$) half of the time and 1 (or $|-\rangle$) the other half:

$$\text{Pr}\left(\langle+|0\rangle\right) = |\langle+|0\rangle|^2 = \left((\langle+|+\rangle + \langle+|-\rangle) / \sqrt{2}\right)^2 = (1+0)^2/2 = 1/2$$

Exercise 3.3: Measuring qubits in different bases

Using the previous example as a guide,

1   Calculate the probability of getting the measurement outcome $|-\rangle$ when measuring the $|0\rangle$ state in the $|-\rangle$ direction.
2   Also calculate the probability of getting the $|-\rangle$ measurement outcome with the input state of $|1\rangle$.

That tells us that if Eve does not know the right basis to measure in, then the measurements she makes are as good as random guesses. This is because, in the wrong basis, the qubit is in a superposition of the two states that define the basis. One "key" to how QKD works is that without the right additional information (the basis the qubit is encoded in), any measurement of the qubit is basically useless. To ensure our security, we have to make it difficult for an adversary to learn that extra information to know the right basis to measure in. The QKD protocol we'll look at next has a solution for this and a proof (out of scope here) that describes the chance that the attacker has any information about the key!

3.3   *Quantum key distribution: BB84*

We have now seen how to share keys in two different bases and what happens if we and Eve don't use the same basis. Again, you might ask why we use this approach to make sharing the key to our secret keys more secure. There are a wide variety of different QKD protocols, each with specific advantages and use cases (not unlike RPG character classes). The most *common* protocol for QKD is called BB84, named for an appropriately cryptic encoding of the two authors' initials and the year the protocol was published (Bennet and Brassard 1984).

BB84 is very similar to what we have worked out so far to share keys but has a critical difference in how we and Eve choose our bases. In BB84, both parties choose their basis randomly (and independently), which means they will end up using the same basis 50% of the time. Figure 3.7 shows the steps of the BB84 protocol.

As a consequence of randomly choosing bases, we and Eve also have to communicate over authenticated classical channels (like the internet) to each take our key and transform it into a key that we believe is identical to the key our partner has. That's because this is real life, and when the qubits are exchanged, it will be possible for both the environment and third-party individuals to manipulate or modify the state of the qubit.

Key expansion

We glossed over one detail in our description of the classical communication channel we and Eve are using: it must be *authenticated*. That is, when we send classical messages to Eve as part of running BB84, it's OK if someone else can read them, but we need to make sure it's really Eve that we're talking to. To prove that some-one wrote and sent a particular message, we actually *already* need some form of shared secret that we can use to validate the other person's identity. So we must already have a shared secret with the other person in BB84. This secret can be smaller than the message we're trying to send, so BB84 is technically more of a *key expansion* protocol.

BB84 protocol

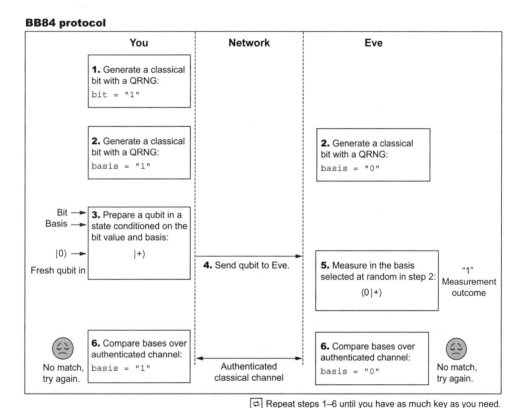

Repeat steps 1–6 until you have as much key as you need.

Figure 3.7 The steps in the BB84 protocol, a particular version of a QKD protocol

The steps of the BB84 protocol are as follows:

1 Choose a random one-bit message to send by sampling our QRNG.
2 We and Eve each choose a random basis with our respective QRNG (no com-munication between them).
3 Prepare a qubit in the randomly selected basis representing our randomly selected message (see table 3.2).
4 Send our prepared qubit in the quantum channel to Eve.

5 Eve measures the qubit when it arrives, performing the measurement in her randomly selected basis and recording the classical bit outcome.

6 Communicate with Eve on an authenticated classical channel, and share which bases we used to prepare and measure the qubit. If they match, keep the bit and add it to the key. Repeat steps 1–6 until we have as much key as we need.

Table 3.2   **What state we should send for each random message and basis choice**

	"0" message	**"1" message**
"0" (or Z) basis	$\lvert 0 \rangle$	$\lvert 1 \rangle = X\lvert 0 \rangle$
"1" (or X) basis	$\lvert + \rangle = H\lvert 0 \rangle$	$\lvert - \rangle = H\lvert 1 \rangle = HX\lvert 0 \rangle$

An error-free world

Since we are simulating the BB84 protocol, we know that the qubit Eve receives will be exactly the same as what we sent. BB84 more realistically will be done in batches where n qubits are exchanged first, followed by a round of sharing the basis values (error correction happens). At the end, we have to shrink the key even further with privacy amplification algorithms to account for the fact that an eavesdropper could have gotten partial information from the errors we detected. We omitted these steps in our implementation of BB84 to keep things simple, but they *are* critical for real-world security 😊.

Let's jump in and implement the BB84 QKD protocol in Python! We will start by writing a function that will run the BB84 protocol (assuming lossless transmission) for a single-bit transmission. That does not guarantee that we get one key bit from this run. However, if we and Eve choose different bases, that exchange will have to be thrown out.

First, it helps to set up some functions that will simplify how we write out the full BB84 protocol. We and Eve need to do things like sample random bits and prepare and measure the message qubit, separated here for clarity.

Listing 3.8   bb84.py: helper functions before the key exchange

```
def sample_random_bit(device: QuantumDevice) -> bool:
    with device.using_qubit() as q:
        q.h()
        result = q.measure()
        q.reset()
    return result
```

sample_random_bit is almost the same as our qrng function before, except here we will reset the qubit after measuring as we know we want to be able to use it more than once.

```
def prepare_message_qubit(message: bool, basis: bool, q: Qubit) -> None:
    if message:
        q.x()
    if basis:
        q.h()
```

The qubit is encoded with the key bit value in the randomly selected basis.

```
def measure_message_qubit(basis: bool, q: Qubit) -> bool:
    if basis:
        q.h()
    result = q.measure()
    q.reset()        <────┐
    return result
```

> **Similar to sample_random_bit after Eve measures the message qubit, she should reset it because in the simulator, we will reuse it for the next exchange.**

> **To help condense the display of long binary keys, a helper function converts the representation to a shorter hex string.**

```
def convert_to_hex(bits: List[bool]) -> str:     <───┐
    return hex(int(
        "".join(["1" if bit else "0" for bit in bits]),
        2
    ))
```

Listing 3.9 bb84.py: BB84 protocol for sending a classical bit

```
def send_single_bit_with_bb84(
    your_device: QuantumDevice,
    eve_device: QuantumDevice
) -> tuple:

    [your_message, your_basis] = [
        sample_random_bit(your_device) for _ in range(2)     <──┐
    ]

    eve_basis = sample_random_bit(eve_device)     <───┐

    with your_device.using_qubit() as q:
        prepare_message_qubit(your_message, your_basis, q)

        # QUBIT SENDING...

        eve_result = measure_message_qubit(eve_basis, q)     <──┐

    return ((your_message, your_basis), (eve_result, eve_basis))     <───┐
```

> **We can randomly choose a bit value and basis using our modified QRNG from before; here, the sample_random_bit function.**

> **With all the preparation done, prepares our qubit to send to Eve**

> **Eve needs to randomly choose a basis with her own qubit, which is why she is using a separate QuantumDevice.**

> **Now Eve has our qubit and measures it in the randomly selected basis she chose earlier.**

> **Since all the computation happens inside a simulator on our computer, nothing needs to be done to "send" the qubit from us to Eve.**

> **Returns the key bit values and bases we and Eve would have at the end of this one round**

Qubits and no-cloning

From what we've seen so far, it seems like our adversary could cheat by eavesdropping on the qubits in the quantum channel and making copies. Here's how: the eavesdropper (called Bob here) first would need to (without detection):

1 Copy qubits as they are being sent between us and Eve, and then store them.
2 While we and Eve finish the classical part of the protocol, listen to the bases we both announce and keep track of ones we both chose the same.
3 For the qubits corresponding to bits where we and Eve used the same basis, measure the copies of the qubits in the same basis as well.

(continued)

Ta-da! We, and Eve, *and* Bob would all have the same key! If you think this seems like a problem, you are right. Don't worry, though; quantum mechanics has the solution. It turns out the problem with Bob's plan is in step 1, where he needs to make *identical* copies of the qubits we and Eve are exchanging. The good news is that making an exact copy of a qubit without knowing what it is beforehand is forbidden by quantum mechanics. The rule that qubits cannot be identically copied without prior knowledge of the state is called the *no-cloning theorem* and is stated as follows:

> No quantum operation can perfectly copy the state of an arbitrary qubit onto another qubit.

If we have some classical description of the state of the qubit, then we can make copies of it. Here we have a qubit in the $|1\rangle$ state, and we can make "copies" of it by preparing more by taking a qubit in the $|0\rangle$ state and applying the x operation.

If we have no prior information about a qubit, then we cannot make perfect copies of it.

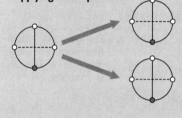

The no-cloning theorem visualized

We will be able to do the simple proof of this in the next chapter, once we learn how to describe the state of more than one qubit 😊.

As an alternative way of thinking about the no-cloning theorem, if Bob could measure a qubit without disturbing it, he could get around needing a copy of the qubits he intercepts. This is not possible because once we measure a qubit, it "collapses" or changes in a way that Eve could detect as additional noise in the measurement results she collects from her qubits. Thus, measuring in transit is not something Bob can do without being detected, so his eavesdropping is doomed to fail.

Exchanging one classical key bit will not be sufficient to send a whole key, so now we need to use the earlier technique to send multiple bits.

Listing 3.10   bb84.py: BB84 protocol for exchanging a key with Eve

```
def simulate_bb84(n_bits: int) -> tuple:
    your_device = SingleQubitSimulator()
    eve_device = SingleQubitSimulator()

    key = []
    n_rounds = 0

    while len(key) < n_bits:
        n_rounds += 1
        ((your_message, your_basis), (eve_result, eve_basis)) =
            ➥ send_single_bit_with_bb84(your_device, eve_device)

        if your_basis == eve_basis:
            assert your_message == eve_result
            key.append(your_message)

    print(f"Took {n_rounds} rounds to generate a {n_bits}-bit key.")

    return key
```

**At this point, we and Eve can publicly announce the bases we each used
to measure this bit. If everything worked right, our results should agree
whenever our bases agree. We check that here with an assert.**

The key is now in the bag, so we can move on to using the key and the one-time pad
encryption algorithm to send a secret message!

3.4   *Using a secret key to send secret messages*

We and Eve have sorted out how to use the BB84 protocol to share a random, binary
key generated by a QRNG. The last step is using this key to share a secret message with
Eve. We and Eve previously decided that the best encryption protocol to use is a one-
time pad to send our secret messages. This turns out to be one of the most secure
encryption protocols, and given that we are sharing keys in one of the most secure
ways possible, it makes sense to keep up that standard!

For example, to tell Eve that we like Python, the message we want to send is
"♡ ⅃ ⌨". Since we are using a binary key, we need to convert the representation of
our Unicode message to binary, which is the following lengthy list of bits:

*"1101100000111101 1101110010010110 1101100000111101
1101110000001101 1101100000111101 1101110010010111011"*

This binary representation of the message is our *message text,* and now we want to combine that with a key to get a ciphertext that is safe to send over the network. Once we
have the key from the BB84 protocol (at least as long as our message), we need to use
a one-time pad encryption scheme to encode our message. We saw this encryption
technique in chapter 2; see figure 3.8 for a quick refresher.

To implement this, we need to use a classical bitwise XOR (the ^ operator in Python)
to combine the message and our key to create the ciphertext that we can safely send to

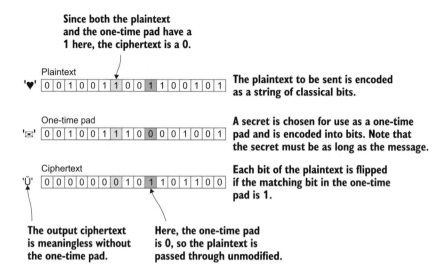

Figure 3.8   An example of one-time pad encryption, which uses random bits to encrypt secret messages

Eve. To decrypt our message, Eve will do the same bitwise XOR operation with the ciphertext and her key (which should be the same as yours). This will give her back the message because any time we XOR a bit string with another one twice, we are left with the original bit string. Here is what this would look like in Python.

Listing 3.11   bb84.py: BB84 protocol for exchanging a key with Eve

```
def apply_one_time_pad(message: List[bool], key: List[bool]) -> List[bool]:
    return [
        message_bit ^ key_bit
        for (message_bit, key_bit) in zip(message, key)
    ]
```

The ^ operator is a bitwise XOR in Python. This applies a single bit of our key as a one-time pad to our message text.

Exercise 3.4: One-time pad encryption

If we had the ciphertext `10100101` and the key `00100110`, what message was originally sent?

Let's put it all together and share the message ("♡ ⺧ ⌨") with Eve by running the bb84.py file we have been building up.

Listing 3.12   bb84.py: using BB84 and one-time pad encryption

```
if __name__ == "__main__":
    print("Generating a 96-bit key by simulating BB84...")
```

```
key = simulate_bb84(96)
print(f"Got key                        {convert_to_hex(key)}.")

message = [
    1, 1, 0, 1, 1, 0, 0, 0,
    0, 0, 1, 1, 1, 1, 0, 1,
    1, 1, 0, 1, 1, 1, 0, 0,
    1, 0, 0, 1, 0, 1, 1, 0,
    1, 1, 0, 1, 1, 0, 0, 0,
    0, 0, 1, 1, 1, 1, 0, 1,
    1, 1, 0, 1, 1, 1, 0, 0,
    0, 0, 0, 0, 1, 1, 0, 1,
    1, 1, 0, 1, 1, 0, 0, 0,
    0, 0, 1, 1, 1, 1, 0, 1,
    1, 1, 0, 1, 1, 1, 0, 0,
    1, 0, 1, 1, 1, 0, 1, 1
]
print(f"Using key to send secret message: {convert_to_hex(message)}.")

encrypted_message = apply_one_time_pad(message, key)
print(f"Encrypted message:             {convert_to_hex(encrypted_messa
    ge)}.")

decrypted_message = apply_one_time_pad(encrypted_message, key)
print(f"Eve decrypted to get:          {convert_to_hex(decrypted_messa
    ge)}.")
```

Listing 3.13 Running the full solution to the chapter scenario

The exact key we generate will be different every time we run the BB84 simulation—that's a huge part of the point of the protocol, after all!

Since our basis and Eve's basis will agree roughly half the time, it should take about two rounds of BB84 for each bit of key we want to generate.

```
$ python bb84.py
Generating a 96-bit key by simulating BB84...
Took 170 rounds to generate a 96-bit key.
```

```
Got key:                        0xb35e061b873f799c61ad8fad.

Using key to send secret message: 0xd83ddc96d83ddc0dd83ddcbb.

Encrypted message:              0x6b63da8d5f02a591b9905316.

Eve decrypted to get:           0xd83ddc96d83ddc0dd83ddcbb.
```

The message we get by writing down each of the Unicode code points for "♡🧡💻"

When we combine our secret message with the key we got earlier, using the key as a one-time pad, our message is scrambled.

When Eve uses the same key, she gets back our original secret message.

Quantum key distribution is one of the most important spin-off technologies from quantum computing and has the potential to make a huge impact on our security infrastructure. While it is currently quite easy to set up QKD for parties that are relatively close to each other (around 200 km or less), there are significant challenges to deploying a global system for QKD. Usually, the physical system used in QKD is a photon, and it is hard to send single particles of light long distances without losing them.

Now that we have built up a single-qubit simulator and programmed some single-qubit applications, we are ready to start playing around with multiple qubits. In the next chapter, we'll take the simulator we have built and add features to simulate multiple qubit states and play nonlocal games with Eve ♡.

Summary

- Quantum key distribution is a protocol that allows us to randomly generate shared keys that we can use to communicate securely and privately.
- When measuring qubits, we can do so in different bases; if we measure in the same basis that we prepare our qubits in, the results will be deterministic, while if we measure in different bases, the results will be random.
- The no-cloning theorem guarantees that eavesdroppers can't guess the right basis to measure in without causing the key distribution protocol to fail.
- Once we have used QKD to share a key, we can use the key with a classical algorithm called a one-time pad to send data securely.

Nonlocal games: Working with multiple qubits

This chapter covers

- Using nonlocal games to check that quantum mechanics is consistent with how the universe works
- Simulating state preparation, operations, and measurement results for multiple qubits
- Recognizing the characteristics of entangled states

In the last chapter, we used qubits to communicate with Eve securely, exploring how we can use quantum devices in cryptography. Working with one qubit at a time is fun, but working with more will be—well, more fun! In this chapter, we'll learn how to model states of multiple qubits and what it means for them to be *entangled*. We will again be playing games with Eve, but this time we will need a referee!

4.1   Nonlocal games

At this point, we have seen how single-qubit devices can be programmed to accomplish useful tasks such as random number generation and quantum key distribution. The most exciting computational tasks, however, require using multiple qubits together. In this chapter, we'll learn about nonlocal games: a way to validate our quantum mechanical descriptions of the universe with friends using multi-qubit systems.

4.1.1   What are nonlocal games?

We have all played games of one type or another, whether sports, board games, video games, or role-playing games. Games are one of the best ways to explore new worlds and test our limits of strength, endurance, and understanding. Turns out Eve loves to play games, and the latest encrypted message from her was the following:

> *"Hi player! I am keen to play a game called CHSH. It is a nonlocal game where we play with a referee. I'll send the instructions in the next message. STOP"*

What makes the game proposed by Eve *nonlocal* is the fact that the players are (sadly) not in the same place while playing the game. The players participate in the game by sending and receiving messages with a central referee but don't have a chance to talk to each other while playing. What is really cool is that by playing the game, we can show that classical physics just doesn't cut it to describe the results we get in these games with particular strategies. The particular winning strategy we will look at here involves the players sharing a pair of qubits before the game starts. We will dive into just what entangling two qubits means as we go through this chapter, but let's start with describing the full rules of our nonlocal game.

> **NOTE**   A referee adjudicating a nonlocal game can ensure that the players don't communicate by separating them by a large enough distance that no light from one player could reach the other before the game ends.

4.1.2   Testing quantum physics: The CHSH game

The nonlocal game Eve has suggested playing is called *the CHSH game*, shown in figure 4.1.[1]

The CHSH game comprises two players and a referee. We can play as many rounds of the game as we like, and each round has three steps. As Eve mentioned in her first message, once a round starts, the players cannot communicate and must make their own (possibly preplanned) decisions.

---

[1] The name CHSH comes from the initials of the researchers who originally created the game: Clauser, Horne, Shimony, and Holt. You can find the original if you are interested: https://journals.aps.org/prl/abstract/10.1103/PhysRevLett.23.880.

1. **A referee sends you and Eve a one-bit question. Your question is labeled a and Eve's is b. Once the game starts, you and Eve can no longer communicate until after the game ends.**

2. **The referee demands a one-bit answer from each player. Here, your answer is labeled x and Eve's is labeled y.**

3. **Both players send a one-bit answer back to the referee. The referee then scores the game and declares if the players won.**

4. **The scoring rules require that you and Eve answer with the correct parity given the input bits from the referee.**

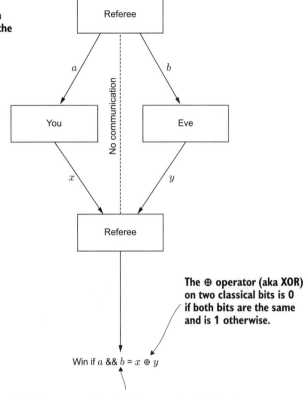

The $\oplus$ operator (aka XOR) on two classical bits is 0 if both bits are the same and is 1 otherwise.

Win if a && $b = x \oplus y$

The && operator (aka AND) on two classical bits is 1 if both bits are 1 and is 0 in all other cases.

Figure 4.1   The CHSH game, a nonlocal game with two players and a referee. The referee gives each player a question in the form of a bit value, and then each player has to figure out how to respond to the referee. The players win if the Boolean AND of their responses is the same as the classical XOR of the referee's questions.

The steps for one round of the CHSH game are as follows:

1 The referee starts the round by giving us and Eve each one classical bit. The referee chooses these bits *independently* and *uniformly at random*, so we could get a 0 or a 1, each with 50% probability, and the same for Eve. This means there are four possible ways the referee can start the game (our bit, Eve's bit): (0,0), (0,1), (1,0), or (1,1).

2 We and Eve must each *independently* decide on a single classical bit to give back to the referee as a response.

3 The referee then calculates the parity (XOR) of our and Eve's classical bit responses.

As listed in table 4.1, in three out of the four cases, we and Eve must respond with *even* parity (our answers must be equal) to win, while in the fourth case, our answers must be different. These are definitely *unusual* rules, but not too bad compared to some multiday board games.

Table 4.1   Win conditions for the CHSH game

Our input	Eve's input	Response parity to win
0	0	Even
0	1	Even
1	0	Even
1	1	Odd

We can expand on table 4.1 to get all of the possible outcomes of the game; see table 4.2.

Table 4.2   All possible states of the CHSH game with win conditions. Input bits come from the referee, and both players respond to the referee.

Our input	Eve's input	Our response	Eve's response	Parity	Win?
0	0	0	0	Even	Yes
0	0	0	1	Odd	No
0	0	1	0	Odd	No
0	0	1	1	Even	Yes
0	1	0	0	Even	Yes
0	1	0	1	Odd	No
0	1	1	0	Odd	No
0	1	1	1	Even	Yes
1	0	0	0	Even	Yes
1	0	0	1	Odd	No
1	0	1	0	Odd	No
1	0	1	1	Even	Yes
1	1	0	0	Even	No
1	1	0	1	Odd	Yes
1	1	1	0	Odd	Yes
1	1	1	1	Even	No

Let's look at some Python code to simulate this game. Since our and Eve's responses to the referee are allowed to depend on the message the referee gives us, we can represent each player's actions as a "function" that the referee calls.

Exercise 4.1: Umpire state of mind

Since the referee is purely classical, we'll model them as using classical random number generators. This leaves open the possibility, though, that we and Eve could cheat by guessing the referee's questions. A possible improvement might be to use the QRNGs from chapter 2. Modify the code sample in listing 4.1 so that the referee can ask questions of us and Eve by measuring a qubit that starts off in the |+⟩ state.

Exercise solutions

All solutions for exercises in this book can be found in the companion code repo: https://github.com/crazy4pi314/learn-qc-with-python-and-qsharp. Just go to the folder for the chapter you are in and open the Jupyter notebook with the name that mentions exercise solutions.

As we can see in listing 4.1, we are declaring a new type `Strategy` to define the tuple of functions representing our and Eve's one-bit functions that represent our individual strategies. We can think of these functions as representing what we and Eve each do with the bits given to us by the referee.

Listing 4.1 chsh.py: Python implementation for the CHSH game

The "strategy" function will assign one-bit functions
representing what "you" and "eve" will do based on our input.

```
import random
from functools import partial
from typing import Tuple, Callable
import numpy as np

from interface import QuantumDevice, Qubit
from simulator import Simulator

Strategy = Tuple[Callable[[int], int], Callable[[int], int]]

def random_bit() -> int:
    return random.randint(0, 1)

def referee(strategy: Callable[[], Strategy]) -> bool:
    you, eve = strategy()
    your_input, eve_input = random_bit(), random_bit()
    parity = 0 if you(your_input) == eve(eve_input) else 1
    return parity == (your_input and eve_input)
```

Using Python's typing module lets us document that a value of type Strategy is a tuple of two functions, each of which takes an int and returns an int.

The classical random number generator the referee will use

The referee picks two random bits, one for each player.

Check table 4.1 to see if the players won.

Gives each player their random bit and then computes the parity of their responses

```
def est_win_probability(strategy: Callable[[], Strategy],
                        n_games: int = 1000) -> float:
    return sum(
        referee(strategy)
        for idx_game in range(n_games)
    ) / n_games
```

We can use Python's built-in sum function to count the number of times referee returns True for a particular strategy—in other words, how many times we have won the game.

Divides by the number of games we played and then estimates the probability that our and Eve's strategy wins the CHSH game

Note that in listing 4.1, we don't have a definition yet for the input `strategy` to the referee. Now that we have implemented the rules of the game in Python, let's talk *strategy* and get to implementing a classical strategy for playing the CHSH game.

> **TIP** It's helpful to choose variable naming conventions that make it obvious what role each variable plays in our code. We chose to use the prefix `n_` in the variable `n_games` to indicate that the variable refers to a number or size, and we use the prefix `idx_` to refer to the index for each individual game. Much like driving, it's good if our code is predictable.

4.1.3 Classical strategy

The simplest strategy for both us and Eve to pursue is to ignore our inputs entirely. Looking at table 4.3, if both of us agree before the game that we will never change our outputs (i.e., always return 0), we will win 75% of the time (this does assume the referee chooses the random bits for each player uniformly).

Table 4.3 Best classical strategy for the CHSH game, where we both always respond with 0 with win conditions

Our input	Eve's input	Our response	Eve's response	Parity	Win?
0	0	0	0	Even	Yes
0	1	0	0	Even	Yes
1	0	0	0	Even	Yes
1	1	0	0	Even	No

If we were to write this strategy as a Python function, we would have the following code.

Listing 4.2 chsh.py: an easy, constant strategy for the CHSH game

```
def constant_strategy() -> Strategy:
    return (
        lambda your_input: 0,
        lambda eve_input: 0
    )
```

Now we can test how often we expect to win a round the CHSH game using `constant _strategy`:

```
>>> est_win_probability(constant_strategy)
0.771
```

Note that you may get slightly more or less than 75% when you try this. This is because the win probability is estimated using a finite number of rounds (in stats, this is called a binomial distribution). For this example, we'd expect error bars of about 1.5%.

OK, so that's an easy strategy, but is there anything cleverer we can do? Given that we and Eve only have classical resources, sadly, this is *provably* the best we can do. Short of cheating 😊 (e.g., communicating with Eve or guessing the referee's inputs), we cannot win this game more than 75% of the time on average.

This all leads to the obvious question: what if we and Eve could use qubits? What would be our best strategy then, and how often would we win? What does it say about our understanding of the universe if we have proof that we cannot win CHSH more than about 75% of the time, and then we find a way that we *can* beat that win rate? As you might guess, we can do better than a 75% win rate playing CHSH if the players share quantum resources, i.e., have qubits. Later in the chapter, we will get into quantum-based strategies for CHSH, but spoiler: we will need to simulate more than one qubit.

4.2 Working with multiple qubit states

So far, in this book, we've only worked with one qubit at a time. To play a nonlocal game, for example, each player will need their own qubit. This raises the question, how do things change when the system we are considering has more than one qubit? The main difference is that we cannot describe each qubit individually and have to think in terms of a state that describes the whole system.

> **NOTE** When describing a group or register of qubits, we generally *cannot* just describe each qubit individually. The most useful quantum behaviors can only be seen when we describe the state of a group or register of qubits.

The next section will help relate this system-level view with a similar classical programming concept of a register.

4.2.1 Registers

Suppose that we have a *register* of classical bits: that is, a collection of many classical bits. We can index through each bit in that register and look at its value independently, even though it is still a part of that register. The contents of the register can represent a more complex value, like bits that together represent a Unicode character (as we saw in chapter 3), but this higher-level interpretation is not necessary.

When we store information in a classical register, the number of different states of that register grows very rapidly as we add more bits. For example, if we have three bits, there are eight different states that our register can be in; see listing 4.3 for an example. We say for the classical register state `101` that the zeroth bit is a 1, the first is 0, and the second is 1. When these values are concatenated together, they give us the string 101.

Listing 4.3   Listing all states of a classical three-bit register

```
>>> from itertools import product
>>> ", ".join(map("".join, product("01", repeat=3)))
'000, 001, 010, 011, 100, 101, 110, 111'
```

If we have four bits, we can store one of 16 different states; if we have n bits, we can store one of 2^n. We say that the number of different possible states of a classical register *grows exponentially* with the number of bits. The bit strings output by listing 4.3 show the actual data in the register for each state of the register. They also serve as convenient labels for one of eight possible messages that we can encode with three classical bits.

What does all this have to do with qubits? We saw in chapters 2 and 3 that any state of the classical bit also describes a qubit state. The same holds for registers of qubits as well. For instance, the three-bit state "010" describes the three-qubit state $|010\rangle$.

> **TIP**   In chapter 2, we saw that qubit states described by classical bits in this way are called *computational basis states*; here, we use the same term for states of multiple qubits that are described by strings of classical bits.

Just as with single qubits, however, the state of a register of multiple qubits can also be made up by adding different qubit states together. In the exact same way that we can write $|+\rangle$ as $(|0\rangle + |1\rangle) / \sqrt{2}$ to get another valid qubit state, our three-qubit register can be in a wide variety of different states:

- $(|010\rangle + |111\rangle) / \sqrt{2}$
- $(|001\rangle + |010\rangle + |100\rangle) / \sqrt{3}$

> **TIP**   We'll see more as we go along, but just as we needed the square root of 2 to make the measurement probabilities work out for $|+\rangle = (|0\rangle + |1\rangle) / \sqrt{2}$, we need to divide by $\sqrt{2}$ and $\sqrt{3}$ in our examples to make sure all the probabilities for each measurement are realistic: i.e., add up to one.

This example of the linearity of quantum registers is called the *superposition principle*.

> **DEFINITION**   The *superposition principle* tells us that we can add together two different states of a quantum register to get another valid state. The $|+\rangle$ state we saw before is a good example of this, except each register has only one qubit.

To write the state of a quantum register in a computer, we'll again use vectors, just as we did in chapter 2. The main difference is how many numbers we list in each vector. Let's see what it looks like to write the state of a two-qubit register on a computer. For example, the vector for the two-qubit state $(|00\rangle + |11\rangle) / \sqrt{2}$ can also be written as the state $(1 \times |00\rangle + 0 \times |01\rangle + 0 \times |10\rangle + 1 \times |11\rangle) / \sqrt{2}$. If we make a list of what we had to multiply each computational basis state by to get the state we wanted, we have precisely the information we need to write in our vector. In listing 4.4, we've written down $(|00\rangle + |11\rangle) / \sqrt{2}$ as a vector.

Listing 4.4   Using Python to write an example of a two-qubit state

```
>>> import numpy as np
>>> two_qubit_state = np.array([[
...
...        1,
...
...        0,
...
...        0,
...        1
... ]]) / np.sqrt(2)
```

We start the same way, using the np.array function to make a new vector.

Each entry in this vector describes a different computational basis state. This entry tells us that we have to multiply $|00\rangle$ by 1.

Similarly, this entry tells us how much of the $|01\rangle$ state we need to add to get the state we want.

Finally, we divide by $\sqrt{2}$ to make sure all the measurement probabilities work out, just as we did with the $|+\rangle$ state in chapters 2 and 3.

The numbers in the vector from listing 4.4 are coefficients that we multiply by each of the computational basis states, which we then add together to make a new state. These coefficients are also called the *amplitudes* for each of the basis states in the sum.

Thinking with directions

Another way to think about this example is in terms of directions on a map, similar to how vectors are discussed in appendix C. Each different computational basis state tells us about a *direction* that a qubit state can be pointed in. We can think of a two-qubit state as a direction in four dimensions instead of the two-dimensional maps we see in appendix C. Since this book is two-dimensional rather than four-dimensional, we unfortunately can't draw a picture here, but sometimes thinking of vectors as directions can be more helpful than thinking of vectors as lists of numbers.

4.2.2   *Why is it hard to simulate quantum computers?*

We have seen that as the number of bits grows, the number of different states a register can be in grows exponentially. While this won't be a problem for us in playing a nonlocal game with only two qubits, we'll want to use more than just two qubits as we proceed through this book.

When we do, we'll also have exponentially many different computational basis states for our quantum register, meaning that we will need exponentially many different amplitudes in our vectors as we grow the size of our quantum register. To write the state of a 10-qubit register, we'll need to use a vector that is a list of $2^{10} = 1024$ different amplitudes. For a 20-qubit register, we'll need about 1 million amplitudes in our vectors. By the time we get to 60 qubits, we'll need about 1.15×10^{18} numbers in our vectors. That's about one amplitude for each grain of sand on the planet.

In table 4.4, we summarize what this exponential growth means as we try to simulate quantum computers using classical computers like phones, laptops, clusters, and cloud environments. This table shows that even though it's very challenging to reason about quantum computers using classical computers, we can pretty easily reason about small examples. With a laptop or desktop, we can simulate up to about 30 qubits without too much hassle. As we'll see throughout the rest of the book, this is more than enough to understand how quantum programs work and how quantum computers can be used to solve interesting problems.

Table 4.4   How much memory is required to store a quantum state?

# of qubits	# of amplitudes	Memory	Size comparison
1	2	128 bits	
2	4	256 bits	
3	8	512 bits	
4	16	1 kilobit	
8	256	4 KB	Tap-enabled credit card
10	1024	16 KB	
20	1,048,576	16 MB	
26	67,108,864	1 GB	Raspberry Pi RAM
28	268,435,456	4 GB	iPhone XS Max RAM
30	1,073,741,824	16 GB	Laptop or desktop RAM
40	1,099,511,627,776	16 TB	
50	1,125,899,906,842,624	16 petabytes	
60	1,152,921,504,606,846,976	16 exabytes	
80	1,208,925,819,614,629,174,706,176	16 yottabytes	Approximate size of the internet
410	2.6×10^{123}	4.2×10^{124} bytes	Computer the size of the universe

---

Deep dive: Are quantum computers exponentially more powerful?

You may have heard that the number of different numbers we have to keep track of to simulate a quantum computer using a classical computer is why quantum computers are more powerful, or that a quantum computer can store that much information. This isn't exactly true. A mathematical theorem known as *Holevo's theorem* tells us that a quantum computer made up of 410 qubits can store at most 410 classical bits of information, even if it would take a classical computer about the size of the entire universe to write the state of that quantum computer.

Put differently, *just because it's hard to simulate a quantum computer doesn't mean it does something useful*. Throughout the rest of the book, we'll see that it takes a bit of art to figure out how to use a quantum computer to solve useful problems.

4.2.3 *Tensor products for state preparation*

Describing quantum registers as vectors describing computational basis states is all well and good, but even if we know the state we want to get to, we need to know how to prepare it. For example, if one player in a nonlocal game has a qubit in the $|0\rangle$ state and the other has a qubit in the $|1\rangle$ state, we can combine those two single-qubit states in a straightforward way to describe the state of the game as $|01\rangle$. What does it mean to "combine" the states of two (or more) qubits? We can do this by adding one more concept to our mathematics toolbox, called the *tensor product*.

In the same way that we used the product function in listing 4.3 to combine labels for a three-classical-bit register, we can use the concept of a tensor product, written as $\otimes$, to combine the quantum states for each qubit to make a state that describes multiple qubits. The output of product was a list of all possible states of those three classical bits. The output of a tensor product is, similarly, a state that lists all computational basis states for a quantum register. We can use NumPy to compute tensor products; NumPy provides an implementation of the tensor product as the function np.kron, as shown in listing 4.5.

> **Why kron?**
>
> The name np.kron may seem odd for a function that implements tensor products, but the name is short for a related mathematical concept called the *Kronecker product*. NumPy's use of kron as short for *Kronecker* follows the convention used in MATLAB, R, Julia, and other scientific computing platforms.

Listing 4.5 A two-qubit state, using NumPy and tensor products

```
>>> import numpy as np
>>> ket0 = np.array([[1], [0]])
>>> ket1 = np.array([[0], [1]])
>>> np.kron(ket0, ket1)
array([[0],
       [1],
       [0],
       [0]])
```

Defines vectors for the single-qubit states $|0\rangle$ and $|1\rangle$, just as in chapters 2 and 3

We can build the vector for $|0\rangle \otimes |1\rangle$ by calling NumPy's implementation of the tensor product. For historical reasons, the tensor product is represented in NumPy by the kron function.

The vector returned by np.kron has a 1 for the entry corresponding to the $|01\rangle$ computational basis state and 0s everywhere else, so we recognize this vector as being the state $|01\rangle$.

This example shows us that $|0\rangle \otimes |1\rangle = |01\rangle$. That is, if we have the state of each qubit individually, we can combine them by using the tensor product to describe the state of the whole register.

We can combine as many qubits as we want this way. Say we had four qubits, all in the $|0\rangle$ state. The register of all four qubits could be described as $|0\rangle \otimes |0\rangle \otimes |0\rangle \otimes |0\rangle$.

Listing 4.6   Making |0000⟩ as the tensor product of 4 copies of |0⟩

```
>>> import numpy as np
>>> ket0 = np.array([[1], [0]])
>>> from functools import reduce
>>> reduce(np.kron, [ket0] * 4)
array([[1],
       [0],
       [0],
       [0],
       [0],
       [0],
       [0],
       [0],
       [0],
       [0],
       [0],
       [0],
       [0],
       [0],
       [0],
       [0]])
```

The reduce function provided with the Python standard library lets us apply a two-argument function like kron between each element in a list. Here, we use reduce instead of np.kron(ket0, np.kron(ket0, np.kron(ket0, ket0))).

We get back a four-qubit state vector representing |0⟩ ⊗ |0⟩ ⊗ |0⟩ ⊗ |0⟩ = |0000⟩.

NOTE   The two-qubit state $(|00⟩ + |11⟩) / \sqrt{2}$ that we saw earlier *cannot* be written as the tensor product of two single-qubit states. Multiple-qubit states that can't be written out as tensor products are called *entangled*. We'll see a lot more about entanglement throughout the rest of this chapter and in the rest of the book.

4.2.4   *Tensor products for qubit operations on registers*

Now that we know how to use the tensor product to combine quantum states, what is np.kron actually doing? In essence, the tensor product is a table of every different way of combining its two arguments, as shown in figure 4.2.

The same tensor product shown in figure 4.2 of two matrices in Python is also shown in the following listing.

Listing 4.7   Finding the tensor product of *A* and *B* with NumPy

```
>>> import numpy as np
>>> A = np.array([[1, 3], [5, 7]])
>>> B = np.array([[2, 4], [6, 8]])
>>> np.kron(A, B)
array([[ 2,  4,  6, 12],
       [ 6,  8, 18, 24],
       [10, 20, 14, 28],
       [30, 40, 42, 56]])
>>> np.kron(B, A)
array([[ 2,  6,  4, 12],
       [10, 14, 20, 28],
       [ 6, 18,  8, 24],
       [30, 42, 40, 56]])
```

Matrices A and B are arbitrary 2 × 2 matrices used as examples here.

As we saw earlier, np.kron is NumPy's implementation of the tensor product.

Note that the order of the arguments to the tensor product matters. Although both np.kron(A, B) and np.kron(B, A) contain the same information, the entries in each are ordered quite differently!

Let's consider a simple example and take the tensor product of two matrices A and B:

$$A = \begin{bmatrix} 1 & 3 \\ 5 & 7 \end{bmatrix}$$

$$B = \begin{bmatrix} 2 & 4 \\ 6 & 8 \end{bmatrix}$$

The tensor product is denoted using the ⊗ operator, just like products are indicated with ×.

$$C = A \otimes B$$

$$= \begin{bmatrix} 1 \times B & 3 \times B \\ 5 \times B & 7 \times B \end{bmatrix}$$

To start, you first need to make copies of B for each element in A. It's a bit like making a big matrix by tiling B.

$$= \begin{bmatrix} 1 \times 2 & 1 \times 4 & 3 \times 2 & 3 \times 4 \\ 1 \times 6 & 1 \times 8 & 3 \times 6 & 3 \times 8 \\ 5 \times 2 & 5 \times 4 & 7 \times 2 & 7 \times 4 \\ 5 \times 6 & 5 \times 8 & 7 \times 6 & 7 \times 8 \end{bmatrix}$$

After that, you can expand each copy of B to get the pairs of numbers you need to multiply together to find the big matrix.

$$= \begin{bmatrix} 2 & 4 & 6 & 12 \\ 6 & 8 & 18 & 24 \\ 10 & 20 & 14 & 28 \\ 30 & 40 & 42 & 56 \end{bmatrix}$$

At this point, you can find the answer by using ordinary (aka scalar) multiplication.

Each element of the resulting big matrix tells us the product of one element from A and one element from B. That is, the tensor product $A \otimes B$ is made up of all possible products of elements from A and B.

Figure 4.2 The tensor product of two matrices shown step by step. We start by multiplying each term in A by a full copy of B. The resulting matrix dimensions of the tensor product are the product of the dimensions of the input matrices.

Using the tensor product between two matrices, we can find how different quantum operations transform the state of a quantum register. We can also understand how a quantum operation transforms the state of multiple qubits by taking the tensor product of two matrices instead, letting us understand how our and Eve's moves in a nonlocal game affect our shared state.

For example, we know that we can write $|1\rangle$ as $X|0\rangle$ (that is, the result of applying the x instruction to an initialized qubit). This also gives us another way to write out multiple-qubit states like the $|01\rangle$ state we saw earlier. In this case, we can get $|01\rangle$ by applying an x instruction *only* to the second qubit of a two-qubit register. Using the tensor product, we can find a unitary matrix to represent this.

Listing 4.8 Calculating the tensor product of two matrices

```
>>> import numpy as np
>>> I = np.array([[1, 0], [0, 1]])
>>> X = np.array([[0, 1], [1, 0]])
>>> IX = np.kron(I, X)
>>> IX
array([[0, 1, 0, 0],
       [1, 0, 0, 0],
       [0, 0, 0, 1],
       [0, 0, 1, 0]])
```

Defines a matrix that represents doing nothing to the first qubit, known as the identity matrix 𝟙. Since 𝟙 is hard to write in Python, we use I instead.

Defines the unitary matrix X that lets us simulate the x instruction

Combines the two using the tensor product I ⊗ X

The matrix 𝟙 ⊗ X consists of two copies of X representing what happens to the second qubit for each possible state of the first qubit.

```
>>> ket0 = np.array([[1], [0]])
>>> ket00 = np.kron(ket0, ket0)
>>> ket00
array([[1],
       [0],
       [0],
       [0]])
>>> IX @ ket00
array([[0],
       [1],
       [0],
       [0]])
```

◁— **Let's see what happens when we use $1 \otimes X$ to simulate how the x instruction transforms the second qubit in a two-qubit register. We'll start with that register in the $|00\rangle = |0\rangle \otimes |0\rangle$ state.**

◁— **We recognize the state we get back as the $|01\rangle$ state from earlier in this section. As expected, that is the state we get by flipping the second qubit from $|0\rangle$ to $|1\rangle$.**

Exercise 4.2: Hadamard operation on a two-qubit register

How would you prepare a $|+0\rangle$ state? First, what vector would you use to represent the two-qubit state $|+0\rangle = |+\rangle \otimes |0\rangle$? You have an initial two-qubit register in the $|00\rangle$ state. What operation should you apply to get the state you want?

Hint: Try $(H \otimes 1)$ if you're stuck!

Deep dive: Finally proving the no-cloning theorem

Learning that operations on multiple qubits are also represented by unitary matrices lets us finally prove the no-cloning theorem that we've seen a few times so far. The key insight is that cloning a state isn't linear and thus cannot be written as a matrix.

As with many proofs in mathematics, the proof of the no-cloning theorem works by *contradiction*. That is, we assume the opposite of the theorem and then show that we get something false due to that assumption.

Without further ado, then, we start by assuming that we have some wondrous clone instruction that can perfectly copy the state of its qubit. For instance, if we have a qubit q1 whose state starts in $|1\rangle$ and a qubit q2 whose state starts in $|0\rangle$, then after calling q1.clone(q2), we would have the register $|11\rangle$.

Similarly, if q1 starts in $|+\rangle$, then q1.clone(q2) should give us a register in the state $|++\rangle = |+\rangle \otimes |+\rangle$. The problem comes in reconciling what q1.clone(q2) should do in these two cases. We know that any quantum operation other than measurement must be linear, so let's give the matrix that lets us simulate clone a name: C seems pretty reasonable.

Using C, we can break down the case that we want to clone $|+\rangle$ into the case in which we want to clone $|0\rangle$ plus the case in which we want to clone $|1\rangle$. We know that $C|+0\rangle = |++\rangle$, but we also know that $C|+0\rangle = C(|00\rangle + |10\rangle) / \sqrt{2} = (C|00\rangle + C|10\rangle) / \sqrt{2}$. Since clone needs to clone $|0\rangle$ and $|1\rangle$ as well as $|+\rangle$, we know that $C|00\rangle = |00\rangle$ and $C|10\rangle = |11\rangle$. That gives us that $(C|00\rangle + C|10\rangle) / \sqrt{2} = (|00\rangle + |11\rangle) / \sqrt{2}$, but we concluded earlier that $C|+0\rangle = |++\rangle = (|00\rangle + |01\rangle + |10\rangle + |11\rangle) / 2$.

We thus have a contradiction and can conclude that we went wrong at the very first step, where we assumed that `clone` could exist! Thus, we have shown the no-cloning theorem.

One important thing to note from this argument is that we can always copy information from one qubit to another *if we know the right basis*. The problem came in when we didn't know if we should copy information about $|0\rangle$ vs. $|1\rangle$ or $|+\rangle$ vs. $|-\rangle$, as we could copy either $|0\rangle$ or $|+\rangle$, but not both. This isn't a problem classically, as we only ever have the computational basis to work with.

Up to this point, we've used NumPy to write our qubit simulator, `SingleQubit-Simulator()`. This is very helpful, as without NumPy, we'd need to write our own matrix analysis functions and methods. However, it is often convenient to rely on Python packages with special support for quantum concepts, building on the excellent numerical support provided by NumPy and SciPy (an extension to the NumPy numerical capabilities). In the next chapter, we will look at a Python package designed for quantum computing called QuTiP (Quantum Toolbox in Python), which will help us finish the upgrades to our simulator to simulate our CHSH game.

Summary

- Nonlocal games such as the CHSH game are experiments that can be used to check that quantum mechanics is consistent with how our universe actually works.
- It takes exponentially many classical bits to write the state of a quantum register, making it very hard to simulate more than about 30 qubits using traditional computers.
- We can combine single-qubit states together using the tensor product, allowing us to describe multi-qubit states.
- Multi-qubit states that can't be written by combining single-qubit states represent qubits that are entangled with each other.

Nonlocal games: Implementing a multi-qubit simulator

This chapter covers

- Programming a simulator for multiple qubits using the QuTiP Python package and tensor products
- Recognizing the proof that quantum mechanics is consistent with our observations of the universe by simulating experimental results

In the previous chapter, we learned about nonlocal games and how we can use them to validate our understanding of quantum mechanics. We also learned how to represent states of multiple qubits and what *entanglement* is.

In this chapter, we will dive into a new Python package called QuTiP that will allow us to program quantum systems faster and has some cool built-in features for simulating quantum mechanics. Then we'll learn how to use QuTiP to program a simulator for multiple qubits and see how that changes (or doesn't!) the three main tasks for our qubits: state preparations, operations, and measurement. This will let us finish the implementation of the CHSH game from chapter 4!

5.1   *Quantum objects in QuTiP*

QuTiP (Quantum Toolbox in Python, www.qutip.org) is a particularly useful package that provides built-in support for representing states and measurements as bras and kets, respectively, and for building matrices to represent quantum operations. Just as `np.array` is at the core of NumPy, all of our use of QuTiP will center around the `Qobj` class (short for *quantum object*). This class encapsulates vectors and matrices, providing additional metadata and useful methods that will make it easier for us to improve our simulator. Figure 5.1 shows an example of creating a `Qobj` from a vector, where it keeps track of some metadata:

- `data` holds the array representing the `Qobj`.
- `dims` is the size of our quantum register. We can think of it as a way of keeping track of how we record the qubits we are dealing with.
- `shape` keeps the dimension of the original object we used to make the `Qobj`. It is similar to the `np.shape` attribute.
- `type` is what the `Qobj` represents (a state = `ket`, a measurement = `bra`, or an operator = `oper`).

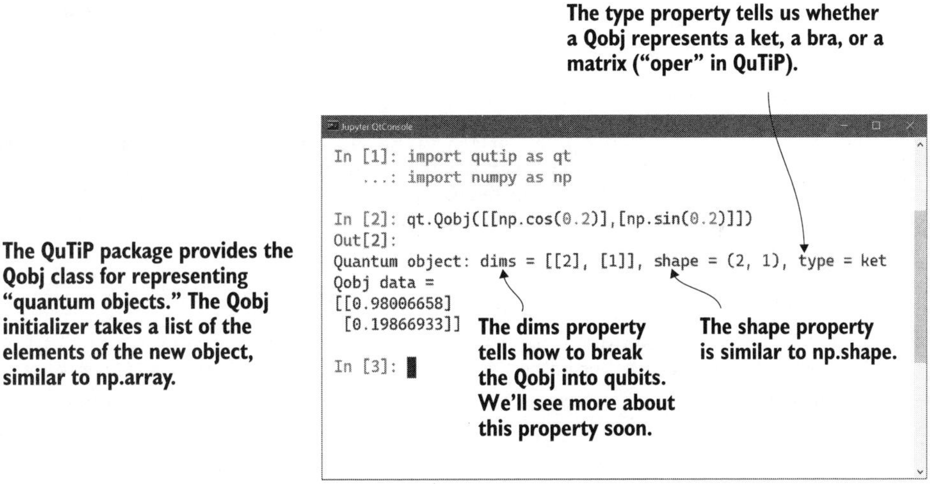

The type property tells us whether a Qobj represents a ket, a bra, or a matrix ("oper" in QuTiP).

The QuTiP package provides the Qobj class for representing "quantum objects." The Qobj initializer takes a list of the elements of the new object, similar to np.array.

```
In [1]: import qutip as qt
   ...: import numpy as np

In [2]: qt.Qobj([[np.cos(0.2)],[np.sin(0.2)]])
Out[2]:
Quantum object: dims = [[2], [1]], shape = (2, 1), type = ket
Qobj data =
[[0.98006658]
 [0.19866933]]

In [3]:
```

The dims property tells how to break the Qobj into qubits. We'll see more about this property soon.

The shape property is similar to np.shape.

Figure 5.1   Properties of the `Qobj` **class in the QuTiP Python package. Here we can see things like the** `type` **and** `dims` **properties that help both us and the package keep track of metadata about our quantum objects.**

Let's try importing QuTiP and asking it for the Hadamard operation; see listing 5.1.

NOTE   Make sure as you run things that you are in the right `conda` env; for more information, see appendix A.

Listing 5.1   QuTiP's representation of the Hadamard operation

```
>>> from qutip.qip.operations import hadamard_transform
>>> H = hadamard_transform()
>>> H
Quantum object: dims = [[2], [2]], shape = (2, 2), type = oper, isherm = True
Qobj data =
[[ 0.70710678  0.70710678]
 [ 0.70710678 -0.70710678]]
```

Note that QuTiP prints out some diagnostic information about each `Qobj` instance along with the data itself. Here, for instance, `type = oper` tells us that H represents an operator (a more formal term for the matrices we've seen so far) along with some information about the dimensions of the operator represented by H. Finally, the `isherm = True` output tells us that H is an example of a special kind of matrix called a *Hermitian operator*.

We can make new instances of `Qobj` in much the same way we made NumPy arrays, by passing in Python lists to the `Qobj` initializer.

Listing 5.2   Making a `Qobj` from a vector representing a qubit state

One key difference between creating Qobj instances and arrays is that when we create Qobj instances, we always need two levels of lists. The outer list is a list of rows in the new Qobj instance.

```
>>> import qutip as qt
>>> ket0 = qt.Qobj([[1], [0]])
>>> ket0
Quantum object: dims = [[2], [1]], shape = (2, 1), type = ket
Qobj data =
[[1.]
 [0.]]
```

QuTiP prints some metadata about the size and shape of the new quantum object, along with the data contained in the new object. In this case, the data for the new Qobj has two rows, each with one column. We identify that as the vector or ket that we use to write the $|0\rangle$ state.

Exercise 5.1: Creating the Qobj for other states

How would you create a `Qobj` to represent the $|1\rangle$ state? How about the $|+\rangle$ or $|-\rangle$ state? If you need to, check back to section 2.3.5 for what vectors represent those states.

Exercise solutions

All solutions for exercises in this book can be found in the companion code repo: https://github.com/crazy4pi314/learn-qc-with-python-and-qsharp. Just go to the folder for the chapter you are in, and open the Jupyter notebook with the name that mentions exercise solutions.

QuTiP really helps by providing a lot of nice shorthand for the kinds of objects we need to work with in quantum computing. For instance, we could have also made `ket0` in the previous sample by using the QuTiP `basis` function; see listing 5.3. The basis function takes two arguments. The first tells QuTiP that we want a qubit state: 2 for a single qubit because the length of a vector that is needed to represent it. The second argument tells QuTiP which basis state we want.

Listing 5.3 Using QuTiP to easily create |0⟩ and |1⟩

```
>>> import qutip as qt
>>> ket0 = qt.basis(2, 0)      ◁———  Passes a 2 as the first argument to indicate we want a single qubit,
>>> ket0                              and passes a 0 for the second argument because we want |0⟩
Quantum object: dims = [[2], [1]], shape = (2, 1), type = ket   ◁———┐  Note that we get
Qobj data =                                                         │  exactly the same
[[1.]                        We can also construct a               │  output here as
 [0.]]                       quantum object for |1⟩ by             │  in the previous
>>> ket1 = qt.basis(2, 1)    passing a 1 instead of a 0.   ◁——     │  example.
>>> ket1
Quantum object: dims = [[2], [1]], shape = (2, 1), type = ket
Qobj data =
[[0.]
 [1.]]
```

...basis?

As we have seen before, the states |0⟩ and |1⟩ make up the *computational basis* for a single qubit. The QuTiP function `basis` gets its name from this definition, as it makes quantum objects to represent computational basis states.

There are more things in heaven and earth than our qubits

It may seem a little odd that we had to tell QuTiP that we wanted a qubit. After all, what else *could* we want? As it turns out, quite a bit (yes, pun very much intended)!

There are many other ways to represent classical information than bits, such as *trits*, which have three possible values. However, we tend not to see classical information represented using anything other than bits when we write programs, as it's very useful to pick a convention and stick with it. Things other than bits still have their uses, though, in specialized domains such as telecommunications systems.

In the exact same fashion, quantum systems can have any number of different states: we can have qutrits, qu4its, qu5its, qu17its, and so forth, collectively known as qu*dits*. While representing quantum information using qu*dits* other than qubits can be useful in some cases and can have some very interesting mathematical properties, qubits give us all we need to dive into quantum programming.

Exercise 5.2: Using qt.basis for multiple qubits

How could you use the `qt.basis` function to create a two-qubit register in the |10⟩ state? How could you create the |001⟩ state? Remember that the second argument to `qt.basis` is an index to the computational basis states we saw earlier.

QuTiP also provides a number of different functions for making quantum objects to represent unitary matrices. For instance, we can make a quantum object for the X matrix by using the `sigmax` function.

Listing 5.4   Using QuTiP to create an object for the X matrix

```
>>> import qutip as qt
>>> qt.sigmax()
Quantum object: dims = [[2], [2]], shape = (2, 2), type = oper, isherm = True
Qobj data =
[[0. 1.]
 [1. 0.]]
```

As we saw in chapter 2, the matrix for `sigmax` represents a rotation of $180°$ (figure 5.2).

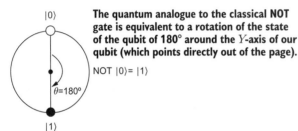

$|0\rangle$

The quantum analogue to the classical NOT gate is equivalent to a rotation of the state of the qubit of $180°$ around the Y-axis of our qubit (which points directly out of the page).

NOT $|0\rangle = |1\rangle$

$\theta = 180°$

$|1\rangle$

Figure 5.2   A visualization of the quantum equivalent of a NOT operation operating on a qubit in the $|0\rangle$ state, leaving the qubit in the $|1\rangle$ state

QuTiP also provides a function `ry` to represent rotating by whatever angle we want instead of $180°$ like the x operation. We saw the operation that `ry` represents in chapter 2 when we considered rotating $|0\rangle$ by an arbitrary angle θ. See figure 5.3 for a refresher on the operation we now know as `ry`.

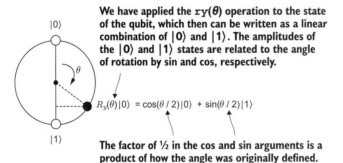

$|0\rangle$

We have applied the `ry($\theta$)` operation to the state of the qubit, which then can be written as a linear combination of $|0\rangle$ and $|1\rangle$. The amplitudes of the $|0\rangle$ and $|1\rangle$ states are related to the angle of rotation by sin and cos, respectively.

θ

$R_y(\theta)|0\rangle = \cos(\theta/2)|0\rangle + \sin(\theta/2)|1\rangle$

$|1\rangle$

The factor of ½ in the cos and sin arguments is a product of how the angle was originally defined.

Figure 5.3   A visualization of QuTiP function `ry`, which corresponds to a variable rotation of θ around the Y-axis of our qubit (which points directly out of the page)

Now that we have a few more single-qubit operations down, how can we easily simulate multi-qubit operations in QuTiP? We can use QuTiP's `tensor` function to quickly get up and running with tensor products to make our multi-qubit registers and operations, as we show in listing 5.5.

NOTE Since identity matrices are often written using the letter *I*, many scientific computing packages use the name eye as a bit of a pun to refer to the identity matrix.

Listing 5.5 Tensor products in QuTiP

```
>>> import qutip as qt
>>> from qutip.qip.operations import hadamard_transform
>>> psi = qt.basis(2, 0)
```
Sets psi to represent
$|\psi\rangle = |0\rangle$

```
>>> phi = qt.basis(2, 1)
>>> qt.tensor(psi, phi)
```
Sets phi to represent
$|\phi\rangle = |1\rangle$

```
Quantum object: dims = [[2, 2], [1, 1]], shape = (4, 1), type = ket
Qobj data =
[[ 0.]
 [ 1.]
 [ 0.]
 [ 0.]]
>>> H = hadamard_transform()
```
After calling tensor, QuTiP tells us the amplitudes for each classical label in $|\psi\rangle \otimes |\phi\rangle = |0\rangle \otimes |1\rangle = |01\rangle$, using the same order as listing 4.3.

Sets H to represent the Hadamard operation discussed earlier

```
>>> I = qt.qeye(2)
```
We can use the qeye function provided by QuTiP to get a copy of a Qobj instance representing the identity matrix that we first saw in listing 4.8.

```
>>> qt.tensor(H, I)
Quantum object: dims = [[2, 2], [2, 2]], shape = (4, 4),
type = oper, isherm = True
Qobj data =
[[ 0.70710678  0.          0.70710678  0.         ]
 [ 0.          0.70710678  0.          0.70710678]
 [ 0.70710678  0.         -0.70710678  0.         ]
 [ 0.          0.70710678  0.         -0.70710678]]
```

The unitary matrices representing quantum operations combine using tensor products in the same way as states and measurements.

We can use a common math trick to prove how applying tensor products of states and operations works. Say we want to prove this statement:

If we apply a unitary to a state and then take the tensor product, we get the same answer as if we applied the tensor product and then the unitary.

In math, we would say that for any unitary operators *U* and *V* and for any states $|\psi\rangle$ and $|\phi\rangle$, $(U|\psi\rangle) \otimes (V|\phi\rangle) = (U \otimes V)(|\psi\rangle \otimes |\phi\rangle)$. The math trick we can use is to take the left side and subtract from it the right. We should end up with 0. We give this a try in the following listing.

Listing 5.6 Verifying the tensor product in QuTiP

```
>>> (
...     qt.tensor(H, I) * qt.tensor(psi, phi) -
```
The right side of the statement we are trying to prove, where we use *H* and *I* as *U* and *V*: $(U \otimes V)(|\psi\rangle \otimes |\phi\rangle)$.

```
...        qt.tensor(H * psi, I * phi)
... )
Quantum object: dims = [[2, 2], [1, 1]], shape = (4, 1), type = ket
Qobj data =
[[ 0.]
 [ 0.]
 [ 0.]
 [ 0.]]
```

The left side of the statement we are trying to prove, where we use H and I as U and V: $(U|\psi\rangle) \otimes (V|\phi\rangle)$.

Yay! The two sides of the equation are equal if their difference is 0.

NOTE For a list of all the built-in states and operations in QuTiP, see http://qutip.org/docs/latest/guide/guide-basics.html#states-and-operators.

5.1.1 *Upgrading the simulator*

The goal now is to use QuTiP to upgrade our single-qubit simulator to a multi-qubit simulator with some of the features of QuTiP. We will do this by adding a few features to our single-qubit simulator from chapters 2 and 3.

The most significant change we'll need to make to our simulator from previous chapters is that we can no longer assign a state to each qubit. Rather, we must assign a state to the entire *register* of qubits in our device since some of the qubits may be *entangled* with each other. Let's jump into making the modifications necessary to separate the concept of the state to the device level.

NOTE To look at the code we wrote earlier, as well as the samples for this chapter, see the GitHub repo for the book: https://github.com/crazy4pi314/learn-qc-with-python-and-qsharp.

To review, we have two files for our simulator: the interface (interface.py) and the simulator itself (simulator.py). The device interface (`QuantumDevice`) defines a way of interacting with an actual or simulated quantum device, which is represented in Python as an object that lets us allocate and deallocate qubits.

We won't need anything new for the `QuantumDevice` class in the interface to model our CHSH game since we'll still need to allocate and deallocate qubits. Where we can add features is in the `Qubit` class provided along with our `SingleQubitSimulator` in simulator.py.

Now we need to consider what, if anything, needs to change in our interface for a `Qubit` we allocate from the `QuantumDevice`. In chapter 2, we saw that the Hadamard operation was useful for rotating qubits between different bases to make a QRNG. Let's build on this by adding a new method to `Qubit` to allow quantum programs to send a new kind of rotation instruction that we will need to use the quantum strategy for CHSH.

Listing 5.7   interface.py: adding a new `ry` operation

```
class Qubit(metaclass=ABCMeta):
    @abstractmethod
    def h(self): pass
```

```
@abstractmethod
def x(self): pass

@abstractmethod
def ry(self, angle: float): pass        ◁——  The abstract method ry, which takes
                                               an argument angle to specify how far
                                               to rotate the qubit around the Y-axis
@abstractmethod
def measure(self) -> bool: pass

@abstractmethod
def reset(self): pass
```

That should cover all the changes we need to make to our `Qubit` and `QuantumDevice` interface for playing CHSH with Eve. We need to address what changes we need to make to simulator.py to allow it to allocate, operate, and measure multi-qubit states.

The main changes to our `Simulator` class that implements a `QuantumDevice` are that we need attributes to track how many qubits it has and the register's overall state. The next listing shows these changes as well as an update to allocation and deallocation methods.

Listing 5.8 simulator.py: the multi-qubit `Simulator`

We have changed the name from SingleQubitSimulator to Simulator to indicate that it is more generalized. That means we can simulate multiple qubits with it.

The more general Simulator class needs a few attributes, the first being capacity, which represents the number of qubits it can simulate.

```
class Simulator(QuantumDevice):        ◁——
    capacity: int                                        ◁——
    available_qubits: List[SimulatedQubit]               ◁——
    register_state: qt.Qobj               ◁——
    def __init__(self, capacity=3):
        self.capacity = capacity
        self.available_qubits = [             ◁——
            SimulatedQubit(self, idx)
            for idx in range(capacity)
        ]
        self.register_state = qt.tensor(       ◁——
            *[
                qt.basis(2, 0)
                for _ in range(capacity)
            ]
        )
    def allocate_qubit(self) -> SimulatedQubit:       ◁——
        if self.available_qubits:
            return self.available_qubits.pop()

    def deallocate_qubit(self, qubit: SimulatedQubit):
        self.available_qubits.append(qubit)
```

available_qubits is a list containing the qubits the Simulator is using.

register_state uses the new QuTiP Qobj to represent the state of the entire simulator.

A list comprehension allows us to make a list of available qubits by calling SimulatedQubit with the indices from the range of capacity.

register_state is initialized by taking the tensor product of a number of copies of the |0⟩ state equal to the simulator's capacity. The *[...] notation turns the generated list into a sequence of arguments for qt.tensor.

The allocate_qubit and deallocate_qubit methods are the same as from chapter 3.

Peer not into the box, mortal!

Just as we used NumPy to represent a simulator's state, the `register_state` property of our newly upgraded simulator uses QuTiP to predict how each instruction has transformed the state of our register. When we write quantum programs, though, we do so against the interface in listing 5.7, which doesn't have any way to let us access `register_state`.

We can think of the simulator as a kind of black box that *encapsulates* the notion of a state. If our quantum programs were able to look inside that box, they would be able to cheat by copying the information in ways forbidden by the no-cloning theorem. This means for a quantum program to be correct, we cannot look inside the simulator to see its state.

In this chapter, we'll cheat a little; but in the next chapter, we'll fix that to make sure our programs can be run on actual quantum hardware.

We also will add a new *private* method to our `Simulator` that allows us to apply operations to specific qubits in our device. This will let us write methods on our qubits that send operations back to the simulator to be applied to the state of an entire register of qubits.

TIP   Python is not strict about keeping methods or attributes private, but we will prefix this method name with an underscore to indicate that it is meant for use in the class only.

Listing 5.9   simulator.py: one additional method for `Simulator`

The private method _apply takes an input unitary of type Qobj representing a unitary operation to be applied and a list of int to indicate the indices of the available_qubits list where we want to apply the operation. For now, that list will only ever contain one element since we're only implementing single-qubit operations in our simulator. We'll relax this in the next chapter.

```python
def _apply(self, unitary: qt.Qobj, ids: List[int]):
    if len(ids) == 1:
        matrix = qt.circuit.gate_expand_1toN(
            unitary, self.capacity, ids[0]
        )
    else:
        raise ValueError("Only single-qubit unitary matrices are supported.")

    self.register_state = matrix * self.register_state
```

If we want to apply a single-qubit operation to a qubit in a register, we can use QuTiP to generate the matrix we need. QuTiP does this by applying the matrix for our single-qubit operation to the correct qubit, and by applying 𝟙 everywhere else. This is done for us automatically by the gate_expand_1toN function.

Now that we have the right matrix to which to multiply our entire register_state, we can update the value of that register accordingly.

Let's get to the implementation of `SimulatedQubit`, the class that represents how we simulate a single qubit, given that we know it is part of a device that has multiple qubits. The main difference between the single- and multi-qubit versions of `SimulatedQubit` is that we need each qubit to remember its "parent" device and location or `id` in that device so that we can associate the state with the register and not each qubit. This is important, as we will see in the next section, when we want to measure qubits in a multi-qubit device.

Listing 5.10 simulator.py: single-qubit operations on a multi-qubit device

> **To initialize a qubit, we need the name of the parent simulator (so we can easily associate it) and the index of the qubit in the simulator's register. __init__ then sets those attributes and resets the qubit to the $|0\rangle$ state.**

```
class SimulatedQubit(Qubit):
    qubit_id: int
    parent: "Simulator"

    def __init__(self, parent_simulator: "Simulator", id: int):    ◁
        self.qubit_id = id
        self.parent = parent_simulator

    def h(self) -> None:
        self.parent._apply(H, [self.qubit_id])

    def ry(self, angle: float) -> None:
        self.parent._apply(qt.ry(angle), [self.qubit_id])    ◁

    def x(self) -> None:
        self.parent._apply(qt.sigmax(), [self.qubit_id])
```

> **We can also pass the parameterized qt.ry operation from QuTiP to _apply to rotate our qubit about the Y-axis by an angle "angle".**

To implement the h operation, we ask the parent of SimulatedQubit (which is an instance of Simulator) to use the _apply method to generate the right matrix that would represent the operation on the complete register, then update the register_state.

Great! We are almost finished upgrading our simulator to use QuTiP and support multiple qubits. We will tackle simulating measurement on multi-qubit states in the next section.

5.1.2 Measuring up: How can we measure multiple qubits?

TIP This section is one of the most challenging in the book. Please don't worry if it doesn't make a lot of sense the first time around.

In some sense, measuring multiple qubits works the same way we're used to from measuring single-qubit systems. We can still use Born's rule to predict the probability of any particular measurement outcome. For example, let's return to the $(|00\rangle + |11\rangle) / \sqrt{2}$ state that we've seen a few times already. If we were to measure a pair of qubits in that state, we would get either "00" or "11" as our classical outcomes with equal probability since both have the same amplitude: $1 / \sqrt{2}$.

Similarly, we'll still demand that if we measure the same register twice in a row, we get the same answer. If we get the "00" outcome, for instance, we know that qubits are left in the $|00\rangle = |0\rangle \otimes |0\rangle$ state.

This gets a little bit trickier, however, if we measure *part* of a quantum register without measuring the whole thing. Let's look at a couple of examples to see how that could work. Again taking $(|00\rangle + |11\rangle) / \sqrt{2}$ as an example, if we measure *only* the first qubit and we get a "0", we know that we need to get the same answer again the next time we measure. The only way this can happen is if the state transforms to $|00\rangle$ as a result of having observed "0" on the first qubit.

On the other hand, what happens if we measure the first qubit from a pair of qubits in the $|+\rangle$ state? First, it's helpful to refresh our memory as to what $|+\rangle$ looks like when written as a vector.

Listing 5.11   Representing the $|++\rangle$ state with QuTiP

Start by writing $|+\rangle$ as $H|0\rangle$. In QuTiP, we use the hadamard _transform function to get a Qobj instance to represent H, and we use basis(2, 0) to get a Qobj representing $|0\rangle$.

We can print out ket_plus to get a list of the elements in that vector; as before, we call each of these elements an amplitude.

```
>>> import qutip as qt
>>> from qutip.qip.operations import hadamard_transform
>>> ket_plus = hadamard_transform() * qt.basis(2, 0)
>>> ket_plus
Quantum object: dims = [[2], [1]], shape = (2, 1), type = ket
Qobj data =
[[0.70710678]
 [0.70710678]]
>>> register_state = qt.tensor(ket_plus, ket_plus)
>>> register_state
Quantum object: dims = [[2, 2], [1, 1]], shape = (4, 1), type = ket
Qobj data =
[[0.5]
 [0.5]
 [0.5]
 [0.5]]
```

To represent the state $|+\rangle$, we use that $|+\rangle = |+\rangle \otimes |+\rangle$.

This output tells us that $|++\rangle$ has the same amplitude for each of the four computational basis states $|00\rangle$, $|01\rangle$, $|10\rangle$, and $|11\rangle$, just as ket_plus has the same amplitude for each of the computational basis states $|0\rangle$ and $|1\rangle$.

Suppose that we measure the first qubit and get a "1" outcome. To ensure that we get the same result the next time we measure, the state after measurement can't have any amplitude on $|00\rangle$ or $|01\rangle$. If we only keep the amplitudes on $|10\rangle$ and $|11\rangle$ (the third and four rows of the vector we calculated previously), then we get that the state of our two qubits becomes $(|10\rangle + |11\rangle) / \sqrt{2}$.

Where did the $\sqrt{2}$ come from?

We included a $\sqrt{2}$ to ensure that all our measurement probabilities still sum to 1 when we measure the second qubit. For Born's rule to make any sense, we always need the sum of the squares of each amplitude to sum to 1.

There's another way to write this state, though, that we can check using QuTiP.

Listing 5.12 Representing the |1+⟩ state with QuTiP

```
>>> import qutip as qt
>>> from qutip.qip.operations import hadamard_transform
>>> ket_0 = qt.basis(2, 0)
>>> ket_1 = qt.basis(2, 1)
>>> ket_plus = hadamard_transform() * ket_0        ⟵─┐  Recall that we can
>>> qt.tensor(ket_1, ket_plus)                           write |+⟩ as H|0⟩.
Quantum object: dims = [[2, 2], [1, 1]], shape = (4, 1), type = ket
Qobj data =
[[0.        ]
 [0.        ]
 [0.70710678]
 [0.70710678]]
```

This tells us that if we only keep the parts of the state |+⟩ that are consistent with getting a "1" outcome from measuring the first qubit, then we get $|1\rangle = |1\rangle \otimes |+\rangle$. That is, nothing happens at all to the second qubit in this case!

Exercise 5.3: Measuring the other qubit

In the example where our two qubits begin in the |++⟩ state, suppose we measured the second qubit instead. Check that no matter what result we get, nothing happens to the state of the first qubit.

To work out what it means to measure part of a register more generally, we can use another concept from linear algebra called *projectors*.

DEFINITION A *projector* is the product of a state vector (the "ket" or |+⟩ part of a bra-ket) and a measurement (the "bra" or ⟨+| part of a bra-ket) and represents our requirement that *if* a certain measurement outcome occurs, *then* we must transform to a state consistent with that measurement.

See figure 5.4 for a quick example of a single-qubit projector. Defining projectors on multiple qubits works exactly the same way.

In QuTiP, we write the bra corresponding to a ket by using the .dag() method (short for *dagger*, a call-back to mathematical notation we see in figure 5.4). Fortunately, even if the math isn't straightforward, it winds up not being that bad to write in Python, as we can see next.

Listing 5.13 simulator.py: measuring individual qubits in a register

```
def measure(self) -> bool:                  Uses QuTiP to make a list of projectors, one
    projectors = [          ⟵─┐             for each possible measurement outcome
        qt.circuit.gate_expand_1toN(                              ⟵──────────────┐
            qt.basis(2, outcome) * qt.basis(2, outcome).dag(),
            self.parent.capacity,           As in listing 5.9, uses the gate_expand_1toN
            self.qubit_id                   function to expand each single-qubit projector
        )                                   into a projector that acts on the whole register
```

Uses each projector to pick out the parts of a state that are consistent with each measurement outcome

```
        for outcome in (0, 1)
    ]
    post_measurement_states = [
        projector * self.parent.register_state
        for projector in projectors
    ]
    probabilities = [
        post_measurement_state.norm() ** 2
        for post_measurement_state in post_measurement_states
    ]
    sample = np.random.choice([0, 1], p=probabilities)
    self.parent.register_state = post_measurement_states[sample].unit()
    return bool(sample)

def reset(self) -> None:
    if self.measure(): self.x()
```

The length of what each projector picks (written as the .norm() method in QuTiP) tells us about the probability of each measurement outcome.

Once we have the probabilities for each outcome, we can pick an outcome using NumPy.

If the result of a measurement is $|1\rangle$, then flipping with an x instruction resets back to $|0\rangle$.

Uses the .unit() method built-in to QuTiP to ensure that the measurement probabilities still sum up to 1

This is an example of a projector: that is, a matrix that squares to itself. In this example, we get our projector by multiplying a ket with a bra. When we compute inner products such as for Born's rule, we've generally done the opposite: multiplied a bra with a ket.

When we do so, we get that the bra is represented by a row vector, so that the projector is a product of a column with a row.

$$|0\rangle\langle0| = \begin{bmatrix} 1 \\ 0 \end{bmatrix} \left(\begin{bmatrix} 1 \\ 0 \end{bmatrix}\right)^{\dagger} = \begin{bmatrix} 1 \\ 0 \end{bmatrix} \begin{bmatrix} 1 & 0 \end{bmatrix} = \begin{bmatrix} 1 & 0 \\ 0 & 0 \end{bmatrix}$$

Recall that we can turn a ket like $|0\rangle$ into a bra like $\langle0|$ by taking the conjugate transpose (written as a dagger).

Working through the matrix multiplication, we get a 1 in the $|0\rangle$ row and the $|0\rangle$ column, and zeroes everywhere else.

$$\begin{bmatrix} 1 & 0 \\ 0 & 0 \end{bmatrix} \begin{bmatrix} \alpha \\ \beta \end{bmatrix} = \begin{bmatrix} \alpha \\ 0 \end{bmatrix}$$

When we multiply an arbitrary state vector by this projector, it projects out or filters out all but the part corresponding to the $|0\rangle$ computational basis state.

What we're left with might no longer be a valid state, as it might not have the right length. The length tells us about how much of the original state vector was picked out by our projector. In our simulator, we'll use this to find the probability for each measurement outcome, giving us another way to compute Born's rule.

Figure 5.4   An example of a projector acting on a single-qubit state

5.2   CHSH: Quantum strategy

Now that we have expanded our simulator to handle multiple qubits, let's see how we can simulate a *quantum*-based strategy for our players that will result in a win probability higher than could be possible with any classical strategy! See figure 5.5 for a reminder of how the CHSH game is played.

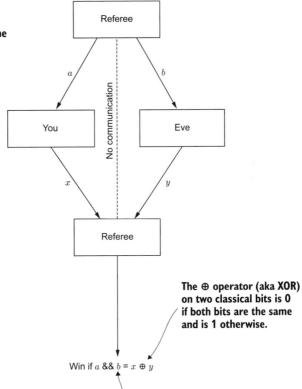

1. A referee sends you and Eve a one-bit question. Your question is labeled a and Eve's is b. Once the game starts, you and Eve can no longer communicate until after the game ends.

2. The referee demands a one-bit answer from each player. Here, your answer is labeled x and Eve's is labeled y.

3. Both players send a one-bit answer back to the referee. The referee then scores the game and declares if the players won.

4. The scoring rules require that you and Eve answer with the correct parity given the input bits from the referee.

The $\oplus$ operator (aka XOR) on two classical bits is 0 if both bits are the same and is 1 otherwise.

Win if a && $b = x \oplus y$

The && operator (aka AND) on two classical bits is 1 if both bits are 1 and is 0 in all other cases.

Figure 5.5 The CHSH game, a nonlocal game with two players and a referee. The referee gives each player a question in the form of a bit value, and then each player has to figure out how to respond to the referee. The players win if the Boolean XOR of their responses is the same as the classical AND of the referee's questions.

You and Eve now have quantum resources, so let's start with the simplest option: You each have one qubit allocated from the same device. We'll use our simulator to implement this strategy, so this isn't really a test of quantum mechanics as much as that our simulator agrees with quantum mechanics.

NOTE   We can't simulate the players being truly nonlocal, as the simulator parts need to communicate to emulate quantum mechanics. Faithfully simulating quantum games and quantum networking protocols in this manner exposes a lot of interesting classical networking topology questions that are well beyond the scope of this book. If you're interested in simulators intended more for use in quantum networking than quantum computing, we recommend looking at the SimulaQron project (www.simulaqron.org) for more information.

Let's see how often we and Eve can win if we each start with a single qubit, and if those qubits start in the $(|00\rangle + |11\rangle) \, / \, \sqrt{2}$ state that we've seen a few times so far in this chapter. Don't worry about how to prepare this state; we'll learn how to do that in chapter 6. For now, let's just see what we can do with qubits in that state once we have them.

Using these qubits, we can form a new quantum strategy for the CHSH game we saw at the start of the chapter. The trick is that we and Eve can each apply operations to each of our qubits once we get our respective messages from the referee.

As it turns out, ry is a very useful operation for this strategy. It lets us and Eve trade off slightly between how often we win when the referee asks us to output the same answers (the 00, 01, and 10 cases) to do slightly better when we need to output different answers (the 11 case), as shown in figure 5.6.

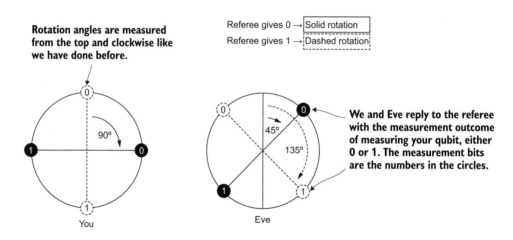

Figure 5.6   Rotating qubits to win at CHSH. If we get a 0 from the referee, we should rotate our qubit by 45°; and if we get a 1, we should rotate our qubit by 135°.

We can see from this strategy that both we and Eve have a pretty easy, straightforward rule for what to do with our respective qubits before we measure them. If we get a 0 from the referee, we should rotate our qubit by 45°; and if we get a 1, we should rotate our qubit by 135°. If you like a table approach to this strategy, table 5.1 shows a summary.

Table 5.1 Rotations we and Eve will do to our qubits as a function of the input bit we receive from the referee. Note that they are all `ry` rotations, just by different angles (converted to radians for `ry`).

Input from referee	Our rotation	Eve's rotation
0	`ry(90 * np.pi / 180)`	`ry(45 * np.pi / 180)`
1	`ry(0)`	`ry(135 * np.pi / 180)`

Don't worry if these angles look random. We can check to see that they work using our new simulator! The next listing uses the new features we added to the simulator to write out a quantum strategy.

Listing 5.14   chsh.py: a quantum CHSH strategy, using two qubits

To start the quantum strategy, we need to create a QuantumDevice instance where we will simulate our qubits.

```
import qutip as qt
def quantum_strategy(initial_state: qt.Qobj) -> Strategy:
    shared_system = Simulator(capacity=2)
    shared_system.register_state = initial_state
    your_qubit = shared_system.allocate_qubit()
    eve_qubit = shared_system.allocate_qubit()

    shared_system.register_state = qt.bell_state()
    your_angles = [90 * np.pi / 180, 0]
    eve_angles = [45 * np.pi / 180, 135 * np.pi / 180]

    def you(your_input: int) -> int:
        your_qubit.ry(your_angles[your_input])
        return your_qubit.measure()

    def eve(eve_input: int) -> int:
        eve_qubit.ry(eve_angles[eve_input])
        return eve_qubit.measure()

    return you, eve
```

Labels can be assigned to each qubit as we allocate them to the shared_system.

Angles for the rotations we and Eve need to do based on our input from the referee

Strategy for playing the CHSH game starts with us rotating our qubit based on the input classical bit from the referee.

The classical bit value our strategy returns is the bit value we get when we measure our qubit.

Eve's strategy is similar to ours; she just uses different angles for her initial rotation.

We cheat a little to set the state of our qubits to the entangled state $(|00\rangle + |11\rangle) / \sqrt{2}$. We will see in chapter 6 how to prepare this state from scratch and why the function to prepare this state is called bell_state.

Just like our classical strategy, quantum_strategy returns a tuple of functions that represent our and Eve's individual actions.

Now that we have implemented a Python version of quantum_strategy, let's see how often we can win by using our CHSH game est_win_probability function.

Listing 5.15   Running CHSH with our new `quantum_strategy`

```
>>> est_win_probability(quantum_strategy)
0.832
```

You may get slightly more or less than 85% when you try this, because the win probability is estimated under the hood using a binomial distribution. For this example, we'd expect error bars of about 1.5%.

The estimated win probability of 83.2% in listing 5.15 is higher than what we can get with any classical strategy. This means that we and Eve can start winning the CHSH game more frequently than any other classical players—awesome! What this strategy shows, though, is an example of how states like $(|00\rangle + |11\rangle)$ / $\sqrt{2}$ are important resources provided by quantum mechanics.

> **NOTE**   States like $(|00\rangle + |11\rangle)$ / $\sqrt{2}$ are called *entangled* because they can't be written as the tensor product of single-qubit states. We'll see many more examples of entanglement as we go along, but entanglement is one of the most amazing and fun things that we get to use in writing quantum programs.

As we saw in this example, entanglement allows us to create correlations in our data that can be used to our advantage when we want to get useful information out of our quantum systems.

The speed of light is still a thing

If you've read about relativity (if you haven't, no worries), you may have heard that it's impossible to send information faster than the speed of light. It may seem from what we've learned about entanglement so far that quantum mechanics violates this, but as it turns out, entanglement can *never* be used on its own to communicate a message of our choosing. We always need to send something else along with using entanglement. This means the speed of light still constrains how fast information can travel through the universe—phew!

Far from being strange or weird, entanglement is a direct result of what we've already learned about quantum computing: it is a direct consequence of quantum mechanics being *linear*. If we can prepare a two-qubit register in the $|00\rangle$ state and the $|11\rangle$ state, then we can also prepare a state in a linear combination of the two, such as $(|00\rangle + |11\rangle)$ / $\sqrt{2}$.

Since entanglement is a direct result of the linearity of quantum mechanics, the CHSH game also gives us a great way to check that quantum mechanics is really correct (or to the best our data can show). Let's go back to the win probability in listing 5.15. If we do an experiment, and we see something like an 83.2% win probability, that tells us our experiment couldn't have been purely classical since we know a classical strategy can *at most* win 75% of the time. This experiment has been done many times throughout history and is part of how we know that our universe isn't just classical—we need quantum mechanics to describe it.

> **NOTE**   In 2015, one experiment had the two players in the CHSH game separated by more than a kilometer!

The simulator that we wrote in this chapter gives us everything we need to see how those kinds of experiments work. Now we can plow ahead to use quantum mechanics and qubits to do awesome stuff, armed with the knowledge that quantum mechanics really is how our universe works.

Self-testing: An application for nonlocal games

This hints at another application for nonlocal games: if we can play *and win* a nonlocal game with Eve, then along the way, we must have built something we can use to send quantum data. This sort of insight leads to ideas known as *quantum self-testing*, where we make parts of a device play nonlocal games with other parts of the device to make sure the device works correctly.

Summary

- We can use the QuTiP package to help us work with tensor products and other computations we need to write a multi-qubit simulator in Python.
- The Qobj class in QuTiP tracks many useful properties of the states and operators we want to simulate.
- We and Eve can use a quantum strategy to play the CHSH game, where we share a pair of entangled qubits before we start playing the game.
- By writing the CHSH game as a quantum program, we can prove that players using entangled pairs of qubits can win more often than players that only use classical computers, which is consistent with our understanding of quantum mechanics.

Teleportation and entanglement: Moving quantum data around

This chapter covers

- Moving data around a quantum computer using classical and quantum control
- Visualizing single-qubit operations with the Bloch sphere
- Predicting the output of two-qubit operations, and Pauli operations

In the last chapter, we added support for multiple qubits to our quantum device simulator with the help of the QuTiP package. That allowed us to play the CHSH game and show that our understanding of quantum mechanics is consistent with what we observe in the real world.

In this chapter, we'll get to see how we can move data between different people or registers in a quantum device. We will take a look at how things like the no-cloning theorem affect how we manage our data on a quantum device. We will also get to check out a uniquely quantum protocol our quantum device can perform, called *teleportation*, which moves data (as opposed to copies).

6.1 Moving quantum data

Just as with classical computing, sometimes in a quantum computer, we have some data *here* that we would very much appreciate being somewhere over *there*. Classically, this is an easy problem to solve by copying data; but as we saw in chapters 3 and 4, the no-cloning theorem means in general, we *can't* copy data stored in qubits.

Moving data classically

In some parts of classical computing, we run into the same problem of not being able to copy information, but for different reasons. Copying data in a multithreaded application can introduce subtle race conditions, while performance considerations can prompt us to reduce the amount of data that we copy.

The solution embraced by many classical languages (e.g., C++11 and Rust) focuses on *moving* data. Thinking in terms of moving data is helpful in quantum computing, although we'll implement moves in a very different way.

So what can we do if we want to move data in a quantum device? Fortunately, there are a number of different ways to move quantum data instead of copying it. In this chapter, we'll see a few of these approaches and add the last couple of features to our simulator to implement them. Let's get to sharing quantum information!

Suppose Eve has some qubits that encode data she'd like to share with us:

Hey player! I have some quantum information I want to share with you. Can I send it over to you?

Here, Eve is referring to the swap instruction—it's a bit different than the instructions we've seen so far in that it operates on *two* qubits at once. By contrast, every operation we've seen so far operates on only one qubit at a time.

Looking at what swap does, the name is pretty descriptive: it literally swaps the state of two qubits in the same register. For example, say we have two qubits in the $|01\rangle$ state. If we use the swap instruction on both qubits, our register will now be in the $|10\rangle$ state. Let's look at an example of using the swap matrix built into QuTiP.

Listing 6.1 Using QuTiP's swap on $|+0\rangle$ to get the $|0+\rangle$ state

```
>>> import qutip as qt
>>> from qutip.qip.operations import hadamard_transform
>>> ket_0 = qt.basis(2, 0)
>>> ket_plus = hadamard_transform() * ket_0
>>> initial_state = qt.tensor(ket_plus, ket_0)
>>> initial_state
Quantum object: dims = [[2, 2], [1, 1]], shape = (4, 1), type = ket
Qobj data =
```

> Uses qt.basis, hadamard_transform, and qt.tensor to define a variable for our old friend from chapter 5: the state vector $|+0\rangle$

```
[[0.70710678]
 [0.        ]
 [0.70710678]
 [0.        ]]
>>> swap_matrix = qt.swap()
>>> swap_matrix * initial_state
Quantum object: dims = [[2, 2], [1, 1]], shape = (4, 1), type = ket
Qobj data =
[[0.70710678]
 [0.70710678]
 [0.        ]
 [0.        ]]
>>> qt.tensor(ket_0, ket_plus)
Quantum object: dims = [[2, 2], [1, 1]], shape = (4, 1), type = ket
Qobj data =
[[0.70710678]
 [0.70710678]
 [0.        ]
 [0.        ]]
```

As we saw in chapter 4, this state has equal amplitudes on the $|00\rangle$ and $|10\rangle$ computational basis states.

Gets a copy of the unitary matrix for the swap instruction by calling qt.swap

When we do so, we end up in a superposition between $|00\rangle$ and $|01\rangle$ instead of between $|00\rangle$ and $|10\rangle$.

Quickly checks that the result of using the swap instruction on a register of two qubits that start in the $|+0\rangle$ state is $|0+\rangle$

The same way that we've simulated single-qubit operations, we can multiply our state by the unitary matrix for swap to find the state of our two-qubit register after applying a swap instruction.

Looking at listing 6.1, we can see that the swap instruction did pretty much what its name suggests. In particular, swap took two qubits that started in the state $|+0\rangle$ to the $|0+\rangle$ state. More generally, we can read what the swap instruction does by looking at the unitary matrix we used to simulate it.

Listing 6.2   Unitary matrix for the swap instruction

```
>>> import qutip as qt
>>> qt.swap()
Quantum object: dims = [[2, 2], [2, 2]],
    shape = (4, 4), type = oper, isherm = True
Qobj data =
[[1. 0. 0. 0.]
 [0. 0. 1. 0.]
 [0. 1. 0. 0.]
 [0. 0. 0. 1.]]
```

The unitary matrix we use to simulate the swap instruction is a 4 × 4 matrix because it acts on two-qubit states.

Each column of this unitary matrix tells us what happens to one of the computational basis states; here, the swap instruction does nothing to qubits that start in the $|00\rangle$ state.

On the other hand, the $|01\rangle$ and $|10\rangle$ states are swapped by the swap instruction.

The swap instruction also leaves $|11\rangle$ alone.

Each column of this unitary matrix tells us what happens to one of the computational basis states. For instance, the first column tells us that the $|00\rangle$ state is mapped to the vector [[1], [0], [0], [0]], which we recognize as $|00\rangle$.

NOTE   The unitary matrix for the swap instruction *cannot* be written as the tensor product of any two single-qubit unitary matrices. That is, we can't understand what swap does by considering one qubit at a time—we need to work out what it does to the state of the pair of qubits that the swap instruction acts on.

Figure 6.1 shows that we can see what swap does in general, regardless of what state our two qubits start in.

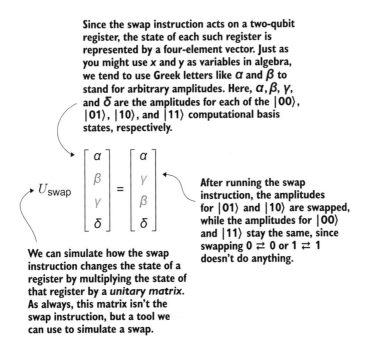

Since the swap instruction acts on a two-qubit register, the state of each such register is represented by a four-element vector. Just as you might use *x* and *y* as variables in algebra, we tend to use Greek letters like α and β to stand for arbitrary amplitudes. Here, $\alpha, \beta, \gamma,$ and δ are the amplitudes for each of the $|00\rangle$, $|01\rangle$, $|10\rangle$, and $|11\rangle$ computational basis states, respectively.

$$U_{swap}\begin{bmatrix}\alpha\\\beta\\\gamma\\\delta\end{bmatrix}=\begin{bmatrix}\alpha\\\gamma\\\beta\\\delta\end{bmatrix}$$

After running the swap instruction, the amplitudes for $|01\rangle$ and $|10\rangle$ are swapped, while the amplitudes for $|00\rangle$ and $|11\rangle$ stay the same, since swapping $0 \rightleftarrows 0$ or $1 \rightleftarrows 1$ doesn't do anything.

We can simulate how the swap instruction changes the state of a register by multiplying the state of that register by a *unitary matrix*. As always, this matrix isn't the swap instruction, but a tool we can use to simulate a swap.

Figure 6.1 The two-qubit operation swap exchanges the states of two qubits in a register. We can see this in the generic example shown here because the terms describing the $|01\rangle$ and $|10\rangle$ states are swapped. The other two are not because we can't tell the difference when the two qubits are in the same state.

Remember that in chapter 2, we saw that a unitary matrix is a lot like a truth table. That is, unitary matrices like what we get back from qt.swap are useful in that they help us simulate what the swap instruction does. Just as a classical adder isn't its truth table, though, it's helpful to remember that these unitary matrices aren't quantum programs but tools that we use to simulate how quantum programs work.

Exercise 6.1: Swapping the second and third qubits in a register

Say you have a register with three qubits in the state $|01+\rangle$. Using QuTiP, write out this state, and then swap the second and third qubits so your register is in the $|0+1\rangle$ state.

Hint: Since nothing will happen to the first qubit, be sure take the tensor product of an identity matrix and qt.swap to build up the correct operation for your register.

> ### Exercise solutions
>
> All solutions for exercises in this book can be found in the companion code repo: https://github.com/crazy4pi314/learn-qc-with-python-and-qsharp. Just go to the folder for the chapter you are in and open the Jupyter notebook with the name that mentions exercise solutions.

At this point, Eve is positively *dying* waiting to send her qubits. Let's add what we need to our simulator to not keep her waiting any longer!

6.1.1 *Swapping out the simulator*

The simulator we worked on in chapter 4 needs just a couple of tweaks to be able to use two-qubit operations like swap. The changes we need to make are as follows:

- Modify _apply to work with two-qubit operations.
- Add swap and other two-qubit instructions.
- Add the rest of the single-qubit rotation instructions.

As we saw in chapter 4, if a matrix acts on a single-qubit register, we can use QuTiP to apply that to a register with an arbitrary number of qubits by using the gate_expand _1toN function. This takes the tensor product of identity operators on each qubit except the qubits we're working with.

In the same way, we can call QuTiP's gate_expand_2toN function to turn two-qubit unitary matrices into matrices that we can use to simulate how two-qubit operations like swap transform the state of a whole register. Let's add that to our simulator now (listing 6.3).

> **TIP** We've made a couple of small changes to the code in this chapter to help make the printed output look a little nicer. These changes, along with all the samples for this and other chapters, are on the GitHub repo for this book: https://github.com/crazy4pi314/learn-qc-with-python-and-qsharp.

Listing 6.3   simulator.py: applying two-qubit unitary matrices

To simulate two-qubit operations, we need two indices for qubits in the register: one for each qubit that our instruction acts on.

The call to gate_expand_2toN looks very similar to our call to gate_expand_ltoN, except that we pass a 4 × 4 matrix instead of a 2 × 2 matrix.

```
def _apply(self, unitary: qt.Qobj, ids: List[int]):
    if len(ids) == 1:
        matrix = qt.circuit.gate_expand_1toN(unitary,
                                             self.capacity, ids[0])
    elif len(ids) == 2:
        matrix = qt.circuit.gate_expand_2toN(unitary,
                                             self.capacity, *ids)
    else:
        raise ValueError("Only one- or two-qubit unitary matrices
supported.")

    self.register_state = matrix * self.register_state
```

We saw that QuTiP provides the function `swap` to give us a copy of the unitary matrix that simulates the `swap` instruction. This can be used to pretty quickly add the `swap` instruction to our simulator using the changes we made to `Simulator._apply`.

Listing 6.4   simulator.py: adding a swap instruction

```
def swap(self, target: Qubit) -> None:
        self.parent._apply(
            qt.swap(),
            [self.qubit_id, target.qubit_id]
        )
```

To get the 4 × 4 unitary matrix, we need to pass to "apply"; we just use the qt.swap function we've seen a few times so far in this chapter.

We need to make sure we pass the indices for both qubits we want to swap between so that gate_expand_2toN correctly applies the unitary matrix for our new swap instruction to the state of an entire register.

While we're working with the simulator, let's add one more instruction to print out its state more easily without having to access its internals.

Listing 6.5   simulator.py: adding a dump instruction

```
def dump(self) -> None:
        print(self.register_state)
```

This way, we can ask the simulator to help us debug quantum programs, but in a way that can be safely stripped out for devices that don't support it (e.g., actual quantum hardware).

TIP Remember that a qubit is not a state. A state is just a convenient way of representing how the quantum system will behave.

With both these changes in place, we're all set to use the `swap` instruction. Let's use it to repeat the experiment where we swapped two qubits starting in the |0+⟩ state to transform them into the |+0⟩ state.

TIP As always, for the full sample files, see the GitHub repo for this book: https://github.com/crazy4pi314/learn-qc-with-python-and-qsharp.

Listing 6.6   Testing the swap instruction on the |0+⟩ state

```
>>> from simulator import Simulator
>>> sim = Simulator(capacity=2)
>>> with sim.using_register(n_qubits=2) as (you, eve):
...     eve.h()
...     sim.dump()
...     you.swap(eve)
...     sim.dump()
Quantum object: dims = [[2, 2], [1, 1]], shape = (4, 1), type = ket
Qobj data =
[[0.70710678]
 [0.70710678]
 [0.        ]
 [0.        ]]
```

Since we'll be working a lot with multiple-qubit registers in this chapter, we've added a new convenience method that lets us allocate several qubits at once.

The first dump comes from our first call to sim.dump and confirms that eve.h() prepared the qubits in the |0+⟩ state.

```
Quantum object: dims = [[2, 2], [1, 1]], shape = (4, 1), type = ket
Qobj data =
[[0.70710678]
 [0.        ]
 [0.70710678]
 [0.        ]]
```

After calling you.swap(eve), our qubit ends up in the $|+\rangle$ state, with Eve's qubit ending the way ours started: in the $|0\rangle$ state.

Great: we now have a way to share quantum data with Eve! Well, at least *as long as we're sharing a single quantum device* so that we can apply the swap instruction to both our qubits at the same time.

What happens if we want to share quantum information *between* devices? Fortunately, quantum computing gives us a way to send qubits by only communicating classical data, as long as we both start with some entanglement between our qubits. Like much in quantum computing, this technique is given a whimsical name: *quantum teleportation.* Don't let the name fool you, however. When we get right down to it, teleportation uses what we learned in chapter 4 to let us share quantum data in a useful way. Figure 6.2 shows a list of the steps in a teleportation program.

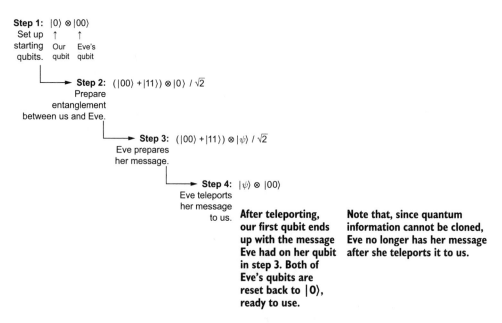

Step 1: $|0\rangle \otimes |00\rangle$
Set up $\quad\uparrow\qquad\uparrow$
starting $\quad$ Our $\quad$ Eve's
qubits. $\quad$ qubit $\quad$ qubit

Step 2: $(|00\rangle + |11\rangle) \otimes |0\rangle / \sqrt{2}$
Prepare
entanglement
between us and Eve.

Step 3: $(|00\rangle + |11\rangle) \otimes |\psi\rangle / \sqrt{2}$
Eve prepares
her message.

Step 4: $|\psi\rangle \otimes |00\rangle$
Eve teleports
her message
to us.

After teleporting, our first qubit ends up with the message Eve had on her qubit in step 3. Both of Eve's qubits are reset back to $|0\rangle$, ready to use.

Note that, since quantum information cannot be cloned, Eve no longer has her message after she teleports it to us.

Figure 6.2   The steps in the teleportation program. We prepare and entangle a register of qubits, and then Eve can prepare and teleport her state to us. Note that she will not have the state after teleportation.

What's really neat about teleportation is that, while we and Eve still need to do some two-qubit operations between our respective qubits, Eve can decide what data she wants to send us *after* we've done those operations. This means we could prepare the entangled qubits before we needed to exchange quantum data and just use them as needed.

Using the simulator that we've developed throughout the past several chapters, we might write up teleportation with a quantum program like that shown in the following listing.

Listing 6.7 A teleportation program in Python

```python
def teleport(msg : Qubit, here : Qubit, there : Qubit) -> None:
    here.h()
    here.cnot(there)

    msg.cnot(here)
    msg.h()

    if msg.measure(): there.z()
    if here.measure(): there.x()

    msg.reset()
    here.reset()
```

There are a few new instructions in this program, though. In the rest of this chapter, we'll see the other pieces required to get up and running with quantum teleportation using our simulator.

6.1.2 What other two-qubit gates are there?

As you may guess, swap is not the only two-qubit operation. Indeed, as shown in listing 6.7, to get teleportation working, we need to add another two-qubit instruction called cnot to the simulator. The cnot instruction does something similar to swap, except it switches the $|10\rangle$ and $|11\rangle$ computational basis states instead of the $|01\rangle$ and $|10\rangle$ states. Another way to think of this is that cnot flips the second qubit *controlled* on the state of the first qubit being $|1\rangle$. This is where the name cnot comes from: it's shorthand for "controlled NOT."

> **TIP** We often call the first qubit passed to a cnot instruction the *control qubit* and the second qubit the *target qubit*. As we will see in chapter 7, though, there is a bit of subtlety to these names.

Let's jump right in and see how the cnot instruction works by applying it to that lovely example, the $|+0\rangle$ state:

```
>>> import qutip as qt
>>> from qutip.qip.operations import hadamard_transform
>>> ket_0 = qt.basis(2, 0)
>>> ket_plus = hadamard_transform() * ket_0
>>> initial_state = qt.tensor(ket_plus, ket_0)
>>> qt.cnot() * initial_state
Quantum object: dims = [[2, 2], [1, 1]], shape = (4, 1), type = ket
Qobj data =
[[0.70710678]
 [0.         ]
 [0.         ]
```

Initializes two qubits so that they start in the $|+0\rangle = (|00\rangle + |10\rangle)/\sqrt{2}$ state

QuTiP provides the unitary matrix for the cnot instruction as the qt.cnot function.

The cnot instruction leaves our qubits in the state $(|00\rangle + |11\rangle)/\sqrt{2}$.

```
    [0.70710678]]
>>> qt.cnot()
Quantum object: dims = [[2, 2], [2, 2]], shape = (4, 4), type = oper,
    isherm = True    ◁
Qobj data =
[[1. 0. 0. 0.]
 [0. 1. 0. 0.]
 [0. 0. 0. 1.]
 [0. 0. 1. 0.]]
```

The matrix for cnot maps the $|10\rangle$ computational basis state to $|11\rangle$ and vice versa, just as we expected from the description.

NOTE   The cnot instruction is *not* the same as if statements in classical programming languages, in that a cnot instruction preserves superposition. If we wanted to use an if statement, we'd have to measure the control qubit, causing it to collapse any superposition on the control qubit. We'll actually use both cnot instructions and if statements conditioned on measurement results when we write out our teleportation program at the end of this chapter—both can be useful! In chapters 8 and 9, we'll see more about how controlled operations differ from if statements.

Figure 6.3 shows how the cnot instruction acts on two-qubit states in general. For now, though, we recognize the output state that we got in the previous code snippet by applying cnot on two qubits in the $|0\rangle$ state as the entangled we needed to play the CHSH game in chapter 4, $(|00\rangle + |11\rangle) / \sqrt{2}$.

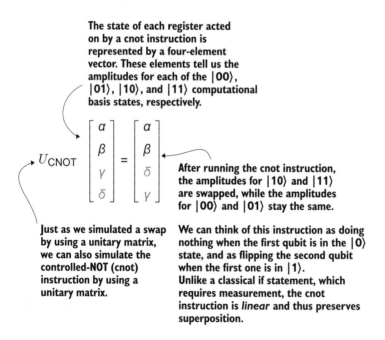

The state of each register acted on by a cnot instruction is represented by a four-element vector. These elements tell us the amplitudes for each of the $|00\rangle$, $|01\rangle$, $|10\rangle$, and $|11\rangle$ computational basis states, respectively.

$$U_{\text{CNOT}} \begin{bmatrix} \alpha \\ \beta \\ \gamma \\ \delta \end{bmatrix} = \begin{bmatrix} \alpha \\ \beta \\ \delta \\ \gamma \end{bmatrix}$$

After running the cnot instruction, the amplitudes for $|10\rangle$ and $|11\rangle$ are swapped, while the amplitudes for $|00\rangle$ and $|01\rangle$ stay the same.

Just as we simulated a swap by using a unitary matrix, we can also simulate the controlled-NOT (cnot) instruction by using a unitary matrix.

We can think of this instruction as doing nothing when the first qubit is in the $|0\rangle$ state, and as flipping the second qubit when the first one is in $|1\rangle$. Unlike a classical if statement, which requires measurement, the cnot instruction is *linear* and thus preserves superposition.

Figure 6.3   The two-qubit operation cnot applies a not operation conditioned on the state of a control qubit.

This means we have everything we need to write a quantum program that entangles two qubits that start in the |00⟩ state. All we need to do is add the cnot instruction to our simulator, the same way we added swap earlier.

Listing 6.8 simulator.py: adding the cnot instruction

```
def cnot(self, target: Qubit) -> None:
        self.parent._apply(
            qt.cnot(),
            [self.qubit_id, target.qubit_id]
        )
```

Now we can write a program to prepare two qubits in an entangled pair:

```
>>> from simulator import Simulator
>>> sim = Simulator(capacity=2)
>>> with sim.using_register(2) as (you, eve):
...     eve.h()
...     eve.cnot(you)
...     sim.dump()
...
Quantum object: dims = [[2, 2], [1, 1]],
    shape = (4, 1), type = ket
Qobj data =
[[0.70710678]
 [0.        ]
 [0.        ]
 [0.70710678]]
```

At this point, it's helpful to pause a moment (sorry, Eve!) and reflect on what we just did. In chapter 4, when we simulated playing the CHSH game with Eve, we had to "cheat" by assuming that we and Eve could have access to two qubits that magically start in the entangled state $(|00⟩ + |11⟩) / \sqrt{2}$. Now, though, we see exactly how we and Eve can prepare that entanglement by running another quantum program before playing CHSH. The h instruction prepares the superposition that we need, while the new cnot instruction allows us to prepare entanglement with Eve. This entanglement "shares" that superposition across our two qubits. (Sharing is caring, after all.)

Just like preparing entanglement between us and Eve was how we got ready for the CHSH game in chapter 4, it is the first step we need for Eve to teleport her quantum data to us. This makes cnot a very important instruction going forward.

Getting back to Eve, though, the next step for her to teleport her data to us is using one of four different single-qubit operations to *decode* the quantum data she sends us (recall figure 6.2). Let's look at those next.

6.2 *All the single (qubit) rotations*

The last thing we need to program quantum teleportation is to apply a correction based on some classical data that Eve sends us. To do so, we need a couple of new single-qubit instructions. For that, it's helpful to revisit the pictures we've been using to depict quantum instructions as rotations, because we may have been cheating a little. We have depicted our qubits so far as any position on a circle, but in reality, we are missing a dimension for our model of a qubit. The state of a *single* qubit is represented by any point on the surface of a sphere, generally referred to as the *Bloch sphere*.

> ### Single qubits only!
> This (and the previous) way of visualizing the state of a qubit *only* works if that qubit is not entangled with any other qubits. Another way of saying this is that we cannot easily visualize a multi-qubit state. Even trying to visualize the state of a two-qubit register with entanglement would involve drawing pictures in seven dimensions. While 7D might be nice for advertising a ride at Niagara Falls, it is much harder to draw useful pictures that way.

The circle we are familiar with was really just a slice through the sphere, and all the rotations we were doing resulted in states still on that circle. Figure 6.4 shows how the previous qubit model compares to the Bloch sphere.

In chapters 2 through 5, we saw that the state of a single qubit can be thought of as a point on a circle.

In this chapter, we'll see that single-qubit states can also be rotated "out of the page," giving an entire sphere instead of just the circle.

Figure 6.4   Comparison of our previous model for a qubit (a point on a circle) and the Bloch sphere. The Bloch sphere is a more general model for the state of a single qubit. We need another dimension to capture that state of a qubit represented by a vector of *complex* numbers, but it only works for single qubits.

> **TIP** You might have inferred from the fact that we showed the *Z*-axis and the *X*-axis that the *Y*-axis was hiding somewhere! As it turns out, when we move from a circle to a sphere, the axis that goes out of the page is often called the "*Y*-axis."

When we first introduced the vector representation of a qubit state in chapter 2, you may recall that the amplitudes in each vector were *complex numbers*. In the rest of this chapter, we'll see that in general, when we use rotation instructions to transform the state of a single qubit, we get complex numbers. Complex numbers are an incredibly useful tool for keeping track of rotations and thus play a large role in quantum computing. Primarily they help us understand the angles and phases between differ-ent quantum states. Don't worry if you're a little rusty with complex numbers, as you'll get plenty of chances to practice with them throughout the rest of the book.

6.2.1 Relating rotations to coordinates: The Pauli operations

In figure 6.5, let's take a moment to quickly review a couple of the single-qubit opera-tions we have seen so far: x and ry.

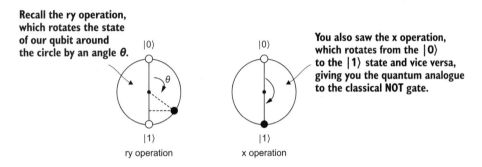

Recall the ry operation, which rotates the state of our qubit around the circle by an angle θ.

You also saw the x operation, which rotates from the |0⟩ to the |1⟩ state and vice versa, giving you the quantum analogue to the classical NOT gate.

ry operation   x operation

Figure 6.5 Illustrations of what x and ry do to a qubit. We have seen both operations in previous chapters. The ry instruction rotates the state of our qubit by an angle theta, and x takes qubits in the |0⟩ state to the |1⟩ and vice versa.

Now that we know the state of our qubit can be rotated on the surface of a sphere, what other rotations can help us rotate the state out of the plane? We can add a rota-tion about the line between the |+⟩ and |−⟩ states. This line is conventionally called the *X*-axis to distinguish it from the *Z*-axis that connects the |0⟩ and |1⟩ states. The rx func-tion in QuTiP gives us a Qobj encapsulating the rotation matrix for a *X*-axis rotation.

Listing 6.9 Using the QuTiP built-in function `qt.sigmaz`

```
>>> import qutip as qt
>>> import numpy as np
>>> qt.rx(np.pi).tidyup()
Quantum object: dims = [[2], [2]], shape = (2, 2),
    type = oper, isherm = False
Qobj data =
[[ 0.+0.j   0.-1.j]
 [ 0.-1.j   0.+0.j]]
```

QuTiP Qobj instances have a tidyup method to help make matrices more readable, as floating-point arithmetic on classical computers can result in small errors.

Up to a coefficient of −*i* (written in Python as −1j), rotating by 180° about the *X*-axis results in the x (NOT) instruction that we first saw in chapter 2.

TIP In Python, the complex number *i* is represented by 1.0j: 1 times *j*, which is sometimes what the imaginary number *i* is called in other fields.

This snippet illustrates something very important: the x operation is precisely what we get by rotating around the *X*-axis by an angle of 180° (π).

DEFINITION As noted in the callouts for listing 6.1, we can check that `qt.rx(np.pi)` is actually off by a factor of $-i$ from `qt.sigmax()`. That factor is an example of a *global phase*. As we will see shortly, global phases *cannot* affect the results of the measurement. Thus, `qt.rx(np.pi)` and `qt.sigmax()` are different unitary matrices that represent the same operation. We'll get more practice with global and local phases in chapters 7 and 8.

By analogy, we call rotating by 180° about the *Z*-axis a z operation. In chapter 3, QuTiP provided the `qt.sigmax` function that simulates the x instruction. Similarly, `qt.sigmaz` provides the unitary matrices we need to simulate the z instructions. The next listing shows an example of using `qt.sigmaz`. Note that we've included the coefficient (that is, the global phase) of $-i$ by multiplying by i right away; this works since $-i \times i = -(-1) = 1$.

Listing 6.10   Using the QuTiP functions `qt.rz` and `qt.sigmaz`

```
>>> import qutip as qt
>>> import numpy as np
>>> 1j * qt.rz(np.pi).tidyup()
Quantum object: dims = [[2], [2]], shape = (2, 2), type = oper, isherm = True
Qobj data =
[[ 1.   0.]
 [ 0.  -1.]]
>>> qt.sigmaz()
Quantum object: dims = [[2], [2]], shape = (2, 2), type = oper, isherm = True
Qobj data =
[[ 1.   0.]
 [ 0.  -1.]]
```

> Cancelling out the global phase this way makes it easier to read the output.

> As promised, up to the coefficient of $-i$, the z instruction applies a 180° rotation about the *Z*-axis.

In the same way that the X operation flips between $|0\rangle$ and $|1\rangle$ while leaving $|+\rangle$ and $|-\rangle$ alone, the z operation flips between $|+\rangle$ and $|-\rangle$ while leaving $|0\rangle$ and $|1\rangle$ alone.

Table 6.1 shows a truth table like the ones we made for the Hadamard operation in chapter 2. By looking at the truth table, we can confirm that, if we do a z operation twice on any input state, we will be back where we started. In other words, z squares to the identity operation $\mathbb{1}$ in the same way that $X^2 = \mathbb{1}$.

Table 6.1   Representing the z instruction as a table

Input state	Output state
$|0\rangle$	$|0\rangle$
$|1\rangle$	$-|1\rangle$
$|+\rangle$	$|-\rangle$
$|-\rangle$	$|+\rangle$

NOTE We listed four rows in table 6.1, but we need only two rows to completely specify how *Z* acts for any input. The other two rows serve to emphasize that we can choose between defining Z by its action on $|0\rangle$ and $|1\rangle$ or by its action on $|+\rangle$ and $|-\rangle$.

Exercise 6.2: Practice using rz and z

Suppose you prepare a qubit in the $|-\rangle$ state and apply a z rotation. If you measure along the X-axis, what do you get? What do you measure if you apply two z rotations? If you implement those same two rotations with rz, what angles should you use?

We can define one more rotation the same way: the rotation about an axis coming "out of the page." This axis connects the states $(|0\rangle + i\,|1\rangle) \, / \, \sqrt{2} \, = R_x(\pi/2)|0\rangle$ and $(|0\rangle - i\,|1\rangle) \, / \, \sqrt{2} \, = R_x(\pi/2)|1\rangle$ and is conventionally called the Y-axis. A 180° rotation about the Y-axis both flips bit labels ($|0\rangle \leftrightarrow |1\rangle$) and phases ($|+\rangle \leftrightarrow |-\rangle$) but leaves alone the two states along the Y-axis.

Exercise 6.3: Truth table for sigmay

Use the `qt.sigmay()` function to make a table similar to table 6.1, but for the y instruction.

DEFINITION   Together, the three matrices X, Y, and Z representing the x, y, and z operations are called the *Pauli matrices* in honor of physicist Wolfgang Pauli. The identity matrix $\mathbb{1}$ is sometimes included as well, representing the "do nothing" or identity operation.

Playing rock-paper-scissors with the Pauli matrices

The Pauli matrices have a number of useful properties that we'll use throughout the rest of the book. Many of these properties make it easy to work out different equations involving the Pauli operators. For example, if we multiply X by Y, we get iZ, but if we multiply YX, we get $-iZ$.

QuTiP can help explore what happens when we multiply Pauli matrices together: for example, multiplying X and Y together in both possible orderings:

```
>>> import qutip as qt
>>> qt.sigmax() * qt.sigmay()
Quantum object: dims = [[2], [2]], shape = (2, 2), type = oper, isherm =
    False
Qobj data =
[[0.+1.j 0.+0.j]
 [0.+0.j 0.-1.j]]
>>> qt.sigmay() * qt.sigmax()
Quantum object: dims = [[2], [2]], shape = (2, 2), type = oper, isherm =
    False
Qobj data =
[[0.-1.j 0.+0.j]
 [0.+0.j 0.+1.j]]
```

> **(continued)**
> Similarly, $YZ = iX$ and $ZX = iY$, but $ZY = -iX$ and $XZ = -iY$. One way to remember this is to think of X, Y, and Z as playing a little game of rock-paper-scissors: X "beats" Y, Y "beats" Z, and Z "beats" X in turn.

We can think of these matrices as establishing a kind of coordinate system for qubit states, called the *Bloch sphere*. As shown in figure 6.6, the X- and Z-axes form the circle we've seen in the book thus far, while the Y-axis comes out of the page.

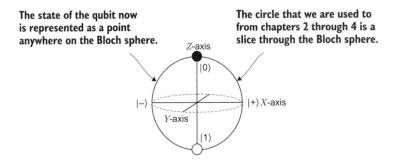

Figure 6.6 **The Bloch sphere, in all its spherical glory. Here, each of the axes is labeled with the corresponding Pauli operator representing rotations around that axis.**

Describing states with Pauli measurements

Any single-qubit state can be entirely specified up to a global phase by the measurement probabilities for X, Y, and Z measurements. That is, if we tell you the probability of getting a "1" outcome for each of the three Pauli measurements that we could perform, you can use that information to write a state vector that is identical to ours, up to the global phase. This makes the analogy to points in three dimensions useful for thinking about single-qubit states.

The *i*s have it

The states at the ends of the Y-axis are usually labeled $|i\rangle$ and $|-i\rangle$ but are not often used on their own. We will just stick to the labeled states we were using before: $|0\rangle$, $|1\rangle$, $|+\rangle$, and $|-\rangle$.

With this picture in mind, it's easier to see why some rotations don't affect the results of measurements. For instance, as illustrated in figure 6.7, the Bloch sphere picture helps us understand what happens if we rotate $|0\rangle$ about the Z-axis.

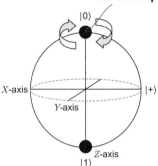

If we rotate around the Z-axis, the $|0\rangle$ and $|1\rangle$ states will stay in the same place.

Figure 6.7 The Bloch sphere illustrating how an rz rotation leaves the $|0\rangle$ state unchanged

In the same way that the North Pole stays in the same spot no matter how much we spin a globe, if we rotate a state about an axis parallel to that state, there is no observable effect on our qubit. We can also see this effect come out of the math.

Listing 6.11 How the $|0\rangle$ state is unaffected by rz rotations

Defines a variable to represent the state $|0\rangle$

Introduces a new state $|\psi\rangle$ that's a 60° (π / 3 in radians) rotation of $|0\rangle$ about the Z-axis

```
>>> ket0 = qt.basis(2, 0)
>>> ket_psi = qt.rz(np.pi / 3) * ket0
>>> ket_psi
Quantum object: dims = [[2], [1]], shape = (2, 1),
    type = ket
Qobj data =
[[ 0.8660254-0.5j]
 [ 0.0000000+0.j ]]
>>> bra0 = ket0.dag()
>>> bra0
Quantum object: dims = [[1], [2]], shape = (1, 2),
    type = bra
Qobj data =
[[ 1.  0.]]
>>> np.abs((bra0 * ket_psi)[0, 0]) ** 2
1.0
```

The resulting state is $|\psi\rangle = [\cos(60° / 2) - i \sin(60° / 2)] |0\rangle = [\sqrt{3} / 2 - i / 2] |0\rangle$.

Recall that in QuTiP, we write out the "dagger" operator $^{+}$ by calling the .dag method of Qobj instances, in this case giving us the row vector for $\langle 0 |$.

As before, the probability of observing a "0" when measuring along the Z-axis hasn't changed.

Taking the inner product $\langle 0 | \psi \rangle$, we can compute Born's rule $\Pr(0 | \psi) = |\langle 0 | \psi \rangle|^2$. Note that we need to index by [0, 0], since QuTiP represents the inner product of $|0\rangle$ with $|\psi\rangle$ as a 1×1 matrix.

TIP When writing down states, $|\psi\rangle$ is often used as an arbitrary name, similar to how x is often used to represent an arbitrary variable in algebra.

In general, we can always multiply a state by a complex number whose absolute value is 1 without changing the probabilities of any measurement. Any complex number $z = a + bi$ can be written as $z = re^{i\theta}$ for real numbers r and θ, where r is the absolute value of

> ### Exercise 6.4: Verifying that applying rz doesn't change |0⟩
>
> We've only checked that one measurement probability is still the same, but maybe the probabilities have changed for *X* or *Y* measurements. To fully check that the global phase doesn't change anything, prepare the same state and rotation as in listing 6.11 and check that the probabilities of measuring the state along the *X*- or *Y*-axis aren't changed by applying an `rz` instruction.

z and where θ is an angle. When *r* = 1, we have a number of the form $e^{i\theta}$, which we call a *phase*. We then say that multiplying the state by a phase applies a *global phase* to that state.

NOTE   No global phase can ever be detected by any measurement.

The states $|\psi\rangle$ and $e^{i\theta}|\psi\rangle$ are in every conceivable way two different ways of describing the exact same state. There is no measurement we can do *even in principle* to learn about global phases. On the other hand, we've seen that we can tell apart states like $|+\rangle$ = (|0⟩ + |1⟩) / $\sqrt{2}$ and |−⟩ = (|0⟩ − |1⟩) / $\sqrt{2}$ that differ only in the *local* phase of the |1⟩ computational basis state.

Taking a step back, let's summarize what we've learned about the x, y, and z instructions so far and about the Pauli matrices we use to simulate those instructions. We've seen that the x instruction flips between |0⟩ and |1⟩, while the z instruction flips between the |+⟩ and |−⟩ states. Put differently, the x instruction flips bits, while the z instruction flips phases.

Looking at the Bloch sphere, we can see that rotating about the *Y*-axis should do both of these. We can also see this via $Y = -iXZ$, as it is straightforward to check with QuTiP. We summarize what each Pauli instruction does in table 6.2.

Table 6.2   Pauli matrices as bit and phase flips

Instruction	Pauli matrix	Flips bits (|0⟩ ↔ |1⟩)?	Flips phases (|+⟩ ↔ |−⟩)?
(no instruction)	$\mathbb{1}$	No	No
x	X	Yes	No
y	Y	Yes	Yes
z	Z	No	Yes

> ### Exercise 6.5: Hmm, that rings a Bell
>
> The (|00⟩ + |11⟩) / $\sqrt{2}$ state that we've seen a few times now isn't the only example of an entangled state. In fact, if we pick a two-qubit state at random, it is almost certainly going to be entangled. Just as the computational basis {|00⟩, |01⟩, |10⟩, |11⟩} is a particularly useful set of unentangled states, there's a set of four particular entangled states known as the *Bell basis* after physicist John Stewart Bell:

Name	Expansion in computational basis
$|\beta_{00}\rangle$	$(|00\rangle + |11\rangle) / \sqrt{2}$
$|\beta_{01}\rangle$	$(|00\rangle - |11\rangle) / \sqrt{2}$
$|\beta_{10}\rangle$	$(|01\rangle + |10\rangle) / \sqrt{2}$
$|\beta_{11}\rangle$	$(|01\rangle - |10\rangle) / \sqrt{2}$

Using what you've learned about the cnot instruction and the Pauli instructions (x, y, and z), write programs to prepare each of the four Bell states in the table.

Hint: Table 6.2 should be very helpful in this exercise.

We finish our discussion of single-qubit operations by adding instructions to our Qubit interface and simulator for the x, y, and z operations. To do this, we can implement the rotation instructions rx, ry, and rz using the corresponding QuTiP functions qt.rx, qt.ry, and qt.rz to get copies of the unitary matrices we need to simulate each instruction. Here is how we can do this in our simulator.

Listing 6.12 simulator.py: adding all of the Pauli rotations

```python
def rx(self, theta: float) -> None:
    self.parent._apply(qt.rx(theta), [self.qubit_id])

    def ry(self, theta: float) -> None:
        self.parent._apply(qt.ry(theta), [self.qubit_id])

    def rz(self, theta: float) -> None:
        self.parent._apply(qt.rz(theta), [self.qubit_id])

    def x(self) -> None:
        self.parent._apply(qt.sigmax(), [self.qubit_id])

    def y(self) -> None:
        self.parent._apply(qt.sigmay(), [self.qubit_id])

    def z(self) -> None:
        self.parent._apply(qt.sigmaz(), [self.qubit_id])
```

QuTiP uses the notation σ_x instead of X for the Pauli matrices. Using this notation, the function sigmax() returns a new Qobj representing the Pauli matrix X. This way, we can implement the x, y, and z instructions corresponding to each Pauli matrix.

No one can be told what the Matrix is; you have to see it for yourself

We've talked a lot about matrices in part 1 of this book. A *lot*. It's tempting to say that quantum programming is all about matrices and that qubits are really just vectors. In reality, though, matrices are how we *simulate* what a quantum device does. We'll see more in part 2, but quantum programs don't manipulate matrices and vectors at all—they manipulate classical data such as what instructions to send to a quantum device and what to do with the data we get back from devices. For instance, if we run an instruction on a device, there's no simple way to see what matrix we should use to simulate that instruction—rather, we have to reconstruct that matrix from many repeated measurements using a technique called *process tomography*.

When we write a matrix, whether in code or on a piece of paper, we're implicitly simulating a quantum system. If that really bakes your noodle, don't worry; this will make a lot more sense as you go through the rest of the book.

6.3   *Teleportation*

OK, now we have everything we need to write out what teleportation looks like as a quantum program. As a quick review, figure 6.8 is what we want this program to do.

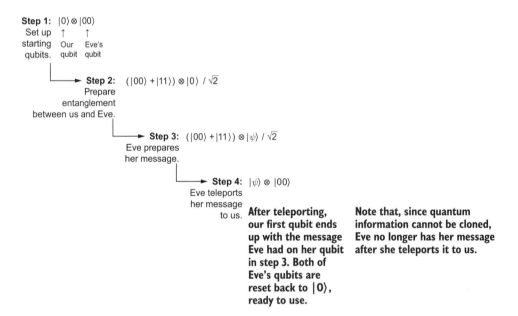

Figure 6.8   Recall the steps of the teleportation program.

We will assume you can prepare some entangled qubits while they are in the same device and that we and Eve have a means of classical communication that we can use to signal the right correction to use. We can now use the features we added to our simulator in this chapter to implement the teleportation program.

Listing 6.13   teleport.py: quantum teleportation in just a few lines

We need to start with some entanglement between "here" and "there". We can use our old friend, the h instruction, together with our new friend, the cnot instruction.

The teleport function takes two qubits as input: the qubit we want to move (msg) and where we want it to be moved ("there"). We also need one temporary qubit, which we call "here". We presume by convention that both "here" and "there" start in the $|0\rangle$ state.

```
from interface import QuantumDevice, Qubit
from simulator import Simulator

def teleport(msg: Qubit, here: Qubit, there: Qubit) -> None:
    here.h()
    here.cnot(there)

    # ...
    msg.cnot(here)
    msg.h()

    if msg.measure(): there.z()
    if here.measure(): there.x()

    msg.reset()
    here.reset()
```

At this point in the program, "here" and "there" are in the $(|00\rangle + |11\rangle) / \sqrt{2}$ state that we first saw in chapter 4.

Runs the program we used to prepare the $(|00\rangle + |11\rangle) / \sqrt{2}$ state backward, but on the msg and "here" qubits that live entirely on our device. We can think of running a preparation backward as a kind of measurement, such that these steps set us up to measure the quantum message we're trying to send Eve in an entangled

When we actually do that measurement, we get classical data to send Eve. Once she has that data, she can use the x and z instructions to decode the quantum message.

The only instruction in this program that needs to act on both "here" and "there". After running this, we can send Eve our qubit, and both of us can run the rest of the program with only classical communication.

Now that we're done with our qubits, it's good to put them back into $|0\rangle$ so they're ready to be used again. This doesn't affect the state of "there", though, as we've only reset our qubits, not the one we gave to Eve!

---

c what we did there?

Suppose we didn't need to send Eve a classical measurement result as a part of teleportation. In that case, we could use teleportation to send both classical and quantum data faster than the speed of light. Just as we couldn't communicate with Eve when we played the CHSH game in chapter 5, the speed of light means we need to communicate with Eve classically to use entanglement to send quantum data. In both cases, entanglement can help us communicate, but it doesn't let us communicate all on its own: we always need some other kind of communication as well.

To see that this actually works, we can prepare something on our qubit and send it to Eve, and then she can undo our preparation on her qubit. Thus far, the messages we and Eve have been sending have been classical, but here the message is *quantum*. We can and will measure the quantum message to get a classical bit, but we can also use the quantum message we get from Eve like any other quantum data. For example, we can apply whatever rotations and other instructions we like.

> **What is this good for?**
> Sending quantum data may not seem that much more useful than sending classical data; after all, sending classical data has gotten us a lot of neat things thus far. In contrast, applications for sending quantum data tend to be a bit more niche at the moment.
>
> That said, moving quantum data is a really useful example to help us understand how quantum computers work. The ideas developed in this chapter aren't often *directly* useful but will help us build great stuff going forward.

Let's say we prepare a *quantum* message by using the operation `msg.ry(0.123)`. The following listing shows how we can teleport this message to Eve.

Listing 6.14   teleport.py: using teleportation to move quantum data

```
if __name__ == "__main__":
    sim = Simulator(capacity=3)
    with sim.using_register(3) as (msg, here, there):
        msg.ry(0.123)
        teleport(msg, here, there)

        there.ry(-0.123)
        sim.dump()
```

As before, allocates a register of qubits and gives each qubit a name

Prepares a message to send to Eve. Here, we've shown using a particular angle as the message, but it can be anything.

Checks the output of the dump instruction to see that the register we allocated is back in the |000⟩ state

Calls the teleportation program we wrote earlier to move the message we prepared onto Eve's qubit

If Eve then undoes our rotation by rotating by the opposite angle, we can check that the register we allocated is back in the |000⟩ state. This shows that our teleportation worked! When you run this program, you'll get output similar to the following:

```
Quantum object: dims = [[2, 2, 2], [1, 1, 1]],
⮕ shape = (8, 1), type = ket
Qobj data =
[[1.]
 [0.]
 [0.]
 [0.]
 [0.]
 [0.]
 [0.]
 [0.]]
```

NOTE   Your output may differ by a global phase, depending on what measurement outcomes you got.

To verify that the teleportation worked, if Eve undoes the instruction that we did on her qubit (`there.ry(0.123)`), she should get back the $|0\rangle$ state that we started with. With teleportation, we and Eve can send quantum information using entanglement and classical communication, as you can prove to yourself in exercise 6.6.

Exercise 6.6: What if it didn't do anything?
Try changing your operation or Eve's operation to convince yourself that you only get a $|000\rangle$ state at the end if you undo the same operation that Eve applied to her qubit.

Now we can brag to all our friends (making whatever sci-fi references we want) that we can do teleportation. Hopefully you see why this is *not* the same as getting beamed down to a planet from orbit and that when you teleport a message, it does not communicate faster than the speed of light.

Summary

- The no-cloning theorem prevents us from copying arbitrary data stored by quantum registers, but we can still move data using the `swap` operation and algorithms like teleportation.
- When a qubit isn't entangled with any other qubits, we can visualize its state as a point on a sphere, known as the *Bloch sphere*.
- In general, we can rotate the state of a single qubit around the X-, Y-, or Z-axis. The operations that apply rotations of 180° about each of these axes are called the *Pauli operations* and describe flipping either or both bits and phases.
- In quantum teleportation, entanglement is used together with Pauli rotations to transfer quantum data from one qubit to another qubit without copying it.

Part 1: Conclusion

We have made it to the end of part 1 of the book, but sadly our qubits are in another castle ☺. Getting through this part was no mean feat, as we were building a simulator for a quantum device while learning a whole host of new quantum concepts. You are probably a bit shaky on some questions or topics, and that's OK.

> **TIP** Appendix B contains some quick references (glossary and definitions) that may be helpful as you move forward in this book and your subsequent quantum development endeavors.

We will be using and practicing these skills to develop more complicated quantum programs for cool applications like chemistry and cryptography. Before we move on to that, though, give yourself a pat on the back: you've done a lot so far! Let's summarize some of what you've accomplished:

- Refreshed your linear algebra and complex number skills
- Learned what a qubit is as well as what you can do with one

- Built a multiple-qubit simulator in Python
- Wrote quantum programs for tasks like quantum key distribution (QKD), playing nonlocal games, and even quantum teleportation
- Learned braket notation for the states of quantum systems

Your Python simulator will continue to be a useful tool for trying to understand what is happening when we get to larger applications. In part 2, we will switch to primarily using Q# as our tool of choice to write quantum programs. We will talk in the next chapter about why we will write more advanced quantum programs in Q# rather than Python, but the main reasons are speed and extensibility. Plus, you can use Q# from Python or with a Q# kernel for Jupyter, so you can work with whatever development environment you like best.

See you in part 2!

Part 2

Programming quantum algorithms in Q#

Wh-en working as a developer, it helps to have the right tool for the right job—and quantum computing is no exception. Quantum computing software stacks tend to be pretty diverse. In part 2, we expand our stack to include Q#, a *domain-specific* programming language for working with quantum devices. Just as domain-specific languages can help with specialized classical hardware like GPUs and FPGA, Q# helps us get the most out of quantum computing by providing the right tools to implement and apply quantum algorithms. As with other specialized languages, Q# works great when interoperating alongside more general-purpose languages and platforms like Python and .NET.

With all that in mind, we start Q-sharpening our skills and learning the basics of writing quantum algorithms. In chapter 7, we revisit quantum random number generators to learn the basics of the Q# language, building on the skills we developed in chapter 2. Next, in chapter 8, we expand our toolbox of quantum programming techniques by learning about *phase kickback*, *oracles*, and other new tricks, and we use them to play some fun new games. Finally, in chapter 9, we learn about the phase-estimation technique, building the skills we will need as we start working on more applied problems in part 3.

Changing the odds:
An introduction to Q#

This chapter covers

- Using the Quantum Development Kit to write quantum programs in Q#
- Using Jupyter Notebook to work with Q#
- Running Q# programs using a classical simulator

Up to this point, we've used Python to implement our own software stack to simulate quantum programs. If you recall, figure 2.1 (appearing again as figure 7.1), was a good model for how the programs we are writing interact with the quantum simulator and devices that we use and build as quantum developers.

Moving forward, we'll be writing more intricate quantum programs that will benefit from specialized language features that are hard to implement by embedding our software stack in Python. Especially as we explore quantum algorithms, it's helpful to have a language tailor-made for quantum programming at our disposal. In this chapter, we'll get started with Q#, Microsoft's domain-specific language for quantum programming, included with the Quantum Development Kit.

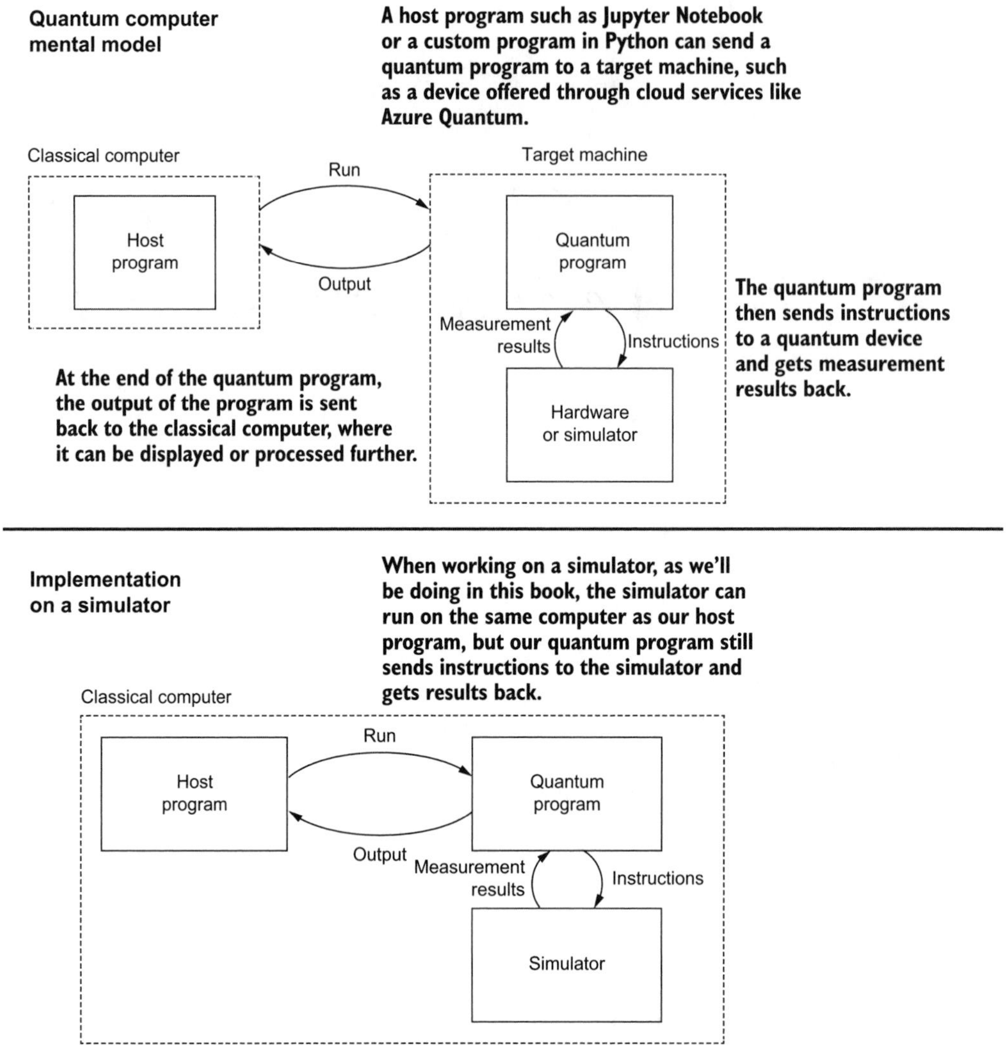

**Quantum computer
mental model**

**A host program such as Jupyter Notebook
or a custom program in Python can send a
quantum program to a target machine, such
as a device offered through cloud services like
Azure Quantum.**

Classical computer

Target machine

Run

Host
program

Output

Quantum
program

Measurement
results

Instructions

Hardware
or simulator

**The quantum program
then sends instructions
to a quantum device
and gets measurement
results back.**

**At the end of the quantum program,
the output of the program is sent
back to the classical computer, where
it can be displayed or processed further.**

**Implementation
on a simulator**

**When working on a simulator, as we'll
be doing in this book, the simulator can
run on the same computer as our host
program, but our quantum program still
sends instructions to the simulator and
gets results back.**

Classical computer

Run

Host
program

Output

Quantum
program

Measurement
results

Instructions

Simulator

Figure 7.1   A mental model for how we can use a quantum computer. The top half of the figure is the general
model for a quantum computer. Given we are using local simulators for this book, the bottom half represents
what we are building and using.

7.1   *Introducing the Quantum Development Kit*

The Quantum Development Kit provides a new language, Q#, to write quantum programs and simulate them using classical resources. Quantum programs written in Q#
are run by thinking of quantum devices as a kind of accelerator, similar to how we
might run code on a graphics card.

> **TIP**   If you've ever used a graphics card programming framework like CUDA
> or OpenCL, this is a very similar model.

A Q# program can include both classical and quantum instructions.

The QuantumSimulator target machine acts very similarly to the simulator that we implemented in part 1 and uses matrix multiplication to simulate how quantum operations would behave on a real quantum system.

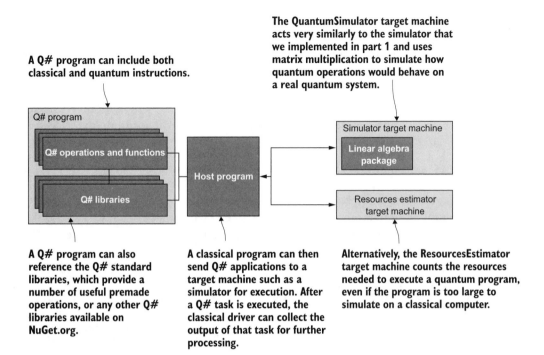

A Q# program can also reference the Q# standard libraries, which provide a number of useful premade operations, or any other Q# libraries available on NuGet.org.

A classical program can then send Q# applications to a target machine such as a simulator for execution. After a Q# task is executed, the classical driver can collect the output of that task for further processing.

Alternatively, the ResourcesEstimator target machine counts the resources needed to execute a quantum program, even if the program is too large to simulate on a classical computer.

Figure 7.2   The Microsoft Quantum Development Kit software stack on a classical computer. We can write a Q# program consisting of functions and operations, referencing any Q# libraries we want to include. A host program can then coordinate communication between our Q# program and the target machine (e.g., a simulator running locally on our computer).

Let's take a look at the software stack for Q# in figure 7.2.

A Q# program consists of operations and functions that instruct quantum and classical hardware to do certain things. There are also many libraries provided with Q# that have helpful, premade operations and functions to use in our programs.

Once the Q# program is written, we need a way for it to pass instructions to the hardware. A classical program sometimes called a *driver* or *host program* is responsible for allocating a target machine and running a Q# operation on that machine.

The Quantum Development Kit includes a plugin for Jupyter Notebook called IQ# that makes it easy to get started with Q# by providing host programs automatically. In chapter 9, we'll see how to write host programs using Python, but for now, we'll focus on Q#. See appendix A for instructions on setting up your Q# environment to work with Jupyter Notebook.

Using the IQ# plugin for Jupyter Notebook, we can use one of two different target machines to run Q# code. The first is the `QuantumSimulator` target machine, which is very similar to the Python simulator we have been developing. It will be a lot faster than our Python code for simulating qubits.

The second is the `ResourcesEstimator` target machine, which will allow us to estimate how many qubits and quantum instructions we would need to run it without fully simulating it. This is especially useful for getting an idea of the resources we would need to run a Q# program for our application, as we'll see when we look at larger Q# programs later in the book.

To get a sense of how everything works, let's start by writing a purely classical Q# "hello, world" application. First, start Jupyter Notebook by running the following in a terminal:

```
jupyter notebook
```

This automatically opens a new tab in our browser with the home page for our Jupyter Notebook session. From the New ↓ menu, select Q# to make a new Q# notebook. Type the following into the first empty cell in the notebook, and press Ctrl-Enter or ⌘-Enter to run it:

> **Defines a new function that takes no arguments and returns the empty tuple, whose type is written as Unit**

```
function HelloWorld() : Unit {      ⟵
    Message("Hello, classical world!");      ⟵
}
```

> **Tells the target machine to collect a diagnostic message. The QuantumSimulator target machine prints all diagnostics to the screen, so we can use Message like print in Python.**

You should get something that looks like figure 7.3.

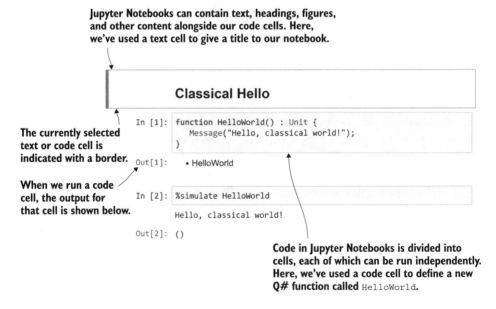

Jupyter Notebooks can contain text, headings, figures, and other content alongside our code cells. Here, we've used a text cell to give a title to our notebook.

Classical Hello

The currently selected text or code cell is indicated with a border.

When we run a code cell, the output for that cell is shown below.

```
In [1]:   function HelloWorld() : Unit {
              Message("Hello, classical world!");
          }
Out[1]:   • HelloWorld

In [2]:   %simulate HelloWorld
          Hello, classical world!
Out[2]:   ()
```

Code in Jupyter Notebooks is divided into cells, each of which can be run independently. Here, we've used a code cell to define a new Q# function called `HelloWorld`.

Figure 7.3   Getting started with IQ# and Jupyter Notebook. Here, a new Q# function called `HelloWorld` is defined as the first cell in a Jupyter Notebook, and the results from simulating that function are in the second cell.

TIP Unlike Python, Q# uses semicolons rather than newlines to end statements. If you get a lot of compiler errors, make sure you remembered your semicolons.

You should get a response that the HelloWorld function was successfully compiled. To run the new function, we can use the %simulate command in a new cell.

Listing 7.1 Using the %simulate magic command in Jupyter

```
In [2]: %simulate HelloWorld
Hello, classical world!
```

A bit of classical magic

The %simulate command is an example of a *magic command*, in that it's not actually part of Q# but is an instruction to the Jupyter Notebook environment. If you're familiar with the IPython plugin for Jupyter, you may have used similar magic commands to tell Jupyter how to handle Python plotting functionality.

In this book, the magic commands we use all start with % to make them easy to tell apart from Q# code.

In this example, %simulate allocates a target machine for us and sends a Q# function or operation to that new target machine. In chapter 9, we'll see how to accomplish something similar using Python host programs instead of using Jupyter Notebook.

The Q# program is sent to the simulator, but in this case, the simulator just runs the classical logic since there are no quantum instructions to worry about yet.

Exercise 7.1: Changing the greeting

Change the definition of HelloWorld to include your name instead of "classical world," and then run %simulate again using your new definition.

Exercise solutions

All solutions for exercises in this book can be found in the companion code repo: https://github.com/crazy4pi314/learn-qc-with-python-and-qsharp. Just go to the folder for the chapter you are in and open the Jupyter notebook with the name that mentions exercise solutions.

7.2   *Functions and operations in Q#*

Now that we have the Quantum Development Kit up and running with Jupyter Notebook, let's use Q# to write some quantum programs. Back in chapter 2, we saw that a useful thing to do with a qubit is to generate random numbers one classical bit at a time. Revisiting that application makes a great place to start with Q#, especially since random numbers are useful if we want to play games.

7.2.1   *Playing games with quantum random number generators in Q#*

Long ago, in Camelot, Morgana shared our love for playing games. Being a clever mathematician with skills well beyond her own day, Morgana was even known to use qubits from time to time as a part of her games. One day, as Sir Lancelot lay sleeping under a tree, Morgana trapped him and challenged him to a little game: each of them must try to guess the outcome of measuring one of Morgana's qubits.

> ### Two sides of the same ... qubit?
> In chapter 2, we saw how to generate random numbers one bit at a time by preparing and measuring qubits. That is, qubits can be used to implement *coins*. We'll use the same kind of idea in this chapter and think of a coin as a kind of interface that allows its user to "flip" it and get a random bit. That is, we can implement the coin interface by preparing and measuring qubits.

If the result of measuring along the Z-axis is a 0, then Lancelot wins their game and gets to return to Guinevere. If the result is a 1, though, Morgana wins, and Lancelot has to stay and play again. Notice the similarity to our earlier QRNG program. Just as in chapter 2, we'll measure a qubit to generate random numbers, this time to play a game. Of course, Morgana and Lancelot could flip a more traditional coin, but where is the fun in that?

Here are the steps of Morgana's side game:

1   Prepare a qubit in the $|0\rangle$ state.
2   Apply the Hadamard operation (recall that the unitary operator H takes $|0\rangle$ to $|+\rangle$ and vice versa).
3   Measure the qubit in the Z-axis. If the measurement result is a 0, then Lancelot can go home. Otherwise, he has to stay and play again!

Sitting at a coffee shop watching the world go by, we can use our laptops to predict what will happen in Morgana's game with Lancelot by writing a quantum program in Q#. Unlike the `HelloWorld` function that we wrote earlier, our new program will need to work with qubits, so let's take a moment to see how to do so with the Quantum Development Kit.

The primary way we interact with qubits in Q# is by calling *operations* that represent quantum instructions. For instance, the `H` operation in Q# represents the Hadamard instruction we saw in chapter 2. To understand how these operations work, it's helpful to know the difference between Q# operations and the functions we saw in the `Hello-World` example:

- *Functions* in Q# represent *predictable* classical logic: things like mathematical functions (`Sin`, `Log`). Functions always return the same output when given the same input.
- *Operations* in Q# represent code that can have *side effects,* such as sampling random numbers or issuing quantum instructions that modify the state of one or more qubits.

This separation helps the compiler figure out how to automatically transform our code as a part of larger quantum programs; we'll see more about this later.

Another perspective on functions vs. operations

Another way of thinking of the difference between functions and operations is that functions compute things but cannot cause anything to *happen*. No matter how many times we call the square root function `Sqrt`, nothing about our Q# program changes. In contrast, if we run the `X` operation, then an `X` instruction is sent to our quantum device, which causes a change in the state of the device. Depending on the initial state of the qubit the `X` instruction was applied to, we can then tell that the `X` instruction has been applied by measuring the qubit. Because functions don't *do* anything in this sense, we can always predict their output exactly, given the same input.

One important consequence is that functions cannot call operations, but operations can call functions. This is because we can have an operation that is not necessarily predictable call a predictable function, and we still have something that may or may not be predictable. However, a predictable function cannot call a potentially unpredictable operation and still be predictable.

We'll see more about the difference between Q# functions and operations as we use them throughout the book.

Since we want quantum instructions to affect our quantum devices (and Lancelot's fate), all quantum operations in Q# are defined as operations (hence the name). For instance, suppose that Morgana and Lancelot prepare their qubit in the $|+\rangle$ state using the Hadamard instruction. Then we can predict the outcome of their game by writing the quantum random number generator (QRNG) example from chapter 2 as a Q# operation.

There may be side effects to this operation...

When we want to send instructions to our target machine to do something with our qubits, we need to do so from an operation since sending an instruction is a kind of *side effect*. That is, when we run an operation, we aren't just computing something: we're *doing* something. Running an operation twice isn't the same as running it once, even if we get the same output both times. Side effects aren't deterministic or predictable, so we can't use functions to send instructions for manipulating our qubits.

In listing 7.2, we do just that, starting with writing an operation called GetNextRandom-Bit to simulate each round of Morgana's game. Note that since GetNextRandomBit needs to work with qubits, it must be an operation and not a function. We can ask the target machine for one or more fresh qubits with the use statement.

Allocating qubits in Q#

The use statement is one of the only two ways to ask the target machine for qubits. There's no limit to the number of use statements we can have in Q# programs, other than the number of qubits that each target machine can allocate.

At the end of a block (i.e., an operation, for, or if body) containing a use statement, the qubits go back to the target machine. Often, qubits are allocated this way at the start of an operation body, so one way to think of use statements is to make sure each qubit that is allocated is "owned" by a particular operation. This makes it impossible to "leak" qubits within a Q# program, which is very helpful given that qubits are likely to be very expensive resources on actual quantum hardware.

If we need more control over when qubits are deallocated, use statements can also optionally be followed by a block, denoted with { and }. In that case, qubits are deallocated at the end of the block instead of at the end of the operation.

Q# also offers one other way to allocate qubits, known as *borrowing*. Unlike when we allocate qubits with use statements, the borrow statement lets us borrow qubits owned by different operations without knowing what state they start in. We won't see much borrowing in this book, but the borrow statement works very similarly to the use statement in that it makes it impossible to forget that we've borrowed a qubit.

By convention, all qubits start in the $|0\rangle$ state right after we get them, and we promise the target machine that we'll put them back into the $|0\rangle$ state at the end of the block so they're ready for the target machine to give to the next operation that needs them.

Listing 7.2   Operation.qs: Q# to simulate a round of Morgana's game

Declares an operation, as we want to use qubits and return a measurement Result to its caller

The use keyword in Q# asks the target machine for one or more qubits. Here, we ask for a single value of type Qubit, which we store in the new variable qubit.

```
operation GetNextRandomBit() : Result {
    use qubit = Qubit();
    H(qubit);
    return M(qubit);
}
```

After calling H, qubit is in the $H|0\rangle = |+\rangle$ state.

Uses the M operation to measure our qubit in the Z-basis. The result will be either Zero or One with equal probability. After measuring, we can return that classical data back to the caller.

Here, we use the M operation to measure our qubit in the Z-basis, saving the result to the result variable we declared earlier. Since the state of the qubit is in an equal superposition of $|0\rangle$ and $|1\rangle$, result will be either Zero or One with equal probability.

Standalone Q# applications

We can also write Q# applications like the QRNG as standalone applications, rather than calling them from Python or IQ# notebooks. To do so, we can designate one of the Q# operations in the quantum application as an *entry point*, which is then called automatically when we run our application from the command line.

For this book, we'll stick with Jupyter and Python to work with Q#. But check out the sample at https://github.com/crazy4pi314/learn-qc-with-python-and-qsharp/tree/master/ch07/Qrng for information on writing standalone Q# applications.

In listing 7.2, we also see our first example of opening a *namespace* in Q#. Like namespaces in C++ and C# or packages in Java, Q# namespaces help keep functions and operations organized. For example, the H operation called in listing 7.2 is defined in the Q# standard library as `Microsoft.Quantum.Intrinsic.H`; that is, it lives in the `Microsoft.Quantum.Intrinsic` namespace. To use H, we can either use its full name, `Microsoft.Quantum.Intrinsic.H`, or an open statement to make all of the operations and functions in a namespace available:

```
open Microsoft.Quantum.Intrinsic;
```
◁── **Makes all of the functions and operations provided in Microsoft.Quantum.Intrinsic available to use within a Q# notebook or source file without having to specify their full names**

TIP When writing Q# in Jupyter Notebook, the `Microsoft.Quantum.Intrinsic` and `Microsoft.Quantum.Canon` namespaces from the Q# standard library are always opened automatically for us, as they're used in most Q# code. For example, when we called `Message` earlier, that function was provided in the `Microsoft.Quantum.Intrinsic` namespace that the Q# kernel opened automatically. To check which namespaces are open in a Q# notebook, we can use the `%lsopen` magic command.

Exercise 7.2: Generating more bits

Use the `%simulate` magic command to run the `GetNextRandomBit` operation a few times. Do you get the results you'd expect?

Next, we'll see how many rounds it takes for Lancelot to get the `Zero` he needs to go home. Let's write an operation to play rounds until we get a `Zero`. Since this operation simulates playing Morgana's game, we'll call it `PlayMorganasGame`.

TIP All Q# variables are immutable by default.

Listing 7.3 Operations.qs: Simulating many rounds of Morgana's game using Q#

```
operation PlayMorganasGame() : Unit {
    mutable nRounds = 0;
```
◁── **Uses the mutable keyword to declare a variable indicating how many rounds have passed. We can change the value of this variable later with the "set" keyword.**

```
mutable done = false;
repeat {
    set nRounds = nRounds + 1;
    set done =
        (GetNextRandomBit() == Zero);
}
until done;

Message($"It took Lancelot {nRounds}
    turns to get home.");
}
```

Q# allows operations to use a repeat-until-success (RUS) loop.

Inside our loop, we call the QRNG that we wrote earlier as the **GetNextRandomBit** operation. We check to see if the result is a Zero and, if it is, set "done" to true.

We use Message again to print the number of rounds to the screen. To do so, we use $"" strings, which let us include variables in the diagnostic message by using {} placeholders inside the string.

If we got a Zero, then we can stop the loop.

TIP   Q# strings denoted with $"" are called *interpolated strings* and work very similarly to f"" strings in Python.

Listing 7.3 includes a Q# control flow called a repeat-until-success (RUS) loop. Unlike a while loop, RUS loops also allow us to specify a "fixup" that runs if the condition to exit the loop isn't met.

When do we need to reset qubits?

In Q#, when we allocate a new qubit with use, we promise the target machine that we will put it back in the |0⟩ state before deallocating it. At first glance, this seems unnecessary, as the target machine could just reset the state of qubits when they are deallocated—after all, we often call the Reset operation at the end of an operation or use block. Indeed, this happens automatically when a qubit is measured, right before it is released!

It is important to note that the Reset operation works by making a measurement in the Z-basis and flipping the qubit with an X operation if the measurement returns One. In many quantum devices, measurement is much more expensive than other operations, so if we can avoid calling Reset, we can reduce the cost of our quantum programs. Especially given the limitations of medium-term devices, this kind of optimization can be critical in making a quantum program practically useful.

Later in the chapter, we will see examples where we know the state of a qubit when it needs to be deallocated, such that we can "unprepare" the qubit instead of measuring it. We don't have a final measurement in those cases, so the Q# compiler doesn't add an automatic reset for us, avoiding the need for a potentially expensive measurement operation.

We can run this new operation with the %simulate command in a fashion very similar to the HelloWorld example. When we do so, we can see how long Lancelot has to stay:

```
In []: %simulate PlayMorganasGame
It took Lancelot 1 turns to get home.
Out[]: ()
```

Looks like Lancelot got lucky that time! Or perhaps unlucky, if he was bored hanging round the table in Camelot.

Deep dive: open vs. import

At first glance, the `open` statement in Q# may feel a lot like the `import` statement in Python, JavaScript, or TypeScript. Both `open` and `import` make code from libraries available to use in our programs and applications. The main difference is that opening a namespace with the `open` statement only does just that: it opens a namespace and makes it available, but it doesn't cause any code to run and doesn't change the way our code compiles and finds libraries.

In principle, we could write every Q# program without a single `open` statement by explicitly referring to each function and operation by its full name, including its namespace (i.e., calling `Microsoft.Quantum.Intrinsic.H` instead of just `H`). In that sense, `open` is similar to the `using` statement in C++ or C#, the `open` statement in F#, and the `import` statement in Java.

In contrast, `import` in Python, JavaScript, and TypeScript not only makes the names from a library available to our code but also causes parts of those libraries to run. When a Python module is first imported, the Python interpreter uses the module's name to look for where that module is defined and then runs the module along with any initialization code it has. Often, to use these modules, we need to first install one or more *packages* using a tool like pip or conda for Python packages or npm for JavaScript and TypeScript.

The same concept can be used to add new libraries to our Q# programs with the *NuGet package manager*. In a Q# notebook, the `%package` command instructs the Q# kernel to download a given Q# library and add it to our session. For example, when we open a new notebook, the Q# standard library is automatically downloaded and installed from the `Microsoft.Quantum.Standard` package on nuget.org (https://www.nuget.org/packages/Microsoft.Quantum.Standard). Similarly, when writing command-line Q# applications, running `dotnet add package` adds the needed metadata to our project's Q# compiler to find the package we need.

For more details, check out the Quantum Development Kit documentation at https://docs.microsoft.com/azure/quantum/user-guide/libraries/additional-libraries.

7.3 Passing operations as arguments

Suppose that, in Morgana's game, we were interested in sampling random bits with non-uniform probability. After all, Morgana didn't promise Lancelot *how* she prepared the qubit they measure; she can keep him playing longer if she makes a biased coin with their qubit instead of a fair coin.

The easiest way to modify Morgana's game is to, instead of calling H directly, take as an input an operation representing what Morgana does to prepare for their game. To take an operation as input, we need to write the *type* of the input, just as we can write `qubit : Qubit` to declare an input `qubit` of type `Qubit`. Operation types are indicated by thick arrows (`=>`) from their input type to their output type. For instance, H has type `Qubit => Unit` since H takes a single qubit as input and returns an empty tuple as its output.

TIP   In Q#, functions are denoted by thin arrows (`->`), while operations are denoted by thick arrows (`=>`).

Listing 7.4   Using operations as inputs to predict Morgana's game

```
operation PrepareFairCoin(qubit : Qubit) : Unit {
    H(qubit);
}

operation GetNextRandomBit(
        statePreparation : (Qubit => Unit)
) : Result {
    use qubit = Qubit();
    statePreparation(qubit);
    return Microsoft.Quantum.Measurement.MResetZ(qubit);
}
```

We've added a new input called **statePreparation to GetNextRandomBit,** representing the operation we want to use to prepare the state we use as a coin. In this case, **Qubit => Unit** is the type of any operation that takes a single qubit and returns the empty tuple type **Unit.**

In **GetNextRandomBit,** the operation passed as **statePreparation** can be called like any other operation.

The Q# standard libraries provide **Microsoft.Quantum.Measurement.MResetZ** as a convenience for measuring and resetting a qubit in one step. In this case, the MResetZ operation does the same thing as the **return M(qubit);** statement in the previous example. The difference is that MResetZ always resets its input qubit, not just when it is used before a qubit is released. We'll see more about this operation later in the chapter, as well as how to use a shorter name when calling this operation.

Exercise 7.3: Type of GetNextRandomBit

What's the type of our new definition of `GetNextRandomBit`?

Tuple in, tuple out

All functions and operations in Q# take a single tuple as an input and return a single tuple as an output. For instance, a function declared as `function Pow(x : Double, y : Double) : Double {…}` takes as input a tuple `(Double, Double)` and returns a tuple `(Double)` as its output. This works because of a property known as *singleton-tuple equivalence*. For any type `'T`, the tuple `('T)` containing a single `'T` is equivalent to `'T` itself. In the example of `Pow`, we can think of the output as a tuple `(Double)` that is equivalent to `Double`.

No matter how many inputs an operation takes, we can always think of that operation as taking exactly one input: a tuple containing all of the inputs.

Similarly, every operation can be thought of as returning exactly one output.

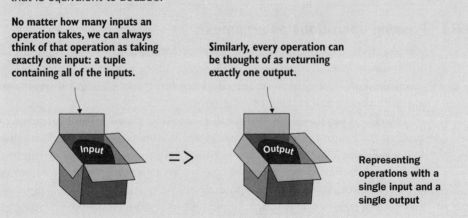

Representing operations with a single input and a single output

With this in mind, a function or operation that returns no outputs can be thought of as returning a tuple with no elements, `()`. The type of such tuples is called `Unit`, similar to other tuple-based languages such as F#. If we think of a tuple as a kind of box, then this is distinct from `void` as used in C, C++, or C# because there still is *something* there: a box with nothing in it.

In Q#, we always return a box, *even if that box is empty*. There's no meaning in Q# for a function or operation that returns "nothing." For more details, see section 7.2 of *Get Programming with F#* by Isaac Abraham (Manning, 2018).

If an operation doesn't take any inputs or doesn't return any outputs, we represent that with an empty tuple, written in Q# as ().

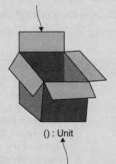

() : Unit

Void

Just like any other value in Q#, the empty tuple has a type. The type of () is called Unit. Most quantum operations that don't involve a measurement return Unit.

In other languages, like C, C++, C#, and Java, we'll sometimes see the keyword void used to indicate that a function or method doesn't return anything. Unlike Unit, void represents that there isn't a value at all, not even an empty box.

`Unit` **vs.** `void`

In listing 7.4, we see that `GetNextRandomBit` treats its input `statePreparation` as a "black box." The only way to learn anything about Morgana's preparation strategy is to *run* it.

Put differently, we don't want to do anything with `statePreparation` that implies we know what it does or what it is. The only way that `GetNextRandomBit` can interact with `statePreparation` is by calling it, passing it a `Qubit` to act on.

This allows us to reuse the logic in `GetNextRandomBit` for many different kinds of state preparation procedures that Morgana might use to cause Lancelot a bit of trouble. For example, suppose she wants a biased coin that returns a `Zero` three-quarters of the time and a `One` one-quarter of the time. We might run something like the following to predict this new strategy.

> **Listing 7.5   Passing different state preparation strategies to `PlayMorganasGame`**

```
open Microsoft.Quantum.Math;
```
◁— Classical math functions such as Sin, Cos, Sqrt, and ArcCos as well as constants like PI() are provided by the Microsoft.Quantum.Math namespace.

```
operation PrepareQuarterCoin(qubit : Qubit) : Unit {
    Ry(2.0 * PI() / 3.0, qubit);
}
```
◁— The Ry operation implements a *Y*-axis rotation. Q# uses radians rather than degrees to express rotations, so this is a rotation of 120° about the *Y*-axis.

The `Ry` operation implements the *Y*-axis rotation that we saw in chapter 2. Thus, when we rotate the state of `qubit` by 120° in listing 7.5, if `qubit` starts in the $|0\rangle$ state, that prepares `qubit` in the state $R_y(120°)|0\rangle = \sqrt{3/4}\,|0\rangle + \sqrt{1/4}\,|1\rangle$. As a result, the probability of observing 1 when we measure `qubit` is $\sqrt{1/4}^2 = 1/4$.

We can make this example even more general, allowing Morgana to specify an arbitrary bias for her coin (which is implemented by their shared qubit).

> **Listing 7.6   Passing operations to implement arbitrary coin biases**

```
operation PrepareBiasedCoin(
    morganaWinProbability : Double, qubit : Qubit
) : Unit {
    let rotationAngle = -2.0 * ArcCos(
        Sqrt(1.0 - morganaWinProbability));
    Ry(rotationAngle, qubit);
}
```
◁— Finds out what angle to rotate the input qubit by to get the right probability of seeing a One as our result. This takes a bit of trigonometry; see the next sidebar for details.

```
operation PrepareMorganasCoin(qubit : Qubit)
: Unit {
    PrepareBiasedCoin(0.62, qubit);
}
```
◁— This operation has the right type signature (Qubit => Unit), and we can see that the probability Morgana will win each round is 62%.

Working out the trigonometry

As we've seen several times, quantum computing deals extensively with rotations. To figure out what angles we need for our rotations, we rely on trigonometry (literally, "the study of triangles"): a branch of mathematics that describes rotation angles. For instance, as we saw in chapter 2, rotating $|0\rangle$ by an angle θ about the *Y*-axis results in a state $\cos(-\theta/2)\,|0\rangle + \sin(-\theta/2)\,|1\rangle$. We know we want to choose θ such that $\cos(-\theta/2) = \sqrt{100\% - 62\%}$ so we get a 62% probability of a One result. That means we need to "undo" the cosine function to figure out what θ needs to be.

In trigonometry, the inverse of the cosine function is the arccosine function and is written arccos. Taking the arccosine of both sides of $\cos(-\theta/2) = \sqrt{100\% - 62\%}$ gives us $\arccos(\cos(-\theta/2)) = \arccos(\sqrt{100\% - 62\%})$. We can cancel out arccos and cos to find a rotation angle that gives us what we need, $-\theta/2 = \arccos(\sqrt{100\% - 62\%})$.

Finally, we multiply both sides by –2 to get the equation used in line 4 of listing 7.6. We can see this argument visually in the following figure.

If a measurement along the Z-axis results in a zero, then Lancelot wins and can go home.

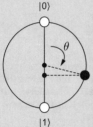

Morgana can control how probable a one outcome is by choosing θ, the angle that she rotates about the Y-axis.

If Morgana chooses θ to be close to π / 2 (90°), then both zero and one results will be approximately as probable.

On the other hand, the closer Morgana picks to (180°), the closer the projection of the state onto the Z-axis is to $|1\rangle$.

If she picks θ to be exactly π, then the result will always be a one: she can keep Lancelot playing indefinitely.

If a measurement along the Z-axis results in a one, then Morgana wins, and Lancelot has to play another round.

How Morgana can choose θ to control the game. The closer to π she picks θ to be, the longer Morgana can keep poor Lancelot playing.

This is somewhat unsatisfying, though, because the operation PrepareMorganasCoin introduces a lot of boilerplate just to lock down the value of 0.62 for the input argument morganaWinProbability to PrepareBiasedCoin. If Morgana changes her strategy to have a different bias, then using this approach, we'll need another boilerplate operation to represent it. Taking a step back, let's look at what PrepareMorganasCoin actually *does*. It starts with an operation PrepareBiasedCoin : (Double, Qubit) => Unit and wraps it into an operation of type Qubit => Unit by locking down the Double argument as 0.62. That is, it removes one of the arguments to PrepareBiasedCoin by fixing the value of that input to 0.62.

Fortunately, Q# provides a convenient shorthand for making new functions and operations by locking down some (but not all!) of the inputs. Using this shorthand, known as *partial application*, we can rewrite PrepareMorganasCoin from listing 7.6 in a more readable form:

```
let flip = GetNextRandomBit(PrepareBiasedCoin(0.62, _));
```

The _ indicates that part of the input to PrepareBiasedCoin is *missing*. We say Prepare-BiasedCoin has been partially applied. Whereas PrepareBiasedCoin had type (Double,

Qubit) => Unit, because we filled in the Double part of the input, PrepareBiased-Coin(0.62, _) has type Qubit => Unit, making it compatible with our modifications to GetNextRandomBit.

> **TIP**   Partial application in Q# is similar to functools.partial in Python and the _ keyword in Scala.

Another way to think of partial application is as a way to make new functions and operations by specializing existing functions and operations.

Listing 7.7   Using partial application to specialize an operation

```
function BiasedPreparation(headsProbability : Double)
: (Qubit => Unit) {                              ◄──────────────   The output type is an operation that
    return PrepareBiasedCoin(                                      takes a qubit and returns the empty
        headsProbability, _);      ◄──────────────┘                tuple. That is, BiasedPreparation
}                                                                  is a function that makes new
                                                                   operations!
```

Makes the new operation by passing headsProbability but leaving a blank (_) for the target qubit. This gives us an operation that takes a single Qubit and substitutes in the blank.

> **TIP**   In listing 7.7, we return PrepareBiasedCoin(headsProbability, _) as a value in its own right, just as we may return 42 from a function or operation with Int as its output type. In Q#, functions and operations are values in precisely the same sense that 42, true, and (3.14, "hello") are all values in Q#, and just as the Python function (lambda x: x ** 2) is a value in Python. Formally, we say that functions and operations are *first-class* values in Q#.

It may seem a bit confusing that BiasedPreparation returns an operation from a function, but this is completely consistent with the split between functions and operations described previously since BiasedPreparation is still predictable. In particular, Biased-Preparation(p) always returns the same operation for a given p, no matter how many times we call the function. We can assure ourselves that this is the case by noticing that BiasedPreparation only partially applies operations but never calls them.

Exercise 7.4: Partial application
Partial application works for functions as well as operations! Try it by writing a function Plus that adds two integers, n and m, and another function PartialPlus that takes an input n and returns a function that adds n to its input.

Hint: You can get started using the following code snippet as a template:

```
function Plus(n : Int, m : Int) : Int {
    // fill in this part
}

function PartialPlus(n : Int) : (Int -> Int) {
    // fill in this part
}
```

7.4 Playing Morgana's game in Q#

With first-class operations and partial application at the ready, we can now make a more complete version of Morgana's game.

The Q# standard libraries

The Quantum Development Kit comes with various standard libraries that we'll see throughout the rest of the book. In listing 7.8, for example, we use an `MResetZ` operation that both measures a qubit (similar to `M`) and resets it (similar to `Reset`). This operation is offered by the `Microsoft.Quantum.Measurement` namespace, one of the main standard libraries that come with the Quantum Development Kit.

A full list of the operations and functions available in that namespace can be found at https://docs.microsoft.com/qsharp/api/qsharp/microsoft.quantum.measurement. For now, though, don't worry too much about it; we'll see more of the Q# standard libraries as we go.

Listing 7.8   Complete Q# listing for biased `PlayMorganasGame`

```
open Microsoft.Quantum.Math;              ←┐ Opens namespaces from the Q# standard
open Microsoft.Quantum.Measurement;        │ library to help with classical math and
                                           │ measuring qubits

operation PrepareBiasedCoin(winProbability : Double, qubit : Qubit)
: Unit {
    let rotationAngle = 2.0 * ArcCos(
        Sqrt(1.0 - winProbability));      ←┐ The rotation angle
    Ry(rotationAngle, qubit);              │ chooses the coin's bias.
}


operation GetNextRandomBit(statePreparation : (Qubit => Unit))
: Result {                                 ┌ Uses the operation we passed in as
    use qubit = Qubit();                   │ statePreparation and applies it to the qubit.
    statePreparation(qubit);           ←──┘
    return MResetZ(qubit);             ←┐ The MResetZ operation is defined in the Microsoft.Quantum
}                                        │ .Measurement namespace that we open at the beginning of the
                                         │ sample. It measures the qubit in the Z-basis and then applies
                                         │ the operations needed to return the qubit to the |0⟩ state.

operation PlayMorganasGame(winProbability : Double) : Unit {
    mutable nRounds = 0;
    mutable done = false;                         ┌ Uses partial application to specify
    let prep = PrepareBiasedCoin(                 │ the bias for our state preparation
        winProbability, _);               ←────   │ procedure but not the target qubit.
    repeat {                                      │ While PrepareBiasedCoin has type
        set nRounds = nRounds + 1;                │ (Double, Qubit) => Unit,
        set done = (GetNextRandomBit(prep) == Zero);  │ PrepareBiasedCoin(0.2, _) "fills in"
    }                                             │ one of the two inputs, leaving an
    until done;                                   │ operation with type Qubit =>
                                                  │ Unit, as expected by EstimateBias.

    Message($"It took Lancelot {nRounds} turns to get home.");
}
```

Providing documentation for Q# functions and operations

Documentation can be provided for Q# functions and operations by writing small, specially formatted text documents in triple-slash (///) comments before a function or operation declaration. These documents are written in Markdown, a simple text-formatting language used on sites like GitHub, Azure DevOps, Reddit, and Stack Exchange and by site generators like Jekyll. The information in /// comments is shown when we hover over calls to that function or operation and can be used to make API references similar to those at https://docs.microsoft.com/qsharp/api/.

Different parts of /// comments are indicated with section headers such as /// # Summary. For example, we can document the PrepareBiasedCoin operation from listing 7.8 with the following:

```
/// # Summary
/// Prepares a state representing a coin with a given bias.
///
/// # Description
/// Given a qubit initially in the |0⟩ state, applies operations
/// to that qubit such that it has the state √p |0⟩ + √(1 - p) |1⟩,
/// where p is provided as an input.
/// Measurement of this state returns a One Result with probability p.
///
/// # Input
/// ## winProbability
/// The probability with which a measurement of the qubit should return
///       One.
/// ## qubit
/// The qubit on which to prepare the state √p |0⟩ + √(1 - p) |1⟩.
operation PrepareBiasedCoin(
        winProbability : Double, qubit : Qubit
) : Unit {
    let rotationAngle = 2.0 * ArcCos(Sqrt(1.0 - winProbability));
    Ry(rotationAngle, qubit);
}
```

When using IQ#, we can look up documentation comments by using the ? command. For instance, we can look up the documentation for the X operation by running X? in an input cell.

For a full reference, see https://docs.microsoft.com/azure/quantum/user-guide/language/statements/iterations#documentation-comments.

To estimate the bias of a particular state preparation operation, we can run the Play-MorganasGame operation repeatedly and count how many times we get a Zero. Let's pick a value for winProbability and run the PlayMorganasGame operation with that value to see how long Lancelot will be stuck:

```
In []: %simulate PlayMorganasGame winProbability=0.9
It took Lancelot 5 turns to get home.
```

> We can pass inputs to operations using the %simulate command by specifying them after the name of the operation we want to simulate.

Try playing around with different values of `winProbability`. Note that if Morgana really tips the scales, we can confirm that it will take Lancelot quite a long time to make it back to Guinevere:

```
In []: %simulate PlayMorganasGame winProbability=0.999
It took Lancelot 3255 turns to get home.
```

In the next chapter, we'll build on the skills we learned here by going back to Camelot to find our first example of a quantum algorithm: the Deutsch–Jozsa algorithm.

Summary

- Q# is a quantum programming language provided with the open source Quantum Development Kit from Microsoft.
- Quantum programs in Q# are broken down into functions representing classical and deterministic logic, and operations that can have side effects such as sending instructions to quantum devices.
- Functions and operations are first-class values in Q# and can be passed as inputs to other functions and operations. We can use this to combine different parts of quantum programs.
- By passing Q# operations in our program, we can extend our QRNG example from chapter 2 to allow passing in operations that prepare states other than $|+\rangle$; this in turn allows for making biased random numbers.

What is a quantum
algorithm?

This chapter covers

- Understanding what a quantum algorithm is
- Designing oracles to represent classical functions in quantum programs
- Working with useful quantum programming techniques

One important application of quantum algorithms is obtaining speedups for solving problems where we need to search inputs to a function we're trying to learn about. Such functions could be obfuscated (such as hash functions) or computationally difficult to evaluate (common in studying mathematical problems). In either case, applying quantum computers to such problems requires us to understand how we program and provide input to quantum algorithms. To learn how to do so, we'll program and run an implementation of the *Deutsch–Jozsa algorithm*, which will let us learn properties of unknown functions quickly using quantum devices.

8.1　*Classical and quantum algorithms*

> *Algorithm (noun): a step-by-step procedure for solving a problem or accomplishing some end.*
>
> —Merriam-Webster Dictionary

When we talk about classical programming, we sometimes say that a program implements an *algorithm*: that is, a sequence of steps that can be used to solve a problem. For example, if we want to sort a list, we can talk about the quicksort algorithm independently of what language or operating system we are using. We often specify these steps at a high level. In the quicksort example, we might list the steps as something like the following:

1　If the list to be sorted is empty or only has one element, return it as is.
2　Pick an element of the list to be sorted, called the *pivot*.
3　Separate all other elements of the list into those that are smaller than the pivot and those that are larger.
4　Quicksort each new list recursively.
5　Return the first list, then the pivot, and finally the second list.

These steps serve as a guide for writing an implementation in a particular language of interest. Say we want to write the quicksort algorithm in Python.

Listing 8.1　An example implementation of quicksort

```
def quicksort(xs):
    if len(xs) > 1:              ⟵ Checks for the base case by seeing if there
        pivot = xs[0]                are at least two elements in the list
        left = [x in xs[1:] if x <= pivot]    ⟵ Picks the first element to
        right = [x in xs[1:] if x > pivot]       be our pivot for step 2
        return quicksort(left) +
    [pivot] + quicksort(right)   ⟵ Python code that builds two
    else:                           new lists as described in step 3
        return xs
```

Concatenates everything back together as described in steps 4 and 5

A well-written algorithm can help guide how to write implementations by making clear the steps that must be executed. Quantum algorithms are the same in this respect: they list the steps we need to perform in any implementation.

> **DEFINITION**　A *quantum program* is an implementation of a quantum algorithm consisting of a *classical program* that sends instructions to a *quantum device* to prepare a particular state or measurement result.

As we saw in chapter 7, when we write a Q# program, we are writing a classical program that sends instructions to one of several different target machines on our behalf, as illustrated as figure 8.1, returning measurements to our classical program.

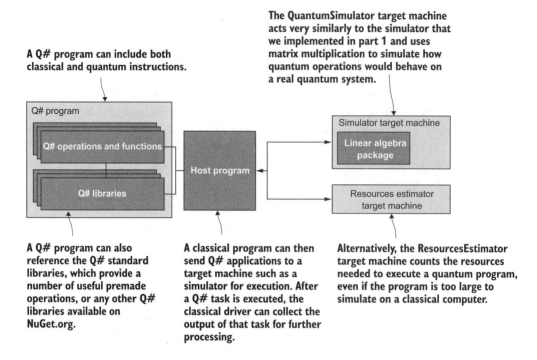

Figure 8.1 The Microsoft Quantum Development Kit software stack on a classical computer. We can write a Q# program consisting of functions and operations and referencing any Q# libraries we want to include. A host program can then coordinate communication between our Q# program and the target machine (e.g., a simulator running locally on our computer).

The art of quantum programming

We cannot copy quantum states, but if they resulted from running a program, we can tell someone else what steps they need to take to prepare the same states. As we saw previously, quantum programs are a special kind of classical program, so we can copy them with reckless abandon. As we will see throughout the rest of the book, any quantum state can either be approximated or written out exactly by the output of a quantum program that starts with only copies of the |0⟩ state. For example, in chapter 2, we prepared the initial state |+⟩ of a QRNG with a program consisting of a single H instruction.

Put differently, we can think of a program as being a recipe for how to prepare a qubit. Given a qubit, we cannot determine what recipe was used to prepare it, but we can copy the recipe itself as much as we like.

Whereas the steps in executing quicksort instruct the Python interpreter to compare values and to move values around in memory, the steps in a Q# program instruct our target machines to apply rotations and measurements to qubits in a device. As shown in figure 8.1, we can use a host program to send Q# applications to each different target machine to run. For now, we'll keep using the IQ# plugin for Jupyter Notebook as our host program; in the next chapter, we'll see how to use C# to write our own host programs as well.

Most of the time in this book, we're interested in simulating quantum programs, so we use the QuantumSimulator target machine. This simulator works very similarly to the ones we developed in chapters 2 and 4, as it executes instructions such as the Hadamard instruction H by multiplying quantum states with unitary operators like *H*.

> **TIP** As in previous chapters, we use fonts to distinguish instructions like H from unitary matrices like *H* that we use to simulate those instructions.

The ResourcesEstimator target machine allows us to not run a quantum program but get estimates of how many qubits *would* be required to run it. This is useful for larger programs that cannot be classically simulated or run on available hardware, to help us learn how many qubits it will take; we'll see more about this target machine later.

Since Q# applications send instructions to the target machines that we use to run them, it's easy to reuse Q# code later across different target machines that share the same instruction set. The QuantumSimulator target machine, for instance, uses the same instructions that we expect actual quantum hardware to take, once it becomes available; thus we can test Q# programs on simulators now using small instances of problems and then run the same programs on quantum hardware later.

What remains in common across these different target machines and applications is that we need to write the program that sends instructions to the target machine to accomplish some goal. Our task as quantum programmers is thus to make sure these instructions have the effect of solving a useful problem.

> **TIP** The way that we use simulators to test Q# programs is a bit similar to how we use simulators to test programs for other specialized hardware like field-programmable gate arrays (FPGAs) or emulators to test applications for mobile devices from our desktops and laptops. The main difference is that we can only use a classical computer to simulate a quantum computer for a very small number of qubits or restricted kinds of programs.

This is much easier to do when we have an algorithm guiding us to organize the steps that need to happen in classical and quantum devices. In developing new quantum algorithms, we can use quantum effects, such as entanglement, which we saw in chapter 4.

> **TIP** To get any advantage from our quantum hardware, we *must* use the unique quantum properties of the hardware. Otherwise, we just have a more expensive, slower classical computer.

8.2   Deutsch–Jozsa algorithm: Moderate improvements for searching

So what might make a good example of a *quantum* algorithm that takes advantage of our shiny new quantum hardware? We learned in chapters 4 and 7 that thinking about games often helps, and this is no exception. To find a game for this chapter, let's take a trip back to Camelot, where Merlin finds himself facing a test.

8.2.1   Lady of the (quantum) Lake

Merlin, the famous and wise wizard, has just encountered Nimue, the Lady of the Lake. Nimue, seeking a capable mentor for the next King of England, has decided to test Merlin to see if he is up to the task. Two bitter rivals, Arthur and Mordred, are vying for the throne, and if Merlin accepts Nimue's task, he must choose whom to mentor as king.

For her part, Nimue does not care who becomes king, as long as Merlin can give them sage council. Nimue *is* concerned about whether Merlin, the appointed instructor for the new king, will be reliable and consistent in his leadership.

Since Nimue shares our love of games, she has decided to play a game with Merlin to test whether he will be a good mentor. Nimue's game, Kingmaker, tests to see if Merlin is *consistent* in his role as advisor to the king. To play Kingmaker, Nimue gives Merlin the name of one of the two bitter rivals, and Merlin must respond with whether Nimue's candidate should be the true heir to the throne. Here are the rules:

- In each round, Nimue asks Merlin a single question of the form "Should *potential heir* be the king?"
- Merlin must answer either "yes" or "no," giving no additional information.

Each round gives Nimue more information about the realm of mortals, so she wants to ask as few questions as is needed to catch Merlin out if he is not trustworthy. Her objectives are as follows:

- Verify that Merlin will be a good mentor to the new King of England.
- Ask as few questions as possible to verify.
- Avoid learning whom Merlin will say yes to mentoring.

At this point, Merlin has four possible strategies:

1. Say "yes" when asked if Arthur should be king and "no" otherwise (good mentor).
2. Say "yes" when asked if Mordred should be king and "no" otherwise (good mentor).
3. Say "yes" regardless of whom Nimue asks about (bad mentor).
4. Say "no" regardless of whom Nimue asks about (bad mentor).

We can think of Merlin's strategies by using the concept of a truth table once again. Suppose, for instance, that Merlin has decided to be singularly unhelpful and deny any candidates to the throne. We might write this down using the truth table in table 8.1.

Table 8.1 Truth table for one possible Kingmaker strategy: Merlin always says no.

Input (Nimue)	Output (Merlin)
"Should Mordred be king?"	"No."
"Should Arthur be king?"	"No."

At this point, Nimue would be right to complain about Merlin's wisdom as a mentor! Merlin has not been consistent with his charge to choose between Arthur and Mordred. While Nimue may not care whom Merlin picks, he surely must pick *someone* to mentor and prepare for the throne.

Nimue needs a strategy to determine in as few rounds of the game as possible if Merlin has strategy 1 or 2 (good mentor) or if Merlin is playing according to 3 or 4 (bad mentor). She could just ask both questions: "Should Mordred be king?" and "Should Arthur be king?" and then compare his answers, but this would result in Nimue knowing for sure whom he chose to be king. With each question, Nimue learns more about the kingdom's mortal affairs—how distasteful!

While it would seem Nimue's game is doomed to force her to learn Merlin's choice of heir, she is in luck. This being a quantum lake, we'll see throughout the rest of this chapter that Nimue can ask a *single* question that will tell her *only* if Merlin is committed to his role as a mentor and not whom he has chosen.

Since we don't have a quantum lake at our disposal, let's try to model what Nimue is doing with quantum instructions in Q# on our classical computer and then simulate it. Let's represent Merlin's strategy by a classical function f, which takes Nimue's question as an input x. That is, we'll write $f(\text{Arthur})$ to mean "what Merlin answers when asked if Arthur should be king." Note that since Nimue will ask one of only two questions, which question she asks is an example of a bit. Sometimes it's convenient to write that bit using the labels "0" and "1", and other times it's helpful to label Nimue's input bit using the Boolean values "False" and "True". After all, "1" would be a pretty strange answer to a question like "Should Mordred be king?"

Using bits, we write $f(0) = 0$ to mean that if Nimue asks Merlin, "Should Mordred be king?" his answer is no. Table 8.2 shows how we can map Nimue's questions to Boolean values.

Table 8.2 Encoding Nimue's question as a bit

Nimue's question	Representation as a bit	Representation as a Boolean
"Should Mordred be king?"	0	False
"Should Arthur be king?"	1	True

If she didn't have any quantum resources, to be sure of what Merlin's strategy is, Nimue would have to try both inputs to f; that is, she'd have to ask Merlin both questions.

Trying all the inputs would give her Merlin's full strategy; and as noted, Nimue is not really interested in it.

Instead of having to ask Merlin about both Mordred and Arthur, we can implement a quantum algorithm in Q# that uses quantum effects to learn whether Merlin is a good mentor by asking him only *one* question. Using the simulators provided with the Quantum Development Kit, we can even run our new Q# program on our laptops or desktops! In the rest of this chapter, we'll look at an example of how to write this quantum algorithm, called the Deutsch–Jozsa algorithm (see figure 8.2).

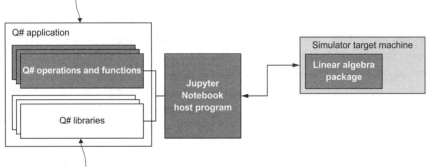

For the rest of chapter 8, we'll be writing Q# applications that we can run on our classical computers using the simulator target machine.

We'll make use of the Q# libraries that come with the Quantum Development Kit, but we won't be writing our own in this chapter.

Figure 8.2   We will be working in the Microsoft Quantum Development Kit software stack for this chapter, writing Q# programs that are run via a Jupyter Notebook host on a simulator target machine.

Let's sketch out what our quantum program will look like. The possible inputs and outputs for *f* (Merlin's strategy) are `True` and `False`. We can write a truth table for *f* using the inputs and outputs we get when we call *f*. For instance, if *f* is the classical NOT operation (often denoted ¬), then we will observe that *f*(`True`) is `False` and vice versa. As shown in table 8.3, using a classical NOT operation as a strategy in our game corresponds to picking Mordred to be king.

Table 8.3   Truth table for the classical NOT operation

Input	Output
`True` ("Should Arthur be king?")	`False` ("No.")
`False` ("Should Mordred be king?")	`True` ("Yes.")

There are four possible options for the definition of our function f, each of which represents one of the four strategies available to Merlin, as summarized in figure 8.3.

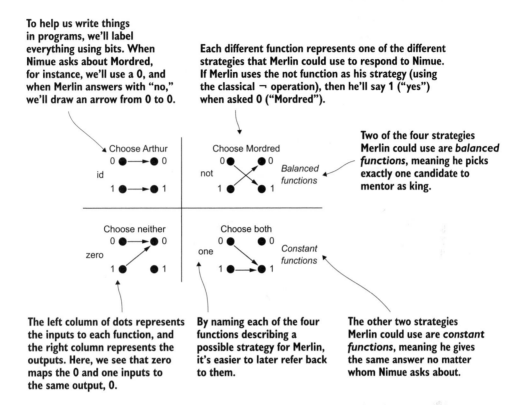

To help us write things in programs, we'll label everything using bits. When Nimue asks about Mordred, for instance, we'll use a 0, and when Merlin answers with "no," we'll draw an arrow from 0 to 0.

Each different function represents one of the different strategies that Merlin could use to respond to Nimue. If Merlin uses the not function as his strategy (using the classical ¬ operation), then he'll say 1 ("yes") when asked 0 ("Mordred").

Two of the four strategies Merlin could use are *balanced functions*, meaning he picks exactly one candidate to mentor as king.

The left column of dots represents the inputs to each function, and the right column represents the outputs. Here, we see that zero maps the 0 and one inputs to the same output, 0.

By naming each of the four functions describing a possible strategy for Merlin, it's easier to later refer back to them.

The other two strategies Merlin could use are *constant functions*, meaning he gives the same answer no matter whom Nimue asks about.

Figure 8.3 Four different functions from one bit to one bit. We call the two functions in the top row *balanced* because equally many inputs map to 0 as inputs that map to 1. We call the two functions in the bottom row *constant* as all inputs map to a single output.

Two of these functions, labeled id and not for convenience, send each of the 0 and 1 inputs to different outputs; we call these functions *balanced*. In our little game, they represent the cases in which Merlin picks exactly one person to be king. All the cases are listed in table 8.4.

Table 8.4 Classifying Merlin's strategies as either constant or balanced

Merlin's strategy	Function	Type	Passes Nimue's challenge?
Choose Arthur	id	Balanced ($f(0) \neq f(1)$)	Yes
Choose Mordred	not	Balanced ($f(0) \neq f(1)$)	Yes
Choose neither	zero	Constant ($f(0) = f(1)$)	No
Choose both	one	Constant ($f(0) = f(1)$)	No

On the other hand, the functions that we label zero and one are *constant* functions since they send both inputs to the same output. Constant functions then represent strategies in which Merlin is decidedly useless, as he's either picked both to be king (a good way to start a bad war) or picked neither.

Classically, to determine if a function is constant or balanced (whether Merlin is a bad or good mentor, respectively), we must learn the entire function by building up its truth table. Remember, Nimue wants to ensure that Merlin is a reliable mentor. If Merlin follows a strategy represented by a constant function, he will not be a good mentor. Looking at the truth tables for the id and one functions, tables 8.5 and 8.6, respectively, we can see how they describe when Merlin is following a strategy that will let him be a good or bad mentor.

Table 8.5   Truth table for the id function, an example of a balanced function

Input	Output
True ("Should Arthur be king?")	True ("Yes")
False ("Should Mordred be king?")	False ("No")

Table 8.6   Truth table for the one function, an example of a constant function

Input	Output
True ("Should Arthur be king?")	True ("Yes")
False ("Should Mordred be king?")	True ("Yes")

Nimue's difficulty in trying to learn whether Merlin is a good or bad mentor (that is, whether *f* is balanced or constant) is that the quality of Merlin's mentorship is a kind of *global* property of his strategy. There's no way to look at a single output of *f* and conclude anything about what *f* would output for different inputs. If we only have access to *f*, then Nimue is stuck: she must reconstruct the entire truth table to decide whether Merlin's strategy is constant or balanced.

On the other hand, if we can represent Merlin's strategy as a part of a quantum program, we can use the quantum effects we've learned about so far in the book. Using quantum computing, Nimue can learn *only* if his strategy is constant or balanced, without having to learn exactly which strategy he's using. Since we are not interested in the information the truth table provides beyond whether Merlin is a good or bad mentor, using quantum effects can help us learn what we care about more directly. With our quantum algorithm, we can do this with one call of the function and without needing to learn any additional information we are not interested in. By not asking for all the details of the truth table but only looking for more general properties of our function, we can best utilize our quantum resources.

> **The power of quantum computing**
>
> If we want to use a *classical* computer to learn whether a function is constant or balanced, we have to solve a harder problem first: identifying exactly which function we have. In contrast, quantum mechanics lets us solve only the problem we care about (constant versus balanced) without solving the more challenging problem a classical computer has to solve.
>
> This is an example of a pattern we'll see throughout the book, in which quantum mechanics lets us specify less powerful algorithms than we can express classically.

To do so, we will use the Deutsch–Jozsa algorithm, which uses a *single query* to our quantum representation of Merlin's strategy to learn whether he is a good or bad mentor. The advantage isn't terribly practical (a savings of only one question), but that's OK; we'll see more practical algorithms later in the book. For now, the Deutsch–Jozsa algorithm is a great place to start learning how to implement quantum algorithms and, even more importantly, what tools we can use to understand what quantum algorithms do.

8.3 Oracles: Representing classical functions in quantum algorithms

Let's see what things look like from Nimue's quantum lake. As we plunge in for a swim, we face a somewhat immediate question: how can we use qubits to implement the function *f* that represents Merlin's strategy? From the previous section, we saw that the classical function *f* is our description of a strategy that Merlin uses to play each round of Kingmaker. Since *f* is classical, it's easy to translate this back into a set of actions that Merlin will take: Nimue gives Merlin a single classical bit (her question), and Merlin gives Nimue a classical bit back (his answer).

To avoid meddling in the affairs of mortals, Nimue now wants to use the Deutsch–Jozsa algorithm, instead. Since she lives in a quantum lake, Nimue can easily allocate a qubit to give Merlin. Lucky for us, Merlin knows how to communicate with qubits, but we still need to figure out what Merlin will do with Nimue's qubits to act on his strategy.

The trouble is, we can't pass qubits to the function *f* that we use to represent Merlin's strategy: *f* takes and returns classical bits, not qubits. For Merlin to use his strategy to guide what he does with Nimue's qubits, we want to turn Merlin's strategy *f* into a kind of quantum program known as an *oracle*. Conveniently for us, Merlin plays the role of an oracle pretty well.

> **NOTE** From the T. H. White treatment of Merlin, we learn that he lives life backward in time. We'll represent that by making sure everything Merlin does is *unitary*. As we saw in chapter 2, one consequence is that the transformations Merlin applies are *reversible*. In particular, Merlin won't be able to measure Nimue's qubits since measurement is not reversible. That privilege is Nimue's alone.

To understand what we need to do to model Merlin's actions as an oracle, we have to figure out two things:

1. What transformation should Merlin apply to Nimue's qubits based on his strategy?
2. What quantum operations will Merlin need to apply to implement that transformation?

Unitary matrices and truth tables

Another way of saying what we need to do in step 1 is that we need to find a *unitary matrix* that represents what Merlin does, similar to how we used classical functions like *f* to represent what Merlin did when Nimue gave him classical bits. As we saw in chapter 2, unitary matrices are to quantum computing as truth tables are to classical computing: they tell us what the effect of a quantum operation is for every possible input. Once we find the right unitary, in step 2 we'll figure out the sequence of quantum operations we can do that will be described by that unitary.

8.3.1   *Merlin's transformations*

To complete step 1, we need to turn functions like *f* into unitary matrices, so let's start by recapping what *f* can be. The possible strategies Merlin can use are represented by the functions id, not, zero, and one (see figure 8.4).

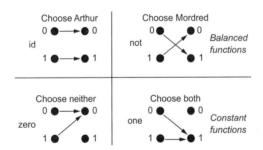

Figure 8.4   **Four different functions from one bit to one bit**

For the two balanced functions id and not in figure 8.4 we can answer question 1 easily. Quantum programs for id and not can be implemented as rotation operations, making it easy to turn them into quantum operations. The quantum NOT operation, for instance, is a rotation of 180° around the X-axis, exchanging the $|0\rangle$ and $|1\rangle$ states with each other.

> **TIP**   Recall from chapter 3 that the quantum operation X, represented by the unitary matrix $X = \begin{pmatrix} 0 & 1 \\ 1 & 0 \end{pmatrix}$, applies a rotation of 180° around the X axis. This operation implements a quantum NOT: since $X|0\rangle = |1\rangle$ and $X|1\rangle = |0\rangle$, we can write it using the ¬ (NOT) operator from chapter 2 as $X|x\rangle = |\neg x\rangle$.

While any rotation can be undone by rotating the same amount in the opposite direction, we run into more problems with the constant functions zero and one. Neither zero nor one can be implemented directly as rotations, so we have a bit more work to do. For instance, if *f* is zero, then the outputs *f*(0) and *f*(1) are both 0. If we only have the output 0, we cannot tell whether we got that output from giving *f* a 0 or a 1 as input (see figure 8.5).

Example 1: We can see with the way the inputs and outputs are mapped that if we know the output of the function, then we can trace it back to what the input was!

Example 2: We can see that with constant functions, although we know the output, it is ambiguous what the input was. It could have been either 0 or 1 but, we can't know...

Figure 8.5 Why can't we reverse the constant zero or one functions? Basically, we lose the information about which input we started with if all inputs map to a single output.

NOTE Once we apply zero or one, we have lost any information about the input.

Since one and zero are both irreversible, and valid operations on qubits are reversible, Merlin needs another way to represent functions like *f* in quantum algorithms such as the one for Nimue's challenge. On the other hand, if we can represent Merlin's strategy with a reversible classical function instead of *f*, it will be much easier to write a quantum representation of his strategy. Here is our strategy for representing classical functions as quantum oracles:

1 Find a way to represent our irreversible classical function with a reversible classical function.

2 Write a transformation on quantum states using our reversible classical function.

3 Figure out what quantum operations we can do that result in that transformation.

Let's use the tried-and-true approach of guessing and checking to see if we can design a valid reversible classical function. The easiest way to figure out whether we were given a 0 or a 1 as an input is to record it somewhere. So let's make a new function that returns two bits instead of one.

For our first attempt, let's record and keep the input:

$$g(x) = (x, f(x))$$

For example, if Merlin uses the strategy one (that is, he says "yes" to Nimue no matter what she asks), then $f(x) = 1$, and $g(x) = (x, f(x)) = (x, 1)$.

This gets us a lot closer since we can now tell whether we started with a 0 or 1 input. But we're not quite there, since *g* has two outputs and one input (see figure 8.6).

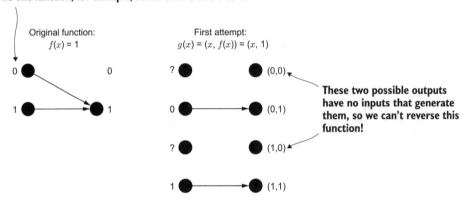

As before, we'll represent functions by drawing arrows from possible inputs to the corresponding outputs. The one function, for example, sends both 0 and 1 to 1.

Original function:
$f(x) = 1$

First attempt:
$g(x) = (x, f(x)) = (x, 1)$

These two possible outputs have no inputs that generate them, so we can't reverse this function!

Figure 8.6   First attempt: keeping input and output with $g(x)$**. Using this approach, some output combinations can't be reached from any input (e.g., no input produces the output (1,0)). Thus it is impossible to reverse the function since there's no input corresponding to those outputs.**

To use *g* as a strategy, Merlin would have to give Nimue back more qubits than she gave him, but she is the keeper of both swords and qubits. More technically, reversing *g* would destroy information, as it would take two inputs and return one output!

Trying one more time, let's define a new classical function *h* that takes two inputs and returns two outputs, $h(x, y)$. Let's again consider the example where we describe Merlin's strategy with the function $f(x) = 1$. Since *g* got us nearly there, we'll choose *h* such that $h(x, 0) = g(x)$. We saw from our first attempt that when Merlin uses the strategy $f(x) = 1$, then $g(x) = (x, 1)$, so we have that $h(x, 0) = (x, 1)$. Now we just need to define what happens when we pass $y = 1$ to *h*. If we want *h* to be reversible, we need that $h(x, 1)$ is assigned to something other than $(x, 1)$. One way to do this is to let $h(x, y) = (x, \neg y)$ so that $h(x, 1) = (x, 0) \neq (x, 1)$. This choice is especially convenient since applying *h* twice gets us back our original input, $h(h(x, y)) = h(x, \neg y) = (x, \neg\neg y) = (x, y)$. If this a bit wordy, take a look at a visual representation of this argument in figure 8.7.

Now that we know how to make a *reversible* classical function from each strategy, let's finish by making a quantum program from our reversible function. In the case of one, we saw that *h* flips its second input, $h(x, y) = (x, \neg y)$. Thus we can write a quantum program that does the same thing as our reversible classical function simply by flipping the second of two input qubits. As we saw in chapter 4, we can do this using the X instruction since $X|x\rangle = |\neg x\rangle$.

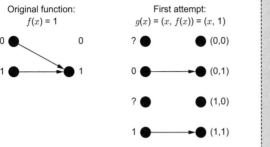

Hurray! By having two input bits and two output bits, our function is reversible. Here, that means we can map every output to a unique input, and vice versa.

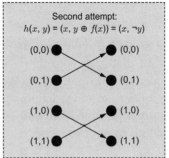

Figure 8.7 Second attempt: $h(x, y)$, **which is reversible and has the same number of inputs and outputs**

8.3.2 Generalizing our results

More generally, we can make a reversible quantum operation in precisely the same way we made reversible classical function h by flipping an output bit based on the output of the irreversible function f. We can define the unitary matrix (that is, the quantum analogue of a truth table) U_f for f for each input state in exactly the same way. Figure 8.8 shows a comparison of how we can do this definition.

$$h(x, y) = (x, y \oplus f(x))$$

We can make a new reversible classical function h from an irreversible function f by flipping a bit based on the output of f.

To define h, we specify what it does for arbitrary classical bits x and y.

$$U_f |x\rangle |y\rangle = |x\rangle |y \oplus f(x)\rangle$$

In exactly the same way, we can define a unitary matrix U_f.

Much like we defined h by saying what it did for each classical bit x and y, we can say what U_f does for input qubits in states labeled by classical bits—that is, the $|0\rangle$ and $|1\rangle$ states.

Figure 8.8 Constructing reversible classical functions and unitary matrices from irreversible classical functions. On the left, we can see that we can build a reversible classical function from an irreversible one if we keep track of the input we are giving to the irreversible function. We can do the same for a unitary matrix that describes a quantum operation by having two registers of qubits: one register keeps track of the input, and the other holds the output of our irreversible function.

Defining U_f this way makes it easy to undo the call to f since applying U_f twice gives us the identity $\mathbb{1}$ (that is, the unitary matrix for the "do nothing" instruction). When we define a unitary matrix this way by applying a function f conditionally to the labels for qubit states, we call this new operation an *oracle*.

DEFINITION   An *oracle* is a quantum operation represented by a unitary matrix U_f that transforms its input state as

$$U_f |x\rangle |y\rangle = |x\rangle |y \oplus f(x)\rangle.$$

The symbol $\oplus$ represents the exclusive OR operator from regular Boolean logic.

All that's left is to figure out what sequence of instructions we need to send to implement each unitary U_f. We've seen the instructions we need to implement an oracle for one: an X instruction on the second qubit. Now let's look at how to write oracles for other possible *f* functions. That way, Merlin will know what he should do no matter what his strategy is.

Deep dive: Why is it called an oracle?

So far, we've seen a few different examples of the kind of whimsical naming that quantum computing owes to its physics history, like bra, ket, and teleportation. It's not just physicists who like to have a bit of fun, though! One branch of theoretical computer science called *complexity theory* explores what it is possible to do efficiently, even in principle, given different kinds of computing machines. You may have heard, for instance, of the "**P** versus **NP**" problem, a classic conundrum in complexity theory that asks whether problems in **P** are as difficult to solve as those in **NP**. The complexity class **P** is the group of questions for which there exists a way to answer them with an algorithm that takes polynomial time. In contrast, **NP** is the group of questions for which we can check a potential answer in polynomial time, but we don't know if we can come up with an answer from scratch in polynomial time.

Many other problems in complexity theory are posed by introducing small games or stories to help researchers remember what definitions to use where. Our own little story about Merlin and Nimue is a nod to this tradition. In fact, one of the most celebrated stories in quantum computing is called **MA** for "Merlin–Arthur." Problems in the class **MA** are thought of using a story in which Arthur gets to ask Merlin, an all-powerful but untrustworthy wizard, a set of questions. A yes/no decision problem is in **MA** if, whenever the answer is "yes," there exists a proof that Merlin can give Arthur and that Arthur can easily check using a **P** machine and a random number generator.

The name *oracle* fits into this kind of storytelling, in that any complexity class **A** can be turned into a new complexity class $\mathbf{A}^{\mathbf{B}}$ by allowing **A** machines to solve a **B** problem in a single step, as though they were consulting an oracle. Much of the history of problems like the Deutsch–Jozsa problem stems from trying to understand how quantum computing affects computational complexity, so many of the naming conventions and much of the terminology has been adopted into quantum computing.

For more on complexity theory and how it relates to quantum computing, black holes, free will, and Greek philosophy, check out *Quantum Computing Since Democritus* by Scott Aaronson (Cambridge University Press, 2013).

In general, finding a sequence of instructions by starting from a unitary matrix is a mathematically difficult problem known as *unitary synthesis*. That said, in this case, we can figure it out by substituting each of Merlin's strategies f into our definition for U_f and identifying what instructions will have that effect—we can guess and check in the same way we did to turn the one function into an oracle. Let's try this for the zero function.

Exercise 8.1: Try writing an oracle!

What would the oracle operation (U_f) be for f if f was zero?

Solution: Let's work it out one step at a time:

1. From the definition for U_f, we know that $U_f \, |xy\rangle = |x\rangle \, |y \oplus f(x)\rangle$.
2. Substituting zero for f, $f(x) = 0$, we get that $U_f \, |xy\rangle = |x\rangle |y \oplus 0\rangle$.
3. We can use that $y \oplus 0 = y$ to simplify this further, getting that $U_f \, |xy\rangle = |x\rangle |y\rangle$.
4. At this point, we notice U_f does nothing to its input state, so we can implement it by—doing nothing.

Exercise solutions

All solutions for exercises in this book can be found in the companion code repo: https://github.com/crazy4pi314/learn-qc-with-python-and-qsharp. Just go to the folder for the chapter you are in and open the Jupyter notebook with the name that mentions exercise solutions.

The function $f = $ id is slightly more subtle than the zero and one cases because $y \oplus f(x)$ cannot be simplified to not depend on x. As summarized in table 8.7, we need U_f $|x\rangle \, |y\rangle = |x\rangle \, |y \oplus f(x)\rangle = |x\rangle \, |y \oplus x\rangle$. That is to say, we need the action of the oracle on the input state ($|x\rangle \, |y\rangle$) to leave x alone and replace y with the exclusive OR of x and y.

Another way to think of this output is to is recall that $y \oplus 1 = \neg y$, so when $x = 1$, we need to flip y. This is precisely how we defined the controlled-NOT (CNOT) instruction in chapter 6, so we recognize that when f is id, U_f can be implemented by applying a CNOT.

This leaves us with how to define the oracle for $f = $ not. Just as the oracle for id flips the output (target) qubit when the input (control) qubit is in the $|1\rangle$ state, the same argument gives us that we need our oracle for not to flip the second qubit when the input qubit is in $|0\rangle$. The easiest way to do this is to first flip the input qubit with an X instruction, apply a CNOT instruction, and then undo the first flip with another X.

> **TIP** If you want to see more about how you can construct the other oracles and use QuTiP to prove they do what you want, check out appendix D.

To review the oracles we have learned to define, we collected all the work in this section in table 8.7.

Table 8.7   Oracle outputs for each one-bit function f

Function name	Function	Output of oracle
zero	$f(x) = 0$	$|x\rangle|y \oplus 0\rangle = |x\rangle|y\rangle$
one	$f(x) = 1$	$|x\rangle|y \oplus 1\rangle = |x\rangle|\neg y\rangle$
id	$f(x) = x$	$|x\rangle|y \oplus x\rangle$
not	$f(x) = \neg x$	$|x\rangle|y \oplus \neg x\rangle$

The uncompute trick: Turning functions into quantum oracles

As it stands, it may seem as though it takes a lot of work to design U_f for each function f. Fortunately, there's a nice trick that lets us build an oracle starting with a somewhat simpler requirement.

Recall that earlier, we attempted to define a reversible version of f by returning $(x, f(x))$ as output when given $(x, 0)$ as input. Similarly, suppose that we are given a quantum operation V_f that correctly transforms $|x\rangle|0\rangle$ to $|x\rangle|f(x)\rangle$. We can always make an oracle U_f by using one additional qubit and calling V_f twice using a technique called the *uncompute trick,* as shown in the following figure.

The uncompute trick: If we add another input $|0\rangle$, then we can make an operation that gives us a way to make the operation from $|x\rangle|y\rangle$ to $|x\rangle|f(x)\rangle$ reversible! This works for any function $f(x)$.

The first step in the uncompute trick is to use a temporary qubit along with the circuit from attempt 2. The math is easiest if we start with it in the $|0\rangle$ state.

We can apply the inverse of the circuit to get rid of the memory leak, cleaning up the temporary register we used.

At the end of the uncompute trick, our temporary register doesn't "remember" anything about x, so we don't have a memory leak!

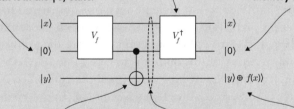

Since the information $f(x)$ is classical, we can then use a CNOT to copy this information onto the $|y\rangle$ register.

The state here would be $|x\rangle|f(x)\rangle|y \otimes f(x)\rangle$ This is a problem because the second qubit leaks information about our system (it's an extra qubit we will recycle after this, so, like a hard drive, we should return it blank).

It's straightforward at this point to check that our new circuit is reversible—it's actually its own inverse and is the same form as the other oracles in this chapter.

Using the uncompute trick to turn an operation that only works when we add an extra $|0\rangle$ input qubit into an operation that can be used as an oracle

> While this doesn't especially help in the case of Deutsch–Jozsa, it shows that the concept of an oracle is very general, as it's often much easier to start with an operation of the form V_f.

NOTE   The oracle construction also works for multiple-qubit functions. As a thought exercise, if we have a function $f(x_0, x_1) = x_0$ AND x_1, how will the oracle U_f transform an input state $|x_0 \, x_1\rangle$? We'll see in later chapters how to code this oracle.

We've thus used the oracle representation to solve the problem that functions like zero and one cannot be represented as rotations. With that dealt with, we can continue to write the rest of the algorithm that Nimue uses to challenge Merlin.

Deep dive: Other ways to represent functions as oracles

This isn't the only way we could have defined U_f. Merlin could have flipped the sign of Nimue's input x when $f(x)$ is one:

$$U_f |x\rangle = (-1)^{f(x)} |x\rangle \, .$$

This turns out to be a more useful representation in some cases, such as in gradient descent algorithms. These algorithms are common in machine learning and minimize functions by searching along directions in which a function changes the fastest. For more information, see section 4.10 of *Grokking Deep Learning* by Andrew Trask (Manning, 2019).

Picking the right way for a particular application to represent classical information such as subroutine calls within a quantum algorithm is a part of the art of quantum programming. For now, we will use the definition of *oracle* introduced earlier.

With the oracle representation of f in hand, the first few steps of the Deutsch–Jozsa algorithm can be written in the same sort of pseudocode that we used to write quick-sort earlier:

1. Prepare two qubits labeled control and target in the $|0\rangle \otimes |0\rangle$ state.
2. Apply operations to the control and target qubits to prepare the following state: $|+\rangle \otimes |-\rangle$.
3. Apply the oracle U_f to the input state $|+\rangle \otimes |-\rangle$. Recall that $U_f |x\rangle |y\rangle = |x\rangle |y \oplus f(x)\rangle$.
4. Measure the control qubit in the X-basis. If we observe a 0, then the function is constant; otherwise, the function is balanced.

TIP   Measuring a qubit in the X-basis always returns a 0 or 1, just like if we measured in the Z-basis. Recall from chapter 3 that if the state of the qubit is

$|+\rangle$, we always get a 0 when we measure in the *X*-basis, while we always get a 1 if the qubit is in $|-\rangle$.

Figure 8.9 illustrates these steps. We'll see at the end of the chapter *why* this algorithm works, but let's jump in and start programming it. To do so, we'll use the Q# language provided by the Quantum Development Kit since this makes it much easier to see the structure of a quantum algorithm from its source code.

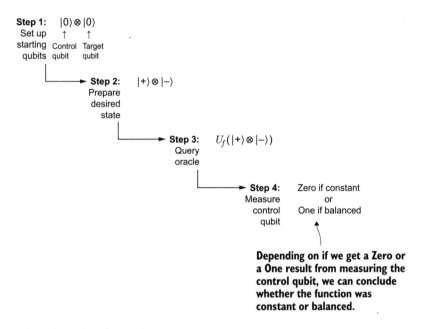

Figure 8.9   Steps in the Deutsch–Jozsa algorithm. We start by preparing the $|+-\rangle$ state, then query the oracle (that is, we ask Merlin the question), and then measure the control qubit to learn whether the oracle represents a constant or balanced function.

8.4   *Simulating the Deutsch–Jozsa algorithm in Q#*

In chapter 7, we tried passing operations as arguments in Q# programs. We can use the same approach of passing operations as inputs to oracles to help predict how Nimue's challenge will turn out. To do so, recall that we can consider four possible functions for this problem, each representing a possible strategy that Merlin could use (see table 8.8).

Table 8.8   Representing one-bit functions as two-qubit oracles

Function name	Function	Output of oracle	Q# operation
zero	$f(x) = 0$	$|x\rangle|y \oplus 0\rangle = |x\rangle|y\rangle$	NoOp(control, target);
one	$f(x) = 1$	$|x\rangle|y \oplus 1\rangle = |x\rangle|\neg y\rangle$	X(target);

Table 8.8 Representing one-bit functions as two-qubit oracles *(continued)*

Function name	Function	Output of oracle	Q# operation
id	$f(x) = x$	$\lvert x\rangle\lvert y \oplus x\rangle$	CNOT(control, target)
not	$f(x) = \neg x$	$\lvert x\rangle\lvert y \oplus \neg x\rangle$	X(control); CNOT(control, target); X(control);

If we represent each function $f(x)$ by an oracle (quantum operation) that maps $\lvert x\rangle\lvert y\rangle$ to $\lvert x\rangle\lvert y \oplus f(x)\rangle$, then we can identify each of the functions zero, one, id, and not from figure 8.3.

Each of the four oracles translates immediately into Q#:

```
namespace DeutschJozsa {
    open Microsoft.Quantum.Intrinsic;

    operation ApplyZeroOracle(control : Qubit, target : Qubit) : Unit {
    }

    operation ApplyOneOracle(control : Qubit, target : Qubit) : Unit {
        X(target);
    }

    operation ApplyIdOracle(control : Qubit, target : Qubit) : Unit {
        CNOT(control, target);
    }

    operation ApplyNotOracle(control : Qubit, target : Qubit) : Unit {
        X(control);
        CNOT(control, target);
        X(control);
    }
}
```

Can't we just look at the source code?

In Oracles.qs, we wrote the source code for each of the four single-qubit oracles `ApplyZeroOracle`, `ApplyOneOracle`, `ApplyIdOracle`, and `ApplyNotOracle`. Looking at that source code, we can tell whether each is constant or balanced without having to call it, so why should we worry about the Deutsch–Jozsa algorithm? Thinking from Nimue's perspective, she doesn't necessarily have the source code that Merlin uses to apply operations to her qubits. Even if she does, Merlin's ways are inscrutable, so she may not be able to easily predict what Merlin does even given the source code he uses.

Practically speaking, while it's hard to obfuscate a two-qubit oracle all that much, the Deutsch–Jozsa algorithm demonstrates a technique that is useful more generally. For example, we might have access to the source code for an operation, but it is a mathematically or computationally difficult problem to extract the answer to a question about that operation. All cryptographic hash functions have this property by design,

(continued)

whether they're used to ensure that a file has been downloaded correctly, to check whether an application has been signed by a developer, or as part of growing a blockchain through mining for collisions.

In chapter 10, we'll see an example that uses techniques like those developed in the Deutsch–Jozsa algorithm to ask questions about such functions more quickly.

With these oracles implemented in Q#, we can write the entire Deutsch–Jozsa algorithm (as well as Nimue's strategy for Kingmaker)! See figure 8.10 for a refresher on the steps of Deutsch-Jozsa.

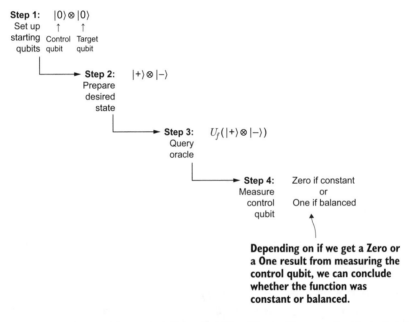

Figure 8.10 Steps of the Deutsch–Jozsa algorithm. We start by preparing the $|+-\rangle$ state, then query the oracle (aka ask Merlin the question), and then measure the control qubit.

Listing 8.2   Algorithm.qs: Q# operation to run Deutsch–Jozsa

```
operation CheckIfOracleIsBalanced(oracle : ((Qubit, Qubit) => Unit))
: Bool {
    use control = Qubit();
    use target = Qubit();

    H(control);
    X(target);
    H(target);
```

Asks the target machine to give us two qubits, control and target, each starting in the $|0\rangle$ state

Prepares the input state $|+-\rangle = (|00\rangle - |01\rangle + |10\rangle - |11\rangle)/2$ on control and target, as shown in step 2 of figure 8.10

```
        oracle(control, target);          ◄──────────┐   Calls the oracle given as the input argument.
                                                      │   Note that the oracle is called only once!
        H(target);                ◄───────────────┐
        X(target);                                 │   We know the target qubit is still in |−⟩, so we
                                                   │   can undo the X(target); H(target); sequence of
        return MResetX(control) == One;   ◄──────┘   operations to reset the target qubit.
}
```

Measures whether the control qubit is in | +⟩ or |−⟩,
corresponding to Zero or One results in the *X*-basis

Like the MResetZ operation provided by the Q# standard libraries, the MResetX operation performs the desired *X*-basis measurement and resets the measured qubit to the |0⟩ state. Now we want to make sure our implementation is good, so let's test it!

Measurement results in Q#

We've now seen both the MResetX and MResetZ operations in Q#, which measure and reset a qubit in the *X*- and *Z*-bases, respectively. Both of these operations return a Result value, which seems a little confusing at first. After all, an *X*-basis measurement tells us whether we were in the |+⟩ or |−⟩ state, so why does Q# use the labels Zero and One?

Conventions used for *X*- and *Z*-basis measurement results in Q#

Result value	*X*-basis	*Z*-basis
Zero	⟨+|	⟨0|
One	⟨−|	⟨1|

We'll see more about this later, but the short version is that a value of type Result tells us how many phases of (−1) are applied to a state by different instructions. For example, $Z|1\rangle = -|1\rangle = (-1)^1 |1\rangle$, while $X|-\rangle = (-1)^1 |-\rangle$. Since in both cases we raise (−1) to the power of 1, |1⟩ and |−⟩ are assigned to the One result when we measure in the *Z*- and *X*-bases, respectively. Similarly, since $Z|0\rangle = (-1)^0|0\rangle$, we assign |0⟩ to the Zero result when we measure *Z*.

We said earlier that Nimue would like to learn as little as she can about humankind's affairs. So, she only asks Merlin to do something with her qubits once, where we call oracle(control, target). Nimue gets only one classical bit of information from the call to MResetX, which isn't enough for her to tell the difference between the id strategy (Merlin selects Arthur to mentor as king) and the not strategy (Merlin selects Mordred to mentor).

To make sure she can still learn what she actually cares about—whether Merlin's strategy is constant or balanced—we can use the Fact function provided with the Q# standard libraries to test that our implementation works. Fact takes two Boolean variables as the first two arguments, checks to see if they are equal, and, if they aren't, issues a message.

> **TIP** Later, we'll see how to use these assertions to write unit tests for quantum libraries.

The first thing we do is pass the `ApplyZeroOracle` operation that we wrote earlier as the oracle for the `zero` function. Since `zero` isn't a balanced function, we expect `CheckIfOracleIsBalanced(ApplyZeroOracle)` to return `false` as its output; this expectation can be checked using the `Fact` function.

Listing 8.3   Algorithm.qs: Q# operation testing Deutsch–Jozsa

```
operation RunDeutschJozsaAlgorithm() : Unit {
    Fact(not CheckIfOracleIsBalanced(ApplyZeroOracle),
        "Test failed for zero oracle.");
    Fact(not CheckIfOracleIsBalanced(ApplyOneOracle),
        "Test failed for one oracle.");
    Fact(CheckIfOracleIsBalanced(ApplyIdOracle),
        "Test failed for id oracle.");
    Fact(CheckIfOracleIsBalanced(ApplyNotOracle),
        "Test failed for not oracle.");

    Message("All tests passed!");
}
```

Runs the Deutsch–Jozsa algorithm for the case in which Merlin uses the zero strategy

Does exactly the same thing for the one strategy, this time calling **CheckIfOracleIsBalanced(ApplyOneOracle)** instead

If all four assertions passed, then we can be sure that our program for the Deutsch–Jozsa algorithm works regardless of which strategy Merlin uses.

If we run this using the `%simulate` magic command, we can confirm that by using the Deutsch–Jozsa algorithm, Nimue can learn exactly what she wants to learn about Merlin's strategy:

```
In [ ]: %simulate RunDeutschJozsaAlgorithm
All tests passed!
```

8.5   *Reflecting on quantum algorithm techniques*

Phew—we've taken a couple of pretty big steps here:

- We've used classical reversible functions to model Merlin's strategy in a way that we can write it as a quantum oracle.
- We've used Q# and the Quantum Development Kit to implement the Deutsch–Jozsa algorithm and test that we can learn Merlin's strategy with a single oracle call.

At this point, it's helpful to reflect on what we learned from taking a splash in Nimue's quantum lake, as the techniques we used in this chapter will be helpful throughout the rest of the book.

8.5.1 *Shoes and socks: Applying and undoing quantum operations*

The first pattern that's helpful to reflect on is one we might have noticed in Algorithm.qs. Let's take another look at the order in which operations are applied to the `target` qubit.

Listing 8.4 Instructions from Deutsch–Jozsa for the `target`

```
// ...
X(target);
H(target);
oracle(control, target);
H(target);
X(target);
// ...
```

One way to think of this sequence is that the `X(target); H(target);` instructions prepare `target` in the |–⟩ state, while the `H(target); X(target);` instructions "unprepare" |–⟩, returning `target` back to the |0⟩ state. We have to reverse the order due to what's often called the *shoes and socks* principle. If we want to put on shoes and socks, we'll have better results if we put on our socks first; but if we want to take them off, we need to take our shoes off first. See figure 8.11 for an illustration of this procedure.

Figure 8.11 We can't take off our socks before our shoes.

The Q# language makes it easier to do shoes-and-socks kinds of transformations of our code using a feature called *functors*. Functors allow us to easily describe new variants of an operation we have already defined. Let's jump right into an example and introduce a new operation, PrepareTargetQubit, that encapsulates the X(target); H(target); sequence.

```
operation PrepareTargetQubit(target : Qubit)
: Unit is Adj {            ◁┐
    X(target);
    H(target);
}
```

> By writing "is Adj" as a part of the signature, we tell the Q# compiler to automatically compute the inverse operation—that is, the adjoint—of this operation.

We can then call the inverse operation generated by the compiler using Adjoint, one of the two functors provided by Q# (we'll see the other one in chapter 9).

```
PrepareTargetQubit(target);
oracle(control, target);
Adjoint PrepareTargetQubit(target);    ◁┐
```

> Adjoint PrepareTargetQubit applies the Adjoint functor to PrepareTargetQubit, giving back an operation that "undoes" PrepareTargetQubit. Following shoes-and-socks thinking, this new operation works by first calling Adjoint H(target); and then Adjoint X(target);.

Self-adjoint operations

In this case, X and Adjoint X are the same operation, since flipping a bit and then flipping it again always gets us back to where we started. Put differently, X undoes X. Similarly, Adjoint H is the same as H, so the previous snippet gives us the sequence H(target); X(target);. We say that the instructions X and H are *self-adjoint*.

Not all operations are their own adjoints, though! For instance, Adjoint Rz(theta, _) is the same operation as Rz(-theta, _).

In more practical terms, the Adjoint functor on the operation *U* is the same as the operation that reverses or undoes the effects of *U*. The name *adjoint* refers to the conjugate transpose U^+ of a unitary matrix *U*. In words, U^+ is called the *adjoint* of *U*. The Adjoint keyword in Q# guarantees that if an operation U is described by the unitary *U*, then if Adjoint U exists, it is described by U^+.

The pattern of performing an instruction is so commonly used that the Q# standard libraries provide the ApplyWith operation to express this pattern of doing and then undoing an operation.

NOTE   The ApplyWith operation is provided by the Microsoft.Quantum .Canon namespace in the Q# standard library. Much like the standard library in other languages, the Q# standard library provides many of the basic tools you'll need for writing programs in Q#. As you go through the rest of the book, you'll see lots of ways the Q# standard library can help make your life as a quantum developer easier.

Using `ApplyWith` and partial application, we can rewrite the `CheckIfOracleIsBalanced` operation in a compact way.

Listing 8.7 `ApplyWith` **and partial application help with shoes-and-socks ordering**

```
H(control);
ApplyWith(PrepareTargetQubit, oracle(control, _), target);
set result = MResetX(control);
```

The `ApplyWith` operation in this sample automatically applies the adjoint of `Prepare-TargetQubit` after `oracle(control, _ )` is done. Note that _ is used to partially apply the `oracle` to the `control` qubit.

Let's expand listing 8.7 step by step to see how it works. The call to `ApplyWith` applies its first argument, then applies its second argument, then applies the adjoint of its first argument to the qubit supplied in the last argument.

Listing 8.8 Expanding `ApplyWith` in listing 8.7

```
H(control);
PrepareTargetQubit(target);
(oracle(control, _))(target);
Adjoint PrepareTargetQubit(target);
set result = MResetX(control);
```

The partial application on the third line can then be replaced by substituting `target` for the `_`.

Listing 8.9 Resolving partial application in listing 8.8

```
H(control);
PrepareTargetQubit(target);
oracle(control, target);
Adjoint PrepareTargetQubit(target);
set result = MResetX(control);
```

Using operations like `ApplyWith` helps reuse common patterns in quantum programming, particularly to make sure we don't forget to take an `Adjoint` in a large quantum program.

Q# also provides another way to represent the shoes-and-socks pattern using blocks of statements instead of passing around operations. For example, we could write listing 8.7 using the `within` and `apply` keywords instead, as shown next.

Listing 8.10 Using `within` and `apply` for shoes-and-socks ordering

```
H(control);
within {
    PrepareTargetQubit(target);
} apply {
    oracle(control, target);
}
set result = MResetX(control);
```

Both forms can be useful in different contexts, so feel free to use whichever works best for you!

8.5.2 Using Hadamard instructions to flip control and target

We can use shoes-and-socks kinds of thinking from the previous section to change which qubits play the roles of control and target in instructions like CNOT. To understand how this works, it's important to keep in mind that quantum instructions transform the entire state of the registers they act on. In cases like the Deutsch–Jozsa algorithm, the control qubit can be affected by applying gates to the control and target qubits together—not just the target qubit. This is an example of a more general pattern: the control and target of a CNOT operation swap roles when we apply a CNOT instruction in the *X*-basis instead of the *Z*- (computational) basis.

To see this, let's look at the unitary operator (the quantum analogue to classical truth tables) for what happens if we use H instructions to transform to the *X*-basis, apply a CNOT instruction, and then use more H instructions to go back to the *Z*-basis.

Listing 8.11 Checking that H flips the control and target of CNOT

It's helpful to define a shorthand for the unitary operator $H \otimes H$
that simulates the sequence of instructions H(control); H(target);.

```
>>> import qutip as qt
>>> from qutip.qip.operations import hadamard_transform
>>> H = hadamard_transform()
>>> HH = qt.tensor(H, H)
>>> HH
Quantum object: dims = [[2, 2], [2, 2]], shape = (4, 4), type = oper,
 isherm = True
Qobj data =
[[ 0.5  0.5  0.5  0.5]
 [ 0.5 -0.5  0.5 -0.5]
 [ 0.5  0.5 -0.5 -0.5]
 [ 0.5 -0.5 -0.5  0.5]]
>>> HH * qt.cnot(2, 0, 1) * HH
Quantum object: dims = [[2, 2], [2, 2]], shape = (4, 4), type = oper,
 isherm = True
```

Looking at the unitary operator $H \otimes H$, we see that $|00\rangle$ is transformed to $(|00\rangle + |01\rangle + |10\rangle + |11\rangle) / 2$, a uniform superposition over all four computational basis states.

Gives the unitary operator representing H(control); H(target); CNOT(control, target); H(control); H(target);. We can think of this sequence of instructions as applying a **CNOT** in the *X*-basis instead of the *Z*-basis.

```
Qobj data =
[[1. 0. 0. 0.]
 [0. 0. 0. 1.]
 [0. 0. 1. 0.]
 [0. 1. 0. 0.]]
>>> qt.cnot(2, 1, 0)
Quantum object: dims = [[2, 2], [2, 2]], shape = (4, 4), type = oper,
  isherm = True
Qobj data =
[[1. 0. 0. 0.]
 [0. 0. 0. 1.]
 [0. 0. 1. 0.]
 [0. 1. 0. 0.]]
```

The unitary operator for this sequence looks a bit like CNOT, but with some of the rows flipped around. What happened?

Reversing the role of the control and target qubits in a call to the CNOT instruction gives us exactly the same unitary operator as using H instructions to apply a CNOT instruction in the X-basis.

To try to figure out what applying H instructions to each qubit did to the CNOT instruction, let's look at the unitary operator for CNOT(target, control).

Figure 8.12 provides a visual representation of the Python code we just ran.

Let's look at two different programs (written as circuits) that each use a CNOT instruction.

When drawn as a picture, the CNOT instruction that you saw in chapter 6 is indicated with a black dot for the control qubit.

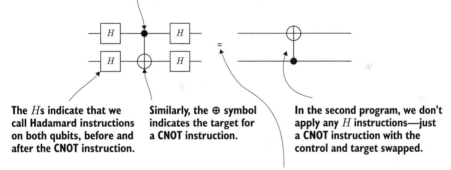

The Hs indicate that we call Hadamard instructions on both qubits, before and after the CNOT instruction.

Similarly, the ⊕ symbol indicates the target for a CNOT instruction.

In the second program, we don't apply any H instructions—just a CNOT instruction with the control and target swapped.

These two programs are completely equivalent. There is no way to tell which sequence of instructions has been applied, as both programs have exactly the same effect.

Figure 8.12 Changing which qubits are the control and target of a CNOT instruction using Hadamard instructions. By applying Hadamards on each qubit, and both before and after the CNOT, we can flip the roles of the control and target qubits.

From the previous calculation, we can conclude that CNOT(target, control) does precisely the same thing as H(control); H(target); CNOT(control, target); H(control); H(target);. In the same way that H flips the role of the X- and Z-bases, H instructions can flip between using a qubit as a control or a target.

8.6   *Phase kickback: The key to our success*

With these techniques in mind, we're now equipped to explore what makes the Deutsch–Jozsa algorithm do its thing: a quantum programming technique called *phase kickback*. This technique lets us write the `CheckIfOracleIsBalanced` operation to work for several different oracles while revealing only the one bit we want to know (whether Merlin was acting as a good mentor).

To see how the Deutsch–Jozsa algorithm uses phase kickback to work in *general*, let's go back to our three ways of thinking and use math to predict what happens when we call any oracle. Recall that we defined the oracle U_f that we constructed from each classical function f such that, for all classical bits x and y, $U_f|xy\rangle = |x\rangle|f(x) \oplus y\rangle$.

> **TIP**   Here we use x and y to represent classical bits that label two-qubit states. This is another example of using the computational basis to reason about how quantum programs behave.

Let's begin the same way we did in our QuTiP programs by expanding the input state $|+-\rangle = |+\rangle \otimes |-\rangle$ in the computational basis. Starting by expanding the state of the control qubit, we have that $|+-\rangle = |+\rangle \otimes |-\rangle = (|0\rangle + |1\rangle) / \sqrt{2} \otimes |-\rangle = (|0-\rangle + |1-\rangle) / \sqrt{2}$. As before, we can check our math using QuTiP.

Listing 8.12   Using QuTiP to check $(|0-\rangle + |1-\rangle) / \sqrt{2} = |+-\rangle$

```
>>> import qutip as qt
>>> from qutip.qip.operations import hadamard_transform
>>> from numpy import sqrt
>>> H = hadamard_transform()
>>> ket_0 = qt.basis(2, 0)       ◁─┐ Starts with useful
>>> ket_1 = qt.basis(2, 1)         │ shorthand notation
>>> ket_plus = H * ket_0
>>> ket_minus = H * ket_1
>>> qt.tensor(ket_plus, ket_minus)
Quantum object: dims = [[2, 2], [1, 1]], shape = (4, 1), type = ket
Qobj data =
[[ 0.5]
 [-0.5]
 [ 0.5]
 [-0.5]]
>>> (
...      qt.tensor(ket_0, ket_minus) +
...      qt.tensor(ket_1, ket_minus)
... ) / sqrt(2)
Quantum object: dims = [[2, 2], [1, 1]], shape = (4, 1), type = ket
Qobj data =
[[ 0.5]     ◁─┐ Both vectors are the same, telling us
 [-0.5]       │ that (|0-⟩ + |1-⟩) / √2 is another
 [ 0.5]       │ way of writing |+-⟩.
 [-0.5]]
```

Next, as we saw in chapter 2, we can use linearity to predict how U_f transforms this input state.

The matrix revisited

We implicitly used linearity earlier in this section when we used matrices to model how the Deutsch–Jozsa algorithm works. As described in chapter 2, matrices are one way of writing linear functions.

Since U_f is a unitary matrix, we know that for *any* states $|\psi\rangle$ and $|\phi\rangle$ and for *any* numbers α and β, $U_f(\alpha\,|\psi\rangle + \beta\,|\phi\rangle) = \alpha U_f|\psi\rangle + \beta U_f|\phi\rangle]$. Using this property with the computational basis, we have that in the same way $|+-\rangle$ and $(|0-\rangle + |1-\rangle)\,/\,\sqrt{2}$ are the same state, $U_f\,|+-\rangle$ and $U_f\,(|0-\rangle + |1-\rangle)\,/\,\sqrt{2}$ are the also same state.

TIP Using our shorthand for multi-qubit states, $|+-\rangle = |+\rangle \otimes |-\rangle$, $|0-\rangle = |0\rangle \otimes |-\rangle$, and $|1-\rangle = |1\rangle \otimes |-\rangle$.

Figure 8.13 gives a visual depiction of linearity.

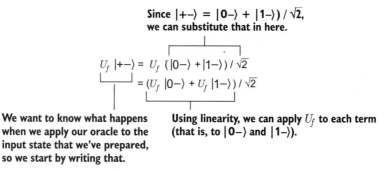

Figure 8.13 **Applying linearity to understand how our oracle transforms the input state**

Written like this, it's not immediately clear what advantage we've obtained by applying U_f to $|0-\rangle$ and $|1-\rangle$. Let's look at how the oracle operation applies to the first term by factoring out the control (first) qubit to consider the effect on the target qubit.

Doing so, we'll again use linearity to understand how U_f works by passing one state at a time to our oracle. As we learned in chapter 2, linearity is a very powerful tool that lets us break down even quite complicated quantum algorithms into pieces that we can understand and analyze more easily. In this case, we can understand how U_f acts on $|0-\rangle$ by using linearity (that is, by breaking $|0-\rangle$ into a superposition between $|00\rangle$ and $|01\rangle$).

We start by using that $|-\rangle = (|0\rangle - |1\rangle)/\sqrt{2}$.

$$U_f|0-\rangle = U_f(|00\rangle - |01\rangle)/\sqrt{2}$$

We can apply U_f to each term by linearity.

$$= (U_f|00\rangle - U_f|01\rangle)/\sqrt{2}$$

The definition of an oracle tells us how U_f transforms states in the computational basis.

$$= (|0(0 \oplus f(0))\rangle - |0(1 \oplus f(0))\rangle)/\sqrt{2}$$

XORing something with 0 does nothing.

$$= (|0f(0)\rangle - |0(1 \oplus f(0))\rangle)/\sqrt{2}$$

XORing something with 1 is the same as NOT.

$$= (|0f(0)\rangle - |0(\neg f(0))\rangle)/\sqrt{2}$$

Since the control qubit is in $|0\rangle$ in both terms, we can factor it out.

$$= |0\rangle \otimes (|f(0)\rangle - |\neg f(0)\rangle)/\sqrt{2}$$

For instance, if we're considering the zero function, then $f(0) = 0$. Thus, $|f(0)\rangle = |0\rangle$ and $|\neg f(0)\rangle = |1\rangle$, so $U_f|0-\rangle = |0-\rangle$.

On the other hand, if $f(0) = 1$, then $U_f|0-\rangle = |0\rangle \otimes (|1\rangle - |0\rangle)/\sqrt{2} = -|0-\rangle$. That is, U_f flips the sign of $|0-\rangle$.

TIP $(|1\rangle - |0\rangle)/\sqrt{2}$ can also be written as $-|-\rangle$, or as $X|-\rangle$.

Note then that U_f either rotates the target qubit by X or not depending on the value of $f(0)$:

$$U_f|0-\rangle = (-1)^{f(0)}|0-\rangle/\sqrt{2}$$

We can use the same technique we used before to understand what U_f does if the control qubit is in the $|1\rangle$ state instead. Doing so, we get a phase of $(-1)^{f(1)}$ instead of $(-1)^{f(0)}$, so that $U_f|1-\rangle = (-1)^{f(1)}|1-\rangle$.

Using linearity again to combine the terms for the two states of the control qubit, we now know how U_f transforms the state of both qubits when the control qubit is in $|+\rangle$:

$$U_f|+-\rangle = \frac{1}{\sqrt{2}}((-1)^{f(0)}|0-\rangle + (-1)^{f(1)}|1-\rangle).$$

The last step is to note that, as we saw in chapter 4, we cannot observe *global* phases. Thus, we can factor out $(-1)^{f(0)}$ to express the output state in terms of $f(0) \oplus f(1)$, the question we were interested in to start with, as shown in figure 8.14.

By using linearity and that $|+-\rangle = (|0-\rangle + |1-\rangle)/\sqrt{2}$, we can apply U_f to both of the cases we've already computed, $U_f|0-\rangle$ and $U_f|1-\rangle$.

In both cases, we get a phase that depends on the value of our irreversible classical function, evaluated at the label of the control qubit; e.g., $U_f|0-\rangle = (-1)^{f(0)}|0-\rangle$.

$$U_f|+-\rangle = \frac{1}{\sqrt{2}}((-1)^{f(0)}|0-\rangle + (-1)^{f(1)}|1-\rangle)$$

Next, we can factor out $f(0)$ so it's easier to see that it's a global phase.

Doing so leaves us with a phase on the $|1-\rangle$ part of the state that depends on $f(0) \oplus f(1)$, which is 0 for constant functions and 1 for balanced functions.

To finish our exploration of the Deutsch–Jozsa algorithm, we need to know what the oracle U_f does to $|+-\rangle$, the input state prepared by our H and X instructions.

$$= \frac{1}{\sqrt{2}}(-1)^{f(0)}(|0-\rangle + (-1)^{f(0)\oplus f(1)}|1-\rangle)$$

$$= \frac{1}{\sqrt{2}}(-1)^{f(0)}(|0\rangle + (-1)^{f(0)\oplus f(1)}|1\rangle) \otimes |-\rangle$$

Finally, we notice that the target qubit is in the same state *regardless of the state of the control qubit*. Thus, we can factor it out and safely measure or reset the target qubit without affecting the control.

Figure 8.14 Working out the last couple of steps in the Deutsch–Jozsa algorithm. By writing the oracle's action on the $|+-\rangle$ state, we can see how measuring the control qubit at the end tells us whether the oracle represents a constant or balanced function.

If $f(0) \oplus f(1) = 0$ (constant), then the output state is $|+-\rangle$; but if $f(0) \oplus f(1) = 1$ (balanced), then the output state is $|--\rangle$. With one call to U_f, we learn whether f is constant or balanced *even though we do not learn what $f(x)$ is for any particular input x*.

One way to think of what happens when we apply U_f with the input qubit in the $|+\rangle$ state is that the state of the input qubit represents the question we are asking about f. If we ask the question $|0\rangle$, we get the answer $f(0)$, while if we ask $|1\rangle$, we get the answer $f(1)$. The question $|+\rangle$ then tells us about $f(0) \oplus f(1)$ without telling us about either $f(0)$ or $f(1)$ alone.

When we ask questions in superposition like this, however, the roles of "input" and "output" aren't as immediately clear as they are classically. In particular, the $|0\rangle$ and $|1\rangle$ inputs both cause the output qubit to flip, while the $|+\rangle$ input causes the *input* qubit to flip, provided we start the output qubit in the $|-\rangle$ state. In general, two-qubit operations like U_f transform the entire space of the qubits they act on—our division into inputs and outputs is one way we interpret the action of U_f.

The fact that the input qubit's state changes based on transformations defined in the output qubit is an example of phase kickback, the quantum effect used by the Deutsch–Jozsa algorithm. In the next two chapters, we'll use phase kickback to explore new algorithms such as those used in quantum sensing and quantum chemistry simulations.

Deep dive: Extending Deutsch–Jozsa

While we only considered functions with one-bit inputs here, the Deutsch–Jozsa algorithm only ever needs one query for any sized input/output of our function.

To encode a two-qubit function $f(x_0, x_1)$, we can introduce a three-qubit oracle U_f $|x_0 x_1 y\rangle = |x_0 \ x_1\rangle \otimes |f(x_0, x_1) \oplus y\rangle$. For example, consider $f(x_0, x_1) = x_0 \oplus x_1$. This function is balanced since $f(0, 0) = f(1, 1) = 0$ but $f(0, 1) = f(1, 0) = 1$. When we apply U_f to the three-qubit state $|++-\rangle = (|00\rangle + |01\rangle + |10\rangle + |11\rangle) \otimes |-\rangle$, we get $(|00\rangle - |01\rangle - |10\rangle + |11\rangle) \otimes |-\rangle = |---\rangle$. Using an X-basis measurement, we can tell this from a constant function like $f(x_0, x_1) = 0$, which will give us an output of $|-\rangle$.

As long as we're promised that f is either constant or balanced, the same pattern holds no matter how many bits f takes as input: we can learn a single bit of data about how f behaves with a single call to U_f. Talk about O(1)! If you are not familiar with Big O notation, see *Grokking Algorithms* by Aditya Bhargava (Manning, 2016).

In the next chapter, we'll build on the skills we've learned here by looking at how the *phase estimation algorithm* enables spin-off technologies like quantum sensors.

Summary

- Quantum algorithms are sequences of steps that we can follow to solve a problem using quantum computers. We can implement quantum algorithms by writing quantum programs in Q#.
- The Deutsch–Jozsa algorithm is an example of a quantum algorithm that lets us solve a computational problem with fewer resources than any possible classical algorithm.
- If we want to embed classical functions into a quantum algorithm or program, we need to do so *reversibly*. We can construct special kinds of quantum operations called oracles that allow us to represent classical functions applied to quantum data.
- The Deutsch–Jozsa algorithm lets us test if both outputs from a one-bit oracle are the same or different using only one call to that oracle; we don't learn any particular output but instead directly learn the global property that we're interested in.
- The Deutsch–Jozsa algorithm demonstrates "shoes-and-socks" patterns that occur commonly in other quantum algorithms as well. We will often need to apply an outer operation, apply an inner operation, and then undo (or take the adjoint of) the outer operation.
- The phase kickback technique lets us associate the phase applied by a quantum operation with a control qubit instead of the target qubit. We will see more of this in the algorithms we learn next.

Quantum sensing: It's not just a phase

This chapter covers

- How quantum operations can learn useful information about unknown operations with phase kickback
- Creating new types in Q#
- Running Q# code from a Python host program
- Recognizing important properties and behaviors of eigenstates and phase
- Programming controlled quantum operations in Q#

In the last chapter, we implemented our first quantum algorithm, Deutsch–Jozsa, in Q#. By helping Nimue and Merlin play Kingmaker, we saw how quantum programming techniques like phase kickback can give us advantages in solving problems. In this chapter, we will take a look at *phase-estimation* algorithms we can use in our quantum programs to solve different types of problems. Again, we will return to Camelot; this time, we will use a game between Lancelot and Dagonet to illustrate the task at hand.

9.1   Phase estimation: Using useful properties of qubits for measurement

Throughout the book, we've seen that games can be a helpful way to learn quantum computing concepts. For instance, in the previous chapter, Nimue's game with Merlin let us explore our first quantum algorithm: the Deutsch–Jozsa algorithm. In this chapter, we'll use another game to discover how to learn the phases of quantum states using phase kickback, the quantum development technique used by Deutsch–Jozsa and many other quantum algorithms.

For this chapter's game, let's go back and see what Lancelot has been up to. While Nimue and Merlin are deciding the fate of kings, we find Lancelot and the court jester, Dagonet, playing a guessing game. Since they've had a while to play, Dagonet has gotten bored and wants to "borrow" some of Nimue's quantum tools to make their game a bit more interesting.

9.1.1   Part and partial application

For Dagonet's new game, rather than having Lancelot guess a number, Dagonet has Lancelot guess what a quantum operation does to a single qubit by letting Lancelot call it with different inputs. Given that all single-qubit operations are rotations, this works well for the game. Dagonet picks a rotation angle about a particular axis, and Lancelot gets to input a number to Dagonet's operation, which changes how to scale the rotation that Dagonet applies. What axis Dagonet picks doesn't really matter, as the game is to guess the rotation angle. For convenience here, Dagonet's rotations are always around the Z-axis. Finally, Lancelot can measure the qubit and use his measurement to guess Dagonet's original rotation angle. See figure 9.1 for a flowchart of the following steps:

1   Dagonet picks a secret angle for a single-qubit rotation operation.
2   Dagonet prepares an operation for Lancelot to use that hides the secret angle and allows Lancelot one additional input of a number (we'll call it a scale) that will be multiplied with the secret angle to give the total rotation angle of the operation.
3   Lancelot's best strategy for the game is to select many scale values and estimate the probability of measuring One for each value. To do this, he needs to perform the following steps many times for each of the many scale values:
   a   Prepare the $|+\rangle$ state, and input the scale value in Dagonet's rotation. He uses the $|+\rangle$ state because he knows Dagonet is rotating around the Z-axis; and for this state, these rotations will result in a local phase change he can measure.
   b   After preparing each $|+\rangle$ state, Lancelot can rotate it with the secret operation, measure the qubit, and record the measurement.
4   Lancelot now has data relating his scale factor and the probability he measured a One for that scale factor. He can fit this data in his head and get Dagonet's angle from the fitted parameters (he *is* the greatest knight in the land). We can use Python to help us do the same!

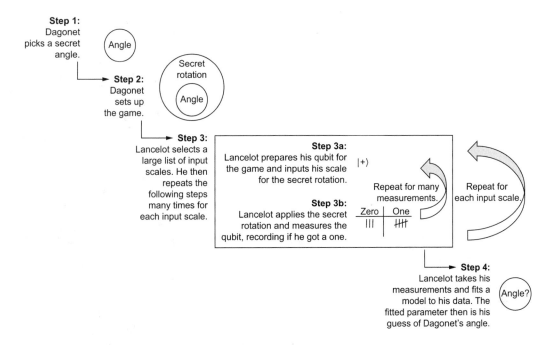

Figure 9.1   Steps in Dagonet and Lancelot's game. Dagonet hides a secret rotation angle in an operation, and Lancelot has to figure out what that angle is.

Note that this *is* a game, as there is no way for Lancelot to measure this rotation directly with just a single measurement. If he could, it would violate the no-cloning theorem, and he would transcend the laws of physics. As a Knight of the Round Table, Lancelot is bound not only by duty and honor but also by the laws of physics, so he must play Dagonet's game by the rules.

Deep dive: Learning the axis with Hamiltonian learning

In this chapter, we focus on the case where Dagonet's rotation axis is known, but we need to learn his angle. This case corresponds to a common problem in physics where we are tasked with learning the *Larmor precession* of a qubit in a magnetic field. Learning Larmor precessions isn't just useful in building qubits; it also allows for detecting very small magnetic fields and building very precise sensors.

More generally, though, we can learn much more than a single rotation angle. The case in which the axis is also unknown is an example of a general kind of problem called *Hamiltonian learning*, a rich area of research in quantum computing. In Hamiltonian learning, we reconstruct a physical model for a qubit or register of qubits using a game very similar to the one explored in this chapter.

Let's jump into prototyping this game in Q#. It will be helpful to have access to different parts of the Q# standard libraries, so we can start by adding the following open statements to the top of our Q# file, operations.qs.

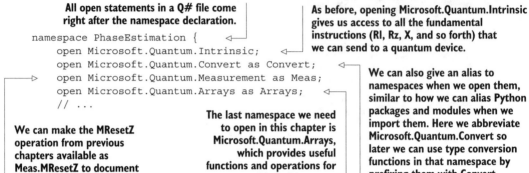

Listing 9.1   operations.qs: opening Q# namespaces for the game

All open statements in a Q# file come right after the namespace declaration.

```
namespace PhaseEstimation {
    open Microsoft.Quantum.Intrinsic;
    open Microsoft.Quantum.Convert as Convert;
    open Microsoft.Quantum.Measurement as Meas;
    open Microsoft.Quantum.Arrays as Arrays;
    // ...
```

As before, opening Microsoft.Quantum.Intrinsic gives us access to all the fundamental instructions (RI, Rz, X, and so forth) that we can send to a quantum device.

We can also give an alias to namespaces when we open them, similar to how we can alias Python packages and modules when we import them. Here we abbreviate Microsoft.Quantum.Convert so later we can use type conversion functions in that namespace by prefixing them with Convert.

We can make the MResetZ operation from previous chapters available as Meas.MResetZ to document where the operation came from.

The last namespace we need to open in this chapter is Microsoft.Quantum.Arrays, which provides useful functions and operations for working with arrays.

Listing 9.2 shows an example of the quantum operation Dagonet needs to implement the rotation he and Lancelot will play with. Like other rotations, our new rotation operation returns Unit (the type of the empty tuple ()), indicating that there's no meaningful return from the operation. For the actual body of the operation, we can find the angle to rotate by multiplying Dagonet's hidden angle angle with Lancelot's scale factor scale.

Listing 9.2   operations.qs: an operation to set up the game

To play the guessing game, we need a quantum operation that takes two classical arguments: one that Dagonet passes and one that Lancelot passes.

```
operation ApplyScaledRotation(
    angle : Double, scale : Double,
    target : Qubit)
: Unit is Adj + Ctl {
    R1(angle * scale, target);
}
```

The Adj + Ctl part of the signature indicates that this operation supports the Adjoint functor that we first saw in chapter 8 as well as the Controlled functor we'll see later in this chapter.

The rotation operation R1 here is almost identical to the Rz operation we've seen a few times so far. The difference between R1 and Rz will become important when we add the Controlled functor.

NOTE   When writing Q# in its own file (that is, not from a Jupyter Notebook), all operations and functions must be defined inside a namespace. This helps keep our code organized and makes it harder for our code to conflict with code in the various libraries we use in our quantum application. For brevity, we often don't show the namespace declarations, but the full code can always be found in the samples repository for this book: https://github.com/crazy4-pi314/learn-qc-with-python-and-qsharp.

To see a visual representation of Dagonet's setup of the game, see figure 9.2.

To start the guessing game, Dagonet first picks an angle that he wants Lancelot to guess.

On his turn, Lancelot can multiply Dagonet's hidden angle by a scale of his choice and then apply a rotation of that angle to a qubit.

Using Q#'s partial application feature, Dagonet can hide his angle inside an operation that he hands to Lancelot.

From Lancelot's perspective, this looks like calling a Q# operation with two inputs: his scale and the target qubit.

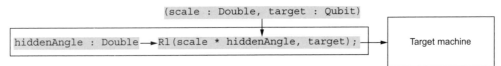

The operation that Dagonet gave Lancelot then multiplies the hidden angle with Lancelot's scale input and uses that to call a quantum instruction that applies a rotation.

That instruction is then sent to the target machine (for instance, a simulator or quantum device), which applies the rotation to the qubit that Lancelot passed.

Because of the no-cloning theorem, Lancelot can't just read out what the actual rotation was; he'll need to use what we learned in the previous several chapters to come up with a way to win Dagonet's game!

Figure 9.2 Using partial application to hide the secret angle while playing Dagonet's guessing game. The oracle that Lancelot gets has an input for his scale parameter, and he can then choose the target machine to use the operation with but cannot "peek inside" the operation to see the secret angle.

Deep dive: Why not just measure the angle?

It may seem like Lancelot has to jump through a lot of hoops to guess Dagonet's hidden angle. After all, what besides duty and honor is stopping Lancelot from passing a scale of 1.0 and then just reading out the angle from the phase applied to his qubit? It turns out that the no-cloning theorem strikes again in this case, telling us that Lancelot can never learn a phase from a single measurement.

The easiest way to see this is to pretend for a moment that Lancelot could do that, and then see what goes wrong. Suppose that Dagonet hides an angle of $\pi/2$ and that Lancelot prepares his qubit in the $|+\rangle = 1 / \sqrt{2} (|0\rangle + |1\rangle)$ state. If Lancelot then passes 1.0 as his scale, his qubit ends up in the $1 / \sqrt{2} (|0\rangle + i |1\rangle)$ state. If Lancelot could directly measure the phase $e^{i\pi/2} = +i$ to guess Dagonet's angle from a single measurement, he could use that to prepare another copy of the $1 / \sqrt{2} (|0\rangle + i |1\rangle)$ state, even though Lancelot didn't know the right basis to measure in. Indeed, Lancelot's magic measurement device should also work if Dagonet hides the angle π, in which case Lancelot winds up with a qubit in the $1 / \sqrt{2} (|0\rangle - |1\rangle)$ state.

Put differently, if Lancelot could figure out Dagonet's angle by measuring phases directly, he could make copies of arbitrary states of the form $1 / \sqrt{2} (|0\rangle + e^{i\phi} |1\rangle)$ for

> *(continued)*
>
> any angle ϕ, *without having to know ϕ ahead of time*. That rather badly violates the no-cloning theorem, so we can safely conclude that Lancelot will need to do a bit more work to win Dagonet's game.

Once we've defined an operation this way, Dagonet can use the partial application feature of Q# that we first saw in chapter 8 to hide his input. Then Lancelot gets an operation that he can apply to his qubits, but not in a way that lets him directly see the angle he is trying to guess.

Using `ApplyScaledRotation`, Dagonet can easily make an operation for Lancelot to call. For instance, if Dagonet picks the angle `0.123`, he can "hide" it by giving Lancelot the operation `ApplyScaledRotation(0.123, _, _)`. As with the examples of partial application in chapter 7, the _ indicates a slot for future inputs.

As shown in figure 9.3, since `ApplyScaledRotation` has type `(Double, Double, Qubit) => Unit is Adj + Ctl`, providing only the first input results in an operation of type `(Double, Qubit) => Unit is Adj + Ctl`. This means Lancelot can provide an input of type `Double`, a qubit he wants to apply his operation to, and use `Adjoint` and the functor we saw in chapter 6.

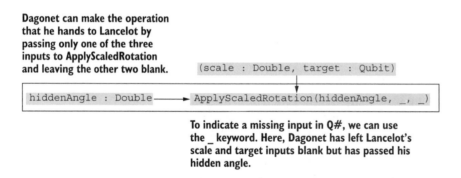

Dagonet can make the operation that he hands to Lancelot by passing only one of the three inputs to ApplyScaledRotation and leaving the other two blank.

`(scale : Double, target : Qubit)`

`hiddenAngle : Double` ⟶ `ApplyScaledRotation(hiddenAngle, _, _)`

To indicate a missing input in Q#, we can use the _ keyword. Here, Dagonet has left Lancelot's scale and target inputs blank but has passed his hidden angle.

Figure 9.3   Partially applying `ApplyScaledRotation` to make an operation for Lancelot

The fact that we can see the value of the angle in the syntax does *not* mean Lancelot can. Indeed, the only things Lancelot can do with a partially applied operation or function are call it, partially apply it further, or pass it to another function or operation. From Lancelot's perspective, `ApplyScaledRotation(0.123, _, _)` is a black box. Thanks to this partial-application trick, he will just have an operation that takes his scale value and can be used to rotate a qubit.

We can simplify our lives as Q# developers by giving a name to the type of Lancelot's operation that's a bit easier to read than `(Double, Qubit) => Unit is Adj + Ctl`.

In the next section, we'll learn how Q# lets us annotate the type signatures we use to play Dagonet and Lancelot's guessing game.

9.2 User-defined types

We have already seen how types play a role in Q#, particularly in the signatures for functions and operations. We have also seen that both functions and operations are tuple-in, tuple-out. In this section, we'll learn how to build up our own types in Q# and why that might be handy.

In Q# (as well as many other languages), several types are defined as part of the language itself: types like `Int`, `Qubit`, and `Result` that we have seen already.

> **TIP** For a complete list of these basic types, see the Q# language docs at https://docs.microsoft.com/azure/quantum/user-guide/language/typesystem/#primitive-types.

Building up from these basic types, we can make array types by adding `[]` after the type. For example, in this chapter's game, we will likely need to input an array of doubles to represent Lancelot's multiple inputs to Dagonet's operation. We can use `Double[]` to indicate an array of `Double` values.

Listing 9.3 Defining an array type of `Doubles` of length `10`

```
let scales = EmptyArray<Double>(10);
```
⟵ **EmptyArray comes from the Microsoft .Quantum.Arrays namespace. Make sure to open it before running this code.**

We can also define our own types in Q# with the `newtype` statement. This statement allows us to declare new *user-defined types* (UDTs). There are two main reasons to use UDTs:

- Convenience
- Communicating intent

The first reason is a matter of *convenience*. Sometimes the type signature for a function or operation can get pretty long, so we can define our own type as a kind of shorthand. Another reason we may want to name our type is to communicate *intent*. Say our operation takes a tuple of two `Double` values that represents a complex number. Defining a new type `Complex` can remind us and our teammates what that tuple represents. The Quantum Development Kit provides several different functions, operations, and UDTs with the Q# libraries, such as the following sample, which defines the type `Complex`.

Listing 9.4 How complex numbers are defined in the Q# runtime

```
namespace Microsoft.Quantum.Math {
    newtype Complex = (
        Real: Double,
        Imag: Double
    );
}
```
⟵ **Complex numbers are implemented as a UDT in the Microsoft.Quantum.Math namespace. We can use this type by including the statement "open Microsoft .Quantum.Math;" in our quantum application.**

The Complex type is defined as a tuple of two Double values, where the first item is named Real and the second is named Imag.

TIP The Quantum Development Kit is open source, so if you're curious, you can always look up how various parts of the Q# language, runtime, compiler, and standard libraries work. For example, the definition of the `Complex` UDT is in the src/Simulation/QSharpFoundation/Math/Types.qs file in the Q# runtime repository at https://github.com/microsoft/qsharp-runtime.

As shown in figure 9.4, there are two ways to get the different items back out of a UDT. We can either use named items together with the `::` operator or "unwrap" the UDT with the `!` operator to get back to the original type wrapped by the UDT:

Since the Complex UDT is defined with a named item called Real, we can access that item as ::Real to get back the real part of our input.

```
function TakesComplex(complex : Complex) : Unit {
    let realFromNamedItem = complex::Real;
    let (real, imag) = complex!;
}
```

Alternatively, since Complex is defined as wrapping a tuple of type (Double, Double), the unwrap operator ! takes us back to the real and imaginary parts of complex without the UDT wrapper.

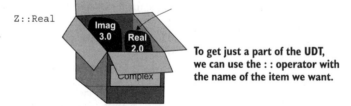

```
let z = Complex(
    2.0, 3.0
);
```

(2.0, 3.0)

When we create a new UDT, we can think of it as a kind of label for a tuple of data. For example, the Complex UDT tells us that its values represent complex numbers.

Z!

(2.0, 3.0)

If we want to just get the data out of a UDT, we can use the ! operator to unwrap it.

Z::Real

Imag 3.0   Real 2.0

To get just a part of the UDT, we can use the :: operator with the name of the item we want.

Figure 9.4   Using the `::` and `!` operators with UDTs. We can think of a UDT as a labeled tuple of data. The `::` operator lets us access that data by name, while the `!` operator unpacks a UDT into its base type.

TIP Both ways of working with UDTs are useful in different cases, but most of the time, we'll stick with using named items and the : : operator in this book.

Once a new UDT has been defined, it can also act as a way to instantiate a new instance of that type. For example, the Complex type acts as a function that creates a new complex number with the input of a tuple of two Double values. This is similar to Python, where types are also functions that create instances of that type.

Listing 9.5 Creating a complex number with the UDT Complex

```
let imaginaryUnit = Complex(0.0, 1.0);                    ◁─────────────────┐
```
Defining a UDT with newtype also defines a new function with the same name as that type that returns values of our new UDT. For instance, we can call Complex as a function with two Double inputs representing the real and imaginary parts of the new Complex value. Here, we define a Complex value representing $0 + 1.0i$ (0+1j in Python notation), also known as the imaginary unit.

Exercise 9.1: UDTs for strategies

In chapter 4, we used Python type annotations to represent the concept of a *strategy* in the CHSH game. UDTs in Q# can be used similarly. Give it a go by defining a new UDT for CHSH strategies, and then use our new UDT to wrap the constant strategy from chapter 4.

Hint: Our and Eve's parts of the strategy can each be represented as operations that take a Result and output a Result: that is, as operations of type Result => Result.

Exercise solutions

All solutions for exercises in this book can be found in the companion code repo: https://github.com/crazy4pi314/learn-qc-with-python-and-qsharp. Just go to the folder for the chapter you are in and open the Jupyter notebook with the name that mentions exercise solutions.

For the game in this chapter, we have defined a new UDT, both to label how we intend to use it and as a convenient shorthand for the operation type that Lancelot gets as his part of the guessing game. In the following listing, we can see the definition of this new type, called ScalableOperation, as a tuple with one named input called Apply.

Listing 9.6 operations.qs: setup for the quantum guessing game

We can declare a new UDT with the newtype statement by giving a name for our new type and defining the underlying type that our new type is based on.

```
newtype ScalableOperation = (                    ◁──────────────────┐
    Apply: ((Double, Qubit) => Unit is Adj + Ctl)         ◁─────────┐
);
```
We can give names to the various items in a UDT using the same syntax as declaring the signature for an operation or a function. Here, the new UDT has a single item named Apply that allows for calling the operation wrapped by ScalableOperation.

```
function HiddenRotation(hiddenAngle : Double)
: ScalableOperation {
    return ScalableOperation(
        ApplyScaledRotation(hiddenAngle, _, _)
    );
}
```

Once defined, we can use a new UDT like any other type. Here, we define a function that outputs values of type ScalableOperation.

We can easily make output values by calling ScalableOperation with the operation to be wrapped in our new UDT. In this example, we can create new instances of ScalableOperation using the same partial application of ApplyScaledRotation that we saw earlier in the chapter.

TIP When we define inputs to functions and operations in Q#, those inputs have names that start with lowercase letters. In listing 9.6, however, the named item `Apply` in `ScalableOperation` starts with an uppercase letter. This is because the inputs to a function or operation only have meaning within that callable, while named items mean something more broadly. We can use the capitalization of inputs and named items to make it obvious where to look for their definitions.

The function `HiddenRotation` defined in listing 9.6 helps us implement Lancelot's and Dagonet's game by giving us a way for Dagonet to hide his angle. Calling `Hidden-Rotation` with Dagonet's angle returns a new `ScalableOperation` that Lancelot can call to gather the data he needs to guess the hidden angle. Figure 9.5 shows Dagonet's new game setup.

By unwrapping the ScalableOperation that Dagonet gives him with ::Apply, Lancelot can now call the operation in which Dagonet hid his angle.

Putting it all together, we now have an operation that Dagonet can call with his angle to hide that angle using partial application and then wrap the result in a user-defined type to make the usage of that operation clear.

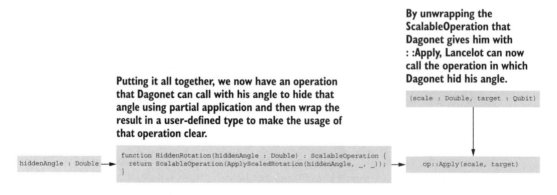

```
(scale : Double, target : Qubit)
```

```
hiddenAngle : Double
```

```
function HiddenRotation(hiddenAngle : Double) : ScalableOperation {
    return ScalableOperation(ApplyScaledRotation(hiddenAngle, _, _));
}
```

```
op::Apply(scale, target)
```

Figure 9.5   Playing Dagonet's guessing game with partial application and UDTs. Dagonet uses a function to construct the UDT that he passes to Lancelot, representing the rotation with his hidden angle.

With some new types and a way for Dagonet to hide his angle, let's continue implementing the rest of the game! We have everything we need for the next step: estimating the probability of each measurement we make during Lancelot's and Dagonet's game. This is very similar to how we would estimate the probability of flipping a coin; see figure 9.6.

Suppose that someone hands us a coin, and we'd like to know the *bias* of that coin: that is, the probability that our shiny new coin lands heads.

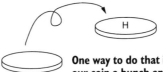

One way to do that is to flip our coin a bunch and make a table of how many times it lands heads and how many times it lands tails.

H	T
III	ℍℍ

If we get 3 heads and 5 tails, we could very reasonably estimate that the probability of getting heads is 3 / 8 = 37.5%. With more flips, we could get a more accurate estimate.

The same idea holds if we're trying to estimate the probability of getting a one from measuring a qubit.

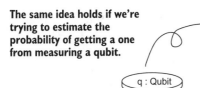

One

Zero	One
III	ℍℍ

For example, suppose we prepare a qubit in the state $|\psi\rangle$ and measure it, repeating the whole process eight times. If we get five one results, we would estimate that $|\langle 1|\psi\rangle|^2 = 5 / 8 = 62.5\%$.

Figure 9.6 Lancelot's estimation is similar to estimating the outcome of a coin flip. He can estimate the bias of a coin by flipping it many times and counting the number of "heads." Similarly, Lancelot can prepare the same qubit in the same state many times, measure it each time, and count the measurement outcomes.

Let's see what the code will look like for this flipping estimation procedure in Dagonet's game. Note that since Lancelot and Dagonet agreed that the Z-axis should be the rotation axis for their game, Lancelot can prepare his target qubit in the $|+\rangle$ state so that Dagonet's rotation does something.

Listing 9.7 operations.qs: estimating the probability of measuring $|1\rangle$

Lancelot's operation needs to take in a Double value representing what scale he picks to run the operation given to him by Dagonet.

```
operation EstimateProbabilityAtScale(
    scale : Double,
    nMeasurements : Int,
```

Lancelot picks a number of times to measure his qubit to get his estimate of the probability.

```
        op : ScalableOperation)
  : Double {
      mutable nOnes = 0;
      for idx in 0..nMeasurements - 1 {
          use target = Qubit();
          within {
              H(target);
          } apply {
              op::Apply(scale, target);
          }
          set nOnes += Meas.MResetZ(target) == One
                         ? 1 | 0;
      }
      return Convert.IntAsDouble(nOnes) /
          Convert.IntAsDouble(nMeasurements);
  }
```

To keep track of the number of |1⟩ outcomes observed so far, we define a mutable variable with the Int value 0.

For each measurement, we need to allocate a qubit that's the target for Dagonet's operation.

Uses the "within" and "apply" keywords for the shoes-and-socks pattern we learned about in chapter 8

Implements Lancelot's strategy by using the H operation to prepare a qubit in the |+⟩ state

Once we have prepared the input to Dagonet's operation, we call it by using ::Apply to unwrap the ScalableOperation UDT.

The ?| ternary operator (much like the if … else operator in Python or the ?: operator in C, C++, and C#) provides a convenient way to increment nOnes.

As output, Lancelot wants to return an estimated probability, so we can declare that as a Double output.

To get our final estimate of the probability of measuring |1⟩, we calculate the ratio of Ones to total counts. The function Convert.IntAsDouble helps us return a floating-point number.

The last input is of type ScalableOperation, the UDT declared earlier in the chapter. This input represents the operation that Dagonet gives Lancelot.

In listing 9.7, the within/apply block makes sure Lancelot's qubit is back in the right axis. We can count how many times the final measurement returns a One result by adding either 1 or 0 to nOnes. Here, the ?| ternary operator (much like the if … else operator in Python or the ?: operator in C, C++, and C#) provides a convenient way to increment nOnes.

An operation by any other name

You may have noticed that operations tend to be named using verbs, while functions tend to be named as nouns. This helps with remembering the distinction you saw in chapter 7: a function *is* something, while an operation *does* something. Being consistent with names can help you make sense of how a quantum program works, so Q# uses conventions like this throughout the language and libraries.

With this in place, we can now write an operation that runs the whole game and returns everything Lancelot needs to guess Dagonet's hidden angle.

Listing 9.8   operations.qs: running the complete game

Makes a new ScalableOperation value that hides Dagonet's angle using the HiddenRotation function we wrote earlier

```
operation RunGame(
    hiddenAngle : Double, scales : Double[], nMeasurementsPerScale : Int
) : Double[] {
    let hiddenRotation = HiddenRotation(hiddenAngle);
```

```
return Arrays.ForEach(
    EstimateProbabilityAtScale(
        _,
        nMeasurementsPerScale,
        hiddenRotation
    ),
    scales
);
}
```

The ForEach operation in Microsoft.Quantum .Arrays (which we gave the shorthand name Arrays) takes an operation and applies it to every element of the scales array.

When we pass "scales" as the second input to ForEach, each element of "scales" is substituted into the partial application slot _.

To get the operation we pass to ForEach, we use partial application to lock down how many measurements Lancelot does at each different scale and what hidden operation he was given by Dagonet.

NOTE It may seem funny that ForEach acts like map in Python and other languages when Q# also has Microsoft.Quantum.Arrays.Mapped. The critical difference is that ForEach takes an operation, while Mapped takes a function.

For Lancelot to actually make sense of all the data he gets out of his Q# program, it might help to use some good old classical data science techniques. Since Python is great at that, running our new RunGame operation from a Python host program can be an excellent way to help Lancelot.

9.3   *Run, snake, run: Running Q# from Python*

In previous chapters, we ran our Q# code in a Jupyter Notebook with a Q# kernel. In this chapter, we want to look at a different way to run Q# code: from Python. Calling Q# from Python can be helpful in different scenarios, especially if we want to preprocess data before using it in Q#, or if we want to visualize the output from our quantum program.

Let's start writing the files to implement Dagonet and Lancelot's game. To try the Q# and Python interop, we will use a Python host program to run the Q# program. This means we will have two files for the game: operations.qs and a host.py file that we will use directly to run the game. Let's dive into the host.py file to see how we can interact with Q# from Python; see figure 9.7.

Instead of using Jupyter Notebook as a premade host program, we can also write our own host program in Python. As in previous chapters, the host program is responsible for sending our Q# program to a target machine.

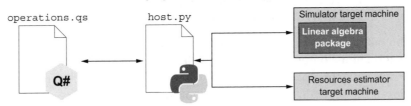

Figure 9.7   Using host programs for Q# written in Python. Like the Jupyter Notebook host, a Python program can coordinate sending the Q# program to a particular target machine and collecting the results.

All of the interoperable functionality we need between Python and Q# is provided by the qsharp Python package.

TIP   Appendix A has full installation instructions for the qsharp Python package.

Once we have the qsharp package, we can import it just like any other Python package. Let's look at a small sample Python file where we can see this in action.

Listing 9.9   qsharp-interop.py: using Q# code directly in Python

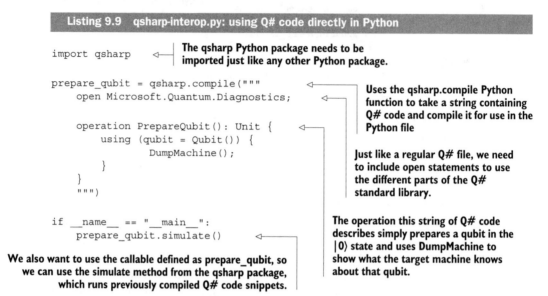

```
import qsharp          ◁──┤   The qsharp Python package needs to be
                              imported just like any other Python package.

prepare_qubit = qsharp.compile("""          ◁─────
    open Microsoft.Quantum.Diagnostics;     ◁──

    operation PrepareQubit(): Unit {        ◁──
        using (qubit = Qubit()) {
                DumpMachine();
        }
    }
    """)

if __name__ == "__main__":
    prepare_qubit.simulate()     ◁─────
```

Uses the qsharp.compile Python function to take a string containing Q# code and compile it for use in the Python file

Just like a regular Q# file, we need to include open statements to use the different parts of the Q# standard library.

The operation this string of Q# code describes simply prepares a qubit in the |0⟩ state and uses DumpMachine to show what the target machine knows about that qubit.

We also want to use the callable defined as prepare_qubit, so we can use the simulate method from the qsharp package, which runs previously compiled Q# code snippets.

Let's try running the qsharp-interop.py script from listing 9.9.

Listing 9.10   Running listing 9.9

```
$ python qsharp-interop.py
Preparing Q# environment...
# wave function for qubits with ids (least to most significant): 0
|0⟩:    1.000000 +  0.000000 i  ==    ******************* [ 1.000000 ]
⇒       --- [  0.00000 rad ]
|1⟩:    0.000000 +  0.000000 i  ==                        [ 0.000000 ]
```

TIP   If you are running code from a Q# Jupyter Notebook, the Q# snippet's output will look different. See figure 9.9 later in the chapter for an example.

From the output in listing 9.10, we can see that it does indeed prepare a |0⟩ state, as the only term in the output that has a coefficient of 1.0 is the |0⟩ state.

The qsharp Python package also looks for Q# operations or functions defined in *.qs files in the same directory as our Python program. In this case, as we proceed through the rest of this chapter, we'll add things to a Q# file called operations.qs. This is a pretty convenient way to start our host.py file for the game. The loaded qsharp package then allows us to import operations and functions from namespaces in Q#

files in the same directory as host.py. We saw `RunGame` previously and will see `RunGame-UsingControlledRotations` shortly.

Listing 9.11 host.py: the start of the phase estimation game

Imports the Q#
Python package

Imports RunGame and RunGameUsingControlledRotations
operations from operations.qs to automatically create Python
objects representing each Q# operation that we import

```
import qsharp      ◁
from PhaseEstimation import RunGame, RunGameUsingControlledRotations      ◁

from typing import Any      ◁
import scipy.optimize as optimization
import numpy as np

BIGGEST_ANGLE = 2 * np.pi
```

The rest of the imports help with type
hinting in Python, visualizing the results of
our Q# simulation, and fitting measurement
data to get Lancelot's final guess.

Now that we have imported and set up our Python file, let's write `run_game_at_scales`: the function that calls the Q# operations.

Listing 9.12 host.py: the Python function that calls Q# operations

Sets the return type hint to Any, which tells Python not to
worry about type checking the return value of this function

```
def run_game_at_scales(scales: np.ndarray,
                       n_measurements_per_scale: int = 100,
                       control: bool = False
    ) -> Any:
        hidden_angle = np.random.random() * BIGGEST_ANGLE      ◁
        print(f"Pssst the hidden angle is {hidden_angle}, good luck!")
        return (
            RunGameUsingControlledRotations
            if control else RunGame
        ).simulate(      ◁
            hiddenAngle=hidden_angle,
            nMeasurementsPerScale=n_measurements_per_scale,
            scales=list(scales)
        )
```

Dagonet chooses
the hidden angle
that he wants
Lancelot to guess.

When qsharp imports
these operations, their
Python representations have
a method called "simulate"
that takes the required
arguments and passes them
along to the Q# simulator.

The return for run_game_at_scales is conditioned on control,
which allows us to choose between two simulations we will
develop for this game (we use control=False for now).

This Python file should be runnable as a script, so we also need to define `__main__`. This is where we can do what Lancelot does in his head by using our host program in Python to take the measurements and scales and fit them to a model for Dagonet's rotation. The best model for how the rotation angle changes the measurement results is given by where θ is Dagonet's hidden angle and `scale` is Dagonet's scale factor:

$$\Pr(1) = \sin\left(\frac{\theta * \text{scale}}{2}\right)^2$$

> ## Exercise 9.2: Born again
>
> This model can be found if we use Born's rule! The definition from chapter 2 is shown next. See if you can plot the resulting value as a function of Lancelot's scale using Python. Does your plot look like a trigonometric function?
>
> $$\Pr(\text{measurement}|\text{state}) = |\langle \text{measurement} \mid \text{state} \rangle|^2$$
>
> *Hint:* For Lancelot's measurements, the $\langle 1 |$ part of Born's rule is given by $\langle 1 |$. Immediately before measuring, his qubit is in the state $HR_1 (\theta * \text{scale}) H|0\rangle$. You can simulate the R1 operation in QuTiP by using the matrix form in the Q# reference at https://docs.microsoft.com/qsharp/api/qsharp/microsoft.quantum.intrinsic.r1.

Once we have that model and data, we can use the `scipy.optimize` function from the SciPy Python package to fit our data to the model. The value it finds for the θ parameter is Dagonet's hidden angle! The next listing shows an example of how to pull this all together.

Listing 9.13   host.py: running host.py as a script

This script plots the data and fitted results, so we need to import the friendly matplotlib.

Lancelot's list of inputs to the game (that is, his scales) are generated as a regularly spaced, sequential list of numbers from np.linspace.

This script runs both versions of the game simulation so they can be compared. Don't worry about the control = True case for now; we'll come back to that shortly.

```python
if __name__ == "__main__":
    import matplotlib.pyplot as plt
    scales = np.linspace(0, 2, 101)
    for control in (False, True):
        data = run_game_at_scales(scales, control=control)

        def rotation_model(scale, angle):
            return np.sin(angle * scale / 2) ** 2
        angle_guess, est_error = optimization.curve_fit(
            rotation_model, scales, data, BIGGEST_ANGLE / 2,
            bounds=[0, BIGGEST_ANGLE]
        )
        print(f"The hidden angle you think was {angle_guess}!")

        plt.figure()
        plt.plot(scales, data, 'o')
        plt.title("Probability of Lancelot measuring One at each scale")
```

Stores the result from the Q# simulation that runs from Python in run_game_at _scales

Represents the operation on the qubit. Lancelot can take the data he gets, fit it to the model, and extract a guess for the angle.

The standard scipy function optimization.curve _fit takes a model of a function, inputs, measured data, and an initial guess to try to fit all the parameters of the model.

Validating the fit found by optimization.curve_fit is important so we can plot both the data and the fitted model to see if it looks right.

```
plt.xlabel("Lancelot's input scale value")
plt.ylabel("Lancelot's probability of measuring a One")
plt.plot(scales, rotation_model(scales, angle_guess))
```

plt.show()   ⟵ | **Displays the plots with the data and fit in a new window**

Now that we have a host program we can use to run the whole game, we can see that Lancelot does a pretty reasonable job of figuring out what angle Dagonet hid in his Q# operation. By taking different measurements and using classical data science techniques, Lancelot can estimate the phase that Dagonet's operation applies to his qubits. Running host.py should generate two pop-up windows that show plots of the measurement probabilities as a function of Lancelot's scale for two strategies he can use (figure 9.8). The first is the approach we have already outlined. We'll implement the latter in the last section of the chapter.

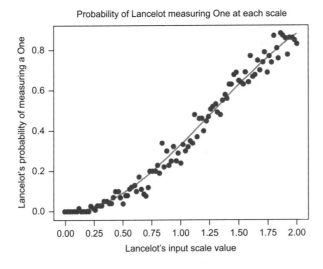

Figure 9.8 An example of one of the two plots that should pop up when we run host.py

TIP Since the SciPy fitting packages are not perfect, sometimes the fitted parameter it finds isn't right. Run it a few times, and hopefully the fitting algorithm will do better next time. If you have any questions about the plotting package `matplotlib`, check out these other titles from Manning: *Data Science Bootcamp* (chapter 2; by Leonard Apeltsin; forthcoming), and *Data Science with Python and Dask* (chapters 7 and 8; by Jesse C. Daniel; 2019).

We can see from these plots that we were able to fit Lancelot's data fairly well. That means the fitted value we find in `angle_guess` is a pretty good approximation of Dagonet's hidden angle!

There's still one more nagging problem with Lancelot's strategy, though: every time he performs a measurement, he needs to prepare the right input to pass to Dagonet's operation. In this particular game, that may not be much of a problem, but as we explore bigger applications of this game in the next chapter, it can be expensive to prepare the input register in the right state every time. Fortunately, we can use *controlled operations* to reuse the same inputs over and over again, as we'll see in the rest of this chapter.

You have seen examples of controlled operations already (like CNOT), but it turns out many other quantum operations can also be applied conditionally, which can be very useful. Controlled operations, along with the last new quantum computing concept we need (eigenstates), will help us to implement a technique we saw at the end of chapter 8: phase kickback.

> **TIP**   There is a lot of discussion about local and global phases in the next few sections. Recall that global phase is a complex coefficient that can be factored out of all the terms of our state and cannot be observed. If you need a refresher on phase, check out chapters 4–6.

9.4   *Eigenstates and local phases*

By now, we've seen that the X quantum operation allows us to flip bits ($|0\rangle \leftrightarrow |1\rangle$) and that the Z operation allows us to flip phases ($|+\rangle \leftrightarrow |-\rangle$). Both of these operations, though, only apply global phases to some input states. As we saw in previous chapters, we can't actually learn anything about global phases, so understanding what states each operation leaves alone is essential to understanding what we can learn by applying that operation.

For example, let's revisit the Z operation. In the following listing, we can see what happens when we try to use Z not to flip a qubit between the $|+\rangle$ and $|-\rangle$ states, but on an input qubit in the $|0\rangle$ state.

> **Listing 9.14   Applying Z to a qubit in the $|0\rangle$ state**

```
use qubit = Qubit();
```
As usual in Q#, we start by allocating a Qubit with a use statement. This provides a fresh qubit in the $|0\rangle$ state.

```
Z(qubit);
```
Applies a Z operation, such that the qubit's state is transformed to $Z|0\rangle = |0\rangle$

```
DumpRegister((), [qubit]);

Reset(qubit);
```
To confirm that the Z operation didn't do anything, we use the DumpRegister function to instruct the simulator to print out the full state vector.

Resets the qubit before releasing it. This isn't strictly needed since we know beforehand that the qubit is still in the $|0\rangle$ state.

In listing 9.14, we can confirm that the Z operation didn't do anything by using the DumpRegister function to instruct the simulator to print out all of its diagnostic information—in this case, the full state vector. Figure 9.9 shows what this diagnostic printout looks like.

> **TIP**   If we run this on a target machine other than a simulator, we get not a state vector but whatever other diagnostics the machine offers (e.g., hardware IDs).

The first line of output from DumpRegister shows the coefficient of the |0⟩ state; here, DumpRegister shows you that the coefficient is simply 1 (written out as 1.0000 + 0.0000i).

The output from DumpRegister also shows other useful information, such as the probability of observing each basis state (the squared absolute value of amplitude, following Born's rule) and the phase associated with each basis state.

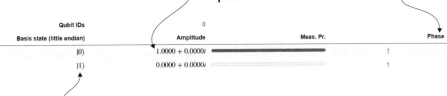

Basis state (little endian)	Qubit IDs Amplitude	0 Meas. Pr.	Phase
|0⟩	1.0000 + 0.0000i		↑
|1⟩	0.0000 + 0.0000i		↑

The second line shows you that the coefficient of the |1⟩ state is 0. Taken with what you learned from the first line, you have that the state being dumped is 1|0⟩ + 0|1⟩ = |0⟩.

Figure 9.9 Output of running listing 9.14

Note that in listing 9.14, Z doesn't do anything to qubit since $Z|0\rangle = |0\rangle$. If we modify the listing to prepare $|1\rangle$ instead by using X before Z, we see something very similar.

Listing 9.15 Applying Z to a qubit in the |1⟩ state

```
use qubit = Qubit();
X(qubit);
```
As before, to prepare a |1⟩ state, we can use that $|1\rangle = X|0\rangle$.

```
Z(qubit);
```
Repeats our experiment from above, but with a different input

```
DumpRegister("1.txt", [qubit]);
Reset(qubit);
```
As before, we can write the state of qubit to a text file, using that we're running on a simulator that keeps the state internally.

The output is as follows:

```
# wave function for qubits with ids (least to most significant): 0
|0>:     0.000000 +  0.000000 i  ==                        [ 0.000000 ]
|1>:    -1.000000 +  0.000000 i  ==  ****************** [ 1.000000 ]
⟹  ---      [  3.14159 rad ]
```
This file represents the vector [[0], [−1]], or −|1⟩ in Dirac notation.

The effect of applying the Z operation to a $|1\rangle$ state is to flip the sign of the state of qubit. This is another example of a *global phase*, as we saw in chapters 6 and 8.

Whenever two states $|\psi\rangle$ and $|\phi\rangle$ are only different by a complex number $e^{i\theta}$, $|\phi\rangle = e^{i\theta}|\psi\rangle$, we say that $|\psi\rangle$ and $|\phi\rangle$ vary by a *global phase*. For example, $|0\rangle$ and $-|0\rangle$ differ by a global phase of $-1 = e^{i\pi}$.

The global phase of a state doesn't affect any measurement probabilities, so we cannot ever detect whether we applied a Z operation when its input is in either the $|0\rangle$ or $|1\rangle$ state. We can confirm this by using the AssertQubit operation, which checks the probability of a particular measurement result.

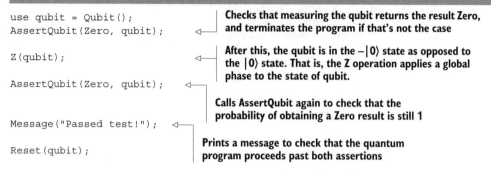

Listing 9.16   Using `AssertQubit` to check a measurement result

```
use qubit = Qubit();
AssertQubit(Zero, qubit);
```
Checks that measuring the qubit returns the result Zero, and terminates the program if that's not the case

```
Z(qubit);
```
After this, the qubit is in the $-|0\rangle$ state as opposed to the $|0\rangle$ state. That is, the Z operation applies a global phase to the state of qubit.

```
AssertQubit(Zero, qubit);
```
Calls AssertQubit again to check that the probability of obtaining a Zero result is still 1

```
Message("Passed test!");
```
Prints a message to check that the quantum program proceeds past both assertions

```
Reset(qubit);
```

Running this snippet simply prints `Passed test!` since the calls to `AssertQubit` don't do anything in the case that the assertion succeeds. Using assertions like this lets us write unit tests that use simulators to confirm our understanding of how particular quantum programs behave. On actual quantum hardware, since we can't do this kind of check due to the no-cloning theorem, assertions can be safely stripped out.

> **IMPORTANT**   Assertions can be really useful tools for writing unit tests and checking the correctness of our quantum programs. That said, it's important to remember that they will be stripped out when running our program on actual quantum hardware, so we don't use assertions to *make* our program run correctly.

> Of course, this is also just good programming practice; assertions in classical languages like Python can often be disabled for performance reasons, such that we can't rely on assertions always being there for us.

Identifying which quantum states are assigned global phases by an operation U gives us a way to understand that quantum operation's behavior. We call such states *eigenstates* of the operation U. If two operations have the same eigenstates and apply the same global phases to each of those eigenstates, there is no way to tell those two operations apart—just as if two classical functions have the same truth table, we can't tell which one is which, no matter what state our qubits are in when we apply each operation. This means we can understand operations not only by a matrix representation of them, but also by understanding what their eigenstates are and what global phase the operation applies to each. As we have seen, we cannot directly learn about the global phase of a qubit; so in the next section, we'll learn how to use controlled versions of an operation to turn that global phase into a local one we can measure. For now, though, let's summarize with a more formal definition of what an eigenstate is.

If, after applying an operation U, the state of a register of qubits qs is only modified by a global phase, we say that the state of that register is an *eigenstate* of U. For example, $|0\rangle$ and $|1\rangle$ are both eigenstates of the Z operation. Similarly, $|+\rangle$ and $|-\rangle$ are both eigenstates of X.

Try the next exercise to practice working with eigenstates.

Exercise 9.3: Diagnostic practice

Try writing Q# programs that use `AssertQubit` and `DumpMachine` to verify the following:

- $|+\rangle$ and $|-\rangle$ are both eigenstates of the X operation.
- $|0\rangle$ and $|1\rangle$ are both eigenstates of the Rz operation, regardless of what angle you choose to rotate by.

For even more practice, try to figure out the eigenstates of the Y and CNOT operations, and write a Q# program to verify your guesses!

Hint: You can find the vector form of the eigenstates of a unitary operation using QuTiP. For instance, the eigenstates of the Y operation are given by `qt.sigmay() .eigenstates()`. From there, you can use what you learned about rotations in chapters 4–6 to determine which Q# operations prepare those states.

Don't forget, you can always test if a particular state is an eigenstate of an operation by writing a quick test in Q#!

Eigenstates are a very useful concept and can be used in a variety of quantum computing algorithms. We'll use them in the next section along with controlled operations to implement a quantum development technique called *phase kickback*, which we were introduced to at the end of chapter 7.

Deep dive: It's only proper

Eigenstates get their name from a concept used throughout linear algebra, known as *eigenvectors*. Just as an eigenstate is a state that is left alone by a quantum operation (i.e., at most a global phase is applied), an eigenvector is a vector that is preserved up to a scaling factor when multiplied by a matrix. That is, if for a matrix A, $A\vec{x} = \lambda\vec{x}$ for some number λ, then $\vec{x}$ is an eigenvector of A. We say that λ is the corresponding *eigenvalue*.

The prefix "eigen-," German for "proper" or "characteristic," indicates that eigenvectors and eigenvalues help us to understand the properties or characteristics of matrices. In particular, if a matrix A commutes with its conjugate transpose (that is, if $AA^\dagger = A^\dagger A$), then it can be *decomposed* into projectors onto eigenvectors, each scaled by its eigenvalues:

$$A = \sum_i \lambda_i \vec{x}_i \vec{x}_i^\dagger$$

Since this condition always holds for unitary matrices, we can always understand quantum operations by decomposing them into their eigenstates and the phases applied to each eigenstate. For example, $Z = |0\rangle\langle 0| - |1\rangle\langle 1|$ and $X = |+\rangle\langle +| - |-\rangle\langle -|$.

One significant consequence of decomposing matrices this way is that if two matrices A and B have the same eigenvectors and eigenvalues, they are the same matrix. Similarly, if two operations can be represented by the same eigenstates and eigenphases, the operations are indistinguishable from each other.

> **(continued)**
> This way of thinking about states and operations can often help us make sense of different quantum computing concepts. Another way of thinking about the phase estimation game you're working on in this chapter is as an algorithm for learning the phases associated with each eigenstate! In chapter 10, you'll see that this connects especially well to certain applications such as learning properties of chemical systems.

9.5   *Controlled application: Turning global phases into local phases*

From what we have seen and can test, *global* phases of states are unobservable, while *local* phases of states can be measured. For example, consider the state $1 / \sqrt{2} \, (-i|0\rangle -i|1\rangle) = -i / \sqrt{2} \, (|0\rangle + |1\rangle)$. There is no measurement we could do to differentiate that state from $(|0\rangle + |1\rangle) / \sqrt{2}$. However, we could distinguish either of those two states from $(|0\rangle - |1\rangle) / \sqrt{2}$ as it differs by a *local* phase; that is, one of the states has a + in front of the $|1\rangle$, and the other has a –.

> **TIP**   If you want a refresher on phases and how to think of them as rotations, see chapters 4 and 5. When you are using the simulator as your target machine, the output of `DumpMachine` and `DumpRegister` can also help you learn about the phases of states.

In the last section, we played around with eigenstates and saw that the global phases of eigenstates can carry information about an operation: let's call it U. If we want to learn this global phase information about the eigenstates, then it seems like we're stuck. If Lancelot were to only prepare eigenstates of Dagonet's operation, he'd never be able to learn what angle Dagonet had hidden.

Quantum algorithms to the rescue! There's a very useful trick we can apply to turn global phases applied by an operation U into *local* phases applied by a closely related operation. To see how this works, let's return to the CNOT operation. Recall from chapter 6 that we can simulate CNOT using a unitary matrix:

$$U_{\text{CNOT}} = \begin{pmatrix} 1 & 0 & 0 & 0 \\ 0 & 1 & 0 & 0 \\ 0 & 0 & 0 & 1 \\ 0 & 0 & 1 & 0 \end{pmatrix}$$

When we first encountered this matrix in chapter 6, we used the analogy between unitary matrices and classical truth tables to work out that the CNOT operation swaps the $|10\rangle$ and $|11\rangle$ states but leaves qubits in the $|00\rangle$ and $|01\rangle$ states alone. That is, CNOT flips the state of its second qubit, *controlled* on the state of the first qubit. As shown in figure 9.10,

Start with the **CNOT** operation that we saw in chapter 6. We can represent it by a unitary matrix. Since **CNOT** acts on two qubits (the control and the target qubits), its unitary matrix is a 4×4 matrix.

The upper-left part of this matrix tells us what the **CNOT** operation does when the control qubit is in the $|0\rangle$ state.

$$U_{\mathrm{CNOT}} = \begin{pmatrix} 1 & 0 & 0 & 0 \\ 0 & 1 & 0 & 0 \\ 0 & 0 & 0 & 1 \\ 0 & 0 & 1 & 0 \end{pmatrix}$$

The lower-right part tells us what happens when the control qubit is in the $|1\rangle$ state. Note that this part of the matrix for **CNOT** is the same as the matrix for the **X** operation.

We can write unitary matrices for other controlled operations the same way. For instance, the controlled-**Z** operation (**CZ** for short) is represented by a matrix with the $\mathbb{1}$ and Z matrices on its diagonal.

$$U_{\mathrm{CZ}} = \begin{pmatrix} 1 & 0 & 0 & 0 \\ 0 & 1 & 0 & 0 \\ 0 & 0 & 1 & 0 \\ 0 & 0 & 0 & -1 \end{pmatrix}$$

Figure 9.10 Writing unitary matrices for controlled operations

we can read the unitary matrix for the CNOT operation as describing a kind of "quantum if" statement: "*If* the control qubit is in the $|1\rangle$ state, *then* apply the X operation to the target qubit."

To use the CNOT operation in Q#, we can try the following code.

Listing 9.17 Using the CNOT operation in Q#

```
use control = Qubit();
use target = Qubit();
H(control);                    Prepares the control qubit in |+⟩
X(target);                     Prepares the target qubit in |1⟩

CNOT(control, target);         Applies CNOT and
DumpMachine();                 prints out the state
                               of the simulator
Reset(control);
Reset(target);
```

By thinking about CNOT as a quantum analogue to a conditional statement, we can write its unitary matrix a bit more directly. In particular, we can look at the unitary matrix for the CNOT operation as a kind of "block matrix" that we can build up using the tensor product we saw in chapter 4:

$$U_{\mathrm{CNOT}} = \begin{pmatrix} \mathbb{1} & 0 \\ 0 & X \end{pmatrix} = |0\rangle\langle 0| \otimes \mathbb{1} + |1\rangle\langle 1| \otimes X$$

Exercise 9.4: Verifying the CNOT matrix

Verify that $|0\rangle\langle0| \otimes \mathbb{1} + |1\rangle\langle1| \otimes X$ is the same as the previous equation.

Hint: You can verify this by hand using NumPy's `np.kron` function or QuTiP's `qt.tensor` function. If you need a refresher, check out how you simulated teleportation in chapter 6, or look at the derivation of the Deutsch–Jozsa algorithm in chapter 8.

We can construct other operations following this pattern, such as the CZ (controlled-Z) operation:

$$U_{CZ} = \begin{pmatrix} 1 & 0 & 0 & 0 \\ 0 & 1 & 0 & 0 \\ 0 & 0 & 1 & 0 \\ 0 & 0 & 0 & -1 \end{pmatrix} = |00\rangle\langle00| + |01\rangle\langle10| + |10\rangle\langle10| - |11\rangle\langle11|$$

Much like the CNOT operation does the same thing as an X operation (applies a bit flip), but controlled on the state of another qubit, when its control qubit is in the $|1\rangle$ state, the CZ operation flips a phase like the Z operation. Figure 9.10 shows an example of how this works. Let's see how controlling Z works in practice by writing some Q# to give CZ a try.

Listing 9.18   Testing the Q# operation CZ

```
use control = Qubit();
use target = Qubit();
H(control);                                    Prepares the control qubit in |+⟩
X(target);                                     Prepares the target qubit in |1⟩

CZ(control, target);
DumpRegister("cz-output.txt", [control, target]);    Applies CZ and
                                                      saves out the
                                                      resulting state
Reset(control);
Reset(target);
```

The output is as follows:

```
# wave function for qubits with ids (least to most significant): 0;1
|0⟩:     0.000000 +  0.000000 i   ==                              [ 0.000000 ]
|1⟩:     0.000000 +  0.000000 i   ==                              [ 0.000000 ]
|2⟩:     0.707107 +  0.000000 i   ==        **********            [ 0.500000 ]
         --- [  0.00000 rad ]
|3⟩:    -0.707107 +  0.000000 i   ==        **********            [ 0.500000 ]
    ---      [  3.14159 rad ]
```

If we run this, the contents of `cz-output.txt` will show that the final state of the [control, target] register is $U_{CZ}|+1\rangle = |-1\rangle$.

Exercise 9.5: Verifying the `cz` output

Either by hand or using QuTiP, verify that the previous output is the same as $|-1\rangle = |-\rangle \otimes |1\rangle$.

If the qubits' order is swapped but, other than that, the answer is correct, note that `DumpMachine` uses a *little-endian* representation to order states. In little-endian, $|2\rangle$ is shorthand for $|01\rangle$, not $|10\rangle$. If this seems confusing, blame the x86 processor architecture.

That is, based on the state of the *target*, the state of the *control* changed as a result, just as we saw in chapter 8 with the Deutsch–Jozsa algorithm! This is because the phase applied by `z` in the case where `control` is in the $|0\rangle$ state is not the same as when `control` is in the $|1\rangle$ state, an effect known as *phase kickback*. In chapter 8, we used phase kickback with a pair of qubits in the $|+-\rangle$ state to tell whether the CNOT operation had been applied. Here, we've seen that we can use the CZ operation to learn about the global phase applied by the Z operation.

IMPORTANT
Even though $|1\rangle$ is an eigenstate of the Z operation, $|+1\rangle$ is *not* an eigenstate of the CZ operation. This means calling CZ on a register in the $|+1\rangle$ state has an observable effect!

Phase kickback is a common quantum programming technique, as it allows us to turn what would otherwise be global phases into a phase between the $|0\rangle$ and $|1\rangle$ branches of the control qubit. In the CZ example, both the input state $|+\rangle|1\rangle$ and the output state $|-\rangle|1\rangle$ are product states, allowing us to measure the control qubit without affecting the target qubit.

Think globally, learn phases locally

Note that a global phase difference between $|1\rangle$ and $Z|1\rangle = -|1\rangle$ became a *local* phase difference between $|1\rangle$ and $U_{CZ}|+1\rangle = |-1\rangle$. That is, by controlling the Z instruction on a qubit in the $|+\rangle$ state, we were able to learn what would have been a global phase without control.

Using the CZ operation, we can implement the phase kickback technique to turn a global phase into a local phase, which we can then measure.

Listing 9.19 Using `cz` to implement phase kickback

```
use control = Qubit();
use target = Qubit();
H(control);
X(target);
```

Prepares the control qubit in $|+\rangle$ and the target qubit in $|1\rangle$

```
CZ(control, target);
if (M(control) == One) { X(control); }

DumpRegister("cz-target-only.txt", [target]);

Reset(target);
```

Fun fact: this is actually how the Reset operation is implemented in Q#.

Now let's dump only the state of the target.

We already reset control, so we don't need to reset it again here.

Applies CZ and saves the resulting state. Before we dump the target qubit's state, though, let's measure and reset the control qubit.

Here's the output:

```
# wave function for qubits with ids (least to most significant): 1
|0):      0.000000 +  0.000000 i   ==                          [ 0.000000 ]
|1):     -1.000000 +  0.000000 i   ==   ******************* [ 1.000000 ]
  --- [  3.14159 rad ]
```

As expected, we get that the target qubit stays in the |1⟩ state, ready to feed into another CZ operation.

9.5.1 Controlling any operation

Thinking back to Lancelot's and Dagonet's game, it would be really useful if we could help Lancelot reuse the qubit that he passes into Dagonet's operation so that he doesn't have to re-prepare it every time. Fortunately, using controlled operations to implement phase kickback gives a hint as to how we can do so. In particular, when we used phase kickback in chapters 7 and 8 to implement the Deutsch–Jozsa algorithm, the target qubit was in the |−⟩ state at both the start and end of the algorithm. That means Lancelot could reuse the same qubit for each round of his game and not need to re-prepare each time. That didn't matter for Deutsch–Jozsa since we only ran one round of Nimue's and Merlin's game. But it's exactly the right trick for Lancelot to win his game with Dagonet, so let's look at how we can help him use phase kickback.

The trouble is that, while phase kickback is a useful tool to have in our toolbox as a quantum developer, so far we have only seen how to use it with the X and Z operations. We know that for our game, Dagonet told Lancelot he will use the R1 operation; is there a way we can use phase kickback to help here? The pattern we used to implement phase kickback in the previous section only required us to control an operation, so what we need is a way to control the op::Apply operation that Dagonet gives Lancelot. In Q#, this is as simple as writing Controlled op::Apply instead of op::Apply, thanks to the Controlled functor. Much like the Adjoint functor in chapter 6, Controlled is a Q# keyword that modifies how an operation behaves: in this case, to turn it into its controlled version.

> **TIP** Just like is Adj indicates that an operation can be used with Adjoint, is Ctl in the type of an operation indicates that it can be used with the Controlled functor. To denote that an operation supports both, we can write is Adj + Ctl. For example, the type of the X operation is (Qubit => Unit is Adj + Ctl), letting us know that X is both adjointable and controllable.

Thus, to help Lancelot, we can change the op::Apply(scale, target) line to Controlled op::Apply([control], (scale, target)), and we have the controlled version of R1.

While that does solve Lancelot's problem, it can be helpful to unpack what's happening under the hood a little more. Any unitary operation (that is, a quantum operation that doesn't allocate, deallocate, or measure qubits) can be controlled, the same way we controlled the Z operation to get CZ, and as we controlled X to get CNOT. For instance, we can define a controlled-controlled-NOT (CCNOT, also known as Toffoli) operation as an operation that takes two control qubits and flips its target if *both* controls are in the $|1\rangle$ state. Mathematically, we write that the CCNOT operation transforms an input state $|x\rangle|y\rangle|z\rangle$ to the output $|x\rangle|y\rangle|z$ XOR $(y$ AND $z)\rangle$. We can also write a matrix that lets us simulate the CCNOT operation:

$$
U_{\text{CCNOT}} = \begin{pmatrix}
1 & 0 & 0 & 0 & 0 & 0 & 0 & 0 \\
0 & 1 & 0 & 0 & 0 & 0 & 0 & 0 \\
0 & 0 & 1 & 0 & 0 & 0 & 0 & 0 \\
0 & 0 & 0 & 1 & 0 & 0 & 0 & 0 \\
0 & 0 & 0 & 0 & 1 & 0 & 0 & 0 \\
0 & 0 & 0 & 0 & 0 & 1 & 0 & 0 \\
0 & 0 & 0 & 0 & 0 & 0 & 0 & 1 \\
0 & 0 & 0 & 0 & 0 & 0 & 1 & 0
\end{pmatrix}
$$

Similarly, the controlled-SWAP operation (also known as the Fredkin operation) transforms its input states from $|1\rangle|y\rangle|z\rangle$ to $|1\rangle|z\rangle|y\rangle$ and leaves its input the same when the first qubit is in the state $|0\rangle$.

> **TIP** We can make a controlled-SWAP out of three CCNOT operations: CCNOT(a, b, c); CCNOT(a, c, b); CCNOT(a, b, c); is equivalent to Controlled SWAP([a], (b, c));. To see this, note that we can also make the uncontrolled SWAP operation from three CNOT operations for the same reason we can swap two classical registers in place using a sequence of three classical XOR operations.

We can generalize this pattern for any unitary operation U (that is, any operation that does not allocate, deallocate, or measure its qubits). In Q#, the transformation performed using the Controlled functor adds a new input to an operation representing which qubits should be used as controls.

> **TIP** This is where the fact that Q# is a tuple-in tuple-out language comes in very handy. Since every operation takes exactly one input, for any operation U, Controlled U takes the original input to U as its second input.

The CNOT and CZ operations are simply shorthand for appropriate calls to Controlled. Table 9.1 shows more examples of this pattern.

TIP Just like Adjoint works on any operation that has is Adj in its type (as we saw in chapter 8), the Controlled functor works on any operation that has is Ctl in its type.

Table 9.1 **Some examples of controlled operations in Q#**

Description	Shorthand	Definition
Controlled-NOT	CNOT(control, target)	Controlled X([control], target)
Controlled-controlled-NOT (Toffoli)	CCNOT(control0, control1, target)	Controlled X([control0, control1], target)
Controlled-SWAP (Fredkin)	n/a	Controlled SWAP([control], (target1, target2))
Controlled Y	CY(control, target)	Controlled Y([control], target)
Controlled-PHASE	CZ(control, target)	Controlled Z([control], target)

As we saw with the CZ example, controlling operations this way lets us turn global phases such as those applied to eigenstates into relative phases that we can learn through measurements.

More than that, by using controlled rotations to kick back phase onto the control register, we can also reuse the same target qubit over and over. When we applied CZ to a target register in an eigenstate of Z, that target register stayed in the same state even though the control register changed. In the rest of this chapter, we'll see how to use that fact to finish Lancelot's strategy for his little game with Dagonet.

9.6 *Implementing Lancelot's best strategy for the phase-estimation game*

We now have everything we need to write a slightly different strategy for Lancelot that will allow him to use controlled operations to reuse the same qubits. As noted before, this may not make a huge impact for Dagonet's game, but it does for other applications of quantum computing.

For example, in chapter 10, we'll see how problems in quantum chemistry can be solved using a game very similar to the one Dagonet and Lancelot are playing. There, however, preparing the right input state can require calling a lot of different quantum operations, such that if we can preserve the target qubit for later use, we can gain quite a lot of performance.

Let's briefly review the game's steps:

1 Dagonet picks a secret angle for a single-qubit rotation operation.
2 Dagonet prepares an operation for Lancelot to use that hides the secret angle and allows Lancelot one additional input of a number (we'll call it a scale) that

will be multiplied with the secret angle to give the total rotation angle of the operation.

3 Lancelot's best strategy for the game is to select many scale values and estimate the probability of measuring One for each value:

  a Prepare the $|+\rangle$ state, and input the scale value in Dagonet's rotation. He uses the $|+\rangle$ state because he knows Dagonet is rotating around the Z-axis; and for this state, these rotations will result in a local phase change he can measure.

  b After preparing each $|+\rangle$ state, Lancelot can rotate it with the secret operation, measure the qubit, and record the measurement.

4 Lancelot now has data relating his scale factor and the probability he measured a One for that scale factor. He can fit this data in his head and get Dagonet's angle from the fitted parameters (he *is* the greatest knight in the land). We can use Python to help us do the same!

The step that needs to change to use our newfound skills with *controlled* rotations is step 3. For step 3a, the *allocation* of the qubits will change. Rather than allocating, preparing, and measuring one qubit per measurement, Lancelot can allocate one `target` qubit to rotate with Dagonet's black box and instead allocate and measure `control` qubits. He still can repeat the measurements but won't have to measure or re-prepare the `target` each time.

We could summarize these changes by rewriting step 3 like this:

3 Lancelot's best strategy for the game is to select many scale values and estimate the probability of measuring One for each value. To do this, he must perform the following steps many times for each of the many scale values. He prepares one qubit in the $|1\rangle$ state to use as the `target` for all of his measurements as it's an eigenstate of the hidden rotation:

  a Prepare a second `control` qubit in the $|+\rangle$ state.

  b Apply the new controlled version of the secret rotation with Lancelot's scale value, un-prepare the `control` qubit and measure it, and then record the measurement.

In our code, these changes can be accomplished by modifying the previous `Estimate-ProbabilityAtScale` operation. Since the rotation axis could be anything Dagonet chooses (here, it's the Z-axis for convenience), Lancelot needs to know how to control an arbitrary rotation. We can do this with the `Controlled` functor before calling the `ScalableOperation` passed from Dagonet. The `Controlled` functor is very similar to the `Adjoint` functor in that it takes an operation and returns a new operation. `Controlled` `U(control, target)` is an example of the syntax that allows us to apply `U` to our `target` qubit, controlled on one or more `control` qubits. The following listing shows how we can modify `EstimateProbabilityAtScale` to use the `Controlled` functor.

Listing 9.20   operations.qs: Lancelot's new strategy

```
operation EstimateProbabilityAtScaleUsingControlledRotations(
    target : Qubit,
    scale : Double,
    nMeasurements : Int,
    op : ScalableOperation)
: Double {
    mutable nOnes = 0;
    for idx in 0..nMeasurements - 1 {
        use control = Qubit();
        within {
            H(control);
        } apply {
            Controlled op::Apply(
                [control],
                (scale, target)
            );
        }
            set nOnes += Meas.MResetZ(control) == One
                          ? 1 | 0;
    }
    return Convert.IntAsDouble(nOnes) /
           Convert.IntAsDouble(nMeasurements);
}
```

The guessing operation now takes the target register as an input and reuses it. Thus, we only need to allocate and prepare the control register each time.

The only other change we need to make is to call Controlled op::Apply instead of op::Apply, passing the new control qubit along with the original inputs.

The other modification we have to make (step 5) is the operation that runs the game. Since using the controlled operation allows Lancelot to reuse the target qubit, it only needs to be allocated once at the beginning of the game. See the next listing for how we can implement this.

Listing 9.21   operations.qs: Implementing `RunGameUsingControlledRotations`

```
operation RunGameUsingControlledRotations(
    hiddenAngle : Double,
    scales : Double[],
    nMeasurementsPerScale : Int)
: Double[] {
    let hiddenRotation = HiddenRotation(hiddenAngle);
    use target = Qubit();
    X(target);
    let measurements = Arrays.ForEach(
        EstimateProbabilityAtScaleUsingControlledRotations(
            target, _, nMeasurementsPerScale, hiddenRotation
        ),
        scales
    );
    X(target);
    return measurements;
}
```

Using EstimateProbability-AtScaleUsingControlledRotations, we can allocate the target qubit once since we use it over and over again through each guess.

Using the X operation, we can prepare the target in the |1⟩ state, an eigenstate of the (uncontrolled) R1 operation in which Dagonet hid his angle.

Using the X operation as in listing 9.21, we can prepare the target in the $|1\rangle$ state, an eigenstate of the (uncontrolled) R1 operation in which Dagonet hid his angle. Since each measurement uses phase kickback to affect only the control register, this preparation can be done once before playing the game.

Summary

- Phase estimation is a quantum algorithm that allows for learning the phase applied to a register of qubits by a given operation.
- In Q#, we can declare new user-defined types to label how a given type is meant to be used in a quantum program or provide a shorthand for long types.
- Quantum programs in Q# can be run on their own or from a host program written in Python; this allows for using Q# programs alongside data science tools like SciPy.
- When an operation leaves inputs in a given state unmodified other than applying a global phase, we say that that input state is an *eigenstate*, and the corresponding phase is an *eigenphase*.
- Using the Controlled functor and phase kickback together, we can turn global eigenphases into local phases that we can observe and estimate.
- Putting everything together, we can use classical data-fitting techniques to learn eigenphases from the measurements returned by running a Q# program that performs phase estimation.

Part 2: Conclusion

In this part of the book, we've had a lot of fun using Q# and quantum computing to help the various denizens of Camelot. Using a quantum random number generator written in Q#, we were able to help Morgana pull one over on poor Lancelot. At the same time, we helped Merlin and Nimue each play their respective roles in deciding the fate of kings, learning about the Deutsch–Jozsa algorithm and phase kickback all the while. With the land at peace and the fires in Castle Camelot burning down for the night, we saw how to use everything we learned to help Lancelot play another game, winning this time by guessing a quantum operation hidden by Dagonet.

Throughout our Camelot escapades, you picked up quite a few new tricks to help you on your way as a quantum developer:

- What a quantum algorithm is, and how to implement it with the Quantum Development Kit and Q#
- How to use Q# from Python and Jupyter Notebook
- How to design oracles to represent classical functions in quantum programs
- User-defined types
- Controlled operations
- Phase kickback

Going forward, it's time to bring what you've learned from Camelot back home and apply these new techniques to something a bit more practical. In the next chapter, you'll see how quantum computing can help in understanding chemistry problems. Don't worry if you don't remember the periodic table; you'll be working with some colleagues who know the chemistry side of things and are looking for your help in using everything you learned in this part of the book to upgrade their workflow with quantum technology.

Part 3

Applied quantum computing

By this point in the book, we have built up a great toolbox of quantum algorithmic techniques—and in this part, we'll see how to apply these techniques to different practical problems. In particular, we'll implement and run small examples of three different quantum programs, each of which addresses a different area in which quantum computing can be applied. These examples are small enough that we can simulate them with classical computers, but they demonstrate how quantum devices can provide computational advantages for problems of practical interest.

In chapter 10, we'll use our quantum programming skills to implement a quantum algorithm that helps solve challenging chemistry problems. We'll build on that in chapter 11 to implement an algorithm for searching through unstructured data; we'll learn how to apply functionality built into Q# and the QDK to estimate the resources required to run a quantum application at scale. Finally, in chapter 12, we'll implement Shor's algorithm for factoring integers, perhaps one of the most famous quantum algorithms owing to its applications in classical cryptography.

10

Solving chemistry problems with quantum computers

This chapter covers

- Solving chemistry simulations with quantum computers
- Implementing the `Exp` operation and the Trotter–Suzuki method
- Creating programs for phase estimation, decomposition, and so on

---

In chapter 9, we used a number of new Q# features like user-defined types (UDTs) and running programs from Python hosts to help us write a quantum program that could estimate phases. As we will see in this chapter, phase estimation is commonly used in quantum algorithms to build up larger and more complex programs. In this chapter, we'll look at our first practical application area: chemistry.

10.1 *Real chemistry applications for quantum computing*

So far in this book, we've learned how to use quantum devices to do everything from chat with our friend Eve to help decide the fate of kings. In this chapter, though, we'll get the chance to do something a bit more *practical.*

> **NOTE** Now that we have what we need to solve harder problems with quantum computers, this chapter's scenario is a little more complicated than most of our earlier games and scenarios. Don't worry if things don't make sense off the bat. Take your time and read things more slowly; we promise it will be worth your while!

As it turns out, our quantum chemist friend Marie has hit the limit of what her classical computer can do to help her model different chemical systems. The problems that Marie solves with computational chemistry techniques can help to combat climate change, understand new materials, and improve energy usage across industries; if we can help her by using Q#, that could have quite a lot of practical applications. Fortunately, by using what we learned about estimating phases in chapter 9, we can do just that, so let's jump in!

Better tasting through chemistry

Any candy maker can tell you the difference that temperature makes: cook sugar to the "soft crack" stage, and we get taffy; but if we add a bit more energy, we can make any number of other delightful confections ranging from toffee to caramels. Everything about sugar—its taste, how it looks, and how it pulls—changes depending on the energy we pour into it via a saucepan. To no small degree, if we understand how the shape of sugar molecules changes as we add energy to a sweet melting pot, we understand sugar itself.

We see this effect not just with candy but throughout our lives. Water, steam, and ice are differentiated by understanding what shapes H_2O can take—what shapes it can arrange itself in—as a function of energy. In many cases, we want to understand how the molecule arranges itself as a function of energy based on simulations rather than experiments. In this chapter, we'll build on the techniques from the previous several chapters, showing how we can simulate the energy of chemical systems so that we can understand them as keenly as a candy maker understands their craft and use these chemical systems to make our lives better—maybe even a little sweeter.

To get a feel for how this works, we agree with Marie that we will start by looking at *molecular hydrogen*, or H_2, as it is a simple enough chemical system that we can compare what we learn from our quantum program with what classical modeling tools can simulate. That way, as we use the same techniques to study molecules that are larger than can be simulated classically, we have a great test case we can fall back on to make sure everything is correct.

The simulation within the simulation

In this chapter, our work with Marie involves two different kinds of simulation: using a classical computer to simulate a quantum computer, and using a quantum computer to simulate a different kind of quantum system. We'll often want to do both, in that it's helpful in building quantum chemistry applications to use a classical computer to simulate how a quantum computer simulates a quantum chemical system. That way, when we run our quantum simulation on actual quantum hardware, we can be assured that it works correctly.

As shown in figure 10.1, Marie will start things off by using her expertise in quantum chemistry to describe a problem that she's interested in solving with a quantum computer: in this case, understanding the structure of H_2. For the most part, these problems consist of learning properties of a special kind of matrix called a *Hamiltonian*. Once we get a Hamiltonian from Marie, we can then write a quantum operation much like the one shown in listing 10.1 to simulate it and learn things about it that Marie can use to understand how different chemicals behave. Throughout the rest of this chapter, we'll develop the concepts and understanding that we need to implement the steps in figure 10.1.

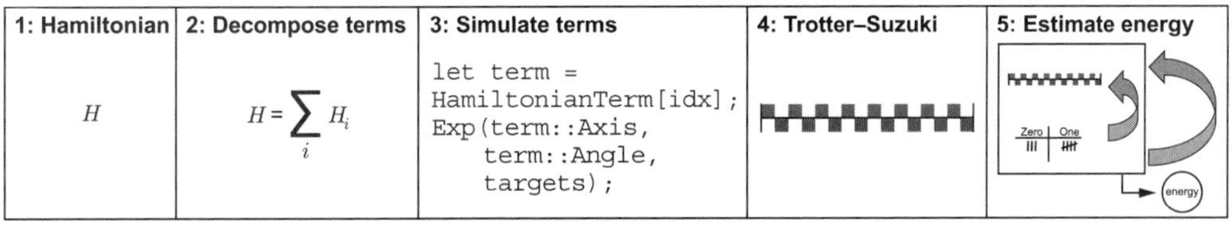

Figure 10.1 Overview of the steps we'll develop in this chapter to help Marie learn her molecule's ground state energy image

We'll implement the following steps in this chapter for our Hamiltonian simulation algorithm:

1. Collaborate with Marie to figure out which Hamiltonian describes the energy levels in the system she is interested in and an approximation of the ground (or lowest energy) state.

2. Prepare that approximation of the ground state, and use the Exp operation in Q# to implement evolution of the quantum system for each term of the Hamiltonian.

3. Using the Trotter–Suzuki decomposition implemented in the Q# function DecomposedIntoTimeStepsCA, simulate evolving our system under the action of all the terms of the Hamiltonian at once by breaking the evolution into small steps.

4. After simulating the evolution of the system under the Hamiltonian, use phase estimation to learn about the change in phase of our quantum device.

5. Make a final correction to the phase we estimate for the system, after which we have the energy of the ground state for H_2.

The following listing shows these steps translated into code.

Listing 10.1   Q# code that estimates the ground state energy of H_2

```
operation EstimateH2Energy(idxBondLength : Int) : Double {
    let nQubits = 2;
    let trotterStepSize = 1.0;
    let trotterStep = EvolveUnderHamiltonian(idxBondLength,
        trotterStepSize, _);
    let estPhase = EstimateEnergy(nQubits,
        PrepareInitalState,
        trotterStep,
        RobustPhaseEstimation(6, _, _));
    return estPhase / trotterStepSize + H2IdentityCoeff(idxBondLength);
}
```

Without further ado, then, let's dive into the first quantum concept we need to help Marie: energy.

10.2 *Many paths lead to quantum mechanics*

Thus far, we've learned about quantum mechanics using the language of computing: bits, qubits, instructions, devices, functions, and operations. Marie's way of thinking about quantum mechanics is very different, though (figure 10.2). For her, quantum

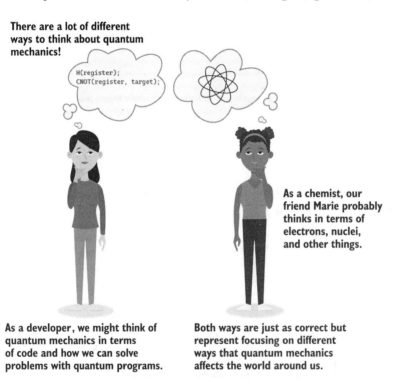

There are a lot of different ways to think about quantum mechanics!

```
H(register);
CNOT(register, target);
```

As a chemist, our friend Marie probably thinks in terms of electrons, nuclei, and other things.

As a developer, we might think of quantum mechanics in terms of code and how we can solve problems with quantum programs.

Both ways are just as correct but represent focusing on different ways that quantum mechanics affects the world around us.

Figure 10.2   Thinking about quantum mechanics in two very different ways

mechanics is a physical theory that tells her how subatomic particles like electrons behave. Thinking in terms of physics and chemistry, quantum mechanics is a theory about the *stuff* that everything around us is made of.

The two ways of thinking meet when it comes time to simulate how physical systems like molecules behave. We can use quantum computers to simulate how other quantum systems evolve and change over time. That is, quantum computing isn't about only physics or chemistry; it can also help us understand scientific problems like the ones Marie runs into.

Information is the core of how we think about quantum computation, but to the physics and chemistry way of thinking, quantum mechanics relies heavily on the concept of *energy*. Energy tells us how physical systems as varied as balls and compasses are affected by the world around them, giving us a consistent way to understand each of these different systems. In figure 10.3, we can see how the state of a ball on a hill and the state of a compass can both be described in the same way using the concept of energy.

As it turns out, energy doesn't just apply to classical systems like balls and compasses. Indeed, we can understand how *quantum* systems like electrons and nuclei

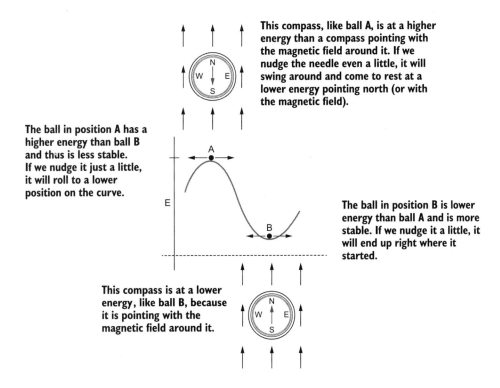

Figure 10.3 Using energy to understand how different physical systems are affected by their environments. A ball at a top of a hill and a compass pointing south are examples of higher-energy systems than a ball in a valley or a compass pointing north.

behave by understanding the energy of different configurations. In quantum mechanics, energy is described by a special kind of matrix called a Hamiltonian. Any matrix that is its own adjoint can be used as a Hamiltonian, and Hamiltonians are *not* operations themselves.

Recall from chapters 8 and 9 that the *adjoint* of a matrix A is its conjugate transpose, $A^\dagger$. This concept is closely related to the `Adjoint` keyword in Q#: if an operation op can be simulated by the unitary matrix U, then the operation `Adjoint op` can be simulated by $U^\dagger$.

In this chapter, we'll learn all the tools and techniques to figure out the energies of quantum systems for which we have a Hamiltonian. Often the process to get the Hamiltonians for systems is a collaboration, but once we have them and a few more pieces of information, we can estimate the energy of that system. This process is called *Hamiltonian simulation* and is critical to many different applications of quantum computing, including chemistry.

> **TIP** We've seen a few examples of Hamiltonians in previous chapters: all of the Pauli matrices (X, Y, and Z) are examples of Hamiltonians as well as being unitary matrices. Not all unitary matrices can be used as Hamiltonians, though! Most of the examples in this chapter take some more work before we can apply them as quantum operations.

Marie is interested in understanding the energy of the bonds in her chemicals. So it makes sense to come up with a Hamiltonian that describes her molecule; then we can help estimate the energy she is interested in. In chemistry, this energy is often called the *ground state energy*, and the corresponding state is known as the *ground state* (or minimum energy state).

Once we have a Hamiltonian, the next step is to figure out how to construct the operations that will simulate how the quantum system changes in time as described by the Hamiltonian. In the next section, we'll learn how to describe the evolution of a quantum system under a Hamiltonian.

Then, with operators in hand that represent the Hamiltonian, the next challenge is to figure out how to simulate the Hamiltonians on our quantum device. There probably won't be just a single operation built into the physical device that will do exactly what we need, so we must find a way to decompose our operations for our Hamiltonian in terms of what our device can provide. In section 10.4, we'll cover how we can take any operations and express them in terms of Pauli operations, which are commonly available as hardware instructions.

Once we have our Hamiltonian expressed as a sum of Pauli matrices, how do we simulate all of them on our system? Likely we will have multiple terms that all sum together to represent the action of the Hamiltonian, and they don't necessarily commute. In section 10.6, we will learn how to use the Trotter–Suzuki method to apply a little of each term in the operation to simulate evolving under the entire thing at once. Then we will have evolved our quantum system in a way that represents Marie's Hamiltonian!

Finally, to work out the energy of the system described by the Hamiltonian we found, we can use phase estimation to help Marie. In section 10.7, we'll get to use the algorithm we learned in chapter 9 to explore the phase applied to our qubits by simulating the Hamiltonian. Let's get to it!

10.3 Using Hamiltonians to describe how quantum systems evolve in time

Figure 10.4 shows a tracker for the steps to simulate another quantum system with our quantum computer. To use a Hamiltonian to describe the energy of a physical or chemical system, we need to look at its eigenstates and their eigenvalues.

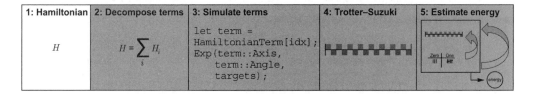

Figure 10.4 We are starting here by learning about Marie's H_2 molecule and which Hamiltonian describes its evolution.

Remember from chapter 9 that if a state $|\psi\rangle$ is an eigenstate of an operation op, then applying op to a register in the state $|\psi\rangle$ at most applies a global phase to $|\psi\rangle$. This phase is called the *eigenvalue* or *eigenphase* corresponding to that eigenstate. Like all other global phases, this eigenphase cannot be directly observed, but we can use the Controlled functor that we learned about in chapter 9 to turn that phase into a local phase.

Each eigenstate of a Hamiltonian is a state of constant energy; just like quantum operations don't do anything to eigenstates, a system that is in an eigenstate of its Hamiltonian will stay at that energy over time. The other property of eigenstates that we saw in chapter 9 still holds here as well: the phase of each eigenstate evolves in time.

The observation that the phases of eigenstates evolve in time is the content of Schrödinger's equation, one of the most important equations in all of quantum physics. Schrödinger's equation tells us that as a quantum system evolves, each eigenstate of a Hamiltonian accumulates a phase proportional to its energy. Using math, we can write Schrödinger's equation as shown in figure 10.5.

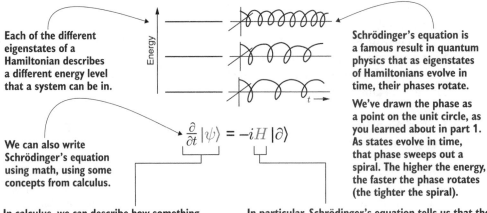

Each of the different eigenstates of a Hamiltonian describes a different energy level that a system can be in.

Schrödinger's equation is a famous result in quantum physics that as eigenstates of Hamiltonians evolve in time, their phases rotate.

We can also write Schrödinger's equation using math, using some concepts from calculus.

We've drawn the phase as a point on the unit circle, as you learned about in part 1. As states evolve in time, that phase sweeps out a spiral. The higher the energy, the faster the phase rotates (the tighter the spiral).

$$\frac{\partial}{\partial t}|\psi\rangle = -iH|\partial\rangle$$

In calculus, we can describe how something changes in time by using a *derivative*. Here, the Schrödinger equation uses a derivative to tell us about how the states of quantum systems change in time.

In particular, Schrödinger's equation tells us that the way a quantum state changes in time (its derivative) is given by the same matrix that describes the energy of each state: the Hamiltonian.

If we use calculus to solve Schrödinger's equation, we get the kind of picture shown here: the Hamiltonian H describes a rotation as states evolve in time. That connection means that learning how quickly each phase rotates in time tells us the energy of the corresponding state!

Figure 10.5   Schrödinger's equation, written out in mathematical notation

The real experts were the friends we made along the way

How can it be that this is chapter 10, and we're seeing the most important equation in quantum physics for the first time? Developing quantum applications may be closely connected to quantum physics, but it's not the same thing, and we don't need to be a physics expert to write quantum applications—we can be, if we're interested, but we don't have to be. Schrödinger's equation only enters the picture here because we need it to understand how quantum computers may be used for practical impact.

Just like our friend Marie is an expert in quantum chemistry and not quantum computing, we don't need to know everything to do something awesome. That's what friends are for!

TIP   Schrödinger's equation relates how phases of different states evolve in time to the energy of those states. Since global phases are unobservable, and since eigenstates of Hamiltonians only acquire global phases as they evolve, Schrödinger's equation tells us that eigenstates of Hamiltonians don't evolve in time.

Schrödinger's equation is most critical for us in this chapter because it relates the energy of a system to phase, a very helpful connection given that in chapter 9, we learned how to do phase estimation! There are other ways Schrödinger's equation is useful, one being another way to look at implementing operations on quantum systems.

One way to implement the rotations we've seen so far in the book is to set up the right Hamiltonian and then—wait. The time derivative $(\partial/\partial t)$ in Schrödinger's equation tells us that the way the state of our qubits rotate is entirely described by the energy associated with each state. For example, Schrödinger's equation tells us that if our Hamiltonian is $H = \omega Z$ for some number ω, if we want to rotate by an angle θ about the Z-axis, we can let our qubit evolve for time $t = \theta / \omega$.

Exercise 10.1: Rotations all around
Try writing other rotations shown earlier in the book (e.g., Rx and Ry) as Hamiltonians.

Exercise solutions
All solutions for exercises in this book can be found in the companion code repo: https://github.com/crazy4pi314/learn-qc-with-python-and-qsharp. Just go to the folder for the chapter you are in and open the Jupyter notebook with the name that mentions exercise solutions.

Listing 10.2 shows a simple Q# operation that simulates evolving under the Hamiltonian $H = \omega Z$.

> **NOTE** In practice, much of the challenge of building a quantum computer is ensuring that qubits *don't* evolve except as instructed by a quantum program. It wouldn't be very useful if walking away from our quantum device for a moment meant that all our qubits were in totally different states when we got back. This is part of why, as quantum developers, we tend to think at the level of instructions sent to a device—that is, quantum operations—and not directly in terms of Hamiltonians.

Switching gears for a moment and temporarily thinking in terms of Hamiltonians gives us a bit of what we need to start making progress on the problem Marie asked us to help with. After all, the problems Marie works with are much easier to describe in that language. For example, in chapter 9, we saw how we can learn about the phase applied by rotations like the one Dagonet hid from Lancelot. We can also express Dagonet's and Lancelot's game in terms of Hamiltonians, though. Suppose that Dagonet was hiding the rotation angle 2.1π; then, since his rotation was about the Z-axis, we could also describe that hidden rotation as a hidden Hamiltonian $H = -2.1\pi Z$.

> **NOTE** We need the – sign due to the – sign in Schrödinger's equation. Getting this wrong is about as common in quantum programming as off-by-one errors in other languages, so don't stress out if you forget once or twice, or if you forget that pesky minus sign almost every time. You're still doing great.

Using this kind of description, Lancelot's scale corresponds to how long he lets his qubits evolve under Dagonet's hidden Hamiltonian. While thinking in terms of a game makes it easier to write quantum programs to learn Dagonet's hidden rotation, thinking in terms of a Hamiltonian makes it easier to map to the kinds of physical concepts that Marie is concerned with, such as field strengths and time. The only tricky part is that we need to multiply the angle for Rz by 2.0, as Rz multiplies its angle by −1 / 2 by convention in Q#. Since Schrödinger's equation tells us that the angle needs a minus sign, the 2.0 gives us the angle we need to match figure 10.5.

Listing 10.2   Evolving under the Hamiltonian H = ωZ

Operation that simulates evolution under H = ωZ using Q#

ω says how large energies described the Hamiltonian are. This plays the role of Dagonet's hidden angle from chapter 9!

```
operation EvolveUnderZ(
    strength : Double,
    time : Double,
    target : Qubit
) : Unit is Adj + Ctl {
    Rz(2.0 * strength * time, target);
}
```

How long we want to simulate the Hamiltonian. This is analogous to Lancelot's scale from chapter 9.

The actual simulation is just one line, since rotations about the Z-axis are built into Q#.

Since Schrödinger's equation tells us that evolving Hamiltonians rotates quantum systems according to their energy, if we can *simulate* the Hamiltonian that Marie gives us, then we can play exactly the same phase estimation game as in chapter 9 to learn the energy levels of that Hamiltonian.

Deep dive: Hamiltonians are the one thing I can control

When we first introduced quantum operations like H, X, and Z, you may have wondered how we would implement them on a real quantum device. Using the concept of a Hamiltonian, we can revisit that question and explore how intrinsic quantum operations work on hardware.

When a magnetic field is applied to a physical system with a magnetic dipole (e.g., an electron spin), the Hamiltonian for that system includes a term that describes how the system interacts with the magnetic field. Typically, we write this as term as $H = \gamma B Z$, where B is the strength of that magnetic field and γ is a number that describes how strongly that system responds to magnetic fields. Thus, to apply an Rz rotation in quantum hardware that uses electron spins to implement qubits, we can turn on a magnetic field and just wait the right length of time. Similar effects can be used to implement other Hamiltonian terms or control the Hamiltonian for other quantum devices.

The same principle is used in other quantum technologies as well, such as nuclear magnetic resonance (NMR) imaging, where good classical algorithms have been developed to build effective Hamiltonians by *pulsing* magnetic fields at the right frequency or building complex shaped pulses to apply a quantum operation. Traditionally, in NMR and in quantum computing more generally, pulse-design algorithms are given whimsical acronyms as names, such as GRAPE, CRAB, D-MORPH, and even ACRONYM. Regardless of whimsy, though, these algorithms let us use classical computers to design quantum operations, given control Hamiltonians like $H = \gamma BZ$. If you're interested in learning more, the original GRAPE paper lays out a lot of the optimal control theory that has been used ever since.[a]

In practice, this isn't the complete story, of course. Not only is there a lot more to designing control pulses, but for fault-tolerant quantum computers, the intrinsic operations that we work with as quantum developers don't directly map to physical operations in the same way as on near-term hardware. Rather, these low-level hardware operations are used to build error-correcting codes such that a single intrinsic operation may decompose into many different pulses being applied across our device.

---

[a] Navin Khaneja et al., "Optimal Control of Coupled Spin Dynamics: Design of NMR Pulse Sequences by Gradient Ascent Algorithms," Journal of Magnetic Resonance 172, no. 2 (2005): 296, https://www.sciencedirect.com/science/article/abs/pii/S1090780704003696.

Suppose that instead of $H = \omega Z$, Marie asks if we can simulate $H = \omega X$. Fortunately, Q# provides rotations about the X-axis as well, so we can modify the call to Rz in listing 10.2 with a call to Rx. Unfortunately, not every Hamiltonian Marie is interested in is as simple as $H = \omega Z$ or $H = \omega X$, so let's look at what quantum development techniques we can use to simulate Hamiltonians that are a bit more difficult.

These aren't the Hamiltonians we are looking for

It is likely that when we start talking to Marie, she will also be working on describing Hamiltonians for her system in her simulation and modeling software. However, these are probably *fermionic Hamiltonians*, which are different from the kind we are using here to describe how quantum devices change in time. As part of the workflow for our collaboration with Marie, we likely need to use some tools like NWChem (https://nwchemgit.github.io) to convert between a Hamiltonian that describes how a chemical changes in time and how qubits change in time. It's out of scope for this book to look at these methods in detail, but there are great software tools that can help with this. Check out the Quantum Development Kit documentation for details if you're interested: https://docs.microsoft.com/azure/quantum/user-guide/libraries/chemistry/. This isn't a big deal for now, just a handy tip for when you are talking to your collaborators!

10.4 *Rotating around arbitrary axes with Pauli operations*

Moving up in complexity, perhaps Marie is interested in something that takes more than a single-qubit Hamiltonian to describe (figure 10.6). If she gives us a Hamiltonian like $H = \omega X \otimes X$, what can we do to simulate it? Fortunately, what we learned about rotations in part 1 of this book is still useful for that kind of two-qubit Hamiltonian, as we can think of it as describing another kind of rotation.

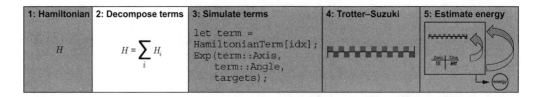

1: Hamiltonian	2: Decompose terms	3: Simulate terms	4: Trotter–Suzuki	5: Estimate energy
H	$H = \sum_i H_i$	```let term = HamiltonianTerm[idx]; Exp(term::Axis, term::Angle, targets);```		

Figure 10.6 In step 2, we look at how to decompose our Hamiltonian into generalized rotations that are easier to simulate.

NOTE In the previous section, we saw that rotations like Rx, Ry, and Rz correspond to Hamiltonians like *X*, *Y*, and *Z*, respectively. We can think of two-qubit Hamiltonians like $X \otimes X$ as specifying an axis in much the same way. It turns out there are 15 possible orthogonal rotation axes for a two-qubit register, as opposed to the 3 dimensions we get for a single-qubit register. So to draw something as a picture, we'd need 13 more dimensions than paper normally has, making it somewhat difficult to illustrate!

This rotation doesn't look like any of the built-in (that is, intrinsic) instructions we've seen so far, so it might seem like we're stuck. As it turns out, though, we can still simulate this Hamiltonian using *single*-qubit rotations like Rx, as long as we use some two-qubit operations on either side. In this section, we'll see how that works and how Q# makes it easy to automate applying multiple-qubit rotations.

By way of getting started, let's look at some of the ways we can change what quantum operations do by surrounding them with other operations. We can always use math to reason about things, as we saw in chapter 9, but fortunately Q# also provides some nice testing functions and operations that can help us. For example, in chapter 9, we saw that surrounding a CNOT operation with H operations gives us a CNOT going in the other direction. Let's see how we can check that using Q#!

TIP Recall that the within/apply block in listing 10.3 applies the shoes-and-socks principle that we first learned about in chapter 9. Most of the code examples in this section use within/apply blocks to help keep track of our shoes-and-socks thinking.

Listing 10.3 Changing the control and target of a CNOT

The operations and functions in the Microsoft.Quantum.Diagnostics namespace help with testing and debugging quantum programs and can be very useful to make sure programs work as intended.

To compare the two ways of writing a **CNOT** operation, we need each to be callable as an operation that takes an array of qubits representing a quantum register.

```
open Microsoft.Quantum.Diagnostics;

operation ApplyCNOT(register : Qubit[])
: Unit is Adj + Ctl {
    CNOT(register[0], register[1]);
}
```

```
operation ApplyCNOTTheOtherWay(register : Qubit[])
: Unit is Adj + Ctl {
    within {
        ApplyToEachCA(H, register);
    } apply {
        CNOT(register[1], register[0]);
    }
}
```

⟵ **To check the equivalence that we first saw in chapter 7, we can write a second operation that reverses the control and target of a CNOT operation.**

```
operation CheckThatThisWorks() : Unit {
    AssertOperationsEqualReferenced(2,
        ApplyCNOT, ApplyCNOTTheOtherWay);
    Message("Woohoo!");
}
```

The first input specifies how large a register each operation acts on, and the second and third inputs represent the operations being compared. If the operations do anything different whatsoever, the assertion fails and the quantum program ends.

⟵ **If we see the message "Woohoo!", we can safely conclude that the two operations cannot be distinguished from each other by looking at what they do to the states of quantum registers.**

NOTE Assertions like AssertOperationsEqualReferenced only make sense when run on a simulator, as running them requires violating the no-cloning theorem. On actual hardware, these kinds of assertions would be stripped out, just as running Python with the -O command-line argument disables the assert keyword. That means Q# assertions give us a way to cheat *safely*, since quantum programs using assertions do the same thing regardless of whether we cheat.

Exercise 10.2: Verifying CNOT identities

Use QuTiP to verify that the two operations ApplyCNOT and ApplyCNOTTheOtherWay can be simulated by the same unitary matrix and thus do the exact same thing.

Exercise 10.3: Three CNOTs make a SWAP

Just as we can use three classical XOR instructions to implement an in-place classical swap, we can use three CNOT operations to do the same thing as a single SWAP operation. The following Q# snippet does the same thing as SWAP(left, right):

```
CNOT(left, right);
CNOT(right, left);
CNOT(left, right);
```

Double-check that this is the same as SWAP(left, right) by using Assert-OperationsEqualReferenced and by using QuTiP.

Extra credit: SWAP(left, right) is the same as SWAP(right, left), so the previous snippet should work even if we start with CNOT(right, left) instead. Double-check that!

Deep dive: The Choi–Jamiłkowski isomorphism

The `AssertOperationsEqualReferenced` operation in listing 10.3 works using a neat piece of mathematics called the *Choi–Jamiłkowski isomorphism*, which says any operation that can be simulated using a unitary matrix is perfectly equivalent to a particular state called its *Choi state*. This means a simulator can effectively find the entire truth table for any adjointable operation (that is, any operation that has `is Adj` in its signature) by finding its Choi state. The `AssertOperationsEqualReferenced` operation uses this concept to prepare a register of qubits in the Choi state for each of the operations passed as inputs. On a simulator, it's easy to cheat and check whether two states are the same even though the no-cloning theorem tells us we can't do that on an actual device.

When writing unit tests and other checks that quantum programs are correct, this can be a powerful technique for making use of classical simulators while still preventing cheating on actual hardware.

When we run `CheckThatThisWorks` either in Jupyter Notebook (as we saw in chapter 7) or at the command line, we should see the message `"Woohoo!"` telling us that our Q# program ran past the call to `AssertOperationsEqualReferenced`. Since that assertion only passes if the two operations that we give it do exactly the same thing for all possible inputs, we know that the equivalence we learned about in chapter 7 works.

We can use the same logic to check how two-qubit operations like `CNOT` transform other operations. For example, transforming a call to `X` with calls to `CNOT` does the same thing as calling `X` multiple times, as demonstrated in the next listing.

Listing 10.4 Applying X on each qubit in a register

```
open Microsoft.Quantum.Diagnostics;
open Microsoft.Quantum.Arrays;

operation ApplyXUsingCNOTs(register : Qubit[])
: Unit is Adj + Ctl {
    within {
        ApplyToEachCA(

            CNOT(register[0], _),

            Rest(register)
        );
    } apply {
        X(register[0]);
    }
}

operation CheckThatThisWorks() : Unit {
    AssertOperationsEqualReferenced(2,
        ApplyXUsingCNOTs,
        ApplyToEachCA(X, _)
    );
}
```

Operation representing a single call to X with CNOTs, using a within/apply block

For the "socks" part of the within/apply block, we can write the CNOT calls we need by using ApplyToEachCA together with the partial application technique we learned in chapter 7.

This part of our call to ApplyToEachCA says to apply a CNOT operation controlled on the first qubit of a register to each element of an array of qubits.

Uses Rest to pick out all but the first (that is, the 0th) element of the register array

The "shoes" part of our within/apply block is a bit simpler: just an X operation on the same qubit we used as a control for our sequence of CNOT calls.

This time, instead of writing our own operation to compare to, we compare to an X operation on each qubit in a register by using partial application.

```
    Message("Woohoo!");
}
```

Exercise 10.4: Unitary equivalence

Using QuTiP, check that when run on two-qubit registers, the two programs in listing 10.4 can be simulated by the same unitary matrix and thus do the same thing to their input registers.

Exercise 10.5: Program equivalence

Try modifying listing 10.4 to see if both programs are equivalent when applied to more than two qubits.

Note: It can be pretty expensive to use `AssertOperationsEqualReferenced` for more than a few qubits.

We can also build up other interesting kinds of operations by using the within/apply concept. In particular, transforming a rotation with CNOT operations the same way as listing 10.4 lets us implement the kinds of multiple-qubit rotations that Marie asked for at the beginning of this section. Using the DumpMachine and DumpRegister features that we learned about in chapter 9, we can see that just as Rx applies an *X*-axis rotation between $|0\rangle$ and $|1\rangle$), we can implement a $(X \otimes X)$-axis rotation between $|00\rangle$ and $|11\rangle$.

Listing 10.5 Creating a a multi-qubit Rx operation

```
open Microsoft.Quantum.Diagnostics;
open Microsoft.Quantum.Math;

operation ApplyRotationAboutXX(
    angle : Double, register : Qubit[]
) : Unit is Adj + Ctl {
    within {
        CNOT(register[0], register[1]);
    } apply {
        Rx(angle, register[0]);
    }
}

operation DumpXXRotation() : Unit {
    let angle = PI() / 2.0;
    use register = Qubit[2];

    ApplyRotationAboutXX(angle, register);

    DumpMachine();
```

For simplicity, we've specialized to the two-qubit case in this listing, but we can use an ApplyToEachCA call the same way to work with registers of more than two qubits.

Instead of applying an X operation to the control qubit, we want to apply an X rotation about an arbitrary angle to the control qubit.

To check what our new ApplyRotationAboutXX operation does, we start by asking our target machine for a two-qubit register with a "using" statement.

We then apply our new rotation about the $(X \otimes X)$-axis to our new register to see what it does.

When run on a simulator, DumpMachine prints out the full state of the simulator, letting us check how our new rotation operation transformed the state of our register.

```
    ResetAll(register);
}
```

> As usual, before releasing our register back to the target machine, we need to reset all of our qubits back into the |0⟩ state.

Exercise 10.6: Predicting ApplyRotationAboutXX

Try preparing the register in states other than |00⟩ before calling `ApplyRotation-AboutXX`. Does the operation do what you expected?

Hint: Recall from part 1 of the book that we can prepare a copy of the |1⟩ state by applying an X operation and that we can prepare |+⟩ by applying an H operation.

Your output from listing 10.5 may look slightly different than figure 10.6, as the IQ# kernel for Jupyter Notebook supports multiple different ways to label qubit states.

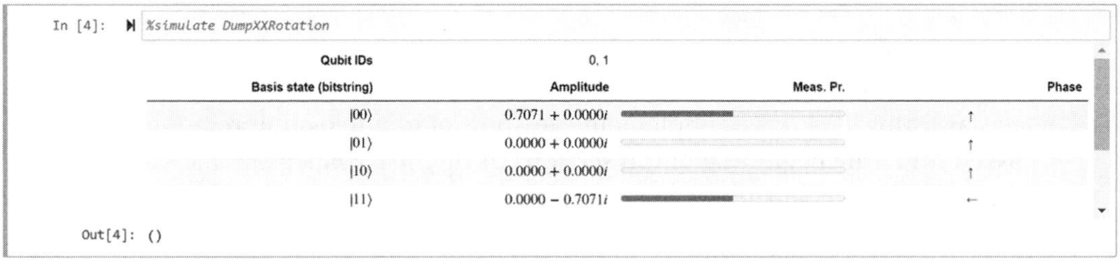

Figure 10.7 Output from running listing 10.5 in a Jupyter Notebook. We can see from the output of DumpMachine in DumpXXRotation, which shows our resulting state is a superposition between |00⟩ and |11⟩.

> **TIP** By default, IQ# uses the "little-endian" convention, useful for arithmetic problems like the ones we'll see in chapter 12. To label qubit states using bit strings like the ones we've seen so far in the book, run `%config dump.basis-StateLabelingConvention = "Bitstring"` from a new Jupyter Notebook cell.

Exercise 10.7: Rx v. rotation about $X \otimes X$

Try using `DumpMachine` to explore how the `Rx` operation acts on a single qubit, and compare to the two-qubit rotation about the $(X \otimes X)$-axis that we implemented in listing 10.5. How are the two rotation operations similar, and how do they differ? Compare rotating about the $(X \otimes X)$-axis with applying an `Rx` operation to each qubit in a two-qubit register.

In general, *any* rotation about an axis given by a tensor product of Pauli matrices (such as $X \otimes X$, $Y \otimes Z$ or $Z \otimes Z \otimes Z$) can be implemented by applying a single-qubit rotation transformed by a sequence of operations like CNOT and H. Finding what the right transformation is, however, can be a bit annoying, so Q# provides a nice built-in operation called Exp to help.

Listing 10.6 Using Exp to figure out how to transform state

```
open Microsoft.Quantum.Diagnostics;
open Microsoft.Quantum.Math;

operation ApplyRotationAboutXX(
    angle : Double, register : Qubit[]
) : Unit is Adj + Ctl {
    within {
        CNOT(register[0], register[1]);
    } apply {
        Rx(angle, register[0]);
    }
}

operation CheckThatThisWorks() : Unit {
    let angle = PI() / 3.0;
    AssertOperationsEqualReferenced(2,
        ApplyRotationAboutXX(angle, _),
        Exp([PauliX, PauliX], -angle / 2.0, _)
    );
    Message("Woohoo!");
}
```

> **WARNING** The conventions used by Exp and Rx to denote angles differ by a factor of $-1 / 2$. When using the Exp operation and single-qubit rotation operations in the same program, make sure to double-check all of your angles!

Using Exp, it's easy to simulate the Hamiltonian $H = \omega X \otimes X$ or any other Hamiltonian made up of tensor products of Pauli matrices (figure 10.8). As shown in the following listing, in Q#, we can specify $(X \otimes X)$ by the Q# value [PauliX, PauliX].

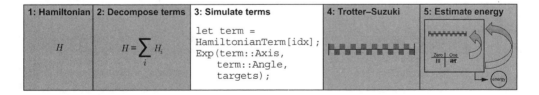

Figure 10.8 In step 3, we look at how to use the Exp operation to program the generalized rotations that represent the Hamiltonian we are trying to simulate.

Listing 10.7   Using `Exp` to simulate evolving under $X \otimes X$

Using what we've learned so far, we can write an operation to simulate evolving under a Hamiltonian proportional to $(X \otimes X)$, just as the operation we wrote in listing 10.2 simulated evolving under a Hamiltonian proportional to Z.

```
operation EvolveUnderXX(
```

Parameter representing the strength of the Hamiltonian: how large the energies described by our Hamiltonian are

```
    strength : Double,
```

Parameter that describes how long to simulate evolution (analogous to Lancelot's scale parameter from chapter 9)

```
    time : Double,
    target : Qubit
) : Unit is Adj + Ctl {
    Exp([PauliX, PauliX], strength * time,
        target);
}
```

Asks for a rotation about the $(X \otimes X)$-axis using the Exp operation provided by the Microsoft.Quantum.Intrinsic namespace

$Z \otimes Z$ is *not* just two Z rotations

It may be tempting to think that we can implement a two-qubit rotation about $Z \otimes Z$ by rotating the first qubit about Z and then rotating the second qubit about Z. These turn out to be very different operations, however:

$$R_z(\theta) \otimes R_z(\theta) = \begin{pmatrix} e^{-i\theta} & 0 & 0 & 0 \\ 0 & 1 & 0 & 0 \\ 0 & 0 & 1 & 0 \\ 0 & 0 & 0 & e^{i\theta} \end{pmatrix} \qquad R_{zz}(\theta) = \begin{pmatrix} e^{-i\theta/2} & 0 & 0 & 0 \\ 0 & e^{i\theta/2} & 0 & 0 \\ 0 & 0 & e^{i\theta/2} & 0 \\ 0 & 0 & 0 & e^{-i\theta/2} \end{pmatrix}$$

One way to think of it is that a rotation about $Z \otimes Z$ is only sensitive to the *parity* of each computational basis state, so $|00\rangle$ and $|11\rangle$ are each rotated by the same phase.

Now that we have the `Exp` operation at our disposal, it's pretty easy to use it to write an operation that simulates each term in the Hamiltonian that Marie gives us.

Listing 10.8   operations.qs: simulating the evolution of a single term

```
operation EvolveUnderHamiltonianTerm(
    idxBondLength : Int,
    idxTerm : Int,
    stepSize : Double,
    qubits : Qubit[])
: Unit is Adj + Ctl {
    let (pauliString, idxQubits) =
        H2Terms(idxTerm);
    let coeff =
```

Index to look up which of the Hamiltonians Marie gave us. Each corresponds to a different bond length.

Term of Marie's Hamiltonian under which we want to simulate evolution

How long to simulate evolution: that is, how long a simulation step to take

Gets the term from the Hamiltonian by using idxTerm together with the H2Terms function provided in the code repository for this book

```
        (H2Coeff(idxBondLength))[idxTerm];
    let op = Exp(pauliString,
        stepSize * coeff, _);
    (RestrictedToSubregisterCA(op, idxQubits))
        (qubits);
}
```

Gets the coefficient of that term by using the H2Coeff function, also provided in the samples repository for this book

Simulates evolution under that term using Exp to do a rotation scaled by the simulation step size, just like the EvolveUnderXX operation from listing 10.7 did

Since not all terms affect all qubits, we can use the RestrictedToSubregisterCA operation provided with Q# to apply our call to Exp to only a subset of the input.

In the next section, we'll see how to use this to simulate evolution under Marie's entire Hamiltonian.

10.5 *Making the change we want to see in the system*

Now that we have learned to describe how a quantum device can change in time using the concept of a Hamiltonian, a very natural question is, how do we implement the particular Hamiltonian we want to simulate? Most quantum devices have some operations that are easy for them to do. For instance, we saw in the previous section that it's straightforward to simulate evolution under any Hamiltonian that is given by a tensor product of Pauli matrices. That said, the Hamiltonian we (and Marie) are interested in is likely *not* a built-in operation but rather something that isn't directly available on our quantum computer.

> **TIP** Usually it easy for devices to implement some of the Pauli operators and maybe a few other operations. The game then becomes figuring out how to transform the operation we *want* into operations the device can easily do.

If there is no easy button to simulate evolution under our Hamiltonian, how can we implement a simulation of a particular Hamiltonian that we can apply to the qubits in our device?

Let's break it down. Literally. We learned all the way back in chapter 2 that we can describe a vector as a linear combination of *basis* vectors or directions. It turns out that we can do the same thing with matrices, and a really convenient basis to do so is the Pauli operators.

Pauli matrix refresher

If you need a refresher on what the Pauli matrices are, no worries, we've got you covered:

$$X = \begin{pmatrix} 0 & 1 \\ 1 & 0 \end{pmatrix} \qquad Y = \begin{pmatrix} 0 & -i \\ i & 0 \end{pmatrix} \qquad Z = \begin{pmatrix} 1 & 0 \\ 0 & -1 \end{pmatrix}$$

Just as we can describe any direction on a map with north and west, we can describe any matrix as a linear combination of Pauli matrices. For example,

$$\begin{pmatrix} 1 & 0 \\ 0 & 0 \end{pmatrix} = \frac{1}{2}\mathbb{1} + \frac{1}{2}Z.$$

Similarly,

$$\begin{pmatrix} 2 & 3 \\ 4 & 5 \end{pmatrix} = \frac{1}{2}\left(7\mathbb{1} + 7X - iY - 3Z\right).$$

The same holds for matrices acting on multiple qubits:

$$U_{\text{SWAP}} = \frac{1}{2}\left(\mathbb{1} \otimes \mathbb{1} + X \otimes X + Y \otimes Y + Z \otimes Z\right).$$

Exercise 10.8: Verifying identities

Use QuTiP to verify the previous equations.

Hint: You can use `qt.qeye(2)` to get a copy of 1, `qt.sigmax()` to get a copy of X, and so forth. To compute tensor products like $X \otimes X$, you can use `qt.tensor`.

This is good news because we can then write the Hamiltonian we want to simulate as a linear combination of Pauli matrices. In the previous section, we saw that we can use Exp to easily simulate Hamiltonians that are made up only of tensor products of Pauli matrices. This makes the Pauli basis very convenient, as it's likely the workflow from Marie's chemistry tools will already output the Hamiltonian for our quantum device in the Pauli basis.

Let's look at the representation of the Hamiltonian that Marie wants us to simulate, using the Pauli basis to expand it. Using her chemistry modeling skills, Marie can helpfully tell us that the Hamiltonian we need to simulate with our qubits is given by the equation below, where each of a, b_0, ..., and b_4 is a real number that depends on the bond length at which she wants to simulate H_2:

$$H = a\mathbb{1} \otimes \mathbb{1} + b_0 Z \otimes \mathbb{1} + b_1 \mathbb{1} \otimes Z + b_2 Z \otimes Z + b_3 Y \otimes Y + b_4 X \otimes X.$$

TIP All the terms and coefficients Marie is using are from the paper "Scalable Quantum Simulation of Molecular Energies."[1] The exact coefficients depend on the length of the bond between the hydrogen atoms, but all of these constants are helpfully typed in for you in the code repo for the book: https://github.com/crazy4pi314/learn-qc-with-python-and-qsharp.

With this representation of Marie's Hamiltonian in hand, it's time to figure out how to actually *use* it. There are six terms to this Hamiltonian, so which term should we apply first? Does the order matter? Unfortunately, the order in which the terms are used often does matter when simulating the evolution of a system under a Hamiltonian. In the next section, we'll learn about a method that allows us to break the evolution of the system into little steps to simulate evolution under all the terms at once.

10.6 Going through (very small) changes

At this point, it's helpful to take a step back and assess where we are in helping Marie. We've seen how to break arbitrary Hamiltonians into sums of Pauli matrices and how to use the Exp operation to simulate evolution under each term in that sum. To simulate arbitrary Hamiltonians, all that's left is to combine those simulations to simulate the entire Hamiltonian (figure 10.9). To do that, we can use one more quantum computing trick called the *Trotter–Suzuki decomposition*.

1: Hamiltonian	2: Decompose terms	3: Simulate terms	4: Trotter–Suzuki	5: Estimate energy
H	$H = \sum_i H_i$	`let term = HamiltonianTerm[idx]; Exp(term::Axis, term::Angle, targets);`		

Figure 10.9 **In this section, we explore how to use the *Trotter–Suzuki decomposition* to simulate the action of the total Hamiltonian by breaking it into much smaller evolutions of each term from step 3.**

Before getting into the details of the Trotter–Suzuki decomposition, though, let's go back to the map analogy that we've used throughout the book to break down linear algebra concepts (discussed in appendix C).

Suppose that we're exploring downtown Phoenix and decide to see what it feels like to go northeast throughout the city. If we start by going north several blocks and then go east several blocks, the route we trace on a map won't look much like a diagonal line. On the other hand, if we switch between going north and east each block, we'll trace out something much closer to a path that looks like it came out of the map of Minneapolis that appears in appendix C. That is, we can simulate the way we might walk through Minneapolis even if we're stuck in Phoenix by quickly switching which way we walk; see figure 10.10.

---

[1] P. J. J. O'Malley et al., "Scalable Quantum Simulation of Molecular Energies" (2015), https://arxiv.org/abs/1512.06860.

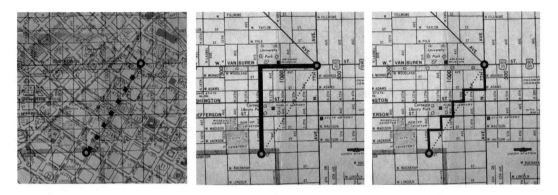

Figure 10.10 If we're in downtown Phoenix, we can still simulate how we might walk through downtown Minneapolis by rapidly alternating directions. Ideally, we would just travel diagonally to our destination, but given the street layout we can approximate the diagonal by making short zigzags. Photo by davecito.

In the previous section, we saw that just like states, the different terms in a Hamiltonian can be thought of as directions on a high-dimensional map. Tensor products of Pauli matrices, such as $Z \otimes \mathbb{1}$ and $X \otimes Z$, play a role similar to the cardinal directions or axes of a map. When we try to simulate Marie's Hamiltonian, though, that doesn't point along a single axis, but along a kind of diagonal in that higher-dimensional space. That's where the Trotter–Suzuki decomposition comes in.

Just as our path looks more diagonal when we quickly switch which direction we walk, we can rapidly switch between simulating different Hamiltonian terms. As illustrated in figure 10.11, the Trotter–Suzuki decomposition tells us that when we rapidly switch this way, we approximately evolve under the sum of the different terms that we're simulating.

Suppose that we have two quantum operations, A and B. Each of them simulates rotation under a different Hamiltonian term.

If we wanted to use them to simulate a combined Hamiltonian, it would be great if we could run both at the same time.

Sadly, we can only apply a single operation to a given set of qubits at a time. One solution might be to use A and then to use B.

However, it turns out to give us a much better approximation if we run A for a short time and then B for a short time, and keep alternating.

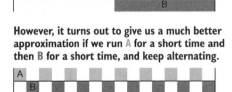

Figure 10.11 Using the Trotter–Suzuki decomposition to approximate evolving under two Hamiltonian terms at once. Just like the map analogy earlier, if we want to apply the effect of two Hamiltonians as quickly as possible, we should alternate evolving a little under each until we reach the full evolution.

We could in principle write this in Q# as a `for` loop. In pseudocode, we might have something like the following.

Listing 10.9   Simulating a Hamiltonian using Trotter–Suzuki

Since this is pseudocode, let's not worry about types for a moment.
This operation won't compile without types, but that's fine for now.

```
operation EvolveUnderHamiltonian(time, hamiltonian,
        ➥ register) {

    for idx in 0..nTimeSteps - 1 {        ◁——————

        for term in hamiltonian {          ◁——
            evolve under term for time / nTimeSteps
        }
    }
}
```

For each step into which we want to divide our simulation (think of city blocks in Phoenix or pixels on a screen), we need to do a bit of each Hamiltonian term.

Within each timestep, we can loop over every term we need to simulate, and simulate each for one step.

Fortunately, Q# provides a standard library function that does precisely this for us: `DecomposedIntoTimeStepsCA`. In listing 10.10, we show how calling `DecomposedIntoTimeStepsCA` makes it easy to use the Trotter–Suzuki decomposition to simulate evolution under Marie's Hamiltonian. The `DecomposedIntoTimeStepsCA` function supports higher-order Trotter–Suzuki decompositions than the first-order approximation we've explored so far in this chapter (represented by a `trotterOrder` of 1). In some cases, this feature can be useful to help increase the accuracy of our simulation, but a `trotterOrder` of 1 works fine for our purposes.

Listing 10.10   operations.qs: using `DecomposedIntoTimeStepsCA`

EvolveUnderHamiltonian applies the appropriate Hamiltonian based on the coefficients for the desired bond length of the H_2 molecule Marie asked us to help with.

```
operation EvolveUnderHamiltonian(
    idxBondLength : Int,
    trotterStepSize : Double,         ◁——
    qubits : Qubit[])
    : Unit is Adj + Ctl {
        let trotterOrder = 1;         ◁——
        let op = EvolveUnderHamiltonianTerm(
                idxBondLength, _, _, _);    ◁——
        (DecomposedIntoTimeStepsCA ((5, op), trotterOrder))
            (trotterStepSize, qubits);   ◁——
    }
```

Step size that represents how long we want to simulate Hamiltonian evolution

In some cases, a trotterOrder >1 can be useful to help increase the accuracy of our simulation, but a trotterOrder of 1 works fine for our purposes.

Partial application can fix the idxBondLength input to EvolveUnderHamiltonian-Term, leaving the idxTerm, stepSize, and qubits arguments blank.

This function outputs an operation that can be used to automatically simulate evolution under the entire Hamiltonian, using the operation that simulates each term one by one, so we can go on and apply it.

10.7   *Putting it all together*

Now that we have a better idea about what Hamiltonians are and how we can simulate evolution under them to understand how quantum systems change in time, we're ready to put together a program that will help Marie solve her question (figure 10.12). As a reminder, Marie is a chemist who studies the ground state energies (aka lowest possible energies) of different chemicals. She has asked us to help figure out the ground state energies for the H_2 molecule with our quantum device. Because the hydrogen atoms that make up H_2 molecules are also quantum systems, it is much easier to simulate the behavior of H_2 with qubits than a classical computer.

1: Hamiltonian	2: Decompose terms	3: Simulate terms	4: Trotter–Suzuki	5: Estimate energy

H	$H = \sum_i H_i$	`let term =`
		`HamiltonianTerm[idx];`
		`Exp(term::Axis,`
		`    term::Angle,`
		`    targets);`		

Figure 10.12   The last step to help Marie simulate her H_2 molecule is to use phase estimation to read the ground state energy.

TIP   Quantum computers are so well suited to simulating the behavior of other quantum systems that this was arguably the first application ever proposed for quantum computing!

Figure 10.13 is a reminder of all the steps and techniques we have learned in this chapter to simulate the evolution of Marie's H_2 molecule in our quantum device.

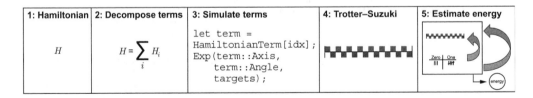

1: Hamiltonian	2: Decompose terms	3: Simulate terms	4: Trotter–Suzuki	5: Estimate energy

H	$H = \sum_i H_i$	`let term =`
		`HamiltonianTerm[idx];`
		`Exp(term::Axis,`
		`    term::Angle,`
		`    targets);`		

Figure 10.13   Overview of the steps developed in this chapter to help Marie learn her molecule's ground state energy

So, being quantum developers, we can collaborate with Marie to simulate the evolution of the H_2 molecule in time and calculate the ground state energy, thanks to Schrödinger's equation. The key point to remember is that the possible energy levels of the H_2 molecule correspond to the different *eigenstates* of the Hamiltonian.

Suppose that our qubits are in an eigenstate of the Hamiltonian. Then, simulating evolution under that Hamiltonian won't change the state of our qubit register, *except* to apply a global phase that is proportional to the energy of that state. That energy tells us exactly what we need to solve Marie's problem, but global phases are unobservable. Fortunately, in chapter 9, we learned from Lancelot's and Dagonet's game how to turn global phases into something we can learn with phase estimation—here is a great place to apply it! Summarizing, the steps to collaborate with Marie and solve her problem are as follows:

1. Prepare the initial state that Marie gives us. In this case, she helpfully tells us to prepare $|10\rangle$.
2. Break the Hamiltonian representing the system into little steps that can be simulated sequentially to represent the entire operation.
3. Apply each step representing the Hamiltonian to our initial state.
4. Use a phase-estimation algorithm to learn about the accumulated global phase on our quantum state, which will be proportional to the energy.

We have the skills and code from the previous sections in this chapter to pull this all together, so let's give it a go.

Starting with the Q# file (here called operations.qs to match what we've seen in previous chapters), we can open some namespaces to utilize premade functions and operations.

Listing 10.11   operations.qs: namespaces needed from the QDK

We have seen **Microsoft.Quantum.Intrinsic** and **Microsoft.Quantum.Canon** before; they have the basic utilities/helper functions and operations we need.

```
namespace HamiltonianSimulation {
    open Microsoft.Quantum.Intrinsic;
    open Microsoft.Quantum.Canon;
    open Microsoft.Quantum.Simulation;
    open Microsoft.Quantum.Characterization;
```

Microsoft.Quantum.Simulation is a namespace for the QDK that has, as we might expect, utilities for simulating systems.

Microsoft.Quantum.Characterization has easy-to-use implementations of the phase-estimation algorithms that we developed in chapter 9.

Next, we need to add the data Marie has about her molecule. All of this is typed out for you in the sample file in the GitHub repo for this book: https://github.com/crazy4pi314/learn-qc-with-python-and-qsharp/blob/master/ch10/operations.qs. The functions H2BondLengths, H2Coeff, and H2IdentityCoeff are what we need (they are kind of long to reproduce here in the text).

Once we have all the coefficient data from Marie in our file, we need the actual terms/structure for the Hamiltonian that we will use with those coefficients we just added. The following listing shows an outline of a function that returns terms of Marie's Hamiltonian expressed as Pauli operators, as well as an operation that will prepare our two-qubit register in the right state for this algorithm.

Listing 10.12   operations.qs: function that returns terms from the Hamiltonian

```
function H2Terms(idxHamiltonian : Int)
: (Pauli[], Int[]) {
    return [
        ([PauliZ], [0]),
        ([PauliZ], [1]),
        ([PauliZ, PauliZ], [0, 1]),
        ([PauliY, PauliY], [0, 1]),
        ([PauliX, PauliX], [0, 1])
    ][idxHamiltonian];
}

operation PrepareInitalState(q : Qubit[])
: Unit {
    X(q[0]);
}
```

The H2Terms function makes it easy to construct the terms of Marie's Hamiltonian.

This function is really just a hard-coded list of tuples that describe the Hamiltonian's terms. This first tuple says that the first term of the Hamiltonian is the PauliZ operation on the zeroth qubit.

Applies PauliZ to both the zeroth and the first qubit

We also need a way to prepare our qubits for the algorithm. Following Marie's advice, we put the first qubit in the $|1\rangle$ state, leaving the rest of the input qubits in the $|0\rangle$ state.

To take care of steps 2 and 3 of our quantum algorithm, we need the operations we defined earlier: EvolveUnderHamiltonianTerm and EvolveUnderHamiltonian.

Global phases and the Controlled functor

Just as we saw in chapter 9, applying EvolveUnderHamiltonian doesn't do anything to qubits prepared in an eigenstate of Marie's Hamiltonian—indeed, that's the whole point! In chapter 9, we were able to solve this by using the Controlled functor to turn the global phase resulting from applying Dagonet's operation on a qubit prepared in an eigenstate into a local phase that can be observed, and then using phase kickback to apply that phase to a control qubit. The EstimateEnergy operation provided by the Quantum Development Kit uses the exact same trick to learn what would otherwise be a global phase of our EvolveUnderHamiltonian operation. This means it's *critical* that our operation supports the Controlled functor by adding is Ctl to the signature for each operation that we pass to EstimateEnergy as part of helping Marie.

Finally, we can use the EstimateEnergy operation provided with the Quantum Development Kit to automate the application of the Trotter–Suzuki steps and the phase-estimation step. We can also use a built-in phase estimation operation that implements a better version of the phase-estimation algorithm we learned about in chapter 9. For example, the Microsoft.Quantum.Simulation library has an operation called EstimateEnergy that uses phase estimation to estimate an eigenstate's energy. It takes a specification for the number of qubits (nQubits), an operation to prepare our desired initial state (PrepareInitialState), how to apply our Hamiltonian (trotterStep), and what algorithm we want to use to estimate the phase resulting from applying our Hamiltonian. Let's check it out in action.

This is it! The operation EstimateH2Energy takes the index of the molecule bond length and returns the energy of its ground state or lowest energy state.

Defines that we need two qubits to simulate this system

```
operation EstimateH2Energy(idxBondLength : Int)
: Double {
    let nQubits = 2;
    let trotterStepSize = 1.0;
    let trotterStep = EvolveUnderHamiltonian(
        idxBondLength, trotterStepSize, _);
    let estPhase = EstimateEnergy(nQubits,
        PrepareInitalState, trotterStep,
        RobustPhaseEstimation(6, _, _));
    return estPhase / trotterStepSize
        + H2IdentityCoeff(idxBondLength);
}
```

Sets a scale parameter for the Trotter–Suzuki steps that apply the terms of our Hamiltonian to our qubits

Builds off of ApplyHamiltonian and gives a convenient name for the operation that applies the terms of our Hamiltonian with our parameters

We have built into the Microsoft.Quantum .Simulation library an operation that estimates the phase resulting from applying our Hamiltonian, which we know represents the energy of the system.

To make sure the units are right for the returned energy, we have to divide by the trotter step size and add the energy from the identity term in the Hamiltonian.

Now to actually run the algorithm! Since the ground state energy is a function of the molecule bond length, we can use a Python host to run the Q# algorithm and then plot the results as a function of the bond length.

Imports the Python package for Q# and then imports the Q# namespace (HamiltonianSimulation) from our operations.qs file. The qsharp Python package makes Q# namespaces available as regular import statements.

```
import qsharp
import HamiltonianSimulation as H2Simulation

bond_lengths = H2Simulation.H2BondLengths.simulate()

def estimate_energy(bond_index: float,
                    n_measurements_per_scale: int = 3
    ) -> float:
    print(f"Estimating energy for bond length of {bond_lengths[bond_index]} Å.")
    return min([H2Simulation.EstimateH2Energy.simulate(idxBondLength=bond_index)
               for _ in range(n_measurements_per_scale)])
```

To make things easier, pulls the list of bond lengths we can simulate for H2 from the Q# function H2BondLengths

The estimate_energy function is a Python wrapper for the EstimateH2Energy Q# operation but runs it a few times to make sure the energy estimate is minimized.

Why do we need to run EstimateH2Energy multiple times?

The state $|01\rangle$ that Marie gave us isn't actually an eigenstate of any H_2 Hamiltonian, but something she computed using a quantum chemistry approximation known as *Hartree–Fock theory*. Since quantum chemistry is her area of expertise, she can help by providing approximations like that.

In practice, this means when we run phase estimation using the tools provided by the `Microsoft.Quantum.Characterization` namespace, we aren't learning the energy of a particular eigenstate; instead, we're randomly projecting onto an eigenstate and learning its energy. Since our initial state is a pretty good approximation, most of the time, we'll project onto the lowest-energy state of Marie's Hamiltonian (that is, the ground state), but we can get unlucky and correctly learn the energy of the wrong eigenstate. Since we're looking for the smallest energy, running multiple times and taking the minimum makes it much more probable that we'll learn the energy we want.

With everything set up in the Python host, all that's left is to write and run the main function.

> **Listing 10.15   host.py: the main program for our simulation**

Running host.py as a script plots the estimated ground state energies from the quantum algorithm in Q#.

```
if __name__ == "__main__":
    import matplotlib.pyplot as plt

    print(f"Number of bond lengths: {len(bond_lengths)}.\n")
    energies = [estimate_energy(i) for i in range(len(bond_lengths))]
    plt.figure()
    plt.plot(bond_lengths, energies, 'o')
    plt.title('Energy levels of H₂ as a function of bond length')
    plt.xlabel('Bond length (Å)')
    plt.ylabel('Ground state energy (Hartree)')
    plt.show()
```

Directly generates the list of estimated energies for each H2 molecule bond length

Sets up the data and style for the plot

Calling plt.show() should pop up or return an image of the plot!

Figure 10.14 shows a sample of what running `python host.py` should output. This plot shows the results of our simulations for various Hamiltonians for different bond lengths of the H_2 molecule. We can see that the energy of the lowest state is much higher when the bond length is short and kind of levels off as the bonds get longer. The lowest energy possible should occur around a bond length of approximately 0.75 Å. If we look it up, the stable (that is, equilibrium) bond length for hydrogen is 0.74 Å! So yeah, it turns out Marie's molecule is pretty well known, but we can see how we could follow this process not only for other chemicals but also for simulating other quantum systems.

Congratulations: we have implemented our first practical application for a quantum computer! Of course, the actual chemical we used here is fairly simple, but this

When we run our Q# program from Python, we get a Matplotlib plot showing the results from simulating our Q# program on our classical computer.

Each dot represents an estimate of the ground state energy of H_2 at a different bond length.

Chemists tend to use a unit called *Hartrees* to describe the energy of different molecules.

For each bond length, measured in Angstroms (written Å, equal to tenths of a nanometer), Marie gives us a different Hamiltonian describing the energy levels of H_2 at that length.

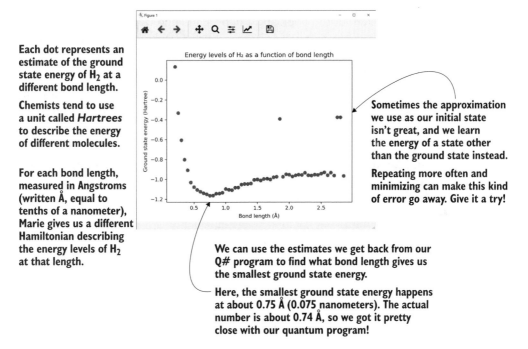

Sometimes the approximation we use as our initial state isn't great, and we learn the energy of a state other than the ground state instead.

Repeating more often and minimizing can make this kind of error go away. Give it a try!

We can use the estimates we get back from our Q# program to find what bond length gives us the smallest ground state energy.

Here, the smallest ground state energy happens at about 0.75 Å (0.075 nanometers). The actual number is about 0.74 Å, so we got it pretty close with our quantum program!

Figure 10.14 A sample of the plot that running host.py should produce. The exact data will likely vary, but in general we should see that the minimum ground state energy happens at about 0.75 Å on the horizontal axis, which is then the bond length with the lowest energy.

process holds for most other quantum systems we might want to simulate. In the next two chapters, we'll explore two other applications of quantum computers: unstructured searching with Grover's algorithm and factoring numbers with Shor's algorithm.

Summary

- One of the most exciting applications of quantum computing is to help us understand the properties of quantum mechanical systems such as chemical interactions.
- We can think about quantum mechanics in many different ways. Using Python and Q#, we've thought about quantum mechanics as a kind of computation, but chemists and physicists may think of quantum mechanics as a set of rules describing how physical systems interact and behave.
- Physicists and chemists use a special kind of matrix called a *Hamiltonian* to predict how quantum mechanical systems change in time. If we can simulate a

Hamiltonian on a quantum computer, then we can simulate physical systems described by those matrices.

- An important special case of a Hamiltonian is a tensor product of Pauli matrices. These Hamiltonians describe a kind of generalization of the rotations we've seen throughout the book and can be simulated using the Q# Exp operation.

- More complicated Hamiltonians can be broken down into sums of simpler Hamiltonians, allowing us to simulate each part of a Hamiltonian at a time.

- If we quickly alternate between the parts of a Hamiltonian we simulate, we can get a better approximation of simulating the full Hamiltonian. This is similar to how quickly alternating between walking north and west looks a bit like walking diagonally northwest when we zoom out.

- Using chemical models (such as we may get from chemist friends), we can write and simulate Hamiltonians for quantum chemistry. Combining this simulation with phase estimation lets us learn the energy structure for different chemicals, helping us predict their behavior.

Searching with quantum computers

In chapter 10, we got to dig into our first application of quantum computing by working with our colleague Marie to help calculate the ground state energy of a hydrogen molecule. To do so, we implemented a Hamiltonian simulation algorithm that used some of the phase-estimation techniques we developed in chapter 9.

In this chapter, we'll look at another application of quantum computing: searching data. This application area is always a hot topic in high-performance computing areas and shows off another way we can use techniques we learned previously to build up another quantum program, in this case based on phase kickback. We also look at the *resources estimator* built into the Quantum Development Kit (QDK) to see how it can help us understand the scaling of our quantum programs, even when they get too big to run locally.

11.1 Searching unstructured data

Suppose we want to search through some data to find a contact's phone number. If the list of contacts is sorted by name, then it's pretty easy to find the phone number associated with a particular name by using a *binary search*:

Algorithm 11.1: Pseudocode for binary search

1   Pick a name/phone number pair in the middle of our list. Call this pair our pivot.

2   If the pivot's name is the name we're looking for, return the pivot's phone number.

3   If the name we're looking for comes before the pivot's name, repeat the search on the first half of the list.

4   Else, if the name we're looking for comes after the pivot's name, repeat the search on the second half of the list.

Not just a character on Star Trek

In this chapter, we'll talk a lot about searching through data. That data can come in a lot of different forms:

- Phone numbers
- Names of dogs
- Weather measurements
- Types of doorbells

What all of these have in common is that we can represent them on classical computers as strings of bits, using a variety of different conventions about how that representation should work.

Searching this way can be done pretty quickly and is key to how we can search databases full of information. The problem is that in algorithm 11.1, we critically depend on our list of names and phone numbers being sorted. If it's not sorted, binary searching simply doesn't work.

> **NOTE**   Now that we have what we need to solve harder problems with quantum computers, this chapter's scenario is a bit more complicated than most of our earlier games and scenarios. Don't worry if things don't make sense off the bat: take your time and read more slowly. We promise it will be worth your while!

Put differently, to search our data quickly, we need to apply some kind of structure to the data: sorting the data or making some other kind of assumption that lets us avoid having to look at every single item. If we don't have any structure, the best thing we can do is to randomly look through the data until we find what we want. The steps listed in algorithm 11.2 show pseudocode for how we would search a list without structure. We might get lucky, but on average, random searching is only ever twice as fast as looking at every single item:

Algorithm 11.2: Pseudocode for searching unstructured lists

1 Pick a random element from our list.
2 If it's the right element, return it. Otherwise, pick a new element and repeat.

The fact that searching unstructured lists is hard is the basis of much of cryptography as well. In that case, rather than writing the list explicitly, our task in trying to break an encryption algorithm is to try different keys until one works. We can think of the decryption function as *implicitly* defining a list, where there's one special "marked item" that corresponds to the correct secret key.

The pseudocode in algorithm 11.3 could represent this decryption task. The random input we pick is the key, which we use with the decryption "function" or algorithm to see if it decrypts the message:

Algorithm 11.3: Pseudocode for searching unstructured inputs to a function

1 Pick a random input.
2 Call our function with that input. If it worked, return our input.
3 Otherwise, pick a new random input and repeat.

If we could search unstructured lists more quickly, that would let us sort through databases, solve mathematical problems, or—yes—even break some kinds of classical encryption.

Perhaps surprisingly, if the function that defines our list can be written out as a quantum operation (using what we learned about oracles in chapter 8), then we can use a quantum algorithm known as *Grover's algorithm* to find an input much faster than with algorithm 11.3.

> **TIP** We're getting toward the end of the book, meaning we have the opportunity to put together what we've learned throughout the book. In particular, in this chapter, we'll use what we learned about *oracles* from Nimue's and Merlin's game in chapter 8 to represent the input to Grover's algorithm. If you need a refresher on what oracles are, no worries; chapter 8 is there to help.

When we run Grover's algorithm, we're searching for one or more particular values of a function over all possible inputs to a function. If we want to search an unstructured list of data, we can consider defining a function that is responsible for looking up a particular entry in the list. We can then search through the inputs to this function to find the particular function output values we want.

Consider a scenario where we need to decrypt a message in 1 minute. There are 2.5 million different keys we need to try, but only one works to decrypt the message, and trying one key at a time will take too long. We can use Grover's algorithm and a function representing the problem, like "Does this cryptographic key decrypt a particular message?" to find the right key much more quickly and without having to test each key individually! This is a lot like the padlock example shown in figure 11.1, where we think of the different possible keys as inputs.

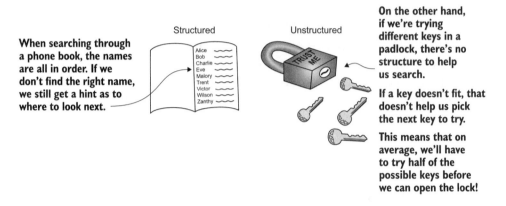

When searching through a phone book, the names are all in order. If we don't find the right name, we still get a hint as to where to look next.

Structured   Unstructured

Alice
Bob
Charlie
Eve
Malory
Trent
Victor
Wilson
Zanthy

On the other hand, if we're trying different keys in a padlock, there's no structure to help us search.

If a key doesn't fit, that doesn't help us pick the next key to try.

This means that on average, we'll have to try half of the possible keys before we can open the lock!

Figure 11.1   Structured and unstructured searches. If we are looking through an alphabetized address book, there is some structure to the data that we can exploit to find data more quickly. In the case of a box of random keys, we just have to keep trying random ones until the lock opens.

We'll make the function we need for Grover's algorithm to represent this problem more precise when we revisit oracles later in the chapter; but it's helpful to remember that when we search with Grover's algorithm, we're searching over *inputs to a function*, not a list of data. With that in mind, here is the pseudocode for Grover's algorithm:

Algorithm 11.4: Pseudocode for performing an unstructured search (Grover's algorithm)

1 Allocate a register of qubits large enough to represent all inputs to the function we are searching over.
2 Prepare the register in a uniform superposition state: i.e., all possible states have the same amplitude. This is because, due to the type of problem, we don't have any additional information about which input is the "correct" one, so this represents a uniform probability distribution (or *prior*) on the data.
3 Reflect the register about the marked state or the state we are searching for. Here, a *reflection* means picking a particular state and flipping the sign on it; we'll see more detail in the next section, as well as how to implement reflections in Q#.
4 Reflect the register about the initial state (uniform superposition).
5 Repeat steps 3 and 4 until the probability of measuring the item we are searching for is sufficiently high. Then measure the register. We can mathematically

work out the optimal number of times we need to do this so that we maximize the correct answer.

Figure 11.2 shows these steps.

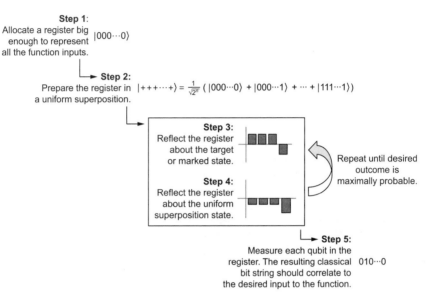

Step 1: Allocate a register big enough to represent all the function inputs. $|000\cdots0\rangle$

Step 2: Prepare the register in $|+++\cdots+\rangle = \frac{1}{\sqrt{2^n}}(|000\cdots0\rangle + |000\cdots1\rangle + \cdots + |111\cdots1\rangle)$ a uniform superposition.

Step 3: Reflect the register about the target or marked state.

Step 4: Reflect the register about the uniform superposition state.

Repeat until desired outcome is maximally probable.

Step 5: Measure each qubit in the register. The resulting classical bit string should correlate to the desired input to the function. $010\cdots0$

Figure 11.2 The steps to Grover's algorithm, which searches over inputs to a function, looking for a particular function output. We start by allocating a register of qubits large enough to represent all of the inputs we want to search over and then put it in a uniform superposition state. Finally, we can reflect the state of the register the right number of times to maximize the probability of measuring the answer we are looking for.

NOTE As we go through this chapter, we'll see that one way to think of Grover's algorithm is as a kind of rotation between the states representing whether we've found the right marked item: the decryption key for our scenario. If we apply steps 3 and 4 of Grover's algorithm too many times, we'll rotate right past the state we're looking for, so choosing the number of iterations is an integral part of the algorithm!

Figure 11.3 shows an example of how the cost of classically searching an unstructured list might compare to using Grover's algorithm.

TIP One way to describe what's shown in figure 11.3 is to use a concept called *asymptotic complexity*. In particular, we say that a classical unstructured search requires $O(N)$ function calls to search through N inputs, while Grover's algorithm requires $O(\sqrt{N})$ calls. Don't worry if this isn't familiar; but if you're curious about how to understand algorithms this way, check out chapter 1 of *Grokking Algorithms* by Aditya Y. Bhargava (Manning, 2016).

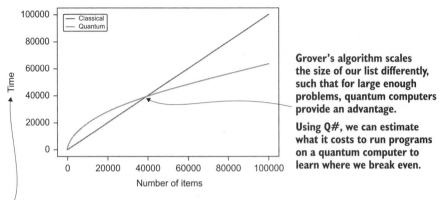

Grover's algorithm scales the size of our list differently, such that for large enough problems, quantum computers provide an advantage.

Using Q#, we can estimate what it costs to run programs on a quantum computer to learn where we break even.

We can measure the amount of time it takes to search a list by how many steps we need to run in our search.

Here, we've used as an example that a quantum computer runs each step 200× as slow as classical computers run corresponding steps.

Figure 11.3   An example of how the time taken to search unstructured lists might scale for classical and quantum computers. We can see that for smaller numbers of items, the quantum approach takes more time; but as we increase the number of items in the search, the quantum approach to search takes less time.

As before, let's jump in and see what that code looks like. Listing 11.1 is an example of a Q# operation that uses Grover's algorithm to search an unstructured list for a marked item. Here, rather than 2.5 million keys, we will reduce the scope to 8 keys, with the marked item or correct key indicated by an integer in the range 0 to 7. Yes, that means we might be able to solve this just as fast on a classical computer. However, at the end of the chapter, we will see how, as the number of keys we need to search through grows, the number of steps or computations required to find the correct key is much lower when using Grover's algorithm. Also, for our sample code here, the function representing the decryption algorithm doesn't really do any decrypting; it just acts like it is playing a guessing game and returns a Boolean if it is given the right key. Implementing a particular decryption algorithm for this chapter is out of scope and would likely need a bit of research to pull off. The goal here is to show how using Grover's algorithm to search through the inputs to a function can speed up particular problems.

Listing 11.1   operations.qs: Q# code that runs Grover's search

```
operation RunGroverSearch(nItems : Int, idxMarkedItem : Int) : Unit {
    let markItem = ApplyOracle(
        idxMarkedItem, _, _);
    let foundItem = SearchForMarkedItem(
```

We can use partial application to include the index of the marked item in the oracle that we provide to the search algorithm.

```
                nItems, markItem);        ◄──────    Runs Grover's search
    Message(                                         algorithm on a register of
        $"Marked {idxMarkedItem} and found           three qubits and provides
  ➥  {foundItem}.");       ◄────                     the oracle markItem that
}                                 Issues a message to   we defined earlier
                                  verify that it found
                                  the right item
```

If we run the sample in listing 11.1, we should get the following output:

```
In [1]: %simulate RunGroverSearch nItems=7 idxMarkedItem=6
Out[1]: Marked 6 and found 6
```

We can see from running the sample of Grover's algorithm that the decryption key we were looking for was the one indexed or marked by the number 6, and the algorithm found the key as number 6 as well. Now, since the `SearchForMarkedItem` operation is really the meat of this example, let's look at its implementation.

Listing 11.2   operations.qs: writing Grover's as a Q# operation

The next input is a representation of our search problem. We can implicitly define our search problem by an oracle that marks whether an item in our list is the right one.

As usual, we start by defining a new operation, using the "operation" keyword.

The first input our operation needs is the number of items in our list.

When we're done with our search, we'll have an index for where the marked item was. Defining our output as an Int lets us return that index.

```
operation SearchForMarkedItem(       ◄──
    nItems : Int,                      ◄──
    markItem : ((Qubit[], Qubit) => Unit is Adj)
) : Int {                                         ◄──
    use qubits = Qubit[BitSizeI(nItems)];    ◄──
    PrepareInitialState(qubits);

    for idxIteration in
            0..NIterations(BitSizeI(nItems)) - 1 {
        ReflectAboutMarkedState(markItem, qubits);
        ReflectAboutInitialState(PrepareInitialState, qubits);
    }

    return MeasureInteger(LittleEndian(qubits));    ◄──
}
```

To start the search, we need to allocate a big enough register to store an index into our list.

The heart of Grover's algorithm comes down to repeatedly reflecting about our start state and the index of the item we're looking for.

Once we're done, measuring our qubit register tells us the index of the item that Grover's algorithm found.

Since we're starting a search on an unstructured list, all items are equally good places to look. We represent this by preparing a uniform superposition over all indices into our list.

The Q# standard library provides a useful operation, `MeasureInteger`, that interprets measurement results as a classical integer. To use `MeasureInteger` as in listing 11.2, we can mark our register as encoding an integer in a little-endian register by using the `Microsoft.Quantum.Arithmetic.LittleEndian` user-defined type.

USER-DEFINED TYPES   If you need a reminder about what user-defined types (UDTs) are and how to use them, check out chapter 9, where we used them to help Lancelot and Dagonet play their angle-guessing game.

By this point in the book, we have almost all the quantum concepts we need to make sense of listing 11.2. In the rest of this chapter, we'll see how to use what we've learned to implement an example oracle that can define a simple search problem and how to implement the two reflections that make up Grover's algorithm to solve that problem.

> **My good fellow—I have a quarrel with your query!**
>
> It may seem a little contrived to use an operation like `ReflectAboutMarkedState` as the oracle to define the query for Grover's algorithm. After all, since the marked item's index is baked in as an input to `ReflectAboutMarkedState`, it may seem as though we're cheating rather badly with this example. That said, `SearchForMarked-Item` only sees our oracle as an opaque box and does not see its inputs, such that baking in the input this way doesn't let us cheat after all.
>
> Using a simple oracle like this helps us focus on how Grover's algorithm works without having to understand a more complicated oracle. In practice, however, we want to use a more sophisticated oracle that represents a more difficult search problem. To search some data represented as a list of items, for example, we could use a technique called *quantum RAM* (qRAM) to turn our list into an oracle. The details of qRAM are beyond the scope of this book, but there are some great resources online about qRAM and how expensive it may be to use in a particular application. Check out https://github.com/qsharp-community/qram for an excellent primer on qRAM and a Q# library you can get started with.
>
> Another area where Grover's algorithm is used a lot is in symmetric key encryption (as contrasted with a public key, which we'll cover in chapter 12). For example, https://github.com/microsoft/grover-blocks provides implementations of oracles representing key parts of the AES and LowMC ciphers so that those ciphers can be understood using Grover's algorithm.

11.2 *Reflecting about states*

In algorithm 11.4 and listing 11.2, we used two operations repeatedly in the `for` loop: `ReflectAboutInitialState` and `ReflectAboutMarkedState`. Let's dig into how these operations help search the input of the function representing our decryption scenario.

Each of these operations is an example of a reflection about a particular state. This is an example of a new kind of quantum operation, but we can still simulate it with a unitary matrix as before. The term *reflecting about a state* means when we have a register of qubits, we pick a particular state it could be in, and if it happens to be in that state, we flip the sign on the state (change the phase of that state). If you think this sounds like some of the controlled operations we looked at before, you are correct; we will use controlled operations to implement these reflections.

11.2.1 *Reflection about the all-ones state*

Let's start by looking at a particularly useful example: a reflection about the all-ones state, $|11\cdots1\rangle$. We can implement this reflection using the CZ (controlled-Z) operation we first saw in chapter 9.

> **TIP** Remember that the Controlled functor isn't just a fancy if block, but rather can be used in superposition. For a review of how the Controlled functor works, check out chapter 9, where we used it to help Lancelot and Dagonet play their game.

Listing 11.3 operations.qs: reflecting about the $|11\cdots1\rangle$ state

```
operation ReflectAboutAllOnes(register : Qubit[]) : Unit is Adj + Ctl {
    Controlled Z(Most(register),
        Tail(register));          ⟵  The Controlled functor allows us to use
}                                      the Z operation in a controlled fashion.
```

Like other Controlled operations, Controlled Z takes two inputs: the register that should be used as control qubits and the qubit the Z operation will be applied to if all the qubits in the control register are in the $|1\rangle$ state. In listing 11.3, we can use the Most function from Microsoft.Quantum.Arrays to get all but the last qubit and Tail to get only the last qubit.

> **TIP** By using CZ together with Most and a Tail, our implementation works no matter how many qubits are in our register. This will be useful later, as we might need different numbers of qubits to represent the data in our list.

Recall from chapter 9 that the CZ operation applies a phase of -1 to the $|11\cdots1\rangle$ state and does nothing to every other computational basis state. Thinking back to chapter 2, where each computational basis state is a kind of direction, that means a single direction is flipped by CZ, while all other input states are left alone. That kind of picture is why we call operations that behave in this way *reflections*, although an actual graphical representation is tricky due to the number of dimensions that can be involved.

Matrix representations of CZ

One way to see that the CZ operation flips the sign of a single input state, as described previously, is to write a unitary matrix that simulates CZ. Here is an example with a single control qubit:

$$U_{\text{CZ}} = \begin{pmatrix} 1 & 0 & 0 & 0 \\ 0 & 1 & 0 & 0 \\ 0 & 0 & 1 & 0 \\ 0 & 0 & 0 & -1 \end{pmatrix}$$

(continued)

And here is an example for two control qubits:

$$U_{\mathrm{CCZ}} = \begin{pmatrix} 1 & 0 & 0 & 0 & 0 & 0 & 0 & 0 \\ 0 & 1 & 0 & 0 & 0 & 0 & 0 & 0 \\ 0 & 0 & 1 & 0 & 0 & 0 & 0 & 0 \\ 0 & 0 & 0 & 1 & 0 & 0 & 0 & 0 \\ 0 & 0 & 0 & 0 & 1 & 0 & 0 & 0 \\ 0 & 0 & 0 & 0 & 0 & 1 & 0 & 0 \\ 0 & 0 & 0 & 0 & 0 & 0 & 1 & 0 \\ 0 & 0 & 0 & 0 & 0 & 0 & 0 & -1 \end{pmatrix}$$

Using what we've learned about unitary matrices throughout the book, these matrices make it clear that the input states $|11\rangle$ and $|111\rangle$, respectively, are flipped by -1, while all other input states are left alone (get a phase of $+1$). The same pattern continues no matter how many control qubits we use with CZ.

Exercise 11.1: Diagnostics on CZ

Use `DumpMachine` to see how CZ acts on the uniform superposition state $|+\cdots\rangle$.

Hint: Recall that $|+\rangle = H|0\rangle$, so we can use the program `ApplyToEachCA(H, register)` to prepare $|+\cdots+\rangle$ on a register that starts in the $|00\cdots0\rangle$ state.

Exercise solutions

All solutions for exercises in this book can be found in the companion code repo: https://github.com/crazy4pi314/learn-qc-with-python-and-qsharp. Just go to the folder for the chapter we are in and open the Jupyter notebook with the name that mentions exercise solutions.

11.2.2 *Reflection about an arbitrary state*

Once we have a reflection about $|11\cdots1\rangle$ under our belt, we can use it to reflect about other states as well. This is important as we probably cannot set up our oracle function representing the decryption algorithm so that the input or key we want is represented by the all-ones input. Also recall from our sample code that the oracle only implements a guessing-game sort of decryption, not a real decryption algorithm.

Deep dive: Reflections are rotations?

Given our geometrical understanding of reflections, it would be natural to think of them as a kind of rotation by 180° degrees. That turns out to be true only because quantum states are vectors of complex numbers; if we only had access to real numbers, we wouldn't be able to get a reflection by using rotations! We can see this by thinking back to how we described states and rotations in chapters 2 and 3: as rotations of a 2D circle.

If we pick up a two-dimensional object, flip it over, and put it back down, there's no way to transform it back to the way it was without picking it back up. On the other hand, three-dimensional space gives us enough extra room to combine different rotations to make a reflection. Since complex numbers give us a third axis when describing the states of qubits (namely, the *Y*-axis), that's also what lets us do the reflections we need in Grover's algorithm.

The trick to reflecting about states other than all-ones is to turn whatever state we want to reflect about into the all-ones state, call `ReflectAboutAllOnes`, and then undo the operation we used to map our reflection onto the all-ones state. We can describe any state by starting from the all-zeros state, so we need a way to go from the all-zeros state to the all-ones state where we can use the reflection we just learned. The following listing shows an example of preparing a register in the all-ones state from the all-zeros state.

Listing 11.4 **operations.qs: preparing the all-ones state**

```
operation PrepareAllOnes(register : Qubit[]) : Unit is Adj + Ctl {
    ApplyToEachCA(X, register);
}
```

The ApplyToEachCA operation allows us to apply the first input (an operation) to each qubit in a register (the second input).

In Q#, all freshly allocated registers start in the $|00\cdots0\rangle$ state. Thus, in listing 11.4, when we apply X to each newly allocated qubit, that prepares our new register it the $|11\cdots1\rangle$ state.

For the next step, we need to consider the operation that prepares the state we want to reflect around. If we have an adjointable operation (`is Adj`) that prepares a particular state that we want to reflect about, then all we have to do is *unprepare* the state, prepare the all-ones state, reflect about the all-ones state ($|11\cdots1\rangle$), unprepare the all-ones state, and then *re-prepare* the state we are trying to reflect about.

Why we love Dirac notation

In understanding the steps in algorithm 11.5, it is helpful to think of what each operation in that sequence of steps does to its input state. Fortunately, Dirac notation (first encountered way back in chapter 2) can help write how unitary matrices transform different states so that we can understand and predict what the corresponding Q# operations will do to our qubits.

For example, consider the Hadamard operation H. As we've seen throughout the book, H can be simulated by the following unitary matrix:

(continued)

$$H = \frac{1}{\sqrt{2}} \begin{pmatrix} 1 & 1 \\ 1 & -1 \end{pmatrix}$$

This unitary matrix acts as a kind of truth table, telling us that H transforms the $|0\rangle$ state into the $1 / \sqrt{2} \, (|0\rangle + |1\rangle)$ state. Using Dirac notation, we can make this clearer by writing $H = |+\rangle\langle 0| + |-\rangle\langle 1|$. By thinking of kets ($|\cdot\rangle$) as denoting inputs and bras ($\langle\cdot|$), we can read this as saying "The H operation transforms $|0\rangle$ into $|+\rangle$ and $|1\rangle$."

This figure shows how Dirac notation acts as a sort of visual language that tells us about the inputs and outputs for different unitary matrices, making it easier to understand how sequences of Q# operations work together.

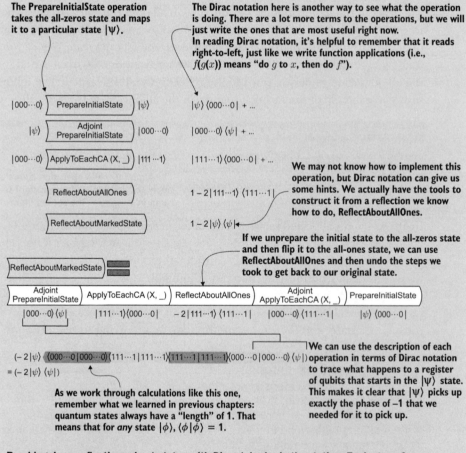

Breaking down reflections about states with Dirac (aka braket) notation. Each step of `ReflectAboutMarkedState` is split up, and we show the Dirac notation for that operation. When all the individual steps are connected, the resulting state is $-2|\psi\rangle\langle\psi|$.

Algorithm 11.5: How to reflect about an arbitrary state

- Using the `Adjoint` functor, "un-prepare" our arbitrary state, mapping it to the all-zeros $|00\cdots0\rangle$ state.
- Prepare the all-ones state $|11\cdots1\rangle$ from the all-zeros state.
- Use `CZ` to reflect about $|11\cdots1\rangle$.
- Un-prepare the all-ones state, mapping it back to the all-zeros state.
- Prepare our state again, mapping the all-zeros state to our arbitrary state.

TIP In algorithm 11.5, steps 1 and 5 cancel adjoints of each other, as do steps 2 and 4. Using what we've learned about "shoes-and-socks" thinking, this makes the procedure of algorithm 11.5 ideal for implementing the `within/apply` feature of Q#! For a reminder of how this feature works, check out chapter 8, where we used `within/apply` blocks to implement the Deutsch–Jozsa algorithm for Nimue and Merlin.

Since we don't have any prior notion about what the right input to our oracle is when we run Grover's algorithm, we want to start our search from the uniform superposition $|+\cdots\rangle$ to represent that any input could be the right one. This gives us a chance to use what we learned from algorithm 11.5 to practice implementing reflections in Q#! Following the steps to reflect the initial state, we can implement the `ReflectAbout-InitialState` operation used in listing 11.2. The following listing shows how we can follow algorithm 11.5 in a Q# operation.

Listing 11.5 operations.qs: reflecting about an arbitrary state

The uniform superposition state represents that we have no prior information for our search (after all, it is an unstructured search problem).

```
operation PrepareInitialState(register : Qubit[]) : Unit is Adj + Ctl {
    ApplyToEachCA(H, register);
}

operation ReflectAboutInitialState(
    prepareInitialState : (Qubit[] => Unit is Adj),
    register : Qubit[])
: Unit {
    within {
        Adjoint prepareInitialState(register);
        PrepareAllOnes(register);
    } apply {
        ReflectAboutAllOnes(register);
    }
}
```

Following algorithm 11.5, to reflect about the initial state, we need to provide an operation that prepares it.

Of course, we also need a register of qubits to apply our reflection to!

Performs steps 1 and 2 from algorithm 11.5

The Adjoint functor indicates that we want to do the "reverse" or opposite of the operation that prepares the initial state. In other words, if we started with the initial state, applying the Adjoint prepareInitialState operation would take us back to the $|00\cdots0\rangle$ state.

We now have the code to reflect about that initial state, so how can we check to see if it does what we expect? When running the simulator target machine, we can use commands like `DumpRegister` to show all the information it uses to simulate our register of qubits. Figure 11.4 shows the output of `DumpRegister` after preparing a uniform superposition.

Preparing initial states

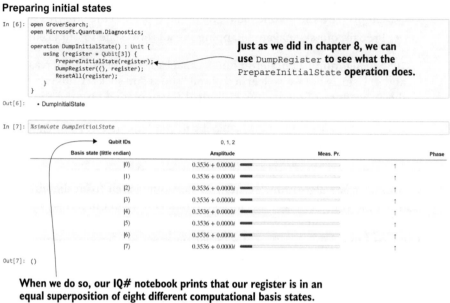

When we do so, our IQ# notebook prints that our register is in an equal superposition of eight different computational basis states.

By default, these basis states are labeled as little-endian, so the dump shows us each basis state as an integer, rather than a bit string.

For example, $|6\rangle$ in little-endian is $|011\rangle$ when written as a bit string.

Figure 11.4   Using `DumpRegister` to view the initial state prepared by our `PrepareInitialState` operation. Each possible basis state has the same amplitude (and so the same measurement probability), which is known as a uniform superposition.

For reflecting about the marked state, the other reflection we need for Grover's algorithm, we must use a slightly different approach. After all, we don't know how to prepare the marked state—that's the problem we're using Grover's algorithm to solve! Fortunately, thinking back to chapter 8, we can use what we learned from Nimue's and Merlin's game to implement a reflection about a state *even when we don't know what that state is.*

NOTE   This is the crux of Grover's algorithm: we can use our oracle to reflect about the marked state by calling it once with the right superposition of inputs. As we see in the next section, each of these reflections gives us some information about the marked item. In contrast, each classical function call can eliminate at most one possible input.

To see how that works in this case, let's first take a step back and look at what our marked state is. Since our list is defined by an oracle, we can write a unitary operator O that lets us simulate that oracle. Here is the Dirac notation:

$$O\,|x\rangle \otimes |y\rangle = |x\rangle \otimes \begin{cases} |\neg y\rangle & x \text{ is the marked item} \\ |y\rangle & \text{otherwise} \end{cases}.$$

In chapter 8, we saw that applying an X operation to a qubit in $|-\rangle$ applied a phase of -1, since $|-\rangle$ is an eigenstate of the X operation. Using the same trick here, we can write what our oracle does when the flag qubit (the $|y\rangle$ register) is in the $|-\rangle$ state:

$$O\,|x\rangle \otimes |-\rangle = \begin{cases} -\,|x\rangle\,|-\rangle & x \text{ is the marked item} \\ |x\rangle\,|-\rangle & \text{otherwise} \end{cases}$$

This is precisely the operation we need to implement the reflection! Thus, following what we learned in chapter 8, we can implement it the same way: simply apply our oracle to a qubit that starts in the $|-\rangle$ state. This oracle then represents the decryption algorithm for the scenario, here simplified to a function that takes possible keys as input and just returns a bool indicating whether it is the correct key. The next listing shows an example Q# operation that uses this approach; recall that in Q#, we can pass an operation as an input to another function or operation.

Listing 11.6 operations.qs: reflecting about a marked state

The operation for our item-marking oracle has type ((Qubit[], Qubit) => Unit is Adj), indicating that it takes a register of qubits plus one additional qubit and is adjointable.

The second input to reflect about the marked state is a register to which we want to apply our reflection.

We need to allocate one additional qubit (called a flag) to apply our oracle, which corresponds to the y register in earlier equations.

In the same way that we used the H and X operations in chapter 8 to prepare Nimue's qubit in the $|-\rangle$ state, we use that $|-\rangle = HX|0\rangle$ here to prepare our flag qubit.

We apply our oracle to use the Deutsch–Jozsa trick and apply a phase of -1 to the state marked by our oracle.

```
operation ReflectAboutMarkedState(
    markedItemOracle :
        ((Qubit[], Qubit) => Unit is Adj),
    inputQubits : Qubit[])
: Unit is Adj {
    use flag = Qubit();
    within {
        X(flag);
        H(flag);
    } apply{
        markedItemOracle(inputQubits,
            flag);
    }
}
```

In listing 11.6, since this preparation is in a within/apply block, Q# automatically puts our qubit back into the $|0\rangle$ state for us by undoing the X and H operations. After all, as we saw in chapter 8, applying our oracle leaves its target in the $|-\rangle$ state.

> ### Exercise 11.2: Flag preparation
> In listing 11.6, we can also write `H(flag); Z(flag);`. Using either or both of QuTiP and `AssertOperationsEqualReferenced` proves that these two ways of preparing our flag qubit give us the same reflection.

What's amazing is that we used the Deutsch–Jozsa trick to reflect about a state that was *implicitly* defined by our oracle! We didn't have to explicitly know what the marked state was to apply the reflection: perfect for use in an unstructured search.

In the next section, we see how to combine the initial and marked state reflections to bring everything together, fully implement Grover's algorithm, and find our key.

11.3   *Implementing Grover's search algorithm*

Now that we have learned about rotating about states and revisited oracles, it's time to put it all together to do some unstructured searching! Let's start by reviewing all the steps to implement Grover's algorithm (figure 11.5):

1 Allocate a register of qubits large enough to index the data set we are searching over.

2 Prepare the register in a uniform superposition state: i.e., all possible states have the same amplitude. This is because due to the type of problem, we don't have any additional information about the data set, so this represents a uniform probability distribution (or prior) on the data.

3 Reflect the register about the marked state or the state we are searching for.

4 Reflect the register about the initial state (uniform superposition).

5 Repeat steps 3 and 4 until the probability of measuring the item we are searching for is sufficiently high. Then measure the register. We can mathematically work out the optimal number of times we need to do this to maximize the probability of getting back the marked item.

> ### As close as you can without going over
> If we apply too many iterations of Grover's algorithm, the amplitude of the state we want to measure decreases. This is because each iteration is effectively a rotation; the trick is to stop that rotation at the right point. To work out the trigonometry for the stopping criteria, we write the state of the register used in Grover's algorithm as a superposition of the unmarked and marked states. We won't cover the details of this derivation here, but check out https://docs.microsoft.com/quantum/libraries/standard/algorithms or section 6.1.3 of *Quantum Computation and Quantum Information* by Michael A. Nielsen and Isaac L. Chuang (Cambridge University Press, 2010) if you're interested in learning more about the math behind the scenes. It is implemented for you in the samples repo for this book, but the formula is below if you want to try to program it in Q# yourself:
>
> $$N_{\text{iterations}} = \text{round}\left(\frac{\pi}{4\arcsin(\frac{1}{\sqrt{2^n}})} - \frac{1}{2} \right)$$

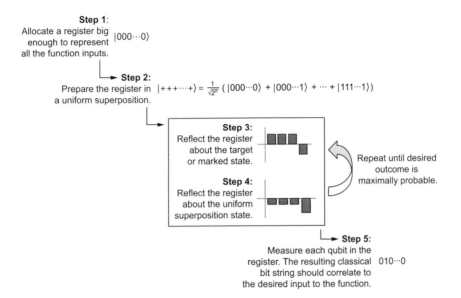

Figure 11.5 Recall the Grover's algorithm steps that search over inputs to a function, looking for a particular function output. We start by allocating a register of qubits large enough to represent all of the inputs we want to search over and then put it in a uniform superposition state. Finally, we can reflect the state of the register the right number of times to maximize the probability of measuring the answer we are looking for.

In the previous section, we developed some of the operations we need for the full implementation. For example, we have implemented step 2 with the PrepareInitial-State operation and the reflections in steps 3 and 4 as the ReflectAboutMarkedState and ReflectAboutInitialState operations, respectively. We still need a function to help figure out how many times to loop over steps 3 and 4 and an implementation of the oracle that identifies the item we are looking for. Let's start with the function that helps define the stopping criteria for Grover's algorithm.

Listing 11.7   operations.qs: the stopping criteria for Grover's

<<< is the left-bitshift operator, used to compute $2^{nQubits}$, which represents the maximum number of items that can be indexed by a quantum register of nQubits.

Figures out the effective rotation angle applied by each iteration of Grover's algorithm

Using the effective rotation angle together with some trigonometry, we can compute how many iterations will maximize the probability that we'll measure the marked item.

```
function NIterations(nQubits : Int) : Int {
    let nItems = 1 <<< nQubits;
    let angle = ArcSin(1. /
        Sqrt(IntAsDouble(nItems)));
    let nIterations =
        Round(0.25 * PI() / angle - 0.5);
    return nIterations;
}
```

Now that we can calculate when to stop the loop in our implementation of Grover's algorithm, the last thing we need is an oracle that can—given the item we are looking for and a potential item from the data set—flip the phase on part of our register if the potential item is the item we are looking for. For the purpose of an example, let's think of the oracle as representing a kind of guessing game. If someone is thinking of the number 4 and asks us to guess their number, that's an example of a kind of classical function:

$$f(x) = \begin{cases} 1 & x = 4 \\ 0 & \text{otherwise} \end{cases}.$$

Classically, we'd have no better strategy than to try different inputs to f until we tried $x = 4$. If we want to try Grover's algorithm instead, using what we learned in chapter 8, we know we need an operation that represents f:

$$U_f\left(|x\rangle \otimes |y\rangle\right) = |x\rangle \otimes \begin{cases} X|y\rangle & x = 4 \\ |y\rangle & \text{otherwise} \end{cases}.$$

It's pretty easy to implement an operation that can be simulated by U_f using the Q# function ControlledOnInt, provided as a part of the Q# standard libraries. Like the Controlled functor, the ControlledOnInt function allows us to control an operation on another register's state. The difference is that while Controlled always controls on the all-ones state $|11\cdots1\rangle$, the ControlledOnInt function allows us to control on a different state, specified by an integer. For example, if Length(register) is 3, then (ControlledOnInt(4, X))(register, flag) flips the state of flag whenever register is in the state $|100\rangle$, since 4 is written as 100 in little-endian notation.

> **Exercise 11.3: Action of ControlledOnInt**
>
> Try writing what (ControlledOnInt(4, X))(register, flag) does to the state of register + [flag] either using Dirac notation (check out chapters 2 and 4 if you need a refresher) or by writing a unitary matrix that can be used to simulate (ControlledOnInt(4, X)) acting on a three-qubit register and a flag qubit.
>
> *Hint*: Since (ControlledOnInt(4, X)) acts on four qubits in this example (three control qubits and a target qubit), the unitary matrix should be a 16 × 16 matrix.
>
> Try doing the same thing, but for (ControlledOnInt(4, Z)).

Using the ControlledOnInt function, we can quickly write an oracle that flips the state of a flag qubit based on an input to that oracle, as shown in the next listing. Here, our oracle should flip its flag qubit whenever the input to the oracle is in the marked state.

Listing 11.8   operations.qs: an oracle marking the state we want

```
operation ApplyOracle(
    idxMarkedItem : Int,
    register : Qubit[],
    flag : Qubit
) : Unit is Adj + Ctl {
    (ControlledOnInt(idxMarkedItem, X))
        (register, flag);
}
```

Indicates the index of the item we are looking for as an integer (the sample here uses three qubits, so we can input any integer 0 to $2^3 - 1 = 7$)

The ControlledOnInt function that we learned about earlier can apply an X on the flag, controlled on the input register being in the right marked item.

With these two code snippets to add, we can return to the sample code from earlier.

Listing 11.9   operations.qs: Grover's algorithm as a Q# operation

As usual, we start by defining a new operation, using the "operation" keyword.

The first input is the number of items in our list.

Just as with the cryptography example, we can implicitly define our list with an oracle that marks whether an item in our list is the right one.

```
operation SearchForMarkedItem(
    nItems : Int,
    markItem : ((Qubit[], Qubit) => Unit is Adj)
) : Int {
    use qubits = Qubit[BitSizeI(nItems)];
    PrepareInitialState(qubits);

    for idxIteration in
            0..NIterations(BitSizeI(nItems)) - 1 {
        ReflectAboutMarkedState(markItem, qubits);
        ReflectAboutInitialState(PrepareInitialState, qubits);
    }

    return MeasureInteger(LittleEndian(qubits));
}
```

When we're done with our search, we have an index for where the marked item was. Defining our output as an Int lets us return that index.

The heart of Grover's algorithm comes down to repeatedly reflecting about our start state and the index for the item that we're looking for.

Once we're done, measuring our qubit register tells us the index of the item that Grover's algorithm found.

Since we're searching an unstructured list, when we first start the search, all items are equally good places to look.

To start the search, we need to allocate a big enough register to store an index into our list.

The Q# standard library provides a useful operation, MeasureInteger, that interprets measurement results as a classical integer. To use MeasureInteger, as in listing 11.10, we can mark our register as encoding an integer in a little-endian register by using the Microsoft.Quantum.Arithmetic.LittleEndian UDT.

We have all the code we need, so let's run an example.

Listing 11.10   operations.qs: a specific example of Grover's

```
operation RunGroverSearch(nItems : Int, idxMarkedItem : Int) : Unit {
    let markItem = ApplyOracle(
        idxMarkedItem, _, _);
    let foundItem = SearchForMarkedItem(
        nItems, markItem);
    Message(
        $"Marked {idxMarkedItem} and found
    {foundItem}.");
}
```

We can use partial application to include the index of the marked item in the oracle we provide to the search algorithm.

Runs Grover's algorithm on a register of three qubits and provides the oracle markItem that we defined earlier

Issues a message to verify that it found the right item

If we run this sample, we should get the following output:

```
In [1]: %simulate RunGroverSearch nItems=7 idxMarkedItem=2
Out[1]: Marked 2 and found 2.
```

Exercise 11.4: Changing oracles
Try changing the definition of the oracle to control on a different integer. Does this change the output when you run Grover's algorithm?

Congratulations: we can now use a quantum program to do unstructured searches! But what's actually going on? The key insight from geometry that makes Grover's algorithm works is that when we reflect about two different axes, we get a rotation. Figure 11.6 shows an example of how that works for maps.

The same idea works for quantum states. In Grover's algorithm, the initial and marked state reflections combine into a single rotation from the unmarked states into the marked state. To understand how that works, we can use the techniques we've learned throughout the book to look at what's happening to the amplitudes of each state of the register as we go through the algorithm's steps.

We can see from figure 11.7 that each round of reflections seems to *amplify* the amplitude of the state that corresponds to the index we are looking for. By rotating between the unmarked and marked states, we can make the state of our qubits line up with the marked state we want to find.

We can use the same kinds of ideas in other applications as well, as it turns out. Grover's algorithm is an example of a broader class of quantum algorithms that do what is called *amplitude amplification*. This means we have greatly amplified the chances that when we measure our qubit register, the classical bit string of measurement results will be the item we are looking for.

Before we close out this chapter, it will be helpful to have a short discussion of how doing searches like the one we just implemented on quantum hardware scales compared to using classical hardware.

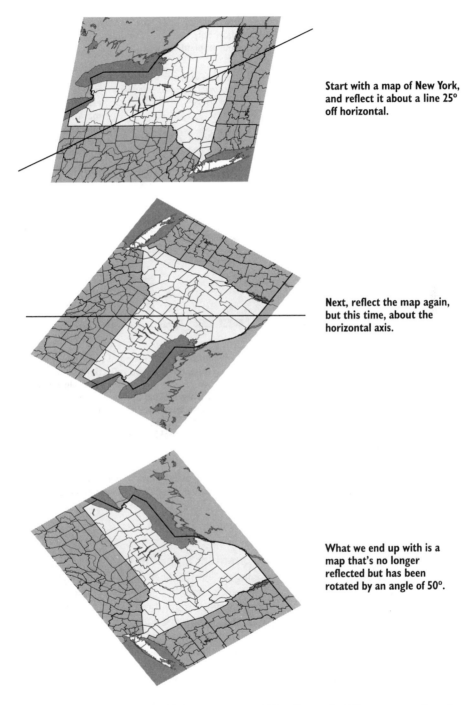

Start with a map of New York, and reflect it about a line 25° off horizontal.

Next, reflect the map again, but this time, about the horizontal axis.

What we end up with is a map that's no longer reflected but has been rotated by an angle of 50°.

Figure 11.6 How pairs of reflections can make a rotation. If we reflect the map over a line at 25° up from the horizontal and then reflect about the horizontal, that's the same as a rotation of the map by 50° down from the horizontal.

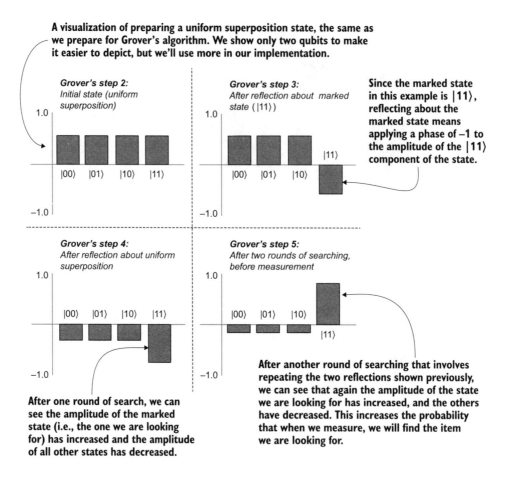

A visualization of preparing a uniform superposition state, the same as we prepare for Grover's algorithm. We show only two qubits to make it easier to depict, but we'll use more in our implementation.

Grover's step 2:
Initial state (uniform superposition)

$|00\rangle$ $|01\rangle$ $|10\rangle$ $|11\rangle$

Grover's step 3:
After reflection about marked state ($|11\rangle$)

$|00\rangle$ $|01\rangle$ $|10\rangle$ $|11\rangle$

Since the marked state in this example is $|11\rangle$, reflecting about the marked state means applying a phase of –1 to the amplitude of the $|11\rangle$ component of the state.

Grover's step 4:
After reflection about uniform superposition

$|00\rangle$ $|01\rangle$ $|10\rangle$ $|11\rangle$

Grover's step 5:
After two rounds of searching, before measurement

$|00\rangle$ $|01\rangle$ $|10\rangle$ $|11\rangle$

After one round of search, we can see the amplitude of the marked state (i.e., the one we are looking for) has increased and the amplitude of all other states has decreased.

After another round of searching that involves repeating the two reflections shown previously, we can see that again the amplitude of the state we are looking for has increased, and the others have decreased. This increases the probability that when we measure, we will find the item we are looking for.

Figure 11.7 A schematic showing how the amplitudes of the state of our qubit register change as we step through Grover's algorithm. As we continue doing reflections, some amplitudes are amplified and the rest are reduced.

Deterministic vs. probabilistic quantum algorithms

Grover's algorithm works by increasing the probability that we get the right answer with each iteration. In general, though, Grover's algorithm may not be able to increase that probability all the way to 100%. Thus, Grover's algorithm is an example of a probabilistic quantum algorithm, meaning we are not guaranteed to get the answer we are looking for every single time we run it. This isn't a problem in practice since we can always run it a small number of times to get an even higher probability of success.

It may be tempting to conclude that all quantum algorithms are probabilistic this way—but that turns out not to be the case. As we saw in chapter 8, the Deutsch–Jozsa algorithm is an example of a *deterministic* quantum algorithm, which gives the same results each time we run it.

Exercise 11.5: Exploring Grover's algorithm with DumpMachine

We've learned a lot about rotations so far in this book, which can help with understanding the rotation applied by each iteration of Grover's algorithm. Try modifying the implementation of Grover's algorithm to apply twice as many iterations, and use DumpMachine to look at the resulting state. Does it seem like what you'd expect from applying a rotation twice?

More general amplitude amplification examples

Along with phase estimation, amplitude amplification is one of the most fundamental techniques used throughout quantum algorithms. In the 25 years since Grover's algorithm first introduced the concept of amplitude amplification, a huge number of variants have been developed to cover a wide range of different problems, such as when there are multiple marked items, when we want to optimize a function rather than find a marked item, or even when we can only *sometimes* correctly prepare the initial state. Many of these techniques are available under the Microsoft.Quantum.Amplitude .Amplification namespace in the Q# standard libraries. Go take a look!

11.4 Resource estimation

We mentioned earlier, when we simplified our scenario from 2.5 million keys to 8, that there would be an advantage to using Grover's algorithm as the number of keys we needed to search grew. So, how long does it take to run Grover's algorithm in practice? This turns out to be a pretty complicated question—we could write several books about it. In part, this is a complicated question because estimating resource requirements necessarily depends on a lot of different parts of our quantum computing stack.

For example, errors are common in quantum devices, so we need to use error correction to protect our computation as it runs. Which error-correction method is used to protect our computation has a massive effect on what's required to run our program. Entire conferences are dedicated to finding better error-correcting codes for just this reason.

Fortunately, Q# and the Quantum Development Kit provide some of the tools we need to start getting a handle on what's required to run different quantum programs. Instead of running our program on a simulator that models how a real quantum computer would work, we can run it on a *resources estimator*, which tells us how many of each kind of intrinsic operation we need to call, how many qubits our program needs, and how many of the quantum operations in our program can be called in parallel. Let's look at a small example, using what we learned about the Deutsch–Jozsa algorithm in chapter 8.

Listing 11.11   Defining the Deutsch–Jozsa algorithm again

```
In [1]: operation ApplyNotOracle(control : Qubit, target : Qubit)
        : Unit {
            within {
                X(control);
            } apply {
                CNOT(control, target);
            }
        }
Out [1]: - ApplyNotOracle
In [2]: open Microsoft.Quantum.Measurement;

        operation CheckIfOracleIsBalanced(
                oracle : ((Qubit, Qubit) => Unit)
        ) : Bool {
            use control = Qubit();
            use target = Qubit();
            H(control);

            within {
                X(target);
                H(target);
            } apply {
                oracle(control, target);
            }

            return MResetX(control) == One;
        }
Out [2]: - CheckIfOracleIsBalanced
In [3]: operation RunDeutschJozsaAlgorithm()
        : Bool {
            return CheckIfOracleIsBalanced(ApplyNotOracle);
        }
Out [3]: - RunDeutschJozsaAlgorithm
```

The same **ApplyNotOracle** we saw earlier, except that now it uses a within/apply flow

Remember that when using Q# Jupyter Notebooks, we have to open namespaces in each cell we want to use them in.

The operation **CheckIfOracleIsBalanced** is the same as before, except that a within/apply block is again used to replace the repeated **H** and **X** operations.

In Q# notebooks, we need an operation with no arguments to use with the %simulate and %estimate commands.

When we run the `%estimate` magic command in an IQ# notebook, we get back a table much like the one shown in figure 11.8. This table reports the kinds of resources the Quantum Development Kit estimates our program would take to run.

Table 11.1   Kinds of resources tracked by the `%estimate` magic command

Resource kind	Description
CNOT	How many times the CNOT operation is called
QubitClifford	How many times the X, Y, Z, H, and S operations are called
R	How many times single-qubit rotation operations are called
Measure	How many measurement operations are called
T	How many times the T operation is called
Depth	How many T operations need to be called in a row on a single qubit

Table 11.1 Kinds of resources tracked by the %estimate magic command *(continued)*

Resource kind	Description
Width	How many qubits our program needs
BorrowedWidth	How many qubits our program needs to be able to borrow (a more advanced technique than we cover in this book)

In [4]: ▶ %estimate RunDeutschJozsaAlgorithm

Out[4]:

Metric	Sum	Max
CNOT	1	1
QubitClifford	8	8
R	0	0
Measure	1	1
T	0	0
Depth	0	0
Width	2	2
QubitCount	2	2
BorrowedWidth	0	0

When we use the %estimate magic command instead of %simulate, IQ# prints the resources required to run our quantum program, broken down by each different kind of resource.

Figure 11.8 Output from running %estimate RunDeutschJozsaAlgorithm on the program in listing 11.11. When we use %estimate, we get a count of various types of resources that our quantum device (or simulator) would need to provide to make it possible to run the program. Check out table 11.1 to learn more about the meaning of each of these counts.

TIP We can also estimate resources from Python! Just use the estimate_ resources method instead of the simulate method that we learned about in previous chapters.

As we can see from running %estimate in the notebook and table 11.1, some categories probably make sense, like the width, how many measurements are made, and R for the number of single-qubit rotations used. Others are new, like counting T operations and depth. We have not seen T operations before, but they are just another kind of single-qubit operation.

Meet Mr. *T*

Like most other operations we've seen so far in this book, the T operation can be simulated by a unitary matrix:

$$T = \begin{pmatrix} 1 & 0 \\ 0 & e^{i\pi/4} \end{pmatrix} = \begin{pmatrix} 1 & 0 \\ 0 & (1+i)/\sqrt{2} \end{pmatrix}$$

(continued)

That is, T is a 45° (π / 4) rotation about the *Z*-axis.

Another way of thinking of the T operation is as the fourth root of the Z operation we've seen quite a bit of. Since 45° × 4 = 180°, if we apply T four times in a row, that's an expensive way of applying the Z operation once.

In Q#, the T operation is made available as `Microsoft.Quantum.Intrinsic.T` and has type `Qubit => Unit is Adj + Ctl`.

Exercise 11.6: Four T's make a Z

Use `AssertOperationsEqualReferenced` to prove that applying the T operation four times does the same thing as applying Z once. There's another operation, S, that can be thought of as the square root of Z (a 90° rotation about the *Z*-axis); check that applying T twice is the same as applying S once.

What makes T operations somewhat special and thus worthy of focusing on so heavily when estimating resources is that they are expensive to use with error-correcting methods that are needed when running on larger quantum devices. Most of the operations we've used so far are part of the *Clifford group*: operations that are easier to use with error correction. As noted before, getting into the details of error correction here is out of scope for this book; but in short, the more operations we have that are not Clifford operations, the harder it will be to implement our program on error-corrected hardware. Thus it is important to count the number of "expensive" operations (like T) for running on our currently available hardware.

> **TIP** At a high level, the number of T operations that must be applied in sequence (that is, that can't be run in parallel) is a pretty good approximation of how long a quantum program takes to run on error-corrected quantum computers. This is reported by the resources estimator as the Depth metric.

So, what are typical or exceptional values for the resources we can count with the resources estimator in Q#? For a simple program like `RunDeutschJozsaAlgorithm`, the resources required are very modest. Looking at table 11.1, though, there's a lot of focus on the T operation, so let's delve into it a bit to see what that operation is and why it's essential for resource estimation. Figure 11.9 shows the output from estimating the resources required to call the `CCNOT` operation that we learned about in chapter 9.

Exercise 11.7: Resetting registers

Why don't we need to reset the register of qubits allocated in `EstimateCcnot-Resources`, as shown in figure 11.9?

Let's see what happens when we run %estimate on the CCNOT operation! To do so, we need to wrap a call to CCNOT in something that allocates a register of qubits.

CCNOT

```
In [1]:  ▶  1  operation EstimateCcnotResources() : Unit {
            2      using (register = Qubit[3]) {
            3          CCNOT(register[0], register[1], register[2]);
            4      }
            5  }
```

Out[1]: • EstimateCcnotResources

```
In [2]:  ▶  1  %estimate EstimateCcnotResources
```

Out[2]:

Metric	Sum	Max
CNOT	10	10
QubitClifford	2	2
R	0	0
Measure	0	0
T	7	7
Depth	5	5
Width	3	3
BorrowedWidth	0	0

The output from %estimate might seem a little surprising, given that we just called a single operation! Behind the scenes, the resources estimator has expanded our call to CCNOT into operations that can be more easily run on error-corrected quantum devices.

Figure 11.9 Output from estimating the resources required to call CCNOT. From the code, it may seem there should be only one operation; but in reality, CCNOT is decomposed into more easily implemented operations depending on the target machine.

This output is a bit surprising, in that our tiny program requires 10 CNOT operations, 5 single-qubit operations, and 7 T operations, even though we don't call any of them directly. As it turns out, it's very difficult to apply operations like CCNOT directly in an error-corrected quantum program. So, the Q# resources estimator first turns our program into something closer to what would actually be run on hardware, using calls to more basic operations like CNOT and T.

Exercise 11.8: T scaling

How does the number of T operation calls change as you increase the number of control qubits? A rough trend is fine.

Hint: As we saw previously, a controlled-NOT operation with an arbitrary number of qubits can be written as `Controlled X(Most(qs), Tail(qs))`; using functions provided by the `Microsoft.Quantum.Arrays` namespace.

This comes in handy when we want to estimate what resources it would take to run a program that is too large for us to simulate on a classical computer. Figure 11.10 shows the output from running Grover's algorithm on a 20-qubit list (about 1 million items).

If we run this for various list sizes, we get a curve like the one shown in figure 11.11. For our scenario with 2.5 million keys, the quantum number of steps is much lower than the classical step cost. That's not the whole story, of course, since each step on a quantum computer will probably be much slower than a corresponding step on a clas-

Counting resources required to run Grover's algorithm

Let's run Grover's algorithm again, this time using a lot more qubits for the list; 20 should do the trick.

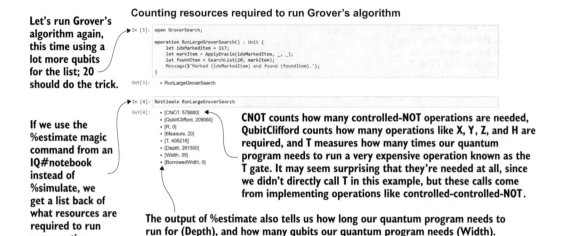

```
In [3]: open GroverSearch;

operation RunLargeGroverSearch() : Unit {
    let idxMarkedItem = 117;
    let markItem = ApplyOracle(idxMarkedItem, _, _);
    let foundItem = SearchList(20, markItem);
    Message($"Marked {idxMarkedItem} and found {foundItem}.");
}

Out[3]:  • RunLargeGroverSearch
```

If we use the %estimate magic command from an IQ#notebook instead of %simulate, we get a list back of what resources are required to run an operation.

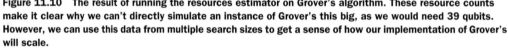

```
In [4]: %estimate RunLargeGroverSearch

Out[4]:  • [CNOT, 578880]
         • [QubitClifford, 209060]
         • [R, 0]
         • [Measure, 20]
         • [T, 405216]
         • [Depth, 261300]
         • [Width, 39]
         • [BorrowedWidth, 0]
```

CNOT counts how many controlled-NOT operations are needed, QubitClifford counts how many operations like X, Y, Z, and H are required, and T measures how many times our quantum program needs to run a very expensive operation known as the T gate. It may seem surprising that they're needed at all, since we didn't directly call T in this example, but these calls come from implementing operations like controlled-controlled-NOT.

The output of %estimate also tells us how long our quantum program needs to run for (Depth), and how many qubits our quantum program needs (Width). Here, searching a list of 2^{20} items (about 1 million) takes about a depth of 261,300 operations—significantly less than 1 million!

Figure 11.10 The result of running the resources estimator on Grover's algorithm. These resource counts make it clear why we can't directly simulate an instance of Grover's this big, as we would need 39 qubits. However, we can use this data from multiple search sizes to get a sense of how our implementation of Grover's will scale.

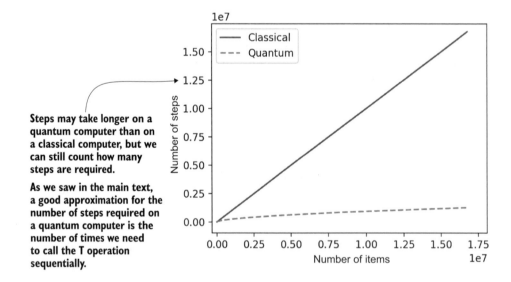

Steps may take longer on a quantum computer than on a classical computer, but we can still count how many steps are required.

As we saw in the main text, a good approximation for the number of steps required on a quantum computer is the number of times we need to call the T operation sequentially.

Figure 11.11 Output from estimating the resources required to run Grover's algorithm for a variety of different-sized lists

sical computer; but it's a really good move toward understanding what it would take to run different quantum programs in practice.

We have now learned how to combine the oracles we learned in chapter 7 and a new flavor of quantum operation (reflections) to search over the inputs to functions. This was helpful in the scenario to help find decryption keys more quickly when there is a tight time constraint.

In the next chapter, we'll use the skills from this chapter to answer one of the most important questions posed by quantum computing: how long would it take a quantum computer to break modern encryption?

Summary

- Another application for quantum computers is to search inputs to an opaque function for an input that produces a desired output (that is, a *marked* input). We can use Grover's algorithm to search using fewer calls to our oracle than is possible with classical computing.
- Grover's algorithm uses reflections, quantum operations in which the phase of one input state is flipped while all other input states are left unmodified. We can build up many different kinds of reflections using rotations together with the shoes-and-socks patterns we saw in chapter 8.
- Using the various rotations provided by Q# together with `within` and `apply`, we can define an oracle that marks a particular item and then reflect about that marked item using a single oracle call. Taken together, these techniques let us implement Grover's algorithm.
- To verify that Grover's algorithm outperforms classical approaches for large enough problems, we can run our Q# program on the resources estimator. Unlike the simulator provided with the Quantum Development Kit, the resources estimator doesn't simulate quantum programs but counts how many qubits they require and how many operations they would need to call on a quantum device.

Arithmetic with quantum computers

This chapter covers

- Programming with the Q# Numerics library
- Implementing Shor's algorithm to factor integers
- Recognizing the implications of quantum computing for security infrastructure

In chapter 11, we used a quantum programming technique called amplitude amplification in Grover's algorithm to speed up searching unstructured data sets. While Grover's was not the most efficient search approach for smaller data sets, as we looked to scaling up to larger and larger problems, our quantum approach offered a clear advantage. In this final chapter, we'll build on the skills we've developed throughout the book to tackle one of the most famous quantum algorithms: Shor's algorithm. We'll implement Shor's and show how it can give us an advantage when trying to factor large integers. While that may not seem like the most interesting task, the difficulty of factoring integers actually underpins much of our current cryptographic infrastructure.

12.1 *Factoring quantum computing into security*

In part 1 of the book, we saw how quantum concepts can be applied to send data securely using techniques such as quantum key distribution. Even without QKD, though, critical data is shared secretly over the internet all the time. The internet is used to share payment data, personal health data, and dating preferences and even to organize political movements. In this chapter, we'll take a look at how classical computers can protect our privacy and how quantum computing changes the way we decide what tools to use to protect our data.

> **NOTE** Now that we have what we need to solve harder problems with quantum computers, this chapter's scenario is a bit more complicated than most of our earlier games and scenarios. Don't worry if things don't make sense off the bat: take your time and read more slowly. We promise it will be worth your while!

To begin, let's look at the state of the art for securing data with classical computers. As it turns out, there are many different problems in classical mathematics, some of which are really easy to solve (e.g., "What's 2 + 2?") and others of which are really difficult to solve (e.g., "Is P equal to NP?"). Between those two extremes, we get problems that are hard to solve unless someone gives us a hint, in which case they become easy. These problems tend to look more like *puzzles* and can be useful for hiding data: we have to know the secret hint or use huge amounts of computing time to solve them.

> **TIP** In chapter 3, we saw quantum key distribution, which is a great way to share information securely that relies on quantum mechanics rather than puzzles. We may not always be able to send qubits to our friends, though, so understanding how to use puzzles to communicate securely and privately still matters.

As we will see later in the chapter, factoring numbers can be one of these puzzles that cryptographic algorithms can rely on for security. A number of very important algorithms and cryptographic protocols are currently in use that rely on the fact that it is difficult for computers to solve puzzles that involve factoring large numbers. If you guessed that quantum computers can help us factor large numbers, you're on the right track.

Enter *Shor's algorithm*. With a classical computer, we can reduce the problem or puzzle of finding factors of integers to solving a kind of puzzle about how quickly functions repeat themselves when using *modular arithmetic* (also known as *clock arithmetic*, as we'll see more of later in the chapter). If we use Shor's algorithm, estimating how quickly functions repeat themselves is precisely the sort of puzzle we can solve easily on a quantum computer. Let's dig into the steps of Shor's and then look at an example of using it:

Scenario: Factoring an integer N

Suppose we're trying to factor the integer N, and we know in advance that N has exactly two prime factors. Using Q#, implement Shor's algorithm to factor N.

Coprime and semiprime

As a helpful bit of terminology, we say two numbers that share no common factors other than 1 are *coprime*. For example, neither 15 nor 16 is prime, but 15 and 16 are coprime with respect to each other.

Similarly, we say that a number with exactly two prime factors is *semiprime*. For example, 15 is semiprime since $15 = 3 \times 5$ and since both 3 and 5 are prime. On the other hand, 28 isn't semiprime since $28 = 4 \times 7 = 2 \times 2 \times 7$. Semiprime numbers come up often when considering cryptography, so it's often useful to make that assumption in our scenarios.

We can perform the steps in algorithm 12.1 (shown as a flowchart in figure 12.1) to use what we learned about phase estimation in chapters 9 and 10 together with some classical math to find the factors of N.

The mod squad

In algorithm 12.1, we need one more bit of classical math: the mod operator. If you haven't seen that operator before, don't worry; we'll go through it in more detail later in the chapter.

Algorithm 12.1: Pseudocode for factoring an integer with Shor's algorithm

1. Pick a random integer g, which we call the *generator*.
2. Check to see if the generator is accidentally a factor by determining whether g and N are coprime. If they share a common factor, then we have a new factor of N; else continue with the rest of the algorithm.
3. Use iterative phase estimation to find the *frequency* of the classical function $f(x) = g^x \bmod N$. The frequency tells us how quickly f returns to the same value as x increases.
4. Use a classical algorithm known as the *continued fractions expansion* to convert the frequency from the previous step into a period (r). The period r should then have the property that $f(x) = f(x + r)$ for all inputs x.
5. If the period r that we find is odd, go back to step 1 and make a new guess. If r is even, go to the next step.
6. Either $g^{r/2} - 1$ or $g^{r/2} + 1$ shares a factor with N.

NOTE In algorithm 12.1, it is important to note that only step 3 involves any quantum computation. Most of the steps for Shor's algorithm are best suited

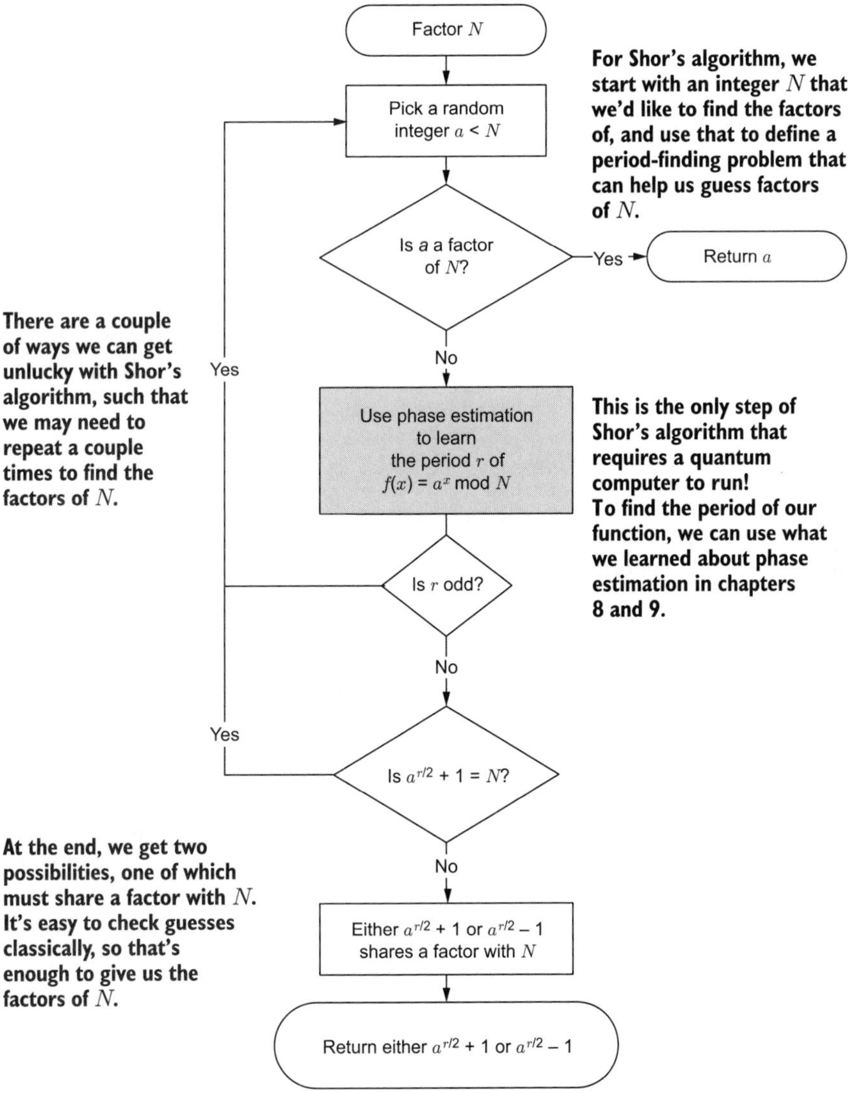
Factor N
Pick a random integer $a < N$
For Shor's algorithm, we start with an integer N that we'd like to find the factors of, and use that to define a period-finding problem that can help us guess factors of N.
Is a a factor of N?
Yes
Return a
There are a couple of ways we can get unlucky with Shor's algorithm, such that we may need to repeat a couple times to find the factors of N.
Yes
No
Use phase estimation to learn the period r of $f(x) = a^x \bmod N$
This is the only step of Shor's algorithm that requires a quantum computer to run! To find the period of our function, we can use what we learned about phase estimation in chapters 8 and 9.
Is r odd?
No
Yes
Is $a^{r/2} + 1 = N$?
No
At the end, we get two possibilities, one of which must share a factor with N. It's easy to check guesses classically, so that's enough to give us the factors of N.
Either $a^{r/2} + 1$ or $a^{r/2} - 1$ shares a factor with N
Return either $a^{r/2} + 1$ or $a^{r/2} - 1$

Figure 12.1 Shor's algorithm represented as a flowchart. To factor an integer *N*, Shor's algorithm uses phase estimation and a quantum computer to find the *period* of a function that takes powers of another integer *a* using modular arithmetic mod *N*. After some classical post-processing, that period can be used to find the factors of *N*.

for classical hardware and demonstrate how quantum hardware will likely be used. That is to say, quantum hardware and algorithms work well as *subroutines* for combined quantum-classical algorithms.

Now that we have seen the steps for Shor's algorithm, listing 12.1 shows what the final implementation might look like. The operation `FactorSemiprimeInteger` is the entry point to the algorithm: it takes as input the integer we want to factor and returns its two factors.

Listing 12.1   Q# code for factoring a semiprime integer

```
operation FactorSemiprimeInteger(number : Int) : (Int, Int) {
    if (number % 2 == 0) {
        Message("An even number has been given; 2 is a factor.");
        return (number / 2, 2);
    }
    mutable factors = (1, 1);
    mutable foundFactors = false;

    repeat {
        let generator = DrawRandomInt(3,number - 2);

        if (IsCoprimeI(generator, number)) {
            Message($"Estimating period of {generator}...");
            let period = EstimatePeriod(generator, number);
            set (foundFactors, factors) = MaybeFactorsFromPeriod(
                generator, period, number
            );
        } else {
            let gcd = GreatestCommonDivisorI(number, generator);
            Message(
                $"We have guessed a divisor of {number} to be " +
                $"{gcd} by accident. Nothing left to do."
            );
            set foundFactors = true;
            set factors = (gcd, number / gcd);
        }
    }
    until (foundFactors)
    fixup {
        Message(
            "The estimated period did not yield a valid factor, " +
            "trying again."
        );
    }
    return factors;
}
```

First checks if we were asked to factor an even number, since then 2 must be a factor

Following step 1 of algorithm 12.1, we pick a random number to define the periodic function that we use to factor "number".

In this chapter, we learn how to write an **EstimatePeriod** operation to handle steps 3 and 4 of algorithm 12.1 using what we've learned about phase estimation.

Once we have the period, we can use steps 5 and 6 of algorithm 12.1 to guess the factors of "number"; we'll write Maybe-FactorsFromPeriod later in the chapter.

If something goes wrong (e.g., our generator has an odd period), we use a repeat/until loop to try again.

Returns the two factors of "number" that we found using our quantum program

---

Luck isn't everything, but it can help!

In listing 12.1, we use IsCoprimeI to check whether generator is a factor of number before proceeding with the rest of Shor's algorithm. If we're really lucky, then generator is already a factor, in which case we don't need a quantum computer to help factor number.

While we may be lucky pretty often in the small examples we can simulate on a laptop or desktop, as number gets bigger, it becomes harder and harder to guess the right factors by accident, such that Shor's algorithm is really helpful almost all the time.

Since this is the last chapter of the book, we have all of the *quantum* concepts we need to understand what's happening in listing 12.1; the only things missing are the classical parts that connect what we've learned so far to the problem of factoring semiprime numbers, as well as a few useful parts of the Q# libraries that can help. As mentioned before, only one step here uses quantum technology, and it does so by creating an oracle that implements the classical function we want to learn about. By using a superposition state, applying the oracle, and doing phase estimation, we can learn properties about the classical function: here, the period. In the rest of the chapter, we'll go through algorithm 12.1 in detail and cover the last pieces that we need to run Shor's algorithm. The first piece we need to understand algorithm 12.1 is a bit of classical math known as *modular arithmetic*, so let's jump on in!

12.2 Connecting modular math to factoring

One way to find puzzles that can be used in security contexts is to look at how *modular arithmetic* works. Unlike normal arithmetic, in modular arithmetic, everything wraps back around like hours on a clock. For instance, if someone asked us what time comes two hours after 11 o'clock, we would get a very odd look if we responded with "13 o'clock." Much more likely, the person was hoping to get an answer like "1 o'clock"— that is, if they don't use 24-hour time.

Using modular arithmetic, we can capture this idea by saying that 11 + 2 = 1 mod. In that equation, mod 12 indicates that we want anything that goes past 12 to wrap around, as illustrated in figure 12.2.

Suppose that at **11 o'clock**, someone asks us what time it will be in two hours.

If we said **13 o'clock**, we'd get some strange looks, but if we said **1 o'clock**, that would be a lot more helpful!

We can think of **(11 + 2)** as having "wrapped around" the **12** on a clock; this is an example of modular arithmetic.

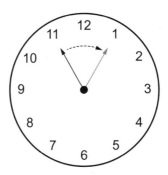

Of course, we don't have to do modular arithmetic only with 12-hour clocks. If clocks had 21 hours, for instance, then using modular arithmetic, $5^2 = 25 = 4$.

Figure 12.2 Using clocks to understand modular arithmetic. When adding and multiplying numbers "mod N," we can think of a normal number line as being wrapped around a clock face with N hours. Just as two hours past 11 o'clock is 1 o'clock, 11 + 2 = 1 when working mod 12.

When arithmetic is allowed to wrap around like this, it can be difficult to figure out where different calculations started. If we're working with ordinary real numbers, for example, it's easy to calculate b if we're given a and a^b; we can take the logarithm of a^b to find b. If we try to solve the same problem in modular arithmetic, it can quickly get tricky. For instance, when computing mod 21, the powers of 5 are 1, 5, 4, 20, 16, 17, 1, ... On the face of it, 5, 4, and 16 don't seem like powers of the same number, much less in increasing order, such that when we're working backward from having taken an exponent mod 21, we have more possible starting places that we need to check.

Exercise 12.1: Powers of 11

What are the powers of 11 when computed mod 21? How long does it take to loop back around to $11^0 = 1$?

Does it matter if you take the modulus by 21 at the end, or whether you compute the modulus at each step?

Hint: Either Python or Q# works great for this, as both define the modulus operator %.

Exercise solutions

All solutions for exercises in this book can be found in the companion code repo: https://github.com/crazy4pi314/learn-qc-with-python-and-qsharp. Just go to the folder for the chapter we are in and open the Jupyter notebook with the name that mentions exercise solutions.

The observation that finding the power b given a^b mod N is hard already gives us a puzzle we can use to hide some data! This puzzle is commonly called the *discrete logarithm* problem. If Alice wants to share a secret with us, we can start by publicly agreeing on a small number like $g = 13$ and a big number like $N = 71$. We then each pick a secret number at random: suppose Alice picks $a = 4$ and we pick $b = 5$. Alice then sends us g^a mod $N = 19$, and we send back g^b mod $N = 34$. If we compute $(g^a)^b$ mod $N = 19^5$ mod 71 = 45 and Alice computes $(g^b)^a$ mod 71 = 34^4 mod 71 = 45, we both get the same number, but an eavesdropper would have to solve the clockface-jumping puzzle we saw earlier to work it out (see figure 12.3). Since $g^{ab} = 45$ is a number that we and Alice know, but no one else knows, we can use g^{ab} as a key to hide our messages using what we learned in chapter 3.

Warning: Don't try this at home

A lot of this protocol's technical conditions go well beyond the scope of this book. Choosing g and N badly can undermine any security offered by this technique, making it trivial for an experienced attacker to break. It's also very easy to introduce bugs by doing this on your own, so please consider this only a conceptual example!

If you're interested in learning more about the practical aspects of using these kinds of puzzles to keep your data secure, *Cryptography Engineering* by Niels Ferguson, Bruce Schneier, and Tadayoshi Kohno (Wiley, 2010) is a great book from which to continue learning.

Step 1: You and Alice each think of a secret random number and agree on a shared **public** number g.

Step 2: You and Alice each compute the g raised to the power of your secret numbers and announce the result.

$g^a \bmod N$

$g^b \bmod N$

Step 3: Using the result you get from Alice together with your own secret number, you can compute the power g^{ab}. Alice can do the same using what she knows.

$(g^b)^a \bmod N$

$(g^a)^b \bmod N$

Step 4: An attacker who overhears the g^a and g^b messages from step 2 needs to solve the discrete logarithm puzzle to get the same answer that you and Alice figured out in step 3.

$g^a \bmod N$, $g^b \bmod N$... $g^{ab} \bmod N = ?$

Figure 12.3 Using the discrete logarithm problem as a puzzle to hide secret messages. Here, the messages we share with Alice are protected if it's hard for someone to compute undo modular arithmetic operations such as the exponential function.

Unlike QKD, this way of sharing secret data (known as the *Diffie–Hellman protocol*) relies on the assumption that the puzzle we and Alice used is hard to solve without a hint that our eavesdropper doesn't have access to. If someone can efficiently work out puzzles like solving $g^a \bmod N$ for a given g and N, our data might as well be public.

One other puzzle that's commonly used to protect data today is the *RSA algorithm*, which uses more advanced classical math to make a puzzle out of factoring really large integers. Just as we can break Diffie–Hellman by solving $g^a \bmod N$, we can break RSA by solving $N = pq$ for p or q given only N. In the RSA puzzle, we call N a *public key* and the factors p and q the *private key*; if we can factor N easily, we can get access to private keys given only public keys. With that in mind, we can make the scenario from earlier a bit more precise:

Scenario: Breaking RSA

Suppose that we know a public key N. Using Q#, implement Shor's algorithm to factor N to recover the private keys p and q.

> ### Break it 'til we make it
>
> This scenario may seem a bit … nefarious when compared to those in previous chapters. In practice, though, it's essential to understand attacks on the tools and protocols that we use to keep our data safe so that we can adjust our approach accordingly. If we use a cryptographic algorithm like RSA to protect data, implementing quantum attacks on that algorithm can help us understand how large a quantum device our attackers would need to compromise our data. After all, there are claims ranging from "There's no problem with RSA at all" to "We should be terrified"; separating those extremes requires understanding the resources an attacker would need.
>
> In other words, by exploring a scenario that puts us in the role of an attacker for a moment, we can understand how much quantum computing power would be required to successfully attack RSA. We'll come back to this point at the end of the chapter, but for now, it helps to think like an attacker. Understanding how quantum computers could attack classical cryptography serves as a great scenario to practice applying our quantum computing skills!
>
> It's worth being cautious in using this example, though. The impact of quantum computing on information security depends on what assumptions we make about classical algorithms, improvements in quantum algorithms, the progress of quantum hardware development, how long we need forward secrecy to last, and many other such concerns. Covering all of these well enough to make *responsible* decisions about how best to deploy cryptography would take more space than is left in this book, unfortunately, so we recommend keeping in mind that the RSA scenario in this chapter is an example and not a complete analysis of the subject.

It turns out that even though Diffie–Hellman and RSA look very different, we can use some classical math to turn the factoring puzzle of RSA into another example of figuring out how quickly we move around a clock face when we perform modular arithmetic (the Diffie–Hellman puzzle). That problem can then be solved easily on a quantum computer using what we learned in chapter 10. Let's run through a quick example of using Shor's algorithm to factor a small integer so that we can see all of those parts at work.

12.2.1 *Example of factoring with Shor's algorithm*

The steps listed for Shor's algorithm can seem very abstract, so before we get into how they work, let's try an example using what we learned earlier about modular arithmetic. Say the number we want to factor is 21; real RSA public keys will be much larger, but let's use 21 for the sake of working through the math by hand. Trust us—it keeps the math much, *much* easier.

Here are the steps from algorithm 12.1 to factor 21:

1 Choose a random integer as a generator; let's say we use 11.
2 We can verify that since 11 shares no common factors with 21, we can use it as the generator for the next step.
3 We can't do the quantum step in our head, unfortunately, so we use the Q# iterative phase estimation operation to estimate the phase generated by applying an oracle that implements the classical function $f(x) = 11^x \bmod 21$. It returns a phase ϕ that we can convert to a frequency of 427 by the following equation: $(\phi * 2^9)) / 2\pi$.
4 We use the continued fractions algorithm on 427 to get a guess for what the period might be. Doing it by hand, we get an estimate of 6 for the period.
5 The period we found is even, so we can continue to the next step.
6 Using the period 6 gives us that either $11^{6/2} - 1 \bmod 21 = 7$ or $11^{6/2} + 1 \bmod 21 = 9$ shares a factor with 21. We can check and verify each possibility to confirm that 7 is indeed a factor of 21.

Exercise 12.2: Looking for common factors

Try step 6 from the previous process, but using 35 as the number to factor, 17 as the generator, and 12 as the period. Check that either or both of the answers that you get from step 6 share a common factor with 35.

Using either Python or Q#, try the same thing with $N = 143$, $g = 19$, and the period $r = 60$.

Note: In the next section, we'll see how to easily use a classical computer to factor a number when given another number that shares some of its factors.

While this is a lot of work to factor a number as small as 21, 35, or 143, the exact same process also works for much larger integers, such as those we might encounter when trying to solve the puzzle that the RSA algorithm uses to protect data.

The rest of the chapter goes through each of these steps in detail and shows how they can work together to factor integers. To kick off that process, let's look at the classical math behind how period finding helps us factor integers and how we can use Q# to implement that classical math.

12.3 *Classical algebra and factoring*

With the concrete example of using Shor's algorithm in mind, we can see how classical arithmetic and algebra help to take advantage of quantum computing. Before going over the core quantum part of the algorithm, it's helpful to explore the classical part a little more to understand why finding the period of generator helps factor integers.

We may remember from algebra that for any number x, $x^2 - 1 = (x + 1)(x - 1)$. As it turns out, that works in modular (clock) arithmetic as well. If we find that the period r of our generator g is even,

- Then that means there's an integer k ...
- Such that $g^r = g^{2k} \bmod N = 1$.

Subtracting one from each side, we get $(g^{2k} - 1) \bmod N = 0$,

- So that using $x^2 - 1 = (x + 1)(x - 1)$ gives us ...
- $(g^k + 1)(g^k - 1) \bmod N = 0$.

Why does this matter? If we have that $x \bmod N = 0$, that tells us x is a multiple of N. Thinking back to the clock analogy, 0, 12, 24, 36, and so forth are all equal to zero mod 12. Put differently, if $x \bmod N = 0$, then there's some integer y such that $x = yN$. Using that with what we got from the period, we know there's some integer y such that $(g^k + 1)(g^k - 1) = yN$. If either $g^k - 1$ or $g^k + 1$ is a multiple of N, we haven't learned much; but in any other case, it tells us that either $g^k - 1$ or $g^k + 1$ has to share a factor with N.

To figure out whether $g^k - 1$ or $g^k + 1$ shares a factor with N, we can compute the *greatest common divisor* (GCD) of each guess with N. This is straightforward to do with a classical computer using a technique called *Euclid's algorithm*.

> **NOTE** Since the GCD is so easy to compute classically, why do we need a quantum computer to help factor? By this point in Shor's algorithm, we've already narrowed the potential factors to two very good guesses and are using the GCD just on those guesses. If we didn't have things narrowed down so well, we'd have to use the GCD on many, many more guesses to have a good chance of finding the factors of N. Even as easy as the GCD is to determine, we still need a good way to narrow it down to a good set of guesses first.

In Q#, we can compute the GCD using the GreatestCommonDivisorI function, as shown in listing 12.2, where the code is run in a Q# Jupyter Notebook. One way we can check that we get the right output from GreatestCommonDivisorI is to start with two integers expressed as the product of prime factors: for example, $a = 2 \times 3 \times 113$ and $b = 2 \times 3 \times 5 \times 13$. Since these two integers only share 2 and 3 as factors, their GCD should be $2 \times 3 = 6$.

The Q# standard library documentation

As usual, listing 12.2 starts with open statements that allow us to use functions and operations provided in the Q# standard library. In this case, the Q# function that computes the GCD of two integers is in the Microsoft.Quantum.Math namespace, so we begin by opening that namespace to make that functionality available. Similarly, the facts and assertions we need to test our new GcdExample function can be used by opening the Microsoft.Quantum.Diagnostics namespace.

For a complete list of what is available in the Q# standard library, check out https://docs.microsoft.com/en-us/qsharp/api/ for a full reference.

Listing 12.2 Finding the greatest common divisor of two integers

```
In [1]: open Microsoft.Quantum.Math;
        open Microsoft.Quantum.Diagnostics;

        function GcdExample() : Unit {
            let a = 2 * 3 * 113;
            let b = 2 * 3 * 5 * 13;
            let gcd = GreatestCommonDivisorI(a, b);
            Message($"The GCD of {a} and {b} is {gcd}.");

            EqualityFactI(gcd, 6, "Got the wrong GCD.");
        }
Out[1]: - GcdExample
In [2]: %simulate GcdExample
The GCD of 678 and 390 is 6.
Out[2]: ()
```

This function is a simple test case to see how the GCD works.

To compute the GCD, we call GreatestCommonDivisorI from the Microsoft.Quantum.Math namespace that we opened earlier.

Uses the EqualityFactI function to confirm that the answer we got matches what we expected (2 × 3 = 6)

As usual, we can use %simulate to run a function or operation on a simulator. Here, we get the output () back since GcdExample returns an output of type Unit.

Input types and naming conventions in Q#

Note the I at the end of the name GreatestCommonDivisorI. This tells us that GreatestCommonDivisorI works on inputs of type Int. When using Shor's algorithm in practice, N will be much, much larger than we can fit into an ordinary Int value, so Q# also provides another type called BigInt to help.

To work with BigInt inputs, Q# also provides the GreatestCommonDivisorL function. Why L and not B? In this case, L stands for "long," helping disambiguate from other types starting with "B," such as Bool.

This convention is used throughout the rest of the Q# standard libraries as well. For instance, the equality fact that we used earlier compared two integers and so is called EqualityFactI. The corresponding fact for comparing two big integers is called EqualityFactL, while the fact for comparing two Result values is called EqualityFactR.

Exercise 12.3: Greatest common denominators

What's the GCD of 35 and 30? Does that help you find the factors of 35?

Hint: Think of this as step 2 of the previous exercise.

Putting everything together, if we have the period of our generator, the following listing shows how we can use that to write MaybeFactorsFromPeriod in Q#. The function name starts with "maybe" because there is a chance the period that was found will not meet conditions necessary to learn something about the factors of the number.

Listing 12.3   operations.qs: computing possible factors from a period

To compute possible factors from a period, we need to take inputs for the number N that we're trying to factor, the period r, and the generator.

If either $g^{r/2} + 1$ or $g^{r/2} - 1$ is a multiple of N, we can't find any factors and need to try again. The Bool output lets the caller know to retry.

```
function MaybeFactorsFromPeriod(
    generator : Int, period : Int, number : Int)
: (Bool, (Int, Int)) {
    if period % 2 == 0 {
```

If the period is odd, we can't use the $x^2 - 1 = (x + 1)(x - 1)$ trick, so we start by checking that the period is even.

```
        let halfPower = ExpModI(generator,
            period / 2, number);
```

Checks that $g^{r/2} + 1$ is not a multiple of N, so we know it's safe to continue

```
        if (halfPower != number - 1) {
            let factor = MaxI(
                GreatestCommonDivisorI(halfPower - 1, number),
                GreatestCommonDivisorI(halfPower + 1, number)
            );
            return (true, (factor, number / factor));
        } else {
            return (false, (1, 1));
        }
    } else {
        return (false, (1, 1));
    }
}
```

The GCD tells us if one of our guesses has a common factor with N. If our guess has no common factors, the GCD returns 1. This checks both guesses and takes whichever gives something other than 1.

The Q# function Microsoft.Quantum.Math.ExpModI returns modular arithmetic exponentials of the form g^x mod N. We can use that to find $g^{r/2}$ mod N given g, r, and N.

Now that we know how to convert a period to potential factors, let's see the core of Shor's algorithm: using phase estimation to estimate the period of our generator. To do so, we'll use what we've learned throughout the rest of the book together with a couple of new Q# operations to do arithmetic on a quantum computer. Let's jump in!

Deep dive: Here's looking at Euclid

Earlier, we used the `GreatestCommonDivisorI` function provided with the Q# standard libraries to compute the GCD of two integers. This function works by using Euclid's algorithm, which recursively attempts to divide an integer into another integer until no remainder is left over.

Suppose that we want to find the GCD of two integers a and b. We begin Euclid's algorithm by finding two additional integers q and r (short for "quotient" and "remainder") such that $a = qb + r$. It's straightforward to find q and r using integer division instructions, so this step isn't too hard on a classical computer. At that point, if $r = 0$, we're done: b is a divisor of both a and of itself, so there can't possibly be a larger common divisor. If not, we know the GCD of a and b has to also be a divisor of r, so we can recurse by finding the GCD of b and r, instead. Eventually, this process has to end, since the integers whose GCD we're looking for get smaller and smaller as we go but never become negative.

To make things a bit more concrete, we can work through the example from listing 12.2, as shown in the following table.

Using Euclid's algorithm to find the GCD of 678 and 390

a	b	q	r
678	390	1	288
390	288	1	102
288	102	2	84
102	84	1	18
84	18	4	12
18	12	1	6
12	6 (answer)	2	0 (done)

12.4 Quantum arithmetic

We have seen quite a few different parts of the Q# standard libraries by now, and with the focus of this chapter on arithmetic, it makes sense to introduce some functions and operations from the `Microsoft.Quantum.Arithmetic` namespace provided by the numerics library for Q#. As you might guess, this namespace provides lots of helpful functions, operations, and types that simplify doing arithmetic in quantum systems. In particular, we can use implementations for things like adding and multiplying numbers represented in qubit registers with support for multiple-qubit register encodings like `BigEndian` (where the least significant bit is on the left) and `LittleEndian` (where the least significant bit is on the right). Let's look at some example code using the Q# numerics library to add two integers.

NOTE A Q# notebook in the samples repo (https://github.com/crazy4pi314/learn-qc-with-python-and-qsharp) has all of these snippets written out for you!

First, since the numerics package is not loaded by default, we need to ask the Q# kernel to load it with the magic command %package. The %package magic command adds a new package to our IQ# session, making the functions, operations, and user-defined types implemented by that package available to us in our session.

To make things easier, we can also turn off displaying small amplitudes from diagnostic outputs like DumpMachine, as shown in the next listing.

Listing 12.4   Loading packages and setting preferences in IQ#

Uses %package to load the Microsoft.Quantum.Numerics package, which provides additional operations and functions for working with numbers represented by registers of qubits

After running %package, IQ# reports what packages are currently available in our IQ# session. Your version numbers will likely vary.

```
In [1]: %package Microsoft.Quantum.Numerics
        Adding package Microsoft.Quantum.Numerics: done!
Out[1]: - Microsoft.Quantum.Standard::0.15.2101125897
        - Microsoft.Quantum.Standard.Visualization::0.15.2101125897
        - Microsoft.Quantum.Numerics::0.15.2101125897
In [2]: %config dump.truncateSmallAmplitudes = "true"
Out[2]: "true"
```

The %config magic command sets various preferences for our current IQ# session. Here, for example, we can use %config to tell the DumpRegister and DumpMachine callables to leave out parts of each state vector that have very small amplitudes. That makes it much easier to visualize states on several qubits, as printing out each computational basis state can quickly get unwieldy.

TIP When we're working with Q# from within Jupyter Notebooks, the IQ# kernel provides several other magic commands to help write quantum programs, in addition to commands like %simulate, %package, and %config that we've seen so far. For a complete list, check out the documentation at https://docs.microsoft.com/qsharp/api/iqsharp-magic.

12.4.1   Adding with qubits

Now, let's get to coding an example that adds two integers while they are encoded in qubit registers. Listing 12.5 uses the AddI operation to add the contents of two quantum registers to each other. This listing uses the LittleEndian UDT provided by the Q# standard library to mark that each register of qubits is meant to be interpreted as an integer using little-endian encoding (also known as *least-significant order*). That is, when interpreting a LittleEndian register as an integer, treat the lowest qubit index as the least significant bit. For instance, to represent the integer 6 as a three-qubit quantum state in little-endian notation, we write $|011\rangle$, since $6 = 0 \times 2^0 + 1 \times 2^1 + 1 \times 2^2 = 2 + 4$.

Listing 12.5   Using the numerics library to add integers encoded in qubits

```
In [3]: open Microsoft.Quantum.Arithmetic;
        open Microsoft.Quantum.Diagnostics;
        open Microsoft.Quantum.Math;
```

```
operation AddCustom(num1 : Int, num2 : Int) : Int {
    let bitSize = BitSizeI(MaxI((num1, num2))) + 1;
    use reg1 = Qubit[bitSize];
    use reg2 = Qubit[bitSize];
    let qubits1 = LittleEndian(reg1);
    let qubits2 = LittleEndian(reg2);

    ApplyXorInPlace(num1, qubits1);
    ApplyXorInPlace(num2, qubits2);

    Message("Before addition:");
    DumpRegister((), reg2);

    AddI(qubits1, qubits2);

    Message("After addition:");
    DumpRegister((), reg2);

    ResetAll(reg1);
    return MeasureInteger(qubits2);
}
```

Out[3]: - AddCustom

Our registers must be big enough to hold the largest possible sum of the two integers. At most, we need one more bit than is required to represent the largest input.

Indicates that we want to interpret reg1 and reg2 as being integers, represented using little-endian encoding

Prepares the LittleEndian representation of an integer into the qubit register, since $x \oplus 0 = x$ whether x is 0 or 1

Using the operation AddI loaded from the numerics package, we can add integers represented by the two input registers qubits1 and qubits2.

Resets the first register so it can be deallocated, and then measures the register with the results

We can see the output of running this snippet in figure 12.4.

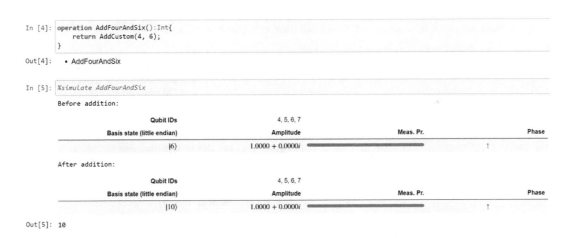

```
In [4]: operation AddFourAndSix():Int{
            return AddCustom(4, 6);
        }
```
Out[4]:   • AddFourAndSix

```
In [5]: %simulate AddFourAndSix
```
Before addition:

	Qubit IDs	4, 5, 6, 7		
Basis state (little endian)		Amplitude	Meas. Pr.	Phase
	6⟩	1.0000 + 0.0000i		↑

After addition:

	Qubit IDs	4, 5, 6, 7		
Basis state (little endian)		Amplitude	Meas. Pr.	Phase
	10⟩	1.0000 + 0.0000i		↑

Out[5]: 10

Figure 12.4   Output of using the numerics library to add integers encoded in qubit registers

12.4.2 *Multiplying with qubits in superposition*

We have seen how to do some basic modular arithmetic in Q#, but like most of our quantum algorithms, unless we use uniquely quantum properties/operations, we just have a very, very expensive calculation. In this section, we'll use the fact that we can have qubits in *superpositions* of numbers to help us gain the advantage we need to make Shor's algorithm work. Fortunately, AddI and many other similar arithmetic operations work in superposition: a property we need to use these arithmetic operations with phase estimation in the next part of the chapter. Before jumping to that, though, it's helpful to play around a little with what it means to add or multiply integers in superposition.

Here, we see how to apply what we've learned about superposition to arithmetic by using `MultiplyByModularInteger` as an example. Shortly, we'll use the same operation to construct the oracle we need for Shor's factoring algorithm later, so it's a pretty practical application.

First, let's look at an operation that we can use to prepare a register in a superposition of two integers. Listing 12.6 shows how to do so using what we learned about the `ApplyXorInPlace` operation in the previous section and the `Controlled` functor in chapter 9.

As we saw with other uses of `Controlled`, controlled operations do something when their control registers are in the all-ones state ($|11\cdots1\rangle$). Listing 12.6 controls on the zero state, instead, by using the `X` operation to map the $|0\rangle$ state to the $|1\rangle$ state. By placing the call to `X` in a `within`/`apply` block, we make sure Q# undoes our call to `X` after we apply our controlled operation.

> **TIP**   Using `within`/`apply` this way achieves something very similar to the `ControlledOnInt` function that we used in chapter 11 and is how that function is implemented in the Q# standard libraries.

Listing 12.6   Preparing a register in a superposition of integers

```
open Microsoft.Quantum.Arithmetic;
open Microsoft.Quantum.Diagnostics;
open Microsoft.Quantum.Math;

operation PrepareSuperpositionOfTwoInts(
    intPair : (Int, Int),
    register : LittleEndian,
) : Unit is Adj + Ctl {
    use ctrl = Qubit();
    H(ctrl);

    within {
        X(ctrl);
    } apply {
        Controlled ApplyXorInPlace(
            [ctrl],
            (Fst(intPair), register)
        );
    }
    Controlled ApplyXorInPlace(
        [ctrl],
        (Snd(intPair), register)
    );
    (ControlledOnInt(Snd(intPair), Y))(register!, ctrl);
}
```

Takes a register and a pair of integers and prepares that register in a superposition of those integers in a LittleEndian encoding

Prepares our control qubit in the $|+\rangle = (|0\rangle + |1\rangle) / \sqrt{2}$ state so that when we control later operations on that qubit, they are also in superposition

As noted previously, using **X** in a within/apply block lets us control on the $|0\rangle$ state instead of on the $|1\rangle$ state.

Adds a new input for the control register (see chapter 9). The other input is a tuple with the original arguments: the integer we want to prepare as a state, and the register on which we want to prepare that state.

Does the same thing with the second integer in intPair, and encodes it in the register as controlled on the ctrl qubit

Adds some phase to one of the two branches of our superposition by using the **Y** operation to rotate, controlled on our control qubit being in the $|1\rangle$ state

TIP The Y operation isn't needed in this case, but it helps us see how the phase applied by the controlled Y operation propagates through later steps.

Once we have a quantum register representing the superposition of two integers, we can apply other arithmetic operations across that superposition. In the following listing, for instance, we use the DumpMachine callable to see how the state of our register changes when using the MultiplyByModularInteger operation provided by the Q# standard libraries.

Listing 12.7 Using the numerics library to multiply in superposition

```
operation MultiplyInSuperpositionMod(
    superpositionInts : (Int, Int),
    multiplier : Int,
    modulus : Int
) : Int {
    use target = Qubit[BitSizeI(modulus - 1)];
    let register = LittleEndian(target);
    PrepareSuperpositionOfTwoInts(superpositionInts, register);

    Message("Before multiplication:");
    DumpMachine();

    MultiplyByModularInteger(
        multiplier, modulus, register
    );

    Message("After multiplication:");
    DumpMachine();

    return MeasureInteger(register);
}
```

The first thing we need to do is allocate a big enough register. Here, since we are doing modular multiplication, the largest possible value our register has to hold is modulus − 1.

Uses the operation we defined in listing 12.6 to prepare our target register in a superposition of integers

The numerics package provides **MultiplyByModularInteger**, which takes a LittleEndian register and multiplies it by the value of a classical multiplier, modulo a given modulus.

Measures a register, and returns the classical Int represented by that register

---

If we run the code in listings 12.6 and 12.7 in the sample notebook, we see the output shown in figure 12.5: the registers correctly show a superposition of 2 and 3 before multiplication and then show a superposition of 1 and 6 afterward. What would we expect the correct output to be? If we multiply as usual, it should be 6 and 9; but since we are doing arithmetic mod 8, the 9 is 1. When we then measure that register, we get 6 half the time and 1 the other half since they are in an equal superposition, as we can see from the state amplitude bars depicted in figure 12.5.

Exercise 12.4: Modular multiplication

Suppose that you have prepared a register in the $1 / \sqrt{2} \, (|2\rangle + |7\rangle)$ state, with each ket representing an integer in little-endian encoding. What state would your register be in after multiplying by 5 modulo 9? Write a Q# program that uses DumpMachine to confirm your answer.

```
In [18]:  operation MultiplyInSuperpostionTest() : Int {
              // Here we are multiplying 3 by a superposition of 2 and
              // 3 all mod 8.
              return MultiplyInSuperpostionMod((2, 3), 3, 8);
          }
```

Out[18]:   • MultiplyInSuperpostionTest

```
In [19]:  %simulate MultiplyInSuperpostionTest
```

Before multiplication:

Qubit IDs		0, 1, 2, 3		
Basis state (little endian)		Amplitude	Meas. Pr.	Phase
$|2\rangle$		$0.7071 + 0.0000i$		↑
$|3\rangle$		$0.0000 - 0.7071i$		←

After multiplication:

Qubit IDs		0, 1, 2, 3		
Basis state (little endian)		Amplitude	Meas. Pr.	Phase
$|1\rangle$		$0.0000 - 0.7071i$		←
$|6\rangle$		$0.7071 - 0.0000i$		↑

Out[19]:   6

Figure 12.5   **Output of multiplying 3 by 2 and 3 in superposition mod 8**

Exercise 12.5: Bonus

If you run the same program as in the previous exercise but try to multiply by 3 modulo 9, you'll get an error. Why?

Hint: Consider what you learned in chapter 8 has to be true of a classical function in order for it to be represented by a quantum oracle. If you're stuck, the answer is provided next, lightly hidden using https://rot13.com.

Answer: Zhygvcylvat ol guerr zbq avar vf abg erirefvoyr. Sbe vafgnapr, obgu bar gvzrf guerr naq sbhe gvzrf guerr zbq avar tvir mreb, rira gubhgu bar naq sbhe nera'g rdhny zbq avar. Fvapr pynffvpny shapgvbaf unir gb or erirefvoyr va beqre gb or ercerfragrq ol dhnaghz bcrengvbaf, gur `ZhygvcylOlZbqhyneVagrtre` envfrf na reebe va guvf pnfr.

NOTE   Notice what we've done here: we've used a quantum program to multiply an integer represented by a quantum register by a classical integer. The computation happens entirely on the quantum device and doesn't use any measurement; that means when our register starts in superposition, *the multiplication happens in superposition* as well.

12.4.3   *Modular multiplication in Shor's algorithm*

Now that we have seen a bit of the numerics library, let's return to the factoring scenario. The main places from algorithm 12.1 where we need to do some modular arithmetic and utilize the numerics library are steps 3 and 4 (repeated next). We can implement three operations to make short work of implementing those steps of Shor's algorithm and help us get to factoring integers.

The first operation we can take a look at from the sample code in this chapter implements step 3 of algorithm 12.1, the EstimateFrequency operation (listing 12.8).

Algorithm 12.1, steps 3 and 4 (pseudocode for factoring an integer with Shor's algorithm)

3 Use iterative phase estimation to find the *frequency* of the classical function $f(x) = a^x \bmod N$. The frequency tells us about how quickly *f* returns to the same value as *x* increases.

4 Use a classical algorithm known as *continued fractions expansion* to convert the frequency from the previous step into a period (*r*). The period *r* should then have the property that $f(x) = f(x + r)$ for all inputs *x*.

TIP This operation uses the phase estimation operations provided with the Q# standard libraries and that we saw in chapter 10. If you need a refresher, head back to chapter 9 for an overview of phase estimation or chapter 10 for how to run phase estimation with the standard libraries.

Listing 12.8   operations.qs: learning a generator's frequency with phase estimation

The freshly allocated register has to specify how to encode the integers it will be representing so we can use the LittleEndian UDT to wrap our newly allocated register.

```
operation EstimateFrequency(
    inputOracle : ((Int, Qubit[]) => Unit is Adj+Ctl),
    nBitsPrecision : Int,
    bitSize : Int)
: Int {
    use register = Qubit[bitSize];

    let registerLE = LittleEndian(register);
    ApplyXorInPlace(1, registerLE);

    let phase = RobustPhaseEstimation(
        nBitsPrecision,
        DiscreteOracle(inputOracle),
        registerLE!
    );
    ResetAll(register);

    return Round(
        (phase * IntAsDouble(2 ^ nBitsPrecision)) / (2.0 * PI())
    );
}
```

Since this is the primary step that uses qubits, we need to allocate a register that is big enough to represent the modulus.

Takes an Int and XORs it with the integer stored in the register provided in the second argument. Since registerLE starts as 0, this prepares the register as 1.

Uses RobustPhaseEstimation (see chapter 10) to learn the phase of inputOracle, and passes a quantum register and the number of bits of precision to which we want the phase estimated

The phase we estimated is just that: a phase. This equation converts it to a frequency: (phase * $2^{nBitsPrecision-1}$) / π.

Once the phase estimation is done, resets all the qubits in the register

Wrapping inputOracle in the DiscreteOracle UDT makes it clear to RobustPhaseEstimation that we want inputOracle to be interpreted as an oracle.

Now that we have the scaffolding for EstimateFrequency under our belt, we can take a look at an operation that implements the oracle we need for this algorithm. The

ApplyPeriodFindingOracle operation is just that: an operation that is structured like an oracle for the function f(power) = generator^{power} mod modulus. The next listing shows an implementation of ApplyPeriodFindingOracle.

Listing 12.9   operations.qs: implementing an oracle for the function f

```
operation ApplyPeriodFindingOracle(
    generator : Int, modulus : Int, power : Int, target : Qubit[])
: Unit is Adj + Ctl {
    Fact(
        IsCoprimeI(generator, modulus),
        "The generator and modulus must be co-prime."
    );
    MultiplyByModularInteger(
        ExpModI(generator, power, modulus),
        modulus,
        LittleEndian(target)
    );
}
```

Does some input checking that the provided generator and modulus are coprime

The same as in listing 12.7. Here, it helps this oracle multiply the integer represented in the target register by f(power) = generator^{power} mod modulus.

Microsoft.Quantum.Math also has the ExpModI function, which allows us to easily calculate f(power) = generator^{power} mod modulus.

LittleEndian tells us that the qubit register that ApplyPeriodFindingOracle takes is interpreted as an integer in the little-endian encoding.

The previous two operations form the basis for step 3 of algorithm 12.1. Now we need an operation that takes care of step 4, where we convert the estimated frequency of the generator to a period. The operation EstimatePeriod in the following listing does just that: given a generator and a modulus, it repeats estimating the frequency using EstimateFrequency and uses the continued fractions algorithm to ensure that the estimated frequency yields a valid period.

Listing 12.10   operations.qs: estimating periods from frequencies

Does some input checking that the provided generator and modulus are coprime

The IsCoprimeI function from the Microsoft.Quantum.Math namespace simplifies checking whether the generator and modulus are coprime.

```
operation EstimatePeriod(generator : Int, modulus : Int) : Int {
    Fact(
        IsCoprimeI(generator, modulus),
        "`generator` and `modulus` must be co-prime"
    );

    let bitSize = BitSizeI(modulus);
    let nBitsPrecision = 2 * bitSize + 1;
    mutable result = 1;
    mutable frequencyEstimate = 0;
```

The largest integer a register of qubits would need to hold is the modulus, so we use BitSizeI to help calculate the number of bits such that modulus $\leq 2^{\{\# \text{ of bits}\}}$.

To use a floating-point to represent k/r where r is the period and k is some other integer, we need enough bits of precision to approximate k/r: that is, one more bit than required to represent both k and r.

The result mutable variable keeps track of our current best guess for a period as we repeat the "repeat" block.

```
      repeat {
            set frequencyEstimate =
               EstimateFrequency(
                   ApplyPeriodFindingOracle(
                       generator, modulus, _, _
                   ),
                   nBitsPrecision, bitSize
               );
```

Repeats the frequency estimation steps as many times as necessary to ensure that we have a viable period estimate to move forward with

Calls the EstimateFrequency operation that we looked at earlier and passes it the appropriate arguments

Partially applies ApplyPeriodFinding-Oracle to ensure that Estimate-Frequency can apply it to the right power and register values

```
            if frequencyEstimate != 0 {
                set result =
                    PeriodFromFrequency(
                        frequencyEstimate, nBitsPrecision,
                        modulus, result
                    );
            } else {
                Message("The estimated frequency was 0, trying again.");
            }
        }
        until ExpModI(generator, result, modulus) == 1
        fixup {
            Message(
                "The estimated period from continued fractions failed, " +
                "trying again."
            );
        }
        return result;
    }
```

Captures step 4 of algorithm 12.1, which uses the continued fractions algorithm in the Q# standard library to calculate the period from the frequency.

Repeats the frequency estimation and period calculation until we have a period such that generatorresult mod modulus = 1.

If the "until" condition is not met, then the fixup block is run, which just issues a message that it is going to try again.

If frequencyEstimate is 0, we need to try again, since that doesn't make sense as a period (1/0). If we get 0, then the "repeat" block runs again, as the "until" condition isn't met in that case.

With this last operation, we have all the code we need to fully implement Shor's algorithm! In the next section, we'll put it all together and explore the implication of this integer factoring algorithm.

12.5 Putting it all together

We have now learned and practiced all the skills it takes to program and run Shor's algorithm. The quantum part of Shor's algorithm was pretty familiar, thanks to what we learned in chapters 9 and 10 about phase estimation; and we worked through classical algebra that links the tasks of factoring numbers and finding the period of a generator. This is no small feat—you should be quite proud of yourself for making it this far in your quantum journey!

Continued fraction convergents

You may have noticed one other bit of classical math happening in Shor's algorithm that we haven't touched on yet. In particular, the `PeriodFromFrequency` function is called on the output we get from phase estimation before continuing:

```
function PeriodFromFrequency(
    frequencyEstimate : Int, nBitsPrecision : Int,
    modulus : Int, result : Int)
: Int {
    let continuedFraction = ContinuedFractionConvergentI(
        Fraction(frequencyEstimate, 2^nBitsPrecision), modulus
    );
    let denominator = AbsI(Snd(continuedFraction!));
    return (denominator * result) / GreatestCommonDivisorI(
        result, denominator
    );
}
```

This is needed because phase estimation doesn't tell us *exactly* what we need. Instead of telling us how *long* it takes our function to spin around a clock (the period of our function), it tells us how *fast* our function spins around said clock: something more like a frequency. Unfortunately, we can't do something like taking the reciprocal of our frequency to get back to our period, as we're looking for the period as an integer. Thus, if we get a frequency estimate of f, we need to search near $f/2n$ for the closest fraction of the form N/r to find our period r.

This is an entirely classical arithmetic problem and has fortunately been well solved using a technique known as *continued fraction convergents*. This solution is made available in the Q# standard libraries by the `ContinuedFractionConvergentI` function, making it easy to go from the estimate we get from phase estimation to something about the period of our function.

Let's take a moment to review the `FactorSemiprimeInteger` operation that we saw at the beginning of the chapter, in light of what we have now learned. If you need a refresher, check out figure 12.6.

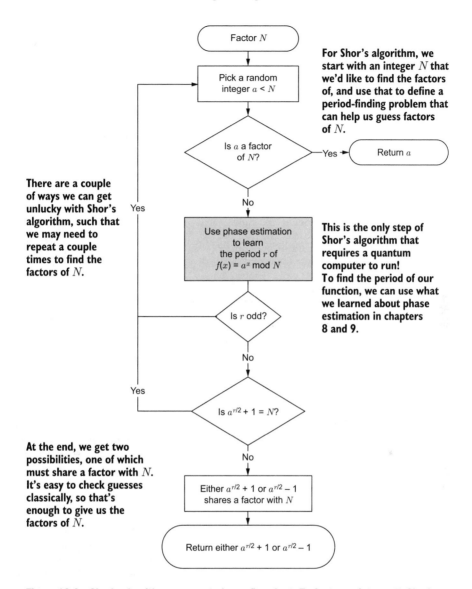

For Shor's algorithm, we start with an integer N that we'd like to find the factors of, and use that to define a period-finding problem that can help us guess factors of N.

There are a couple of ways we can get unlucky with Shor's algorithm, such that we may need to repeat a couple times to find the factors of N.

This is the only step of Shor's algorithm that requires a quantum computer to run! To find the period of our function, we can use what we learned about phase estimation in chapters 8 and 9.

At the end, we get two possibilities, one of which must share a factor with N. It's easy to check guesses classically, so that's enough to give us the factors of N.

Figure 12.6 Shor's algorithm represented as a flowchart. To factor an integer *N*, Shor's algorithm uses phase estimation and a quantum computer to find the *period* of a function that takes powers of another integer *a* using modular arithmetic mod *N*. After some classical post-processing, that period can be used to find the factors of *N*.

Listing 12.11 operations.qs: factoring semiprime integers with Shor's algorithm

Checks whether the integer to factor is even.
If so, then 2 is a factor, and we can stop early.

```
operation FactorSemiprimeInteger(number : Int) : (Int, Int) {
    if number % 2 == 0 {
```

Implements step 1 in algorithm 12.1, using DrawRandomInt to select a random integer in the range from 1 to "number" – 1 as our generator

```
        Message("An even number has been given; 2 is a factor.");
        return (number / 2, 2);
    }
    mutable factors = (1, 1);
    mutable foundFactors = false;

    repeat {
        let generator = DrawRandomInt(
                3, number - 2);
```

Uses the mutable variable factors to keep track of the factors we find for "number" as we step through the algorithm.

Uses the mutable flag foundFactors to keep track of whether we find any factors for "number" as we step through the algorithm

Covers steps 3 and 4 in algorithm 12.1. It returns a period that it computes with continued fractions from the frequency estimation inside EstimatePeriod.

Uses algebra to turn the estimated period into integers that might be factors. Sometimes it fails, so it also returns a Bool value indicating whether it succeeded.

```
    if IsCoprimeI(generator, number) {
        Message($"Estimating period of {generator}...");
        let period = EstimatePeriod(
            generator, number);
        set (foundFactors, factors) =
            MaybeFactorsFromPeriod(
                generator, period, number
            );
    } else {
        let gcd = GreatestCommonDivisorI(
            number, generator);
        Message(
            $"We have guessed a divisor of {number} to be " +
            $"{gcd} by accident. Nothing left to do."
        );
        set foundFactors = true;
        set factors = (gcd, number / gcd);
    }
    }
    until foundFactors
    fixup {
        Message(
            "The estimated period did not yield a valid factor, " +
            "trying again."
        );
    }
    return factors;
}
```

Step 2 in algorithm 12.1, where we verify that the generator is coprime to the integer we want to factor; if it's not, the "else" clause handles returning the common factor between the two.

Handles the case that the generator we guessed at the beginning has a common factor with the number we are trying to factor

Adds the condition for how long we should repeat the preceding block. Here we want to continue looking until we find the factors we are looking for.

Tells the program what to do before repeating the main loop. Here we have it let us know that our Q# program will try again.

Returns the tuple of factors for the input integer

Here's what it looks like if we run this operation in an IQ# notebook to factor 21.

> **Listing 12.12   Output of running `FactorSemiprimeInteger`**

```
In [1]: open IntegerFactorization;
```

To call the FactorSemiprimeInteger operation from within a notebook, it's helpful to write a new operation that provides the input 21.

```
        operation Factor21() : (Int, Int) {
            return FactorSemiprimeInteger(21);
        }
```

```
Out[1]: - Factor21
```

```
In [2]: %simulate Factor21
        We have guessed a divisor of 21 to be 3 by accident. Nothing left to do.
Out[2]: (3, 7)
```

```
In [3]: %simulate Factor21
        Estimating period of 19...
        The estimated period from continued fractions failed, trying again.
Out[3]: (7, 3)
```

```
In [4]: %simulate Factor21
        Estimating period of 17...
        The estimated period did not yield a valid factor, trying again.
        We have guessed a divisor of 21 to be 3 by accident. Nothing left to do.
Out[4]: (3, 7)
```

Each time, our code correctly returned the prime factors of 21: 3 and 7. The operation was run three times to show some possible different outcomes we might get. In In [2], when we tried to guess a generator, our call to DrawRandomInt ended up returning an integer that was not coprime to 21. Thus, we were able to use GreatestCommon-DivisorI to find a factorization. In In [3], our call to DrawRandomInt selected a generator of 19 and then had to run the frequency estimation twice to ensure that the continued fractions algorithm succeeded. In the final run, In [4], one full round of the period-finding task completed but failed to yield a correct factor; and when it tried to pick a new generator, it guessed a factor by accident.

> **NOTE** Given the limitations of running this on simulators or small hardware devices, we will frequently guess the correct factors when selecting the generator. We'll also get unlucky more often with small integers, guessing trivial factors like 1. These edge cases happen less often as the number we are trying to factor increases.

Using a simulator on a laptop, a desktop, or in the cloud, we likely won't be able to factor anything terribly large with Shor's algorithm. For example, it would be quite challenging to factor a 30-bit number by simulating Shor's algorithm on a classical computer, but 40-bit numbers were already considered woefully insufficient at standing up against classical factoring algorithms in 1992. This might seem like it makes Shor's algorithm useless, but all it really tells us is that it's hard to use a classical computer to simulate large quantum programs; we saw why that was the case in chapters 4 and 5.

Indeed, since the same algorithm works for much larger numbers (using 4,096-bit keys isn't overkill for protecting personal data, for example), such as those commonly used to protect data online, understanding how Shor's algorithm and other similar quantum algorithms work can help us appreciate the assumptions that go into modern uses of cryptography and what else we need going forward.

What's next for privacy?

Given what we've learned about Shor's algorithm, it might seem as though the cryptography that protects everything from our health records to our chat history is doomed. Fortunately, there are both quantum technologies (such as quantum key distribution, which we learned about in chapter 3) and new classical technologies meant to resist algorithms such as Shor's. The latter class of technologies, known as *post-quantum cryptography*, is the subject of much ongoing research and exploration.

As it turns out, Q# can play an important role in cryptography research by making it easier to understand how large a quantum computer would be required to attack a given cryptosystem. For instance, researchers at Google recently used Q# and Python to improve the cost required to implement the modular multiplication step of Shor's algorithm,[a] helping them estimate that 20 million qubits would be required to attack reasonable RSA instances using current quantum algorithms.[b] Similarly, https://github.com/Microsoft/grover-blocks is a great example of using Q# to understand how Grover's algorithm (from chapter 11) affects symmetric-key algorithms like AES.

In both cases, Q# is a valuable tool for understanding how much quantum computing power an attacker would need to compromise current cryptosystems. Together with assumptions about the speed at which quantum algorithms and hardware will continue to improve, assumptions about how much quantum computing power will be feasible for attackers to purchase, and requirements for how long algorithms like RSA need to be secure to guarantee our privacy, the understanding developed by using Q# can help us to recognize how quickly current cryptosystems need to be replaced. Like anything in information security, guaranteeing privacy against quantum attackers is a very complex topic, not to mention one without any easy answers. Fortunately, tools like Q# and the Quantum Development Kit help make the problem a bit more tractable.

---

[a]   Craig Gidney, "Asymptotically Efficient Quantum Karatsuba Multiplication" (2018), https://arxiv.org/abs/1904.07356.

[a]   Craig Gidney and Martin Ekerå, "How to Factor 2048-bit RSA Integers in 8 Hours Using 20 Million Noisy Qubits (2019), https://arxiv.org/abs/1905.09749.

Summary

- Modern cryptography works by hiding secrets with mathematical puzzles that are hard for classical computers to solve, like factoring numbers. Large quantum computers can be used to factor numbers, changing how we think about cryptography.
- Modular arithmetic generalizes how the hands of a clock move: for example, 25 + 5 is 3 on a clock face with 27 hours.
- Integers with exactly two prime factors are called *semiprime* and can be factored by using quantum computers to solve modular arithmetic problems together with phase estimation.

- The Q# numerics library provides useful functions and operations for working with modular integers on quantum computers.
- Shor's algorithm combines the classical pre- and post-processing required with phase estimation on a quantum computer to quickly factor integers using modular arithmetic.

Wrapping up

Before we say goodbye, it's helpful to take a step back and appreciate how all the various skills we learned throughout the book came together in this chapter to help us understand a real-world application for quantum computers. In part 1, we learned the basics of how we can describe and simulate quantum computers, and about the basic quantum effects that make quantum computing unique. We learned in chapter 3 how to use single qubits and superposition to share cryptographic keys securely with quantum key distribution. In chapters 4–6, we entangled multiple qubits to play games and move data around a quantum device. We even built our own quantum simulator in Python to implement these games and learn about the math that helps us describe quantum effects.

With all of those basics under our belt, in part 2, we started writing quantum algorithms to help the crew in Camelot play some games. In chapter 7, we learned about Q#, a new programming language specifically designed to easily write programs for a quantum computer. In chapter 8, we implemented the Deutsch–Jozsa algorithm to select a new king, but along the way, we also learned about oracles and how they can help us evaluate classical functions in a quantum program. We also developed our own phase-estimation program in chapter 9, where we learned how to manipulate phase and use it with phase kickback to examine operations in our quantum programs.

Having a new toolbox of quantum development techniques at our disposal, we tackled some of the most exciting applications of quantum computing. In chapter 10, we learned about Hamiltonian simulation and how we can use the quantum systems in our quantum computers to simulate the energy levels in various chemicals. In chapter 11, we implemented Grover's algorithm to search for information in unstructured data with amplitude amplification. In this chapter, we used everything from Q# diagnostic functions and operations to phase estimation and everything from `within`/`apply` blocks to oracle representations of classical functions to factor numbers on a quantum computer. Using what we learned in the rest of the book, most of the hard parts of writing Shor's algorithm were the *classical* parts required to connect the problem of factoring numbers to one of period finding.

While this book did not exhaust all there is to learn about quantum computing—a lot has happened since 1985, after all!—what you've learned gives you what you need to keep learning, exploring, and pushing forward with quantum computing. Using Python and Q# together, you have the tools to take part in one of the most exciting advances in computing, to help your peers and colleagues learn along with you, and to build a community that can put quantum computing to good use. Go have fun!

What's next?

While there's always more to learn about quantum computing, you now have what you need to start developing quantum applications using Python and Q# together. If you're interested in learning and doing more with quantum computing, here are some resources to help you take your next step:

- *Q# Community* (qsharp.community)—An open source community around quantum programming in Q#, including blogs, code repositories, and online meetups
- *Microsoft Quantum Docs* (https://docs.microsoft.com/azure/quantum/)—Full reference documentation for all things related to the Quantum Development Kit
- *arXiv* (arxiv.org)—An online repository for scientific papers and manuscripts, including a huge amount of research about quantum computing
- *Unitary Fund* (unitary.fund)—Nonprofit that provides grants and financial support for open source quantum software, along with neat suggestions for open source projects we can take on
- *Quantum Open Source Foundation* (www.qosf.org)—Foundation for developing open source quantum software, including a list of current projects and resources for further learning
- *QC Ethics* (qcethics.org)—Resources for ethics in quantum computing
- *Q-Turn* (q-turn.org)—An inclusive quantum computing conference series
- *Quantum Algorithm Zoo* (quantumalgorithmzoo.org)—List of known quantum algorithms, with links to papers about each
- *Quantum Computing: A Gentle Introduction* (Jack D. Hidary, Springer, 2019)—More details about the math behind the quantum algorithms we learned about in this book

Many universities and colleges also have courses or research programs that may be of interest as you continue exploring quantum computing. However you decide to continue, we hope you have fun and work to make the quantum computing community even more wonderful!

appendix A
Installing required software

The beginning of almost any project involves finding or setting up a development environment on your computer. This appendix helps you prepare to use the samples for this book online (with Binder or GitHub Codespaces), or to install a Python environment and Microsoft Quantum Development Kit that you can use locally. If you run into issues, please check out the most current documentation for using the Quantum Development Kit (https://docs.microsoft.com/azure/quantum/install-overview-qdk) and/or file an issue on the repo for this book (https://github.com/crazy4pi314/learn-qc-with-python-and-qsharp).

A.1 Running samples online

If you'd like to try out the samples in this book without installing anything, there are two great options to do so:

- Binder (mybinder.org), a free service for exploring hosted Jupyter Notebooks
- GitHub Codespaces, a cloud-hosted development environment

A.1.1 Using Binder

To use Binder, simply go to https://mybinder.org/v2/gh/crazy4pi314/learn-qc-with-python-and-qsharp/master. It may take a few moments, but Binder will spin up a new Jupyter Notebook installation, complete with the Python packages you need and Q# support.

> **WARNING** The Binder service is intended for exploration only and will *delete* your changes after approximately 20 minutes of inactivity. While Binder is a great way to get started, if you would like to continue developing quantum programs, it's helpful to either use GitHub Codespaces or install Python and the Quantum Development Kit locally on your machine.

VT 189 8402

A.1.2 Using GitHub Codespaces

As of the time of this writing, GitHub Codespaces is in early preview at https://github.com/features/codespaces. For instructions on how to use code samples for this book with Codespaces, please check out the sample repository at https://github.com/crazy4pi314/learn-qc-with-python-and-qsharp.

A.2 Installing locally using Anaconda

In part 1 of the book, we make heavy use of Python as a tool to explore quantum programming, while in parts 2 and 3, we use Python and Q# together. In doing so, we rely on the Quantum Development Kit and several Python libraries that make it easier to write scientific programs. As a result, when installing locally, it can be much easier to use a scientific software distribution such as the *Anaconda distribution* (anaconda.com) to help manage Python and other scientific programming tools.

A.2.1 Installing Anaconda

To install Anaconda, follow the instructions at https://docs.anaconda.com/anaconda/install.

> **WARNING** At the time of this writing, the Anaconda distribution is provided with Python 2.7 or 3.8. Python 2.7 officially reached end-of-life as of January 2020, and is provided for compatibility reasons only. We assume Python 3.7 or later in this book, so make sure you install a version of Anaconda that provides Python 3.

A.2.2 Installing packages with Anaconda

Packages are a great way to collaborate and save time when we are trying to learn or develop new code. They are a way of collecting related code and wrapping it up so it is easy to share to other machines. Packages can be installed on our machine with what is sensibly called a *package manager*, of which there are a few common options for Python. We may choose one manager over another because each has its own listing of packages, and the package we want to install may only be known by a particular manager (depending on how the author deployed it). Let's start by looking at the package managers we have already installed as a part of Anaconda.

As a default, Anaconda comes with two package managers: pip and conda. Given we have installed Anaconda, the conda package manager has some additional pip features that make it a good default choice for package management. Conda has support for installing dependencies automatically when you install a package; and it has the concept of *environments*, which are really helpful for creating dedicated Python sandboxes for each project we are working on. A good general strategy is to install packages from conda when they are available and install packages from pip otherwise.

> **NOTE** The conda package manager can be used with most common command-line environments. But to use conda with PowerShell, you need version 4.6.0 or

later. To check your version, run `conda --version`. If you need to update, run `conda update conda`.

Conda environments

We may run into the situation that the packages we need for two different projects contradict each other. To help isolate projects from each other, the Anaconda distribution provides `conda env` as a tool to help manage multiple *environments*. Each environment is a completely independent copy of Python with only the packages needed for a particular project or application. Environments may even use different versions of Python from each other, with one environment using 2.7 and another using 3.8. Environments are also great for collaborating with others, as we can send our teammates a single small text file, environment.yml, to tell their `conda env` how to create an environment that's identical to ours.

For more information, see https://docs.conda.io/projects/conda/en/latest/user-guide/tasks/manage-environments.html.

Following that strategy, let's start by making a new environment with the packages you need. The code samples for this book, found at https://github.com/crazy4pi314/learn-qc-with-python-and-qsharp, come with a file called environment.yml that tells conda what packages you need in your new environment. Clone or download the code from the repository for this book, and then run the following at your favorite command line:

```
conda env create -f environment.yml
```

This command creates a new environment called `qsharp-book` using packages from the `conda-forge` channel and installs Jupyter Notebook, Python (version 3.6 or later), the IQ# kernel for Jupyter, the IPython interpreter, NumPy, the Matplotlib plotting engine, and QuTiP into the new environment. The conda package manager prompts you to confirm the list of packages that will be installed. To proceed, press "y" and then Enter, and grab a cup of coffee.

> **TIP** The environment.yml file provided at https://github.com/crazy4pi314/learn-qc-with-python-and-qsharp also installs the `qsharp` package, which provides integration between Python and the Quantum Development Kit (which you'll install in the next step).

Once conda has finished creating your new environment, let's give it a go. To test your new environment, first activate it:

```
conda activate qsharp-book
```

Once the `qsharp-book` environment has been activated, the `python` command should invoke the version installed into that environment. To check this, you can print the path to the python command for your environment. Run python, and then run the following at the Python prompt:

You may see a different path, depending on your system.

```
>>> import sys; print(sys.executable)
C:\Users\Chris\Anaconda3\envs\qsharp-book\python.exe
```

If your environment was created successfully, you can use it either at the command line with IPython or in your browser with Jupyter Notebook. To get started with IPython, run ipython from your command line (make sure you've activated qsharp-book first):

```
$ ipython
In [1]: import qutip as qt
In [2]: qt.basis(2, 0)
Quantum object: dims = [[2], [1]], shape = (2, 1), type = ket
Qobj data =
[[1.]
 [0.]]
```

If you would like to learn more about using NumPy, continue reading in chapter 2. If you would like to learn more about using QuTiP, continue reading in chapter 5. If you would like to learn about the Quantum Development Kit, continue reading here.

> **For more information**
> - Anaconda documentation: https://docs.anaconda.com/anaconda
> - NumPy documentation: http://numpy.org
> - Jupyter Notebook documentation: https://jupyter-notebook.readthedocs.io/en/stable/notebook.html

A.3   *Installing the Quantum Development Kit*

TIP The latest version of the installation instructions for the Quantum Development Kit can be found at https://docs.microsoft.com/azure/quantum/install-overview-qdk. To use the code samples provided with this book, make sure you install Python and Jupyter Notebook support when following the Quantum Development Kit install guide.

The Quantum Development Kit from Microsoft is a set of tools for working with and programming in Q#, a new language for quantum programming. If you installed your Python environment using Anaconda, then you can get started with the Quantum Development Kit by using conda:

```
conda install -c quantum-engineering qsharp
```

If you would prefer to use Q# with standalone programs or outside of a conda environment, then you can follow the instructions in this section to install the Quantum Development Kit locally on your computer.

NOTE This book focuses on using Visual Studio Code, but the Quantum Development Kit can be used with any other text editor as well by following the command-line instructions in the main text. The Quantum Development Kit can also be used with Visual Studio 2019 or later by using the extension at https://marketplace.visualstudio.com/items?itemName=quantum.DevKit.

Using the Visual Studio Code installation from setting up your Python environment, you need to do a few things to use the Quantum Development Kit with C#, Python, and Jupyter Notebook:

1 Install the .NET Core SDK.
2 Install the project templates for Q#.
3 Install the Quantum Development Kit extension for Visual Studio Code.
4 Install Q# support for Jupyter Notebook.
5 Install the `qsharp` package for Python.

Once you've done this, you have everything you need to write and run quantum programs in Q#.

Meet the .NETs

Answering the question of what .NET is has become a bit more complicated than it used to be. Historically, *.NET* was reasonable shorthand for *.NET Framework*, a virtual machine and compiler infrastructure for any of the .NET languages (most notably, C#, F#, and Visual Basic .NET). The .NET Framework is Windows-only, but third-party reimplementations such as Mono exist for other platforms, including macOS and Linux.

A couple of years ago, though, Microsoft and the .NET Foundation open sourced a new flavor of .NET called .NET Core. Unlike .NET Framework, .NET Core is cross-platform out of the box. .NET Core is also much smaller, with much of the functionality separated into optional packages. This makes it much easier to have multiple versions of .NET Core on the same machine and for new .NET Core features to be introduced without compatibility issues.

However, the bifurcation of .NET into Framework and Core comes with its own foibles. To make .NET Core work better as a cross-platform programming environment, a few things in the .NET standard libraries were changed in ways that aren't entirely compatible with .NET Framework. To resolve this, the .NET Foundation introduced the concept of .NET Standard, a set of APIs offered by both .NET Framework and .NET Core. The .NET Core SDK can then be used to make libraries for either .NET Core or .NET Standard and build applications for .NET Core. Many of the libraries provided in the Quantum Development Kit target .NET Standard, so that Q# programs can be used from traditional .NET Framework applications or new applications built using the .NET Core SDK.

Going forward, the most recent version of .NET is just called ".NET 5," even though it is the next version after .NET Core 3.1. With .NET 5, there is only one .NET platform, instead of .NET Framework, .NET Core, and .NET Standard, reducing much of the confusion. For more, check out https://devblogs.microsoft.com/dotnet/introducing-net-5/.

(continued)

For now, however, .NET Core 3.1 is still the most recent *long-term release* of the .NET platform, making it the best choice for writing stable production software until the next long-term release, .NET 6, comes out. As a result, the Quantum Development Kit is written to use the .NET Core SDK 3.1.

A.3.1   *Installing the .NET Core SDK*

To install the .NET Core SDK, go to https://dotnet.microsoft.com/download/dotnet-core/3.1 and select your operating system from the selections near the top of the page. Under the section labeled "Build Apps—SDK," download an installer for your operating system, and you should be good to go!

A.3.2   *Installing the project templates*

One thing that might be different than you're used to is that .NET development centers around the idea of a *project* that specifies how a compiler is invoked to make a new binary. For instance, a C# project (`*.csproj`) file tells the C# compiler what source files should be built, what libraries are needed, what warnings are turned on and off, etc. In this way, project files work similarly to makefiles or other build-management systems. The big difference is in how project files on .NET Core reference libraries.

  Q# reuses this infrastructure to make it easy to get new libraries for your quantum programs, such as those listed at https://docs.microsoft.com/azure/quantum/user-guide/libraries/additional-libraries, or those made available by community developers at https://qsharp.community/projects/. Using this infrastructure, a Q# project file can specify one or more references to *packages* on NuGet.org, a package repository for software libraries. Each package can then provide a number of different libraries. When a project that depends on a NuGet package is built, the .NET Core SDK automatically downloads the right package and then uses the libraries in that package to build the project.

  From the perspective of quantum programming, this allows for the Quantum Development Kit to be distributed as a small number of NuGet packages that can be installed not on a machine, but into each project. This makes it easy to use different versions of the Quantum Development Kit on different projects or include only the parts you require for a particular project. To help you get started with a reasonable set of NuGet packages, the Quantum Development Kit is provided with templates for creating new projects that reference everything you need.

> **TIP**   If you prefer to work within an IDE, the Visual Studio Code extension for the Quantum Development Kit (see the following) can also be used to create new projects.

To install the project templates, run the following command at your favorite terminal:

```
dotnet new -i "Microsoft.Quantum.ProjectTemplates"
```

Once the project templates are installed, you can use them by running `dotnet new` again:

```
dotnet new console -lang Q# -o ProjectName
```
⊲— Be sure to replace "ProjectName" with the name of the project you would like to create.

A.3.3 Installing the Visual Studio Code extension

Once you have installed Visual Studio Code from https://code.visualstudio.com/, you need the Quantum Development Kit extension to get editor support for Q#, including autocompletion, inline syntax error highlighting, and so forth.

To install the extension, open a new Visual Studio Code window and press Ctrl-Shift-X (Windows and Linux) or ⌘-Shift-X to bring up the extensions sidebar. In the search bar, type `Microsoft Quantum Development Kit` and click the Install button. After Visual Studio Code installs the extension, the Install button changes to a Reload button. Click it to close Visual Studio Code and reopen your window with the Quantum Development Kit extension installed. Alternatively, press Ctrl-P or ⌘-P to bring up the Go To palette. In the palette, type `ext install quantum.quantum-devkit-vscode`, and press Enter.

In either case, once the extension has been installed, to use it, open a folder (Ctrl-Shift-O or ⌘-Shift-O) containing the Q# project you'd like to work on. At this point, you should have everything you need to get up and programming with the Quantum Development Kit!

> **For more information**
> - Quantum Development Kit documentation: https://docs.microsoft.com/azure/quantum/
> - Using the `dotnet` command: https://docs.microsoft.com/dotnet/core/tools/dotnet
> - Getting started with Visual Studio Code: https://code.visualstudio.com/docs/introvideos/basics

A.3.4 Installing IQ# for Jupyter Notebook

Run the following from your favorite command line:

```
dotnet tool install -g Microsoft.Quantum.IQSharp
dotnet iqsharp install
```

> **TIP** On some Linux installations, you may need to run `dotnet iqsharp install --user` instead.

This makes Q# available as a language for Jupyter Notebooks such as the ones used in chapter 7.

appendix B
Glossary and quick reference

This appendix provides a quick reference to many of the quantum concepts covered in this book, as well as to the Q# language (version 0.15). Most of the contents of this appendix are covered in the main body but are collected here for convenience.

B.1 Glossary

adjoint operation A quantum operation that perfectly reverses or undoes the action of another quantum operation. Operations that are their own adjoint, such as X and H, are *self-adjoint*. If an operation can be simulated by the unitary matrix U, its adjoint operation can be simulated by the complex transpose of U, also known as the adjoint of U and written $U^\dagger$. In Q#, operations that have adjoint operations are denoted by is Adj.

algorithm A procedure for solving a problem, typically specified as a sequence of steps.

BB84 Short for "Bennett and Brassard 1984." A protocol for performing quantum key distribution (QKD) by sending single qubits at a time.

Born's rule A mathematical expression that can be used to predict the probability of a quantum measurement, given a description of that measurement and of the state of the register being measured.

classical bit The smallest functional unit of storage and processing in a classical computer. A classical bit can be in either the "0" or "1" state.

classical computer A conventional computer that uses the laws of classical physics to perform computations.

controlled operation A quantum operation applied based on the state of a control register without measuring, such that superpositions are correctly preserved. For example, the CNOT operation is a controlled-NOT or controlled-X operation. Similarly, the Fredkin operation is a controlled-SWAP operation. In Q#, operations that can be controlled are denoted by is Ctl.

complex number A number of the form $z = a + bi$, where $i^2 = -1$.

computational basis state A state labeled by a string of classical bits. For example, $|01101\rangle$ is a computational basis state on a five-qubit register.

computer A device that takes data as input and does some sort of operations on that data.

coprime Two positive integers that share no prime factors. For instance, $21 = 3 \times 7$ and $10 = 2 \times 5$ are coprime, while $21 = 3 \times 7$ and $15 = 3 \times 5$ share 3 as a factor and thus are not coprime.

entanglement When the states of two or more qubits cannot be written out independently. For example, if two qubits are in the state $(|00\rangle + |11\rangle) / \sqrt{2}$, then there are no two single-qubit states $|\psi\rangle$ and $|\phi\rangle$ such that $(|00\rangle + |11\rangle) / \sqrt{2} = |\psi\rangle \otimes |\phi\rangle$, and the two qubits are entangled.

eigenphase The global phase assigned to an eigenstate by a quantum operation. For example, the $|-\rangle = (|0\rangle - |1\rangle) / \sqrt{2}$ eigenstate of the X operation has an eigenphase of -1, since $X|-\rangle = (|1\rangle - |0\rangle) / \sqrt{2} = -|-\rangle$.

eigenstate A state that is unmodified by application of a quantum operation, up to a possible global phase. For example, the $|+\rangle$ state is an eigenstate of the X operation since $X|+\rangle = |+\rangle$.

eigenvalue Given a matrix A, a number λ is an *eigenvalue* of A if $A\vec{x} = \lambda\vec{x}$ for some vector $\vec{x}$.

eigenvector Given a matrix A, a vector $\vec{x}$ of A if $A\vec{x} = \lambda\vec{x}$ for some number λ.

global phase Any two quantum states that are equal up to multiplication by a complex number of magnitude 1 differ by a global phase. In that case, the two states are completely equivalent. For example, $(|0\rangle - |1\rangle) / \sqrt{2}$ and $(|1\rangle - |0\rangle) / \sqrt{2}$ represent the same state, as they differ by a phase of $-1 = e^{i\pi}$.

measurement A quantum operation that returns classical data about the state of a quantum register.

no-cloning theorem The mathematical theorem proving that there cannot exist a quantum operation that perfectly copies quantum information. For example, it is impossible to make an operation that transforms the state $|\psi\rangle \otimes |0\rangle$ to $|\psi\rangle \otimes |\psi\rangle$ for arbitrary quantum states $|\psi\rangle$.

oracle A quantum operation that implements a classical function applied to quantum registers.

Pauli matrices The single-qubit unitary matrices $\mathbb{1}$, X, Y, and Z.

phase A complex number of magnitude 1 (i.e., $a + bi$, where $|a|^2 + |b|^2 = 1$). A phase can be written as $e^{i\theta}$, where θ is a real number. Note that as a shorthand, when it is clear from context, sometimes θ itself is known as a phase.

phase estimation Any quantum algorithm for learning the eigenphase associated with a given eigenstate of a quantum operation.

phase kickback A quantum programming technique for associating the phase applied by a controlled quantum operation to the state of the control register instead of the state of the target register. This technique can be used to convert what would otherwise be a global phase applied by a unitary operation into a physically observable phase.

program A sequence of instructions that can be interpreted by a classical computer to perform a desired task.

quantum computer A quantum device designed and used to solve computational problems that are difficult for classical computers.

quantum device A quantum system built to achieve some purpose or to perform some task.

quantum key distribution (QKD) A communication protocol to share random numbers between two parties such that, when performed by devices that operate correctly, the security of the protocol is guaranteed by quantum mechanics (in particular, by the no-cloning theorem).

quantum operation A subroutine in a quantum program, representing a sequence of instructions sent to a quantum device and classical control flow. Some quantum operations, such as X and H, are built into a quantum device and are said to be *intrinsic*.

quantum program A classical program that controls a quantum device by sending instructions to that device and processing measurement data returned by the device. Typically, quantum programs are written in a quantum programming language such as Q#.

quantum register A collection of qubits. The register can be in any computational basis state, labeled by strings of classical bits, or any superposition thereof.

quantum state The state of a quantum register (that is, a register of qubits), typically written as a vector of 2^n complex numbers, where n is the number of qubits in the register.

quantum system A physical system that requires quantum mechanics to describe and simulate.

qubit The smallest functional unit in a quantum computer. A single qubit can be in the $|0\rangle$ state, the $|1\rangle$ state, or any superposition thereof.

reversible A classical function that can be perfectly inverted. For example, $f(x) = \neg x$ can be inverted, since $f(f(x)) = x$. Similarly, $g(x,y) = (x, x \oplus y)$ is reversible since $g(g(x,y)) = (x,y)$. On the other hand, $h(x,y) = (x, x \text{ AND } y)$ is not reversible, since $h(0,0) = h(0,1) = (0,0)$, so that we cannot determine the input to h given the output $(0,0)$.

semiprime A positive integer with exactly two prime factors. For example, $21 = 3 \times 7$ is semiprime, while $105 = 3 \times 5 \times 7$ has three prime factors and thus is not semiprime.

state A description of a physical system or device that is complete enough to allow simulating that device.

superposition A quantum state that can be written as a linear combination of other states is in a superposition of those states. For example, $|+\rangle = (|0\rangle + |1\rangle) / \sqrt{2}$ is a superposition of the states $|0\rangle$ and $|1\rangle$, while $|0\rangle$ is a superposition of $|+\rangle$ and $|-\rangle = (|0\rangle - |1\rangle) / \sqrt{2}$.

unitary matrix A matrix U such that $UU^\dagger = 1$, where $U^\dagger$ is the conjugate transform, or adjoint of U. Similar to a classical truth table, a unitary matrix is a matrix that describes how a quantum operation transforms the state of its input so that it can be used to simulate that operation for arbitrary inputs.

unitary operation A quantum operation that can be represented by a unitary matrix. In Q#, unitary operations are adjointable and controllable (is Adj + Ctl).

B.2 *Dirac notation*

Often, in quantum computing, we use a kind of compressed notation for vectors and matrices known as *Dirac notation*. This is covered in more detail throughout the book, but a few key points of Dirac notation are summarized in this table.

Dirac notation	Matrix notation
$\lvert 0 \rangle$	$\begin{pmatrix} 1 \\ 0 \end{pmatrix}$
$\lvert 1 \rangle$	$\begin{pmatrix} 0 \\ 1 \end{pmatrix}$
$\langle 0 \rvert$	$(1 \ \ 0)$
$\lvert + \rangle = \frac{1}{\sqrt{2}} (\lvert 0 \rangle + \lvert 1 \rangle)$	$\frac{1}{\sqrt{2}} \begin{pmatrix} 1 \\ 1 \end{pmatrix}$
$\lvert - \rangle = \frac{1}{\sqrt{2}} (\lvert 0 \rangle - \lvert 1 \rangle)$	$\frac{1}{\sqrt{2}} \begin{pmatrix} 1 \\ -1 \end{pmatrix}$
$\lvert 00 \rangle = \lvert 0 \rangle \otimes \lvert 0 \rangle$	$\begin{pmatrix} 1 \\ 0 \\ 0 \\ 0 \end{pmatrix}$
$\lvert ++ \rangle = \lvert + \rangle \otimes \lvert + \rangle = \frac{1}{2}(\lvert 00 \rangle + \lvert 01 \rangle + \lvert 10 \rangle + \lvert 11 \rangle)$	$\frac{1}{2} \begin{pmatrix} 1 \\ 1 \\ 1 \\ 1 \end{pmatrix}$
$\lvert 0 \rangle\langle 0 \rvert$	$\begin{pmatrix} 1 & 0 \\ 0 & 0 \end{pmatrix}$
$\lvert 1 \rangle\langle 1 \rvert$	$\begin{pmatrix} 0 & 0 \\ 0 & 1 \end{pmatrix}$
$\lvert 0 \rangle\langle 0 \rvert \otimes \mathbb{1} + \lvert 1 \rangle\langle 1 \rvert \otimes U$ (controlled-U)	$\begin{pmatrix} 1 & 0 \\ 0 & U \end{pmatrix} = \begin{pmatrix} 1 & \dots & 0 & 0 & \dots & 0 \\ \vdots & \dots & \vdots & \vdots & \dots & \vdots \\ 0 & \dots & 1 & 0 & \dots & 0 \\ 0 & \dots & 0 & u_{11} & \dots & u_{1n} \\ \vdots & \dots & \vdots & \vdots & \dots & \vdots \\ 0 & 0 & 0 & u_{m1} & \dots & u_{mn} \end{pmatrix},$ where $U = \begin{pmatrix} u_{11} & \cdots & u_{1n} \\ \vdots & \dots & \vdots \\ u_{m1} & \cdots & u_{mn} \end{pmatrix}$

B.3   Quantum operations

This section summarizes some common quantum operations that you see throughout the book. In particular, we show how to call each operation from Q# by passing qubits as inputs; how to simulate that operation in QuTiP with a matrix that acts on states, the unitary matrix that we use to simulate each operation; and some examples of how that operation behaves mathematically.

> **NOTE** For a complete listing of all built-in Q# operations, see the Q# API reference at https://docs.microsoft.com/qsharp/api.

For all Q# examples, we have assumed the following open statement:

```
open Microsoft.Quantum.Intrinsic;
```

For all Python/QuTiP examples, we have assumed the following import statements:

```
import qutip as qt
import qutip.qip.operations as qtops
```

The second convention is not used in the book but is used here for brevity.

Q# operations act on *qubits*, while QuTiP represents operations by unitary matrices that multiply *states*. Thus, in contrast with Q# operations, QuTiP objects do not explicitly list their inputs.

Description	Code (Q# and QuTiP)	Unitary matrix	Mathematical examples
Bit flip (Pauli X)	X(target); // Q# qt.sigmax() # QuTiP	$X = \begin{pmatrix} 0 & 1 \\ 1 & 0 \end{pmatrix}$	$X\lvert 0\rangle = \lvert +\rangle$ $X\lvert 1\rangle = \lvert -\rangle$ $X\lvert +\rangle = \lvert +\rangle$ $X\lvert -\rangle = -\lvert -\rangle$
Bit and phase flip (Pauli Y)	Y(target); // Q# qt.sigmay() # QuTiP	$Y = \begin{pmatrix} 0 & -1i \\ 1i & 0 \end{pmatrix}$	$Y\lvert 0\rangle = i\lvert 1\rangle$ $Y\lvert 1\rangle = -i\lvert 0\rangle$ $Y\lvert +\rangle = -i\lvert -\rangle$ $Y\lvert -\rangle = i\lvert +\rangle$
Phase flip (Pauli Z)	Z(target); // Q# qt.sigmaz() # QuTiP	$Z = \begin{pmatrix} 1 & 0 \\ 0 & -1 \end{pmatrix}$	$Z\lvert 0\rangle = \lvert 0\rangle$ $Z\lvert 1\rangle = -\lvert 1\rangle$ $Z\lvert +\rangle = \lvert -\rangle$ $Z\lvert -\rangle = \lvert +\rangle$
Hadamard	H(target); // Q# qtops.hadamard_transform() # QuTiP	$H = \dfrac{1}{\sqrt{2}}\begin{pmatrix} 1 & 1 \\ 1 & -1 \end{pmatrix}$	$H\lvert 0\rangle = \lvert +\rangle$ $H\lvert 1\rangle = \lvert -\rangle$ $H\lvert +\rangle = \lvert 0\rangle$ $H\lvert -\rangle = \lvert 1\rangle$

Description	Code (Q# and QuTiP)	Unitary matrix	Mathematical examples

Controlled-NOT (CNOT)	CNOT(control, target); // Q# (shorthand)
	
	Controlled X(
	  [control],
	  target
	); // Q#
	
	qtops.cnot() # QuTiP
		$U_{\text{CNOT}} = \begin{pmatrix} 1 & 0 & 0 & 0 \\ 0 & 1 & 0 & 0 \\ 0 & 0 & 0 & 1 \\ 0 & 0 & 1 & 0 \end{pmatrix}$	$U_{\text{CNOT}}(\lvert 0\rangle \otimes \lvert x\rangle) = (\lvert 0\rangle \otimes \lvert x\rangle)$
			$U_{\text{CNOT}}(\lvert 1\rangle \otimes \lvert x\rangle) = (\lvert 1\rangle \otimes \lvert \neg x\rangle)$
			$U_{\text{CNOT}}\lvert +-\rangle = -\lvert --\rangle$

CCNOT (Toffoli)	CCNOT(control1, control2, target); // Q# (shorthand)
	
	Controlled X(
	  [control1, control2], target
	); // Q#
	
	qtops.toffoli() # QuTiP
		$U_{\text{CCNOT}} =$
		$\begin{pmatrix} 1 & 0 & 0 & 0 & 0 & 0 & 0 & 0 \\ 0 & 1 & 0 & 0 & 0 & 0 & 0 & 0 \\ 0 & 0 & 1 & 1 & 0 & 0 & 0 & 0 \\ 0 & 0 & 1 & 1 & 0 & 0 & 0 & 0 \\ 0 & 0 & 0 & 0 & 1 & 0 & 0 & 0 \\ 0 & 0 & 0 & 0 & 0 & 1 & 0 & 0 \\ 0 & 0 & 0 & 0 & 0 & 0 & 0 & 1 \\ 0 & 0 & 0 & 0 & 0 & 1 & 0 & 0 \end{pmatrix}$
			$U_{\text{CCNOT}}\lvert 000\rangle = \lvert 000\rangle$
			$U_{\text{CCNOT}}\lvert 110\rangle = \lvert 111\rangle$

X-rotation	Rx(angle, target); // Q# qtops.rx(angle) # QuTiP	$R_x(\theta) = \begin{pmatrix} \cos\dfrac{\theta}{2} & -i\sin\dfrac{\theta}{2} \\ -i\sin\dfrac{\theta}{2} & \cos\dfrac{\theta}{2} \end{pmatrix}$	$R_x(\theta\lvert 0\rangle) = \cos\dfrac{\theta}{2}\lvert 0\rangle - i\sin\dfrac{\theta}{2}\lvert 1\rangle$
Y-rotation	Ry(angle, target); // Q# qtops.ry(angle) # QuTiP	$R_y(\theta) = \begin{pmatrix} \cos\dfrac{\theta}{2} & -\sin\dfrac{\theta}{2} \\ \sin\dfrac{\theta}{2} & \cos\dfrac{\theta}{2} \end{pmatrix}$	$R_y(\theta\lvert 0\rangle) = \cos\dfrac{\theta}{2}\lvert 0\rangle + \sin\dfrac{\theta}{2}\lvert 1\rangle$
Z-rotation	Rz(angle, target); // Q# qtops.rz(angle) # QuTiP	$R_z(\theta) = \begin{pmatrix} e^{-i\theta/2} & 0 \\ 0 & e^{i\theta/2} \end{pmatrix}$	$R_z(\theta\lvert 0\rangle) = e^{i\theta/2}\lvert 0\rangle$
Measure single qubit	M(target); // Q# n/a	n/a	n/a

B.4 Q# Language

B.4.1 Types

In the following table, we use `italic monospace font` to indicate a placeholder. For example, the `BaseType` placeholder in `BaseType[]` can mean `Int`, `Double`, `Qubit`, `(Qubit, Qubit[])`, or any other Q# type.

For emphasis, we have added the type of each example as an annotation after each value in some of the examples. For instance, `Sin : Double -> Double` indicates that `Sin` is a value whose type is `Double -> Double`.

Description	Q# type	Examples

Integers	`Int`	`3`
		`-42`
		`108`

Float	`Double`	`-3.1415` `2.17`
Booleans	`Bool`	`true` `false`

Ranges of integers	`Range`	`0..3`
		`0..Length(arr)`
		`12..-1..0`

Empty tuple	`Unit`	`()`
Measurement results	`Result`	`Zero` `One`

Pauli operators	`Pauli`	`PauliI`
		`PauliX`
		`PauliY`
		`PauliZ`

Strings	`String`	`"Hello, world!"`
Qubits	`Qubit`	(See `use` statement)
Arrays	`BaseType[]`	`new Qubit[0]` `[42, -101]`
Tuples	`(T1)`, `(T1, T2)`, `(T1, T2, T3)`, and so forth	`(PauliX, "X")` `(1, true, Zero)`
Functions	`InputType -> OutputType`	`Sin : Double -> Double` `Message : String -> Unit`

Operations	`InputType => OutputType`
	`InputType => Unit is Adj` (if adjointable)
	
	`InputType => Unit is Ctl` (if controllable)
	
	`InputType => Unit is Adj + Ctl` (if both adjointable and controllable)
		`H : Qubit => Unit is Adj + Ctl`
		`CNOT : (Qubit, Qubit) => Unit is Adj + Ctl`
		`M : Qubit => Result`
		`Measure : (Pauli[], Qubit[]) => Result`

B.4.2   *Q# declarations and statements*

In the following table, we use *italic monospace font* to indicate a placeholder. For example, the *FunctionName* placeholder in function *FunctionName*(input1 : *InputType1*) : *OutputType* stands for the name of the function being defined, while the *InputType1* and *OutputType* placeholders stand for types from the table above.

Q# keywords are indicated in **bold**.

Description	Q# syntax
Comment until end of line	`// comment text`

Documentation comment (before operation or function)	`/// # Summary`
	`/// summary body`
	`///`
	`/// # Description`
	`/// description body`
	`///`
	`/// # Input`
	`/// ## input1`
	`/// description of input`

Namespace declaration	**`namespace`** `NamespaceName {`
	`    // ...`
	`}`

Function declaration	**`function`** `FunctionName(`
	`        input1 : InputType1,`
	`        input2 : InputType2,`
	`        ...`
	`) : OutputType {`
	`    // function body`
	`}`

Operation declaration	**`operation`** `OperationName(`
	`        input1 : InputType1,`
	`        input2 : InputType2,`
	`        ...`
	`) : OutputType {`
	`    // operation body`
	`}`

Operation declaration (adjointable and controllable)	**`operation`** `OperationName(`
	`        input1 : InputType1,`
	`        input2 : InputType2,`
	`        ...`
	`) : Unit `**`is`**` Adj + Ctl {`
	`    // operation body`
	`}`

User-defined type declaration	**`newtype`** `TypeName = (`
	`    ItemType1,`
	`    ItemType2,`
	`    ...`
	`);`

User-defined type declaration with named items	**`newtype`** `TypeName = (`
	`    ItemName1: ItemType1,`
	`    ItemName2: ItemType2,`
	`    ...`
	`);`

Description	Q# syntax
Open namespace (makes items in namespace available in a Q# file or notebook cell)	`open NamespaceName;`

Open namespace with alias	`open NamespaceName as AliasName;`
	Example:
	`open Microsoft.Quantum.Diagnostics as Diag;`

Local variable declaration	`let name = value;`
	Example:
	`let foo = "Bar";`

Mutable variable declaration	`mutable name = value;`
Reassign (update) mutable variable	`set name = newValue;`

Apply-and-reassign mutable variable	`set name operator= expression;`
	Examples:
	`set count += 1;`
	`set array w/= 2 <- PauliX;`
	(see w/ operator)

Classical conditional statement	`if condition {`
	`    // ...`
	`}`

	`if condition {`
	`    // ...`
	`} else {`
	`    // ...`
	`}`

	`if condition {`
	`    // ...`
	`} elseif condition {`
	`    // ...`
	`} else {`
	`    // ...`
	`}`

Iterate over array	`for element in array {`
	`    // loop body`
	`}`
	Note: *array* must be a value of an array type.

Iterate over range	`for index in range {`
	`    // loop body`
	`}`
	Note: *array* must be a value of type `Range`.

Repeat-until-success loop	`repeat {`
	`    // loop body`
	`}`
	`until condition;`

Description	Q# syntax

Repeat-until-success loop with fixup block	```
	repeat {
	    // loop body
	}
	until condition
	fixup {
	    // fixup body
	}
	``

While-loop
(only in functions)
	``
	while condition {
	    // loop body
	}
	``

Terminate with error	`fail "message";`
Return value from function or operation	`return value;`

Apply shoes-and-socks pattern
(see chapter 7 for detail)
	``
	within {
	    // outer body
	} apply {
	    // inner body
	}
	``

Allocate single new qubit (only in operations)	`use name = Qubit();`
Allocate array of qubits (only in operations)	`use name = Qubit[size];`
Allocate a tuple of qubits and registers (only in operations)	`use (name1, name2, ...) = (QubitOrArray1, QubitOrArray2, ...);`

Allocate a single qubit with an explicit scope
(only in operations)
	``
	use name = Qubit() {
	    // ...
	    // name is released here.
	}
	``

B.4.3 Q# expressions and operators

In the following table, we use *`italic monospace font`* to indicate a placeholder. For example, the *`Type`* placeholder in new *`Type[length]`* indicates the base type of the new array, while *`length`* indicates its length.

Q# keywords are indicated in **bold**.

Description	Q# syntax
Arithmetic	`+, -, *, ...`

Format values as a string	`$"... {expression} ..."`
	Example:
	`$"Measurement result was {result}"`

Concatenate two arrays	`array1 + array2`

Description	Q# syntax
Allocate array	**new** *Type*[*length*]
Get element of array	*array*[*index*]
Slice array	*array*[*start*...] *array*[...*end*] *array*[*start*..*end*] *array*[*start*..*step*..*end*]

Copy-and-update item in array	*array* **w/** *index* <- *newValue*
	
	Example:
	`[10, 100, 1000] w/ 1 <- 200`
	`// [10, 200, 1000]`

Access named item of user-defined type	*value*::*itemName*
	
	Example:
	`let imagUnit = Complex(0.0, 1.0);`
	`Message($"{imagUnit::Real}");`
	`// prints 1.0`

Unwrap user-defined type	*value*!
	
	Example:
	`let imagUnit = Complex(0.0, 1.0);`
	`Message($"{imagUnit!}");`
	`// prints (0.0, 1.0)`

Copy-and-update named item of user-defined type	*value* **w/** *itemName* <- *newValue*
	
	Example:
	`let imagUnit = Complex(0.0, 1.0);`
	`let onePlusI = imagUnit w/ Real <- 1.0;`
	`Message($"{onePlusI!}");`
	`// prints (1.0, 1.0)`

B.4.4   *Q# standard libraries*

We have assumed the following open statements:

```
open Microsoft.Quantum.Intrinsic;
open Microsoft.Quantum.Canon;
open Microsoft.Quantum.Arrays as Arrays;
open Microsoft.Quantum.Diagnostics as Diag;
```

For a complete list of Q# functions, operations, and user-defined types, see https://docs.microsoft.com/qsharp/api/.

The suffixes A, C, and CA denote operations that support inputs that are adjointable, controllable, or both (respectively).

Description	Function or operation	Examples
Apply an operation to every element of an array	`ApplyToEachCA`	`ApplyToEachCA(H, register);`
Call an operation several times	`Repeat`	`Repeat(PrintRandomNumber, 10, ());`
Return the first or second item in a pair	`Fst` or `Snd`	■ `Fst((1.0, false)) // 1.0` ■ `Snd((1.0, false)) // false`
Apply an operation to every element of an array, and collect results	`Arrays.ForEach`	`let results = ForEach(M, register);`
Call a function with each element of an array, and collect results	`Arrays.Mapped`	`let sines = Mapped(Sin, angles);`
Fail if a condition is false	`Diag.Fact`	`Fact(2 == 2, "Expected two to equal two.");`
Fail if two measurement results are not equal	`Diag.EqualityFactR`	`EqualityFactR(M(qubit), Zero, "Expected qubit to be in |0) state.");`
Fail if a *hypothetical* measurement does not have an expected result Notes: ■ Only physically possible on simulators ■ Does not actually apply measurement, leaving qubit unaffected	`Diag.AssertMeasurement`	`AssertMeasement([PauliZ], [target], Zero, "Expected qubit to be in |0) state.");`

Fail if two operations are different	`Diag.AssertOperations EqualReferenced`	`AssertOperationsEqualRefer enced(2,`
		`    actualOperation,`
		`    expectedOperation`
		`);`

Ask simulator to display diagnostic info about all allocated qubits	`Diag.DumpMachine`	`DumpMachine();`
Ask simulator to display diagnostic info about a particular register	`Diag.DumpRegister`	`DumpRegister((), register);`

B.4.5   *IQ# magic commands*

For a complete list of IQ# magic commands, see https://docs.microsoft.com/qsharp/api/iqsharp-magic.

Description	Magic command	Example
Simulate a function or operation	`%simulate`	`%simulate PlayMorganasGame winProbability=0.999`
Add new package to IQ# session	`%package`	`%package Microsoft.Quantum.Numerics`
Reload Q# files with current packages	`%workspace reload`	
List all available magic commands	`%lsmagic`	
List currently open namespaces	`%lsopen`	
Run resources estimator on an operation	`%estimate`	`%estimate FindMarkedItem`
Set IQ# configuration options	`%config`	`%config dump.truncateSmallAmplitudes = true`
List all currently defined functions and operations	`%who`	

appendix C
Linear algebra refresher

In this appendix, our goal is to quickly cover some of the linear algebra skills that are useful for this book. We'll discuss what vectors and matrices are, how to work with vectors and matrices to represent linear functions, and how to use Python and NumPy to work with vectors and matrices.

C.1 Approaching vectors

Before we can get to what qubits are, we need to understand the concept of a *vector*.

> *Suppose a friend of ours is having people over to celebrate that they fixed their doorbell, and we'd very much like to find their house and celebrate the occasion with them. How can our friend help us find their home?*

You can see a sketch of our direction dilemma in figure C.1. Vectors are a mathematical tool that can be used to represent a variety of different concepts—basically, anything that we can record by making an ordered list of numbers:

- Points on a map
- Colors of pixels in a display
- Damage elements in a computer game
- Velocity of an airplane
- Orientation of a gyroscope

For instance, if we're lost in an unfamiliar city, someone can tell us where to go by giving us a vector that instructs us to go *a* blocks east and then *b* blocks north (we'll set aside the problem of routing around buildings). We write these instructions with the vector [[a], [b]] (figure C.2).

Like ordinary numbers, we can add different vectors together.

Figure C.1   Looking for our friend's house party

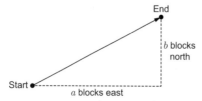

Figure C.2   Vectors as coordinates

NOTE   An ordinary number is often called a *scalar* to distinguish it from a vector.

Using this way of thinking about vectors, we can think of addition between vectors as being defined element-wise. That is, we interpret [[a], [b]] + [[c], [d]] as being instructions to go a blocks east, b blocks north, c blocks east, then finally d blocks north. Since it doesn't matter what order we step in, this is equivalent to taking a + c blocks east, then b + d blocks north, so we write that [[a], [b]] + [[c], [d]] is [[a + c], [b + d]] (figure C.3).

A vector $\vec{v}$ in d dimensions can be written as a list of d numbers. For instance, $\vec{v} =$ [[2], [3]] is a vector in two dimensions (figure C.4).

Similarly, we can multiply vectors by ordinary numbers to transform vectors. We may be lost not just in any city, for example, but a city that uses meters instead of the feet like we're used to. To transform a vector given in meters to a vector in feet, we need to

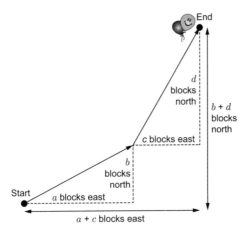

Figure C.3 Adding vectors to find a party

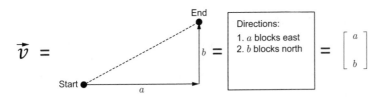

Figure C.4 Drawn vectors have the same information as a list of directions or column of numbers.

multiply each element of our vector by about 3.28. Let's do this using a Python library called *NumPy* to help us manage how we represent vectors in a computer.

TIP Full installation instructions are provided in appendix A.

Listing C.1 Representing vectors in Python with NumPy

Vectors are a special case of NumPy arrays. We create arrays using the "array" function, passing a list of the rows in our vector. Each row is then a list of the columns—for vectors, we only ever have one column per row, but we'll have examples in the book where this isn't true.

```
>>> import numpy as np
>>> directions_in_meters = np.array(
...     [[30], [50]])
>>> directions_in_feet = 3.28 * directions_in_meters
>>> directions_in_feet
array([[ 98.4],
       [164. ]])
```

Starts with an example of going 30 meters east and then 50 meters north

Prints the result of multiplying. We need to go 98.4 feet east and then 164 feet north.

NumPy represents multiplication between scalars and vectors with the Python multiplication operator *.

Exercise C.1: Unit conversion

What are 25 meters west and 110 meters north in feet?

Exercise solutions

All solutions for exercises in this book can be found in the companion code repo: https://github.com/crazy4pi314/learn-qc-with-python-and-qsharp. Just go to the folder for the chapter you are in and open the Jupyter notebook with the name that mentions exercise solutions.

This structure makes it easier to communicate directions. If we didn't use vectors, then each scalar would need its own direction, and it would be critical to keep the directions and scalars together.

C.2   *Seeing the matrix for ourselves*

As we'll see shortly, we can describe how qubits transform as we apply instructions to them in the same way that we describe transforming vectors, using a concept from linear algebra called a *matrix*. This is especially important as we consider transformations of vectors that are more complicated than adding or rescaling.

To see how to use matrices, let's return to the problem of finding the party—that doorbell isn't going to ring itself, after all! Until now, we've simply assumed that each vector's first component means east and the second means north, but someone could well have chosen another convention. Without a way of reconciling the transformation between these two conventions, we'll never find the party. Fortunately, not only will matrices help us model qubits later on in this appendix, but they can also help us find our way to our friends.

Happily, the transformation between listing north first and listing east first is simple to implement: we swap the coordinates `[[a], [b]]` to obtain `[[b], [a]]`. Suppose that this swap is implemented by a function swap. Then swap plays nicely with the vector addition that we saw previously, in that `swap(v + w)` is always the same as `swap(v) + swap(w)`. Similarly, if we stretch a vector and then swap (that is, scalar multiplication), that's the same as if we had swapped and then stretched: `swap(a * v) = a * swap(v)`. Any function that has these two properties is a *linear* function.

A *linear function* is a function f such that $f(ax + by) = af(x) + bf(y)$ for all scalars a and b and all vectors x and y.

Linear functions are common in computer graphics and machine learning, as they include a variety of different ways of transforming vectors of numbers.

These are some examples of linear functions:

- Rotations
- Scaling and stretching
- Reflections

Exercise C.2: Linearity check

Which of the following functions are linear?

- $f(x) = 2^x$
- $f(x) = x^2$
- $f(x) = 2x$

All of these linear functions have in common that we can break them apart and understand them piece by piece. Thinking again of the map, if we're trying to find our way to the party (hopefully there's still some punch left) and the map we've been given has been stretched by 10% in the north-south direction and flipped in the east-west direction, that's not too hard to figure out. Since both the stretching and flipping are linear functions, someone can set us on the right path by telling us what happened to the north-south direction and the east-west direction separately. In fact, we just did that at the beginning of this paragraph!

TIP   If you learn just one thing from this book, the most important takeaway we have to offer is that you can understand linear functions and thus quantum operations by *breaking them into components*. We'll see in the rest of the book that, since operations in quantum computing are described by linear functions, we can understand quantum algorithms by breaking them apart in the same way as we broke up our map example. Don't worry if that doesn't make a lot of sense at the moment—it's a way of thinking that takes some getting used to.

This is because once we understand what happens to the north vector (let's call it `[[1], [0]]` as before) and the west vector (let's call it `[[0], [1]]`), we can figure out what happens to *all* vectors by using the linearity property. For example, if we are told there's a really pretty sight three blocks north and four blocks west of us, and we want to figure out where that is on our map, we can do so piece by piece:

- We need to stretch the north vector by 10% and multiply it by 3, getting `[[3.3], [0]]`.
- We need to flip the west vector and multiply it by 4, getting `[[0], [-4]]`.
- We finish by adding what happens to each direction, getting `[[3.3], [-4]]`.

Linear functions are pretty special! ♡

In the previous example, we were able to stretch our vectors using a linear function. This is because linear functions aren't sensitive to scale. Swapping north–south and east–west does the same thing to vectors, whether they're represented in steps, blocks, miles, furlongs, or parsecs. That's not true of most functions, though. Consider a function that squares its input, $f(x) = x^2$. The larger x is, the more it gets stretched.

(continued)

Linear functions work the same way no matter how large or small their inputs are, which is precisely what lets us break them down piece by piece: once we know how a linear function works at *any* scale, we know how it works at *all* scales.

Thus, we need to look 3.3 blocks north and 4 blocks east on our map.

Later, we'll see how the bits "0" and "1" can be thought of as directions or vectors, not too different from north or east. In the same way that north and east aren't the best vectors to help you understand Minneapolis, we'll find that "0" and "1" aren't always the best vectors to help understand quantum computing (figure C.5).

Figure C.5   North and west aren't always the best directions to use if we want to understand where we're going. In this map of downtown Minneapolis, a large section of the downtown grid is rotated to match the bend in the Mississippi River. Photo by davecito.

This way of understanding linear functions by breaking them apart piece by piece works for rotations, too. If our map has the compass rotated by 45° clockwise (wow, we need a serious lesson in cartography), so that north becomes northeast and west becomes northwest, we can still figure out where things are piece by piece. Using the same example, the north vector is now mapped to approximately [[0.707], [0.707]] on the map, and the west vector is mapped to [[-0.707], [0.707]].

When we sum up what happens in the example, we get 3 * [[0.707], [0.707]] + 4 * [[-0.707], [0.707]], which is equal to (3 - 4) * [[0.707], [0]] + (3 + 4) [[0], [0.707]], giving us [[-0.707], [4.95]]. It might seem that this has less to do with linearity and more to do with north and west being somehow special. However, we could have run through *exactly* the same argument but writing southwest as [[1], [0]] and northwest as [[0], [1]]. This works because southwest and northwest are perpendicular to each other, allowing us to break down any other direction as a combination of northwest and southwest. Other than ease of reading a compass that we buy off a shelf, there's nothing that makes north or west special. If you've ever tried to drive around downtown Minneapolis (see figure C.5), it quickly becomes apparent that north and west aren't always the best way to understand directions!

Formally, any set of vectors that lets us understand directions by breaking them apart piece by piece this way is called a *basis*.

NOTE Technically, we're concerned here with what mathematicians call an *orthonormal basis*, as that's most often useful in quantum computing. All that means is that the vectors in a basis are perpendicular to all the other basis vectors and have a length of 1.

Let's try an example of writing a vector in terms of a basis. The vector $\vec{v}$ = [[2], [3]] can be written as $2\,\vec{b}_0 + 3\,\vec{b}_1$ using the basis $\vec{b}_0$ = [[1], [0]] and $\vec{b}_1$ = [[0], [1]].

BASIS If any vector $\vec{v}$ in d dimensions can be written as a sum of multiples of $\vec{b}_0, \vec{b}_1, ..., \vec{b}_{d-1}$, we say that $\vec{b}_0, \vec{b}_1, ..., \vec{b}_{d-1}$ are a *basis*. In two dimensions, one common basis is horizontal and vertical.

More generally, if we know the output of a function f for each vector in a basis, we can compute f for any input. This is similar to how we use truth tables to describe a classical operation by listing the outputs of an operation for each possible input.

Problem solving with linearity

Let's say f is a linear function that represents how our map is stretched and twisted. How can we find where we need to go? We want to compute the value f(np .array([[2], [3]])) (a somewhat arbitrary value) given our basis f(np.array ([[1], [0]])) (horizontal) and f(np.array([[0], [1]])) (vertical). We also know from looking at parts of the map legend that the map warps the horizontal direction to np.array([[1], [1]]) and the vertical direction to np.array([[1], [-1]]).

The steps to compute f(np.array([[2], [3]])) are as follows:

- We use our basis, np.array([[1], [0]]) and np.array([[0], [1]]), to write that np.array([[2], [3]]) is equal to 2 * np.array([[1], [0]]) + 3 * np.array([[0], [1]]).

(continued)

- Using this new way to write our input to the function, we want to compute `f(2 * np.array([[1], [0]]) + 3 * np.array([[0], [1]]))`.
- We use that `f` is linear to write `f(2 * np.array([[1], [0]]) + 3 * np.array([[0], [1]]))` as `2 * f(np.array([[1], [0]])) + 3 * f(np.array([[0], [1]]))`:

Defines variables horizontal and vertical to represent the basis we will use to represent [[2], [3]]

```
>>> import numpy as np
>>> horizontal = np.array([[1], [0]])
>>> vertical = np.array([[0], [1]])
>>> vec = 2 * horizontal + 3 * vertical
>>> vec
array([[2],
       [3]])
>>> f_horizontal = np.array([[1], [1]])
>>> f_vertical = np.array([[1], [-1]])
>>> 2 * f_horizontal + 3 * f_vertical
array([[ 5],
       [-1]])
```

We can write [[2], [3]] by adding multiples of horizontal and vertical.

Defines how f acts on horizontal and vertical by introducing new variables f_horizontal and f_vertical to represent f(horizontal) and f(vertical), respectively

Because f is linear, we can define how it works for [[2], [3]] by replacing horizontal and vertical by the outputs f_horizontal and f_vertical.

Exercise C.3: Computing linear functions

Suppose that you have a linear function g such that $g([[1], [0]]) = [[2.3], [-3.1]]$ and $g([[0], [1]]) = [[-5.2], [0.7]]$. Compute $g([[2], [-2]])$.

Using this insight, we can make a table of how a linear function transforms each of its inputs. These tables are called *matrices* and are complete descriptions of linear functions. If we tell you the matrix for a linear function, then you can compute that function for *any* vector. For example, the transformation from the north/east convention to the east/north convention for map directions transforms the instruction "go one unit north" from being written as `[[1], [0]]` to being written as `[[0], [1]]`. Similarly, the instruction "go one unit east" goes from being written as `[[0], [1]]` to being written as `[[1], [0]]`. If we stack up the outputs for both sets of instructions, we get the following matrix:

```
>>> swap_north_east = np.array([[0, 1], [1, 0]])
>>> swap_north_east
array([[0, 1],
       [1, 0]])
```

TIP   This is a very important matrix in quantum computing as well! We'll see much more of this matrix throughout the book.

To apply the linear function represented by a matrix to a particular vector, we multiply the matrix and the vector, as illustrated in figure C.6.

A matrix describing a linear function f **can be thought of as a stack of the outputs of** f, **one for each column.**

For instance, the first column tells us that f([[1], [0], [0]]) **is the column vector** [[1], [2], [9]], **while the second column tells us that** f([[0], [1], [0]]) **is** [[3] [4], [8]].

$$\begin{bmatrix} 1 & 3 & 7 \\ 2 & 4 & 6 \\ 9 & 8 & 5 \end{bmatrix} \begin{bmatrix} 3 \\ 1 \\ 2 \end{bmatrix} = \begin{bmatrix} 20 \\ 22 \\ 45 \end{bmatrix} \begin{array}{l} = 1 \times 3 + 3 \times 1 + 7 \times 2 \\ = 2 \times 3 + 4 \times 1 + 6 \times 2 \\ = 9 \times 3 + 8 \times 1 + 5 \times 2 \end{array}$$

Since the first factor had three rows and the second factor had one column, the product has three rows and one column.

The second matrix or vector being multiplied is read out in columns.

Just as the first index of a matrix represents its rows and the second index represents its columns, the first matrix being multiplied is read out row by row.

Figure C.6 How to multiply a matrix by a vector. In this example, the matrix for f tells us that $f([[1], [0], [0]])$ is $[[1], [2], [9]]$.

WARNING While the order in which we add vectors doesn't matter, the order in which we multiply matrices matters quite a lot. If we rotate our map by 90° and then look at it in the mirror, we get a very different picture than if we rotate what we see in the mirror by 90°. Both rotation and flipping are linear functions, so we can write a matrix for each; let's call them R and F, respectively. If we flip a vector $\vec{x}$, we get $F\vec{x}$. Rotating the output gives us $RF\vec{x}$, a very different vector than if we rotated first, $FR\vec{x}$.

Matrix multiplication formalizes the way we computed f given its outputs for a particular set of inputs by "stacking" the outputs of f for vectors like [[1], [0], [0]] and [[0], [1], [0]], as illustrated in figure C.6. While the actual sizes of the matrices and vectors may change, this idea that a matrix can describe a linear transformation stays the same. For the rest of this appendix, we'll look at linear transformations on vectors of length 2. We can think of each row (the outermost index in NumPy) of a matrix as how the function acts on a particular input.

DEEP DIVE: Why do we multiply functions?

When we multiply a matrix by a vector (or even by a matrix by a matrix), we're doing something that seems a bit odd at first. After all, matrices are another way of representing linear functions, so what does it mean to multiply a function by its input, let alone by another function?

(continued)

To answer this, it's helpful to go back to ordinary algebra for a moment, where for any variables a, b, and c, $a(b + c) = ab + ac$. This property, known as the *distributive property*, is fundamental to how multiplication and addition interact with each other. In fact, it's so fundamental that the distributive property is one of the key ways we define what multiplication is—in number theory and other, more abstract, parts of math, researchers often work with objects known as *rings*, where all we really know about multiplication is that it distributes over addition. Although posed as an abstract concept, the study of rings and other similar algebraic objects has broad applications, especially in cryptography and error correction.

The distributive property looks very similar to the linearity property, though, that $f(x + y) = f(x) + f(y)$. If we think of f as being a part of a ring, then the distributive property is identical to the linearity property.

Put differently, just as programmers like to reuse code, mathematicians like to reuse *concepts*. Thinking of multiplying matrices together lets us treat linear functions in many of the same ways we're used to from algebra.

Thus, if we want to know the ith element of a vector $\vec{x}$ that has been rotated by a matrix M, we can find the output of M for each element in $\vec{x}$, sum the resulting vectors, and take the ith element. In NumPy, matrix multiplication is represented by the @ operator.

NOTE   The following code sample only works in Python 3.5 or later.

Listing C.2   Matrix multiplication with the @ operator

```
>>> M = np.array([
...       [1, 1],
...       [1, -1]
... ], dtype=complex)
>>> M @ np.array([[2], [3]], dtype=complex)
array([[ 5.+0.j],
       [-1.+0.j]])
```

Exercise C.4: Matrix multiplication

Let X be the matrix [[0, 1], [1, 0]], and let $\vec{y}$ be the vector [[2], [3]]. Using NumPy, compute $X\vec{y}$ and XX.

Why NumPy?

We could have written all of the previous matrix multiplication by hand, but there are a few reasons it's very nice to work with NumPy instead. Most of the core of NumPy uses constant-time indexing and is implemented in native code so it can take advantage of built-in processor instructions for fast linear algebra. Thus, NumPy is often much, much faster than manipulating lists by hand. In listing C.3, we show an example where NumPy can speed up multiplying even very small matrices by 10×. When we look at larger matrices in chapters 4 and later, using NumPy versus doing things by hand gives us even more of an advantage.

Listing C.3 Timing NumPy evaluation for matrix multiplication

Finds the sizes of each matrix that we need to multiply. If we're representing matrices by lists of lists, then each element of the outer list is a row. That is, an $n \times m$ matrix has n rows and m columns when written out this way.

This time, we use the IPython interpreter for Python, as it provides a few extra tools that are helpful in this example. See appendix A for instructions on how to install IPython.

```
$ ipython
In [1]: def matmul(A, B):
   ...:     n_rows_A = len(A)
   ...:     n_cols_A = len(A[0])
   ...:     n_rows_B = len(B)
   ...:     n_cols_B = len(B[0])
   ...:     assert n_cols_A == n_rows_B
   ...:     return [
   ...:         [
   ...:             sum(
   ...:                 A[idx_row][idx_inner] * B[idx_inner][idx_col]
   ...:                 for idx_inner in range(n_cols_A)
   ...:             )
   ...:             for idx_col in range(n_cols_B)
   ...:         ]
   ...:         for idx_row in range(n_rows_A)
   ...:     ]
   ...:
In [2]: import numpy as np
In [3]: X = np.array([[0+0j, 1+0j], [1+0j, 0+0j]])
In [4]: Z = np.array([[1+0j, 0+0j], [0+0j, -1+0j]])
In [5]: matmul(X, Z)
Out[5]: [[0j, (-1+0j)], [(1+0j), 0j]]
In [6]: X @ Z
Out[6]:
array([[ 0.+0.j, -1.+0.j],
       [ 1.+0.j,  0.+0.j]])
In [7]: %timeit matmul(X, Z)
10.3 µs ± 176 ns per loop (mean ± std. dev. of 7 runs, 100000 loops each)
In [8]: %timeit X @ Z
926 ns ± 4.42 ns per loop (mean ± std. dev. of 7 runs, 1000000 loops each)
```

To actually compute the matrix product of **A** and **B**, we need to compute each element in the product and pack them into a list of lists.

We can find each element by summing over where the output from B is passed as input to A, similar to how we represented the product of a matrix with a vector in figure C.6.

For comparison, we can import NumPy, which provides us with a matrix multiplication implementation that uses modern processor instructions to accelerate the computation.

Initializes two matrices as NumPy arrays as test cases. We'll see much more about these two particular matrices throughout the book.

Matrix multiplication in NumPy is represented by the @ operator in Python 3.5 and later.

The %timeit "magic command" tells IPython to run a small piece of Python code many times and report the average amount of time that it takes.

The inner dimensions of both matrices need to agree in order for matrix multiplication to make sense. Thinking of each matrix as representing a linear function, the first index (the number of rows) tells us how large each output is, while the second index (the number of columns) tells us how large each input is. Thus we need the outputs from the first function to be applied (the one on the right) to be of the same size as the inputs to the second function. This line checks that condition.

C.2.1   *Party with inner products*

There's one last thing we need to worry about to find the party. Earlier, we said we were ignoring the problem of whether there was a road that would let us go in the direction we needed to, but this is a really bad idea when wandering through an unfamiliar city. To make our way around, we need a way to evaluate how far we should walk along a given road to get where we're going. Fortunately, linear algebra gives us a tool to do just that: the *inner product* (figure C.7). Inner products are a way of projecting one vector $\vec{v}$ onto another vector $\vec{w}$, telling us how much of a "shadow" $\vec{v}$ casts on $\vec{w}$.

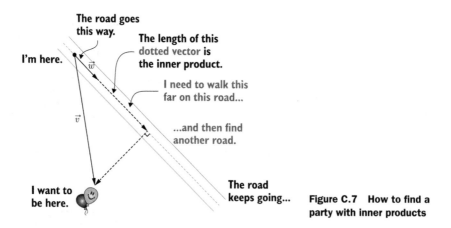

Figure C.7   **How to find a party with inner products**

We can compute the inner product of two vectors by multiplying their respective elements and summing the result. Note that this multiply-and-sum recipe is the same as what we do in matrix multiplication! Multiplying a matrix that has a single row with a matrix that has a single column does exactly what we need. Thus, to find the projection of $\vec{v}$ onto $\vec{w}$, we need to turn $\vec{v}$ into a row vector by taking its *transpose*, written $\vec{v}^{\mathsf{T}}$.

> **Example**
> The transpose of $\vec{w} = \left(\begin{smallmatrix}2\\3\end{smallmatrix}\right)$ is $\vec{w}^{\mathsf{T}} = (2\ \ 3)$.

NOTE   In chapter 3, we'll see that we also need to take the complex conjugate of each element, but we'll set that aside for now.

In particular, the matrix product of $\vec{v}^T$ (the transpose of $\vec{v}$) with $\vec{w}$ gives us a 1×1 matrix containing the inner product we want. Suppose we need to go two blocks south and three blocks east, but we can only go on a road that points more south-southeast. Since we still need to travel south, this road helps us get where we need to go. But how far should we walk before this road stops helping?

Listing C.4 Computing vector dot products with NumPy

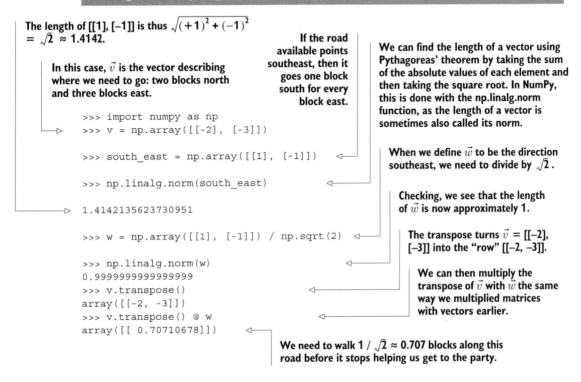

The length of [[1], [–1]] is thus $\sqrt{(+1)^2 + (-1)^2}$ $= \sqrt{2} \approx 1.4142$.

In this case, $\vec{v}$ is the vector describing where we need to go: two blocks north and three blocks east.

If the road available points southeast, then it goes one block south for every block east.

We can find the length of a vector using Pythagoreas' theorem by taking the sum of the absolute values of each element and then taking the square root. In NumPy, this is done with the np.linalg.norm function, as the length of a vector is sometimes also called its norm.

When we define $\vec{w}$ to be the direction southeast, we need to divide by $\sqrt{2}$.

Checking, we see that the length of $\vec{w}$ is now approximately 1.

The transpose turns $\vec{v} = [[-2], [-3]]$ into the "row" [[–2, –3]].

We can then multiply the transpose of $\vec{v}$ with $\vec{w}$ the same way we multiplied matrices with vectors earlier.

```
>>> import numpy as np
>>> v = np.array([[-2], [-3]])

>>> south_east = np.array([[1], [-1]])

>>> np.linalg.norm(south_east)

1.4142135623730951

>>> w = np.array([[1], [-1]]) / np.sqrt(2)

>>> np.linalg.norm(w)
0.9999999999999999
>>> v.transpose()
array([[-2, -3]])
>>> v.transpose() @ w
array([[ 0.70710678]])
```

We need to walk $1 / \sqrt{2} \approx 0.707$ blocks along this road before it stops helping us get to the party.

Exercise C.5: Vector normalization

Given a vector [[2], [3]], find a vector that points in the same direction but with length 1.

Hint: You can do this by using either an inner product or the np.linalg.norm function.

Finally, we have made it to the party (only slightly late) and are ready to try out that new doorbell!

Square roots and lengths

The square root of a number x is a number $y = \sqrt{x}$ such that we get x back when we square y, $y^2 = x$. We use square roots a lot throughout the book, as they are essential for finding the length of vectors. For instance, in computer graphics, quickly finding the lengths of vectors is essential for making games work (see https://en.wikipedia .org/wiki/Fast_inverse_square_root for some fun history about how square roots are used in gaming).

Whether vectors describe how we get to parties or those vectors describe the information that a quantum bit represents, we use square roots to reason about their lengths.

appendix D
Exploring the Deutsch–Jozsa algorithm by example

In this appendix, we do a deep dive on the Deutsch–Jozsa algorithm to show how it works and how we can use the skills and tools we developed in chapter 8 to check our understanding. We implement the Deutsch–Jozsa algorithm in chapter 7 and make heavy use of QuTiP for checking our math at certain steps.

D.1 Using our skills to try things

In chapters 2 and 5, we learn to use NumPy and QuTiP to simulate how the states of qubits are transformed when we send instructions to a quantum computer. We effectively use these packages to do math for us to find out what happens to our quantum states. This is like the "make the computer do the math" approach in figure D.1.

Write the math.

Make the computer do the math.

Push buttons and see what happens.

Figure D.1 Three different approaches to learning how a quantum program or algorithm works

When we program larger algorithms in Q#, we can use both the "make the computer do the math" and a bit of the "push all the buttons" approach to help us predict what a particular operation will do. The three approaches show in figure D.1, used together, are powerful problem-solving tools when learning quantum programming. If we get stuck using one approach, we can always try another to see if that helps.

Let's try to apply this combo approach to the Deutsch–Jozsa algorithm from chapter 8. The following listing shows the four steps of the algorithm.

Listing D.1   The four steps in the Deutsch–Jozsa algorithm

```
H(control);
X(target);        │ Prepare the input
H(target);        │ state |+–⟩.


oracle(control, target);      ◁──┘ Apply the oracle.


H(target);        │ Undo the preparation on the target
X(target);        │ qubit. the input state |+–⟩.


set result = MResetX(control);    ◁──┐ Finally, measure
                                     │ in the X-basis.
```

The key to understanding how the Deutsch–Jozsa algorithm works is understanding the step where we call the oracle, `oracle(control, target)`. Before we can get to that, though, we need to understand step 1, where we prepare our input to `oracle`.

D.2 *Step 1: Preparing the input state for Deutsch–Jozsa*

Let's use Python to try to understand what is happening when we prepare our |+–⟩ state. The operations we use to prep the input state in Q# are as follows:

```
H(control);
X(target);
H(target);
```

Each operation applied here is a single-qubit gate, so we can consider what happens to each qubit independently. Let's look at what happens to the control qubit after the Hadamard operation. We use QuTiP to model the control qubit state preparation:

While H in Q# is an instruction, hadamard_transform in QuTiP gives us a unitary matrix that we can use to simulate how the H instruction transforms states.

```
>>> import qutip as qt
>>> from qutip.qip.operations import hadamard_transform
>>> H = hadamard_transform()
>>> H
Quantum object: dims = [[2], [2]], shape = (2, 2), type = oper,
⇒ isherm = True
Qobj data =
[[ 0.70710678   0.70710678]
 [ 0.70710678  -0.70710678]]
```

$1 / \sqrt{2} \approx 0.707$, so this output tells us that $H = \begin{pmatrix} 1 & 1 \\ 1 & -1 \end{pmatrix} / \sqrt{2}$.

```
>>> control_state = H * qt.basis(2, 0)
>>> control_state
Quantum object: dims = [[2], [1]], shape = (2, 1),
  type = ket
Qobj data =
[[0.70710678]
 [0.70710678]]
```

> Using that $1 / \sqrt{2} \approx 0.707$, we read this as telling us that $|+\rangle = (|0\rangle + |1\rangle) / \sqrt{2}$.

In QuTiP, we can get the vector for the $|0\rangle$ state by calling basis(2, 0). The 2 tells QuTiP we want a qubit (necessary dimension of $|0\rangle$), while the 0 says we want the state to have the value $|0\rangle$. Since $|+\rangle = H|0\rangle$, this sets control_state to $|+\rangle$.

That's a pretty easy one: the control qubit is now in the $|+\rangle$ state. Now let's look at preparing the target qubit in the next snippet.

> **Repeats the same H operation as before, but this time on $X|0\rangle = |1\rangle$**

```
>>> target_state = H * (qt.sigmax() * qt.basis(2, 0))
>>> target_state
Quantum object: dims = [[2], [1]], shape = (2, 1), type = ket
Qobj data =
[[ 0.70710678]
 [-0.70710678]]
```

> **QuTiP tells us that $|-\rangle = (|0\rangle - |1\rangle) / \sqrt{2}$: the same as $|+\rangle$, but with the sign of $|1\rangle$ flipped.**

Now that we have seen how to prepare each qubit, let's have QuTiP help us write the state of our input *register*.

> **As in chapter 4, we combine the states of different qubits to get the state of an entire register of qubits using the tensor function.**

```
>>> register_state = qt.tensor(control_state, target_state)
>>> register_state
Quantum object: dims = [[2, 2], [1, 1]], shape = (4, 1), type = ket
Qobj data =
[[ 0.5]
 [-0.5]
 [ 0.5]
 [-0.5]]
```

> **QuTiP tells us that $|+\rangle \otimes |-\rangle = |+-\rangle = (|00\rangle - |01\rangle + |10\rangle - |11\rangle) / 2$. That is, we have an equal superposition over all four possible computational basis states, with a minus sign in front of computational basis states where the target qubit is in the $|1\rangle$ state.**

NOTE As we see in chapter 4, when writing the state of a multi-qubit system, tensor products can get a little bit verbose. Thus, we often write multi-qubit states like $|0\rangle \otimes |1\rangle$ by concatenating their labels inside a single ket, as in $|01\rangle$. Similarly, $|+-\rangle$ is the same as $|+\rangle \otimes |-\rangle$.

D.3   Step 2: Applying the oracle

Having prepared our input, let's get back to the core of the Deutsch–Jozsa algorithm, where we call into our oracle:

```
oracle(control, target);
```

Just as we can understand operations like H(control) by writing the state of the control qubit and applying the unitary operator H to that state, we can understand what the oracle U_f does by analyzing its action on the state we pass to it.

Recall our game setup in chapter 8, where Nimue and Merlin are playing King-maker. Our quantum oracle operates on two qubits, which raises the question of how we should interpret each of those qubits. In the classical case, the interpretation of the input and output classical bits from f was clear: Nimue asked a one-bit question and got a one-bit answer.

To understand what each qubit does for us, recall that when we use a reversible classical function, we also need two inputs: the first acts like the question we ask in the irreversible case, and the second input gives us somewhere to put the answer (see figure D.2 for a reminder).

$$h(x, y) = (x, y \oplus f(x))$$

We can make a new reversible classical function h from an irreversible function f by flipping a bit based on the output of f.

To define h, we specify what it does for arbitrary classical bits x and y.

$$U_f |x\rangle |y\rangle = |x\rangle |y \oplus f(x)\rangle$$

In exactly the same way, we can define a unitary matrix U_f.

Much like we defined h by saying what it did for each classical bit x and y, we can say what U_f does for input qubits in the labeled by classical bits; that is, in the $|0\rangle$ and $|1\rangle$ states.

Figure D.2   Constructing reversible classical functions and unitary matrices from irreversible classical functions

We can think of the oracle roughly the same way: the first qubit (`control` in the previous snippet) represents our question, while the second qubit (`target`) gives us somewhere for Merlin to apply his answer. This interpretation makes sense when `control` starts in either the $|0\rangle$ or $|1\rangle$ state, but how can we interpret this case where we pass qubits in the $|+-\rangle$ state to the oracle? Our control qubit starts in the $|+\rangle$ state, but $f(+)$ doesn't make any sense. Since f is a classical function, its input has to be either 0 or 1— we can't pass + to the classical function f. It may seem as though we're at a dead end, but fortunately there's a way to figure it out.

Quantum mechanics is linear, which means we can always understand what a quantum operation does by breaking it down into its action on a representative set of states.

> **TIP**   As we see in chapter 2, a set of states that can be used this way is called a *basis*.

To understand what our oracle does when the control qubit is in the $|+\rangle$ state, we can use the fact that $|+\rangle = (|0\rangle + |1\rangle) / \sqrt{2}$ to break the oracle's action down into what it does to $|0\rangle$ *plus* its action on $|1\rangle$ and then sum both parts back together (making sure to divide by $\sqrt{2}$ at the end). This helps because instead of being confused by trying to understand what "$f(+)$" means, we can reduce the action of U_f to cases we do know how to compute, like $f(0)$ and $f(1)$!

> ### Computational basis states
>
> Expanding the action of a quantum operation in terms of how it acts on $|0\rangle$ and $|1\rangle$ is very common in quantum programming. Given how useful this is, we use a special name for these two input states and call $|0\rangle$ and $|1\rangle$ the *computational basis* to set them apart from other bases we might use, like $|+\rangle$ and $|-\rangle$.
>
> Using linearity to understand quantum operations isn't limited to a single qubit, as we see in the rest of the appendix. For two qubits, for instance, the computational basis consists of the states $|00\rangle$, $|01\rangle$, $|10\rangle$, and $|11\rangle$.
>
> If we have even more (say, five) qubits, we can write states like $|1\rangle \otimes |0\rangle \otimes |0\rangle \otimes |1\rangle \otimes |0\rangle$ as strings in the same way, getting $|10010\rangle$. We can write the computational basis for five qubits as $\{|00000\rangle, |00001\rangle, |00010\rangle, ..., |11110\rangle, |11111\rangle\}$.
>
> More generally, if we have n qubits, the computational basis consists of all strings of n classical bits, each as the label of a ket. Put differently, the computational basis for a multiple-qubit system is made up of all tensor products of $|0\rangle$ and $|1\rangle$: that is, all states labeled by a string of classical bits.

With this approach of breaking down how the oracle works, let's look at some examples of the oracles we implemented in chapter 8.

D.3.1 Example 1: The "id" oracle

Suppose we are given an oracle that implements the strategy where Merlin chooses Arthur as king (section 8.2). Recall that the classical one-bit function that represents this strategy is id. From table D.1, we know that this means U_f is implemented by the CNOT instruction, so let's see what that does to `register_state`.

Table D.1 Representing one-bit functions as two-qubit oracles

Function name	Function	Output of oracle	Q# operation
id	$f(x) = x$	$|x\rangle|y \oplus x\rangle$	CNOT(control, target)

TIP Recall that the controlled-NOT instruction flips its second qubit if the first qubit is in $|1\rangle$.

Listing D.2 How the `id` oracle transforms its input state

Asks QuTiP for a matrix that lets us simulate the **CNOT** instruction by using the cnot function. Here, the 2 indicates that we want to simulate **CNOT** on a two-qubit register, the 0 indicates that the 0th qubit is our control, and the 1 indicates that the first qubit is our target.

```
>>> cnot = qt.cnot(2, 0, 1)
>>> cnot
Quantum object: dims = [[2, 2], [2, 2]], shape = (4, 4), type = oper,
    isherm = True
Qobj data =
[[1. 0. 0. 0.]
```

Remember that unitary operators are for quantum computing what truth tables are for classical logic. Each row in this table tells us what happens to a computational basis state.

```
   [0. 1. 0. 0.]
   [0. 0. 0. 1.]
   [0. 0. 1. 0.]]
>>> register_state = cnot * register_state
>>> register_state
Quantum object: dims = [[2, 2], [1, 1]],
➥ shape = (4, 1), type = ket
Qobj data =
[[ 0.5]
 [-0.5]
 [-0.5]
 [ 0.5]]
```

QuTiP tells us that the register with our control and target qubits is now in the state $(|00\rangle - |01\rangle - |10\rangle + |11\rangle) / 2$.

For example, the row at index 2 (zero-indexed) can be written as 10 in binary. Thus, this row is the vector we'll get out if our input is $|10\rangle$, and it tells us that the CNOT instruction leaves our qubits in $|11\rangle$ (3 in decimal, hence there's a 1 in the third column).

Now that we have worked out the action of the id oracle, let's look at what the not oracle does to our input state.

D.3.2   Example 2: The "not" oracle

Let's repeat the analysis using the not oracle, the other balanced function. The oracle representing Merlin choosing Mordred is implemented with a series of X and CNOT operations as in table D.2.

Table D.2   The one-bit function not as a two-qubit oracle

Function name	Function	Output of oracle	Q# operation
not	$f(x) = \neg x$	$|x\rangle|y \oplus \neg x\rangle$	X(control); CNOT(control, target); X(control);

Let's jump to Python to see how to break down the operation of the not oracle.

Listing D.3   Using QuTiP again, now with the not oracle

As in chapter 5, it's helpful to define variables I and X as shorthand for the identity matrix (qt.qeye) and the matrix representing the X operation, respectively.

Prepares the control and target qubits in the $|+-\rangle$ state exactly as before

```
>>> control_state = H * qt.basis(2, 0)
>>> target_state = H * qt.basis(2, 1)
>>> register_state = qt.tensor(control_state, target_state)
>>> I = qt.qeye(2)
>>> X = qt.sigmax()
>>> oracle = qt.tensor(X, I) * qt.cnot(2, 0, 1) *
... qt.tensor(X, I)
>>> oracle
Quantum object: dims = [[2, 2], [2, 2]], shape = (4, 4), type = oper,
➥ isherm = True
Qobj data =
[[0. 1. 0. 0.]
 [1. 0. 0. 0.]
```

This time our oracle is the "not" oracle, which we implement with the sequence of instructions X(control); CNOT(control, target); X(control); as per table D.2.

The unitary operator for the oracle operation looks a bit different this time: it flips the target qubit when the control qubit is a $|0\rangle$.

For instance, row 0 (00 in binary) tells us that $|00\rangle$ is transformed to $|01\rangle$.

```
   [0. 0. 1. 0.]
   [0. 0. 0. 1.]]
>>> register_state = oracle * register_state
>>> register_state
Quantum object: dims = [[2, 2], [1, 1]], shape = (4, 1), type = ket
Qobj data =
[[-0.5]
 [ 0.5]
 [ 0.5]
 [-0.5]]
```

> Similarly, row 2 (10 in binary) tells us that $|10\rangle$ is transformed to $|10\rangle$; the oracle leaves that input alone.

> The state after applying the oracle is $(-|00\rangle + |01\rangle + |10\rangle - |11\rangle)/2 = (-1)|+-\rangle$, precisely the same as before, aside from a global phase of -1.

Looking at these two examples, we got the same output state, except the signs are all flipped. This means if we multiplied one of the state vectors by a -1, they would both be the same. Multiplying an entire vector by a constant is referred to as *adding a global phase*. Since global phases cannot be observed through measurements, we got *exactly* the same information from applying the id and not oracles. We learned nothing about whether we applied id or not; and if we were able to compare the vectors, we would only know that we applied a balanced oracle.

For comparison, let's see what the register looks like after we apply an oracle representing a *constant* function.

D.3.3 Example 3: The "zero" oracle

Once more, with feeling: let's use Python to break down how an oracle representing the constant function zero works. We want to use the zero oracle to show what happens differently when we apply an oracle representing a constant function. This oracle is especially easy to apply since it consists of applying no instructions at all. You can see all the ways to represent this in table D.3.

Table D.3   The one-bit function zero as two-qubit oracles

Function name	Function	Output of oracle	Q# operation
zero	$f(x) = 0$	$|x\rangle|y \oplus 0\rangle = |x\rangle|y\rangle$	(empty)

In listing D.4, we can see that doing nothing on the control qubit and nothing on the target qubit can be simulated by doing nothing on the entire register. Thus, the oracle we create is the two-qubit identity matrix $\mathbb{1} \otimes \mathbb{1}$ for the zero oracle.

Listing D.4   Computing the zero oracle transformation

```
>>> control_state = H * qt.basis(2, 0)
>>> target_state = H * qt.basis(2, 1)
>>> register_state = qt.tensor(control_state, target_state)
>>> X = qt.sigmax()
>>> oracle = qt.tensor(I, I)
>>> oracle
Quantum object: dims = [[2, 2], [2, 2]], shape = (4, 4), type = oper,
➥ isherm = True
```

```
Qobj data =
[[1. 0. 0. 0.]
 [0. 1. 0. 0.]
 [0. 0. 1. 0.]
 [0. 0. 0. 1.]]
>>> register_state = oracle * register_state
>>> register_state
Quantum object: dims = [[2, 2], [1, 1]], shape = (4, 1), type = ket
Qobj data =
[[ 0.5]
 [-0.5]
 [ 0.5]
 [-0.5]]
```

> **Doing nothing on the control qubit and nothing on the target qubit can be simulated by doing nothing on the entire register.**

> **The output state differs by more than a global phase from the id oracle. There's no scalar we can multiply by a global phase to turn the id output into the zero output.**

Here we see our first difference from the previous listing: the minus signs are in different places on our state vector. Before, we used the id oracle and got that the output state was $(|00\rangle - |01\rangle - |10\rangle + |11\rangle) / 2$. Using the zero oracle, the output state is $(|00\rangle - |01\rangle + |10\rangle - |11\rangle) / 2$. There is no number we can multiply the entire vector by to change it into either `[[0.5],[-0.5],[-0.5],[0.5]]` or `[[-0.5],[0.5],[0.5], [-0.5]]`. To see how this difference leads to us telling for sure whether we have a balanced or constant oracle, let's continue to the next step of the Deutsch–Jozsa algorithm.

Exercise D.1: Try the "one" oracle

See if you can use the Python tricks we have used previously to work out how the states of the `target` and `control` qubits change when the `one` oracle is applied.

Exercise solutions

All solutions for exercises in this book can be found in the companion code repo: https://github.com/crazy4pi314/learn-qc-with-python-and-qsharp. Just go to the folder for the appendix we are in and open the Jupyter notebook with the name that mentions exercise solutions.

D.4   Steps 3 and 4: Undo the preparation on the target qubit, and measure

At this point, it is much easier to make sense of the output if we undo the steps we used to prepare $|+-\rangle$ so that everything is back in the computational basis ($|00\rangle$ … $|11\rangle$). To review, table D.4 has the state vectors for all four oracles (three of which we worked out earlier).

Now we want to undo our preparation steps on the target qubit.

Table D.4 The state of the register after applying oracles

Function name	State of the register after applying the oracle
`zero`	[[0.5], [–0.5], [0.5], [–0.5]]
`one`	[[–0.5], [0.5], [–0.5], [0.5]]
`id`	[[0.5], [–0.5], [–0.5], [0.5]]
`not`	[[–0.5], [0.5], [0.5], [–0.5]]

Why do we do "unprepare" the target qubit?

In chapter 7, we see that we need to reset our qubits to the $|0\rangle$ state before returning them to the target machine. At this point, our target qubit is always in the $|-\rangle$ state, *no matter which oracle we use*. This means that after applying the oracle, we know exactly how to put it back to $|0\rangle$. As in chapter 7, this helps us avoid an additional measurement, which can be expensive on some quantum devices.

Note that we can safely return the target qubit to $|-\rangle$ without affecting the results when we measure the control qubit, as the oracle call is the only two-qubit operation in the Deutsch–Jozsa algorithm. As we see in chapter 5, doing single-qubit operations on one qubit can't affect results on another qubit; otherwise, we would be able to send information faster than light!

Let's try this by undoing the preparation on the register from the oracle representing the `id` function.

Listing D.5 The `id` oracle output in the computational basis

It's helpful to define a shorthand for the identity matrix $\mathbb{1}$, which we use to represent what happens to a qubit when we don't apply any instruction to it.

Reproduces the register for the oracle representing the id function, just after the oracle is applied

```
>>> I = qt.qeye(2)
>>> register_state_id = qt.cnot(2,0,1) *
... (qt.tensor(H * qt.basis(2, 0), H * (qt.sigmax() * qt.basis(2, 0))))
...
>>> register_state_id =
⇒ qt.tensor(I, H) * register_state_id
>>> register_state_id
Quantum object: dims = [[2, 2], [1, 1]], shape = (4, 1),
⇒ type = ket
Qobj data =
[[ 0.         ]
 [ 0.70710678]
 [ 0.         ]
 [-0.70710678]]
>>> register_state_id =
⇒ qt.tensor(I, qt.sigmax()) *
⇒ register_state_id
>>> register_state_id
```

Since we're transforming a two-qubit state, we need to say what happens to each qubit to get our matrix. We do this using the tensor function again.

The output is much easier to read: the register is in the state $(|01\rangle - |11\rangle) / \sqrt{2}$.

In our Q# program, we used the X instruction to return the target qubit to $|0\rangle$ before releasing it, simulated by the QuTiP function sigmax().

```
Quantum object: dims = [[2, 2], [1, 1]], shape = (4, 1),
   type = ket
Qobj data =
[[ 0.70710678]
 [ 0.       ]
 [-0.70710678]
 [ 0.      ]]
>>> qt.tensor(H * qt.basis(2, 1), qt.basis(2, 0))
   == register_state_id
True
>>> register_state_id = qt.tensor(H, I) *
   register_state_id
>>> register_state_id
Quantum object: dims = [[2, 2], [1, 1]], shape = (4, 1),
   type = ket
Qobj data =
[[0.]
 [0.]
 [1.]
 [0.]]
```

Since the X instruction flips its argument, applying the X matrix gives us the state $(|00\rangle - |10\rangle) / \sqrt{2}$.

We can use QuTiP to confirm that another way of writing $(|00\rangle - |10\rangle) / \sqrt{2}$ is $(H|1\rangle) \otimes |0\rangle = |-0\rangle$.

We can simulate the MResetX operation by applying H and then measuring in the Z-basis.

The state of our register immediately before measuring has a 1 in row 2 (10 in binary), so the state of our register is $|10\rangle$, and we will measure One with certainty.

TIP   We use the MResetX operation from the Q# standard libraries to measure in the *X*-basis. An *X*-basis measurement returns Zero when its argument is in $|+\rangle$ and returns a One result when its argument is in $|-\rangle$. Thus, we can simulate the MResetX operation by applying *H* and then measuring in the *Z*-basis.

Looking at the final vector in listing D.5, we can see that it represents the state $|10\rangle$. If we were to measure the control qubit from that state, we would get the classical bit One 100% of the time. In the Algorithm.qs file we write in chapter 8, we return to the user that an oracle is balanced if we measured One on the control qubit, so we correctly conclude that id is a balanced oracle! The fact that we will measure One on the control bit every time is really cool.

NOTE   Although some quantum algorithms are random, like the QRNG example from chapter 2 or Morgana's and Lancelot's game from chapter 7, they don't need to be. In fact, the Deutsch–Jozsa algorithm is *deterministic*: we get the same answer every time we run it.

From these examples, we have an important observation (see table D.5): applying an oracle to the control and target qubits can affect the state of the control qubit.

Table D.5   The vectors representing the state of the register after applying the various oracles

Function name	Register state just before measurement	Result of measuring control qubit along *Z*
zero	[[1], [0], [0], [0]]	Zero
one	[[−1], [0], [0], [0]]	Zero
id	[[0], [0], [1], [0]]	One
not	[[0], [0], [−1], [0]]	One

index

Symbols

? command 150
%config magic command 292
%estimate magic command 272
%lsopen magic command 141
%package magic command 292
%simulate magic
    command 137, 141–142,
    174, 292

A

abstractions 26–27
AddI operation 292
Adjoint functor 176, 210, 224,
    261
Adjoint operation 176, 190
adjoint operation 314
algebra
    inner products 338–340
    matrices 330–340
    tensor products 85–89
    vectors 327–330
algorithm 314
algorithms
    classical 153–155
    quantum
        Deutsch-Jozsa algorithm
            156–161, 170–174,
            341–342
        oracles 161–170
        phase kickback 180–184
        techniques 174–179
    Shor's algorithm 287–288,
        296–299

amplitude amplification 268
amplitudes 83
Anaconda 308–310
    installing 308
    installing packages with
        308–310
arguments, passing operations
    as 143–148
arithmetic
    algebra
        inner products 338–340
        matrices 330–340
        tensor products 85–89
        vectors 327–330
    classical algebra and
        factoring 288–290
    connecting modular math to
        factoring 283–288
    quantum arithmetic
        291–299
    adding with qubits
        292–293
    modular multiplication in
        Shor's algorithm
        296–299
    multiplying with qubits
        in superposition
        293–296
    security and factoring
        279–283
AssertionError 65
assert keyword 231
AssertOperationsEqual-
    Referenced 231–232, 264
AssertQubit 203–205
asymptotic complexity 253

B

balanced functions 159
basis 63, 92, 124, 333
BB84 protocol 57, 66–71, 124,
    314
bias 24
BigEndian 291
BigInt type 289
binary search 250
Binder, running samples online
    with 307
bits 22
Bloch sphere 118
bool type 26
Born's rule 39, 41, 314
borrow statement 140
braket 38
bras 28, 38

C

CCNOT operation 211, 274
CheckIfOracleIsBalanced
    operation 174, 177, 180
Choi state 232
CHSH (Clauser, Horne, Shi-
    mony, and Holt) 76–80,
    103–106
ciphertext 41
circuits 27
classical bits 23, 28, 57, 81, 137,
    314
classical computers 6, 161, 314
classical programs 153
classical simulations 27

Clifford group 274
clock arithmetic 279
CNOT (controlled-NOT) 115, 125, 167, 205–206, 233, 345
codes 22
complexity theory 166
complex numbers 45–46, 111, 118, 123, 191–193, 203, 259, 315
Complex type 191
computational basis 93, 345
computational basis states 82, 315
computationally secure 55
computers 5, 315
conda env tool 309
conda-forge channel 309
conda package manager 308–309
conda –version command 309
constant functions 160
continued fraction convergents 300
contradiction 88
Controlled functor 210, 244, 257, 266, 294
ControlledOnInt function 266, 294
controlled operations 202, 314
controlled-Z (CZ) operation 208, 257
control qubit 115, 169, 177, 213, 343–344
coprime 280, 315

D

.dag() method 101
DecomposedIntoTimeStepsCA function 221, 241
Deutsch–Jozsa algorithm 152, 156–161, 341–342
    applying oracles 343–348
    game overview 156–161
    phase kickback 180–184
    preparing input state 342–343
    simulating in Q# 170–174
    undoing preparation on target qubit, and measuring 348–350
Diffie–Hellman protocol 286
digital signal processors (DSPs) 7
Dirac notation 28, 317

discrete logarithm 284
distributive property 336
dotnet iqsharp install –user command 313
dotnet new command 313
Double values 191
DrawRandomInt 303
driver 135
    See also host program
DumpMachine 205–206, 209, 258, 292, 295
DumpRegister 202, 206

E

eigenphase 225, 315
eigenstates 202, 204–206, 242, 315
eigenvalue 205, 225, 315
eigenvectors 205, 315
encapsulation 98
encryption 54–62
    sharing classical bits with qubits 62
encryption algorithms 41, 55
entanglement 86, 96, 106, 114, 117, 129, 315
entry point 141
environments 308
EqualityFactI 289
EqualityFactL 289
EqualityFactR 289
EstimateEnergy operation 244
EstimateFrequency operation 297–298
estimate_resources method 273
Euclid's algorithm 288
Exp operation 221, 235

F

Fact function 173–174
factoring
    classical algebra and 288–290
    connecting modular math to 283–288
    security and 279–283
fair coin 24
fermionic Hamiltonians 229
first-class values 148
fixup blocks 142
ForEach operation 197
for loop 241, 256
frequency 280
functions, in Q# 137–143

functools.partial 148
functors 176

G

gate_expand_1toN function 112
gate_expand_2toN function 112
GCD (greatest common divisor) 288
gedankenexperiment 52
generator 280, 282, 288, 298
GitHub Codespaces 308
global phases 41, 120, 124, 182, 203, 206–212, 315, 347
global property 160
greatest common divisor (GCD) 288
GreatestCommonDivisorI function 288, 303
GreatestCommonDivisorL function 289
ground state 224
ground state energy 224
Grover's algorithm 251

H

Hadamard instructions 21, 48, 178–179
Hadamard operation 43–44, 47, 49–50, 88, 91, 120, 138–139, 259–260, 342–343
Hamiltonian learning 187
Hamiltonian matrix 221, 225–229
Hamiltonian simulation 224–225
Hartree–Fock theory 246
Holevo's theorem 84
H operation 138, 141, 230, 343
host program 135

I

id function 159, 162, 345, 349
if block 257
if statement 116
import statement 143, 318
informationally secure systems 20
inner products 37, 338–340
input qubit 183
interpolated strings 142

Int type 191, 289
ipython command 62, 310
IQ# for Jupyter Notebook,
    installing 313
IQ# magic commands 326
IsCoprimeI function 282

K

ket 28, 33–34, 38–39, 42, 45,
    91–92, 100–102, 166, 295
key expansion protocol 67
keys 55, 251–256, 258, 263
    See also quantum key distribu-
        tion
Kronecker product 85

L

Larmor precession 187
least-significant order 292
linear combination 33
linear function 330
LittleEndian 291–292
little-endian representation 209
local phases
    eigenstates and 202–206
    turning global phases
        into 206–212
Log function 139

M

MA (Merlin-Arthur) 166
magic command 137
many-worlds interpretation 36
matplotlib package 201
matrices 330, 334–340
measure instruction 63
MeasureInteger operation 255,
    267
measurement 315
measuring qubits 34–38, 99–102
    generalizing
        measurement 38–41
    using useful properties of
        qubits 186–191
Merlin-Arthur (MA) 166
message text 71
Microsoft.Quantum.Ampli-
    tude.Amplification
    namespace 271
Microsoft.Quantum.Arithme-
    tic.LittleEndian user-
    defined type 255, 267

Microsoft.Quantum.Arithmetic
    namespace 291
Microsoft.Quan-
    tum.Arrays.Mapped
    function 197
Microsoft.Quantum.Arrays
    namespace 197, 257,
    275
Microsoft.Quantum.Canon
    namespace 176, 243
Microsoft.Quantum.Characteri-
    zation namespace 246
Microsoft.Quantum.Convert
    namespace 188
Microsoft.Quantum.Diagnostics
    namespace 230
Microsoft.Quantum.Intrinsic.H
    operation 141
Microsoft.Quantum.Intrinsic
    namespace 236, 243
Microsoft.Quantum.Intrinsic.T
    operation 274
Microsoft.Quantum.Math
    namespace 191, 289, 298
Microsoft.Quantum.Simulation
    namespace 244
Microsoft.Quantum.Standard
    package 143
modular arithmetic 279, 283
modulus 298
morganaWinProbability 147
Most function 257
moving quantum data
    109–117
    cnot two-qubit operation
        115–117
    single-qubit rotations
        117–126
    swap two-qubit operation
        112–115
    teleportation program
        126–129
MResetX operation 173, 350
MResetZ operation 149, 173
multiple qubit states 81–89
    registers 81–83
    simulating quantum
        computers 83–84
    tensor products for qubit
        operations on
        registers 86–89
    tensor products for state
        preparation 85–86
MultiplyByModularInteger
    operation 294–295

N

namespaces 141
NAND (NOT-AND)
    operation 26
.NET Core SDK, installing 312
.NET Framework 311
newtype statement 191
NMR (nuclear magnetic reso-
    nance) imaging 228
no-cloning theorem 70, 315
nonlocal games 76–81
    CHSH game 76–80, 103–106
    classical strategy 80–81
    defined 76
NOT-AND (NAND)
    operation 26
not function 159, 162
NOT operations 58–61
np.kron function 85, 208
np.linalg.norm function 339
nuclear magnetic resonance
    (NMR) imaging 228
NuGet package manager 143
NumPy library 329

O

-O command-line argument 231
one function 160, 162
open statement 141, 143, 318
operations 138–139
    applying and undoing
        175–178
    in Q# 137–148
    of qubits 30–34
    rx, ry, and rz 94, 119, 125, 205
    tensor products for qubit
        operations on
        registers 86–89
operators 323
oracles 161–170, 251, 315
    Deutsch-Jozsa algorithm
        343–348
    generalizing results 165–170
orthogonal states 40, 63

P

package managers 308
packages 143, 312
partial application 147
Pauli matrices 121, 315
Pauli operations 119–126,
    229–237

perpendicular states 40
phase estimation 186–191, 315
phase kickback 180, 183, 186,
    205, 209, 315
phases 41, 124, 315
photons 62
pip package manager 308
pivot element 153
post-quantum cryptography 304
private method 98
process tomography 126
product function 85
programs 13–15, 315
    classical 13–14
    quantum 14–15
projectors 101
project templates,
    installing 312–313
provably secure 55
public key 286
Python, running Q# from
    197–202
python command 309

Q

Q# 319–326
    declarations and
        statements 320–321
    expressions and
        operators 323
    functions and operations
        in 137–143
    IQ# magic commands 326
    Morgana's game in 149–151
    passing operations as
        arguments 143–148
    Quantum Development
        Kit 134–137
    running from Python
        197–202
    simulating Deutsch-Jozsa
        algorithm in 170–174
    standard libraries 324
    types 319
qRAM (quantum RAM) 256
QRNGs (quantum random num-
    ber generators) 18, 21, 139
    playing games in Q# 138–143
    programming 46–52
    qrng program 22, 48
qsharp-book environment 309
qsharp package 198, 309
qt.basis function 93
qt.rx(np.pi) 120

qt.rx function 125
qt.ry function 125
qt.rz function 125
qt.sigmax() function 120, 238
qt.tensor function 208
quantum advantage 10
quantum algorithms
    classical and quantum
        algorithms 153–155
    Deutsch-Jozsa algorithm
        156–161, 341–342
        game overview 156–161
        phase kickback 180–184
        simulating in Q# 170–174
    oracles 161–170
        generalizing results
            165–170
        Merlin's transformations
            162–164
    techniques 174–179
quantum arithmetic 291–299
    adding with qubits 292–293
    modular multiplication in
        Shor's algorithm
        296–299
    multiplying with qubits in
        superposition 293–296
quantum-based strategy 103
quantum computers 316
    arithmetic with
        classical algebra and
            factoring 288–290
        connecting modular math
            to factoring 283–288
        quantum arithmetic
            291–299
        security and factoring
            279–283
    defined 5–7
    potential of 8–13
        capabilities of 10–11
        limits of 11–13
    programs 13–15
        classical 13–14
        quantum 14–15
    relevance of 4–5
    searching with
        implementing search
            algorithm 264–268
        resource estimation
            271–277
        searching unstructured
            data 250–256
    simulating quantum
        computers 83–84

solving chemistry problems
    with
        different ways of thinking
            about quantum
            mechanics 222–225
        real chemistry
            applications 220–222
        using Hamiltonians to
            describe how quantum
            systems evolve in
            time 225–229
quantum concepts 283
quantum data, moving 109–117
    cnot two-qubit
        operation 115–117
    single-qubit rotations
        117–126
    swap two-qubit operation
        112–115
    teleportation program
        126–129
Quantum Development Kit
    installing 310–313
        IQ# for Jupyter
            Notebook 313
        .NET Core SDK 312
        project templates 312–313
        Visual Studio Code
            extension 313
    Q# 134–137
QuantumDevice 22
QuantumDevice interface 96
quantum foundations 36
quantum key distribution
    BB84 protocol 66–71
    encryption 54–62
    sending secret messages
        71–74
    two bases 63–66
quantum mechanics, different
    ways of thinking
    about 222–225
quantum message 128
quantum NOT operations
    58–61
quantum objects, in QuTiP
    91–102
    measuring multiple
        qubits 99–102
    upgrading simulators 96–99
quantum objects in QuTiP
    91–102
    measuring multiple
        qubits 99–102
    upgrading simulators 96–99

quantum operations 30–31, 40, 43–44, 57, 87, 171, 186, 227, 316, 318
quantum parallelism 12
quantum programs 153, 316
quantum register 100, 316
quantum self-testing 107
QuantumSimulator target machine 135, 155
quantum states 28, 30, 34, 39, 86, 119, 154, 316, 318
    of qubits 28–29, 81–89
    reflecting about 256–264
        reflection about all-ones state 257–259
        reflection about arbitrary states 258–264
    tensor products for state preparation 85–86
quantum systems 223, 316
quantum teleportation 114
qubits 316, 318
    adding with 292–293
    defined 27
    implementing multi-qubit simulators
        quantum objects in QuTiP 91–102
        upgrading simulators 96–99
    measuring 34–38
    measuring multiple qubits 99–102
    multiplying with 293–296
    operations 30–34, 86–89
    programming QRNGs 46–52
    random numbers 19–22
    sharing classical bits with 62
    simulating in code 41–46
    states 28–29, 81–89
Qubit type 143, 145, 191
quicksort 154, 169
QuTiP (Quantum Toolbox in Python), quantum objects in 91–102
    measuring multiple qubits 99–102
    upgrading simulators 96–99

R

R1 operation 200, 215
random bits 24
random numbers 19–22, 41, 47, 51, 54–55, 57–58, 62, 79, 138–143, 282, 285, 316

registers 81–83, 86–89
repeat-until-success (RUS) loops 142
Reset operation 142
resource estimation 271–277
ResourcesEstimator target machine 136, 155
Result type 191
Result value 173, 289
reversible 316
reversible classical function 164
rings 336
rotations 30, 146
RSA algorithm 286
RUS (repeat-until-success) loops 142
rx operations 119, 125
ry operations 94, 125
Rz operations 205
rz operations 125

S

ScalableOperation 193, 213
scalars 328
scale factor 188
Schrödinger's cat 52
scipy.optimize function 200
search
    implementing search algorithm 264–268
    reflecting about states 256–264
        reflection about all-ones state 257–259
        reflection about arbitrary states 258–264
    resource estimation 271–277
    searching unstructured data 250–256
SearchForMarkedItem operation 255–256
self-adjoint 314
semiprime 280, 316
sending qubits 62
Shor's algorithm 279, 287–288, 296–299
side effects 139
sigmax function 94, 125
simulate method 273
simulating
    Deutsch-Jozsa algorithm in Q# 170–174
    implementing multi-qubit simulators
        CHSH 103–106

quantum objects in QuTiP 91–102
    upgrading simulators 96–99
quantum computers 83–84
qubits in code 41–46
Simulator 98
Simulator._apply 113
Sin function 139
single-qubit rotations 117–126, 230
SingleQubitSimulator 89, 96
singleton–tuple equivalence 144
software installation
    installing locally using Anaconda 308–310
    installing Anaconda 308
    installing packages with Anaconda 308–310
    installing Quantum Development Kit 310–313
        IQ# for Jupyter Notebook 313
        .NET Core SDK 312
        project templates 312–313
        Visual Studio Code extension 313
    running samples online 307–308
        using Binder 307
        using GitHub Codespaces 308
Sqrt function 139
standard libraries 324
state 316
statements 320–321
states. See quantum states
Strategy type 79
subroutines 281
superposition 65, 82, 293, 296, 316
swap operation 109, 112–115

T

target qubit 115, 169, 175, 177, 213, 344
teleportation program 126–129
tensor function 94
tensor products
    for qubit operations on registers 86–89
    for state preparation 85–86
T operations 273
trits 93
trotterOrder 241

trotterStep 244
Trotter–Suzuki 221, 224,
    239–242, 245
truth table 26–27, 43, 60, 111,
    120–121, 156–157, 160, 162,
    232, 260

U

UDTs (user-defined types) 191,
    256
uncompute trick 168
uniformly random 77
unitary matrices 27, 43, 162, 316

unitary synthesis 167
user-defined types 191–197
use statement 140

V

vectors 42, 327–330
Visual Studio Code extension,
    installing 313

W

within/apply block 177, 196,
    230, 261, 294

X

X operation 139, 150, 202, 205

Y

Y operation 205

Z

zero function 160, 162, 174,
    182, 347
Z operation 120, 202